Cornell Studies in Political Economy

EDITED BY PETER J. KATZENSTEIN

Governments, Markets, and Growth

FINANCIAL SYSTEMS AND THE POLITICS OF INDUSTRIAL CHANGE

JOHN ZYSMAN

CORNELL UNIVERSITY PRESS

Ithaca and London

First published 1983 by Cornell University Press.
Second printing, 1987.
First published Cornell Paperbacks, 1984.
Third printing, 1990.

Printed in the United States of America

Library of Congress Cataloging in Publication Data

Zysman, John.
    Governments, markets, and growth.

    (Cornell studies in political economy)
    Includes bibliographical references and index.
    1. Economic policy. 2. Industry and state. 3. Economic development. 4. Finance. I. Title. II. Title: Financial systems and the politics of industrial change. III. Series.
    HD87.Z97   1983   338.9   82-49269
    ISBN 0-8014-1597-7 (cloth)
    ISBN 0-8014-9252-1 (paper)

For my parents,
who always wanted me to be a scholar

Contents

Preface

The economic performance of all the advanced countries deteriorated during the 1970s, in many cases quite abruptly. This deterioration has provoked throughout the West a new debate about the proper role of government in the economy. Since solutions always depend on how one perceives a problem, it is not surprising that the sharply different explanations of our current troubles have produced sharply different prescriptions for resolving them.

This book offers an interpretation of contemporary economic difficulties and of the policy debate they have engendered in the advanced countries. It discusses why it has become harder to manage the thousands of micro-changes in production and products which are necessary for economic growth and why attempts to make such changes are met with growing political resistance. The book's general arguments are based on an analysis of the efforts of the governments of the larger advanced countries—the United States, Great Britain, France, West Germany, and Japan—to respond to shifting economic conditions in the years since the Second World War. The discussion focuses on the capacities of the various governments to intervene selectively to shape industrial outcomes and attempts to account for national differences in these capacities and in the strategies adopted. The book argues that there have been three distinct technical-political solutions to the problems of growth: state-led, market-led, and negotiated.

One element of the explanation of the differences in government capacities for industrial leadership is distinct to this book. I contend that an examination of national financial structures can illuminate both government economic strategies and the political conflicts that accompany industrial change. The particular arrangements of national financial systems limit both the marketplace options of firms and the administrative choices of governments. That is, in each country financial markets are one element that delimits the ways in which business and the state can interact. The structure of those markets at once influences the capacity of government to exert industrial leadership and the nature of the political conflicts that arise from its economic objectives. Very simply, in market economies where freely moving prices allocate goods and services, money is not only a medium of exchange but also a means of political and social control: it is one way of deciding who gets what. Therefore, by following the money flows in the market economy and in the institutions that structure that flow we can learn a great deal about the uses to which the society's resources are put, the people who make the allocative decisions, and the process through which control is obtained and exerted.

All long projects require funds to conduct them and the support of friends and colleagues to complete them. This book was no exception. Funding came principally from the German Marshall Fund, the Council on Foreign Relations, and the University of California. Support and advice came from many people over many years. Several are owed special thanks. Peter Gourevitch and Suzanne Berger provided the indispensable encouragement and penetrating analysis that one receives only when the best of friends also happen to be excellent scholars. In our frequent discussions Charles Sabel made me see more clearly what in fact I was attempting with this book. Peter J. Katzenstein clarified the structure the argument should take. Those who worked with me on the sector studies that appear in *American Industry in International Competition*, another volume in this series, kept my eye focused on the real economy and not on the haze of academic arguments about the "crises." Michael Borrus and James E. Millstein both aided my education about the American economy and kept my enthusiasm for the questions fresh. John Ackerman of Cornell University Press worked with patience, exceptional intelligence, and skill to penetrate my arguments and turn my sometimes heavy prose into a more accessible form. Patricia Lockary made my work on successive versions more tolerable by making sure that I kept the whole project in perspective. Her editorial skill, honed in legal practice, and her complete intolerance for social science jargon and vague concepts made this a much better book.

JOHN ZYSMAN

Berkeley, California

Part I

THE ARGUMENT

CHAPTER ONE

The State in the Marketplace

The economic performance of all the advanced countries deteriorated in the 1970s; in many nations the deterioration was quite abrupt. The general signs of trouble were evident in inflation rates that jumped, growth rates that slowed, and the ever-increasing numbers of people out of work. This unfortunate combination was labeled stagflation. In late 1981 and 1982 the inflation rates in many nations slowed; but growth ground virtually to a halt and unemployment mounted further, reaching levels not seen since the Great Depression. The resulting social pain was evident in the many stories about industries, regions, and communities in difficulty. As imports in steel and textiles cut into domestic production, and productivity increases reduced the remaining jobs even further, traditional industrial centers became depressed regions. But the difficulties of the 1970s were not simply the results of recession or of an OPEC-sponsored jump in oil prices. A profound economic transition was underway in the advanced countries, one that involved basic changes in the goods that were produced, how they were made, and where they were made. For while automobile production collapsed in Britain and dropped in the United States, it grew rapidly in Japan. While there were unemployed steelworkers in Pennsylvania, Wales, and the Lorraine, new jobs making steel were being created in Korea, Taiwan, and Brazil. Unemployment among semiskilled textile workers in the Southeast was matched by shortages of trained electronics engineers and computer programmers in other parts of the United States.

The economic deterioration and transition began to provoke political reactions and contribute to shifts in who governed. The state of the economy was not the only partisan issue that affected elections, but it

11

did contribute to changes of government in Sweden, France, Britain, Germany, the United States, and Japan. It is a difficult time for incumbents of all political colors, even entrenched incumbents. The conservatives in France lost power for the first time in nearly a quarter century, while in Sweden more than forty years of Social Democratic rule was interrupted in 1976. Power shifted in an orderly fashion, a hopeful contrast to the tumultuous interwar years when economic conditions had been even more terrible and when social circumstances had been ripe for the emergence of mass political movements. Yet the broad consensus on policy in most countries eroded as more radical economic strategies that broke with the status quo were tried from both the Left and the Right. A vibrant debate about the proper role of government got underway. This debate represents more than disagreement about what government should do; it is indicative of the sharply different explanations offered for our current economic troubles.

To set the present debate we must begin the story in the 1960s when growth was steady. High inflation meant a jump in the price index of a few percent and unacceptable unemployment meant anything in excess of 5 percent in the United States and even less elsewhere. During the first part of the decade it was widely believed that proper government policies could maintain economic stability. The task for government, it was thought, was to find the right apparatus and techniques to balance aggregate demand against the economy's capacity to supply goods and services. Keynesianism was triumphant: John Kennedy and then Richard Nixon had announced their conversion, and policymakers of all political complexions thus assumed that government could assure macroeconomic stability by managing fiscal and monetary aggregates at arm's length. The conventional economic wisdom was that detailed public intervention in the affairs of specific sectors and individual firms was unnecessary. In the United States active government intervention for the purposes of industrial development was limited to the timid trade adjustment and regional programs of the Kennedy years. Since Japan had not yet impinged on its trade partners and the French planning process was being abandoned, state-led growth strategies attracted little attention. During these years it seemed that expanding trade among rich nations, based on technological innovation and specialization of production, was contributing to a general rise in the welfare of all advanced countries. Indeed the 1960s was a liberal moment in which the monetary agreements of Bretton Woods and the trade agreements embodied in GATT (General Agreement on Tariffs and Trade) were being applied and the drive for even freer markets had a full head of steam. The popular emblem of this new international era was the multinational corporation, which symbolized both the new freedoms of the giant corporations that produced around the world and the diminished ability of governments to regulate the behavior of firms that were important to their national economies. As the 1960s advanced, the increasing internationalization of finance began also to place serious constraints on any government's ability to conduct an autonomous aggregate economic policy. Throughout the West some observers proclaimed the death of ideology, arguing that it had become irrelevant as growing wealth seemed to put an end to class conflict. In the America of the 1960s, moreover, the economic limits on political purpose—whether domestic purposes such as the war on poverty or foreign policy purposes such as the war in Vietnam—were not directly debated.

In the 1970s, as the economies of the advanced countries stagnated and projections of the economic future became increasingly pessimistic, the political debate about proper government policy grew acerbic. A resurgence of conflict in tight European labor markets and an American demand for expansion born of the Vietnam War seemed to trigger higher inflation rates and to give early signals that growth might not last forever. Soviet grain purchases pushed up American food prices and the Arab-Israeli war of 1973 provided the impetus for the oil cartel to flex its muscles. The oil crisis of 1973–1974 was clear evidence that the decline in energy costs which had lubricated expansion for decades had been reversed. Slowed growth and rising inflation (see Table 1.1) were clear evidence that the task of assuring macroeconomic stability had become more difficult.

One interpretation held that the troubles facing the advanced countries stemmed from an unfortunate conjuncture of seemingly unrelated difficulties.[1] Consequently, it was argued that if each country could temporarily accept the discipline of restrictive policy, they could all return to the path of growth. In fact, domestic political conflicts over the allocation of the pains of discipline made such restrictive policies difficult to apply. To some this situation suggested a "crisis of democracy," an unrestrained battle among selfish interest groups, each with its hand in the government till and each unconcerned that its individual pilferage would damage the collective welfare.[2] Faced with this same conjuncture of economic difficulties, other analysts began to focus on (and policymakers to press for) "corporatist" solutions, such as income policies, which would structure and regulate economic conflicts through highly organized interest groups.[3] Those groups, it was thought, could negotiate a collective settlement involving both government policies, such as welfare, and market behaviors, such as wage settlements. It seemed to some that the apparently rigid political structures of such small countries as Austria and the Netherlands facilitated such deals and thus, ironically, provided the economic flexibility needed to respond to a changing world economy.

A second interpretation that gained adherents as the decade closed was that the late 1960s had been an economic watershed, a time when long-established growth trends began to change. Distributional conflicts that had been obscured for decades now burst forth as inflation.[4] As unemployment continued to rise in all advanced countries—European countries have produced no new jobs since 1974—the debate about how to maintain stability of prices in an era of unexpected economic shocks had to make room for a debate about whether the growth machine could be restarted. Some voices suggested that the boom years had simply been an anomaly of reconstruction or at best a long economic upswing that had now turned down.[5] Suddenly, attention focused on how to accomplish changes in the multitude of micro-components that constitute the aggregate of economic growth. Growth, it was observed, involved a continuous evolution in who produced what, how, and for which markets.

Firms make the adjustments whether they respond autonomously to price signals or are directed to do so by bureaucratic instruction. The marketplace problem for firms is now to reorganize production, which requires flexibility in the factory, and to shift resources from old uses to new, which requires mobility of labor and capital. The problem is not simply a technical one. The multitude of micro-adaptations often entail social dislocations that provoke conflict. Indeed, economic growth implies changes in the way individuals lead their lives and the manner in which communities are organized. Industrial adjustments are political as much as economic phenomena. The marketplace rules that set the terms on which firms coordinate and compete are established politically. Those rules shape both the allocation of the pains and gains that are generated by industrial development and the price signals that guide the adjustments firms make. Moreover, governments intervene in many markets to set prices, to dictate conditions of supply and demand, and even to organize and direct industrial activities. These government rules and interventions are used both to retard and to facilitate industrial change. For growth to proceed smoothly, both the technical obstacles and the political resistances to development must be overcome. Observing a world of slowed growth and inflation, some have argued that the economic changes themselves have become more numerous and more difficult, that the technical tasks of adjustment are harder and the market conditions for resolving them less favorable. Others note that the political resistance to change has also grown, the result both of the entrenched positions of a new industrial baronry seeking to preserve its position despite market shifts and of interest groups seeking to override the market in pursuit of their special purposes.[6] The position elaborated in this chapter—more in the form of an organizing assumption than a testable proposition—is that the political capacity of the advanced countries for managing change has diminished at the same time that the adjustments they must make have become more difficult.

The liberal international order came under a mercantilist challenge in the same years. It was not simply that American ability to manage the system declined—a decline that was expressed concretely when Nixon was forced in 1971 to break the link between dollar and gold. The premise of the rules of international trade, the GATT system, only awkwardly fit many of the new realities of international trade. The assumption—half truth and half fiction—that governments negotiate about the rules of trade, leaving the market to settle the outcomes, is increasingly less tenable. More than ever, governments are directly negotiating about outcomes. There are three new trade problems—which we examine later in this chapter: (1) the use of state power at home to create competitive advantage in international markets; (2) state negotiation of market shares during periods of surplus capacity; and (3) the state's activities as a trader or salesman for national products. In each case the national debates about the rules of the domestic economy and the appropriate use of national government power in the market become the subject of international debate and negotiation.

As a result of these domestic and international changes, the political *capacity* of government to promote the process of adjustment and the international competitive development of industries suddenly became central.[7] As observers widely agreed that industry's inability to make the changes necessary for adaptation to altered market conditions had contributed to the coincidence of higher inflation and slowed growth, they began to debate how governments could best facilitate "industrial adjustment" and promote the international competitive position of national industry.[8] There was a sharp divergence of opinion. One view held that proper aggregate policies and a stern refusal to grant firms political protections against pains of market change would suffice to set matters right, as Ronald Reagan and Britain's Margaret Thatcher would argue. A second school contended that industrial policies to promote selected industries or resolve the problems of specific firms were required. Opponents of this strategy of industrial policies argue that selective intervention in the affairs of business simply subsidizes those who would resist change. Subsidies to West Virginia steel firms create new competitors for steel producers in other states. Subsidized capital for textiles or steel, which in the United States takes such forms as the sale of investment tax credits by unprofitable firms to profitable firms, means less money or higher rates of interest for expanding high-technology sectors. These domestic distortions, moreover, spill into the international arena. Subsidies that permit uncompetitive plants in Britain may create unemployed steelworkers in Pennsylvania. In reply, the *advocates* of selective industrial policy observe that short-term subsidies can in fact help firms establish long-term strategic advantages in international markets. Japanese promotion of the shipbuilding and steel industries created the conditions for a dominant international market position and, in turn, strategic advantage in these crucial industries provided the basis for a real transformation of the Japanese economy.

The outcome of selective intervention—accelerated development or subsidized resistance—is not really a technical matter that can be predicted by economic logic. As we shall argue in Chapter 2, critics and advocates of government intervention capture different elements of the story. The economic outcome of policy in each country is a political choice that depends in part on the capacity of governments to conduct development policies and in part on the purposes they pursue. As we proceed, we shall explore how these different national policies, resting as they do on distinct government purposes and capacities, influence the competition between companies in international markets.

This book analyzes the efforts made by the governments of the larger advanced countries—the United States, Great Britain, France, West Germany, and Japan—to respond to shifting economic conditions in the years since the Second World War. It focuses on the capacities of the different governments to intervene selectively to shape industrial outcomes. More specifically, the book begins with the notion that an examination of national financial structures can illuminate the economic strategies of these governments and the political conflicts that accompany industrial adjustment. The particular arrangements of national financial systems limit both the marketplace options of firms and the administrative choices of government. That is, financial markets in each country are one element that delimits the ways in which business and the state can interact. The structure of those markets at once influences a government's capacity to exert industrial leadership and the nature of the political conflicts that arise from its economic objectives. Very simply, in market economies where freely moving prices allocate goods and services, money is not only a medium of exchange but also a means of political and social control: it is one way of deciding who gets what. Therefore, by following the money flows in the market economy and dissecting the institutions that structure that flow, we can learn a great deal about the uses to which the society's resources are put, by whom, and how control is obtained and exerted.

Markets and organizations, despite elements common to each, operate according to different logics. Organizations structure human behavior by a set of hierarchies, rules, and commands that mobilize individual efforts toward common purposes. Markets are arenas for buying and selling in which individual activities are connected by conditions of supply and demand as expressed by price. Nonetheless, the fixed character of market arrangements for finance has a political significance similar to that of those enduring arrangements for political administration which we call the state bureaucracy. Both financial systems and state bureaucracies are at once constraints on action and instruments of action. We shall explore how the markets for finance work because we assume here that *how* a thing is done affects not only whether it is possible but also *who* its supporters and opponents will be. The institutional organization of markets and administration—on which the different capacities for government action rest at least in part—also influences the political conflicts about the purposes of intervention. The institutions of the economy and the structure of the markets influence both which interests find political expression and the forms of the conflicts that ensue. Since the different institutions of the economy do shape the actual redeployment of resources, which we have labeled industrial readjustment, they perform the political task of ordering social choices and outcomes.[9] Moreover, these institutions are themselves the subjects of political controversy precisely because they constrain government action and shape the expression of political interests. These market arrangements, such as financial institutions and markets, are linked to the controversies of parties and government both by their histories (the fights that have shaped them) and by the skirmishes that accompany their day-to-day operations.[10] The emphasis on the influence that marketplace arrangements have on political conflict and policy distinguishes this interpretation of industrial change from more conventional accounts that focus primarily on political actors and institutions.

To understand the adjustments the advanced countries are attempting to make to the current economic troubles, we must eliminate the artificial dichotomy that separates the study of markets from the study of politics. Though traditionally viewed as different means of coordinating activities, political command and market prices in fact melt together in the actual workings of the advanced economies. In each case, it is important to determine the character of the mix. Market positions are a source of political power and government choices shape the operations of the market. Thus, any analysis must begin from the understanding that there are no markets apart from politics, that markets were in fact political creations, and that political life is entangled with the workings of markets and market institutions.

The argument here posits three types of financial systems, each of which has specific political implications. First, there is a financial system based on capital markets which allocates resources by competitively established prices. This capital market–based system reinforces arm's-length relations between government and industry. It is associated with a company-led adjustment strategy in which investment and production decisions are the unchallenged prerogatives of management. Though government policies may influence those decisions, they do not add up to a conscious strategy of adjustment or of development. The United States fits into this category. Second, there is a credit-based financial system with government-administered prices which facilitates and encourages government intervention in industrial affairs. This system is a critical component of state-led adjustment strategies in which the government attempts consciously to mold particular sectors. Japan and France both fit into this category. Third, there is a credit-based system dominated by financial institutions whose market power gives them influence in industry and creates what we can term the negotiated style of modern capitalism. The West German system is an example of this model. Each of these models represents a distinct way of resolving both the political and economic problems of growth and, not surprisingly, each has distinct advantages and identifiable weaknesses that will be considered as we proceed.

This first chapter considers the common economic difficulties of the countries in this study in order to set forth the economic pressures their governments confront. The second chapter sets out the political analysis of financial systems and explores the dynamics of industrial adjustment. The varying capacities of governments, and the consequences of their actions, concern us in the rest of the volume.

THE CHANGED CONTEXT of GROWTH: THE BACKGROUND

The changed patterns of growth are evident in both growth and inflation figures.[11] The pace of growth has slowed in all these countries, accompanied by higher unemployment, as illustrated in Table 1.1. Whether judged by mean or average figures, the drop in the pace of growth is clear. At the same time, inflation rates jumped in all these countries, whether measured by mean or average rates (see Table 1.2).

The general trend hides a more complex story. The growth rates of

Table 1.1. Domestic growth and unemployment in five countries, 1954–1981

A. Annual percentage increase in domestic production (constant prices)

Country	1954–1968		1969–1981	
	average	median	average	median
Japan	9.5	9.1	5.7	5.2
West Germany	5.7	5.6	3.2	3.6
France	5.1	5.2	3.8	3.8
United States	3.5	4.1	2.7	2.9
United Kingdom	3.0	3.3	1.8	1.8

SOURCE: Organisation for Economic Cooperation and Development, *National Accounts of the OECD Countries* (Paris: OECD, 1954–1981).

B. Annual unemployment as percentage of total labor force

Country	1954–1968		1969–1981		1954–1981	
	average	median	average	median	average	median
Japan	1.2	1.2	1.7	1.9	1.4	1.3
West Germany	2.3	1.5	2.4	3.1	2.3	1.8
France	1.3	1.3	3.8	3.4	2.4	1.8
United States	5.0	5.2	6.2	5.9	5.6	5.6
United Kingdom	1.8	1.6	4.9	4.1	3.2	2.4

SOURCE: International Labour Organisation, *Yearbook of Labour Statistics* (Geneva: International Labour Office, 1954–1981).

Table 1.2. Annual percentage increase in real consumer prices in five countries, 1954–1981

Country	1954–1968		1969–1981		1954–1981	
	average	median	average	median	average	median
Japan	3.8	3.9	8.4	7.7	5.9	5.2
West Germany	2.2	2.3	4.8	5.4	3.4	3.0
France	3.9	3.2	9.4	9.4	6.4	5.3
United States	1.8	1.5	7.7	6.4	4.5	3.4
United Kingdom	3.2	3.6	12.4	11.9	7.5	4.8

SOURCE: Organisation for Economic Cooperation and Development, *Main Economic Indicators* (Paris: OECD, 1954–1981).

Table 1.3. Average annual percentage increase in domestic
production (constant prices) in five countries, 1954–1981

Country	1954–1981	(excluding 1974–1975)
Japan	7.7	8.2
West Germany	4.6	5.0
France	4.5	4.8
United States	3.1	3.5
United Kingdom	2.5	2.7

SOURCE: Organisation for Economic Cooperation and
Development, *National Accounts of the OECD Countries*
(Paris: OECD, 1954–1981).

Japan, Germany, and France were higher than those of the United
States and Britain throughout the period and their levels of unemployment were lower (see Table 1.3). The high-growth countries were also
the countries that had the highest percentage of the economically active
population engaged in agriculture and the highest rates of increased
productivity (see Tables 1.4 and 1.5). High growth, increased productivity, and the shift of resources out of agriculture are clearly correlated.
We shall consider the link in a moment. These fast-growth countries also
had substantially higher rates of savings and gross investments. The
differences in investment, productivity, and growth finally reflected
themselves in the patterns of international trade. The fast-growth countries saw their share expand while that of the slow-growth countries
contracted (see Chart 1.1 and Table 1.6).

The pattern of inflation rates also suggests an interesting story. Between 1954 and 1968, the ranking was as illustrated in Table 1.7. It
would appear, in fact, that there was a distinct pattern. Japan and
France were high-growth countries whose expansion caused or was
accompanied by inflation. Germany, though expanding rapidly, was
able to contain its inflation. Britain and the United States grew more
slowly, but the British had a high inflation rate.

In general terms the same pattern held in the decade between 1969
and 1978 (see Table 1.8). The constancy of this pattern, however, hid
the fact that British and American inflation rates had accelerated in
these years, in fact altering their ranking in the inflation derby over the
whole period.

The mold broke between 1978 and 1981. Very simply, the United
States and Britain had moved to the head of the inflation league, along
with the French. French and German growth rates fell. Japan continued to grow, although at a much slower rate, and maintained relatively

Table 1.4. Percentage of the economically active population engaged in agriculture in five countries, 1950–1976

Country	1950–1955	1969	1970	1976
Japan	40.3 ('55)	32.6	17.4	12.2
West Germany	23.2 ('50)	11.8	8.5	7.1
France	26.7 ('54)	19.8 ('62)	14.3	10.8
United States	12.2 ('50)	6.5	4.4	3.8
Great Britain	5.1 ('51)	3.8 ('61)	3.2	2.7

SOURCE: Bureau of Labor Statistics, International Economic Performance and Comparative Tax Structure, Office of Economic Policy, Planning, and Research, Department of Economic and Business Development.

Table 1.5. Annual percentage change in manufacturing productivity in 1960–1979, average annual compound rate of change, in percentages

Year	United States	Japan	France	West Germany	United Kingdom
1960–79	2.6	9.2	5.5	5.4	2.9
1960–73	3.1	40.3	5.8	5.5	4.0
1973–79	1.4	6.9	4.8	5.3	0.5
1973–74	−5.0	4.1	3.4	6.0	−0.3
1974–75	5.1	4.0	3.1	4.8	−2.2
1975–76	4.4	9.4	8.2	6.3	3.1
1976–77	3.0	8.8	4.5	5.6	−0.4
1977–78	0.4	6.8	4.9	3.6	1.2
1978–79	0.8	8.1	4.7	5.2	1.7

SOURCE: Bureau of Labor Statistics, International Economic Performance and Comparative Tax Structure, Office of Economic Policy, Planning, and Research, Department of Economic and Business Development.

Table 1.6. Various countries' shares in the value of world exports of manufactures 1950–1977 (percent)

Country	1950	1960	1965	1970	1975	1977
United Kingdom	25.5	16.5	13.9	10.8	9.3	9.3
France	9.9	9.6	8.8	8.7	10.2	9.9
West Germany	7.3	19.3	19.1	19.8	20.3	20.8
Italy		5.1	6.7	7.2	7.5	7.4
Others	26.6	21.0	21.8	23.3	21.4	21.4
Japan	3.4	6.9	9.4	11.7	13.6	15.4
United States	27.3	21.6	20.3	18.5	17.7	15.9

SOURCE: C. J. F. Brown and T. D. Sheriff, "De-industrialization: A Background Paper," in Frank Blackaby, ed., *De-industrialisation* (London: Heinemann, 1979), p. 241.

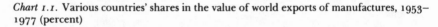

Chart 1.1. Various countries' shares in the value of world exports of manufactures, 1953–1977 (percent)

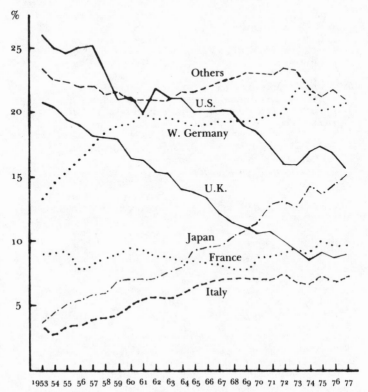

1953 54 55 56 57 58 59 60 61 62 63 64 65 66 67 68 69 70 71 72 73 74 75 76 77

SOURCE: C. J. F. Brown and T. D. Sheriff, "De-industrialisation: A Background Paper," in Frank Blackaby, ed., *De-industrialisation* (London: Heinemann, 1979), pp. 241–242.

low inflation rates. Table 1.9D illustrates the new pattern for the period 1978–1981.

THE NEW POLITICS OF GROWTH: DOMESTIC POLITICAL CIRCUMSTANCES

A look at the transfers surrounding growth in the postwar years may help to clarify the present political challenge.[12] The long expansion in the most rapidly growing countries was facilitated by the shift out of inefficient agriculture into industry. As farming was mechanized, labor

Table 1.7. Growth and inflation in five countries, 1954–1968

A. Average annual percentage increase in
domestic production (constant prices)

Country	Percentage increase
Japan	9.5
West Germany	5.7
France	5.1
United States	3.5
United Kingdom	3.0

B. Average annual percentage increase in
real consumer prices

Country	Percentage increase
France	3.9
Japan	3.8
United Kingdom	3.2
West Germany	2.2
United States	1.8

C. Pattern of growth and inflation in five countries

Inflation rate	Growth rate	
	High (above 5.0%)	Low (below 4.0%)
High (above 3.0%)	Japan France	United Kingdom
Low (below 2.5%)		
	West Germany	United States

SOURCE: See Appendix.

was freed for other uses and, as a result, industrialization did not directly challenge those who owned the land. Even as the countryside emptied of population, patterns of land ownership remained much the same in France, Germany, and Japan; the increase in farm size resulted more from death than from displacement.[13] Precisely because farm ownership did not have to be rapidly or forcibly reorganized to increase production and release workers, governments could purchase the political acquiescence of the farm bloc with subsidies and price supports. The position of the rural elites in the national community changed but their place in the local order was not altered dramatically. Since traditional rural life was the reference used in establishing the levels of agricultural support and subsidies, these government measures did not negate market incentives that could draw labor into in-

Table 1.8. Growth and inflation in five countries, 1969–1978

A. Average annual percentage increase in
domestic production (constant prices)

Country	Percentage increase
Japan	6.1
France	4.5
West Germany	3.6
United States	3.0
United Kingdom	2.3

B. Pattern of growth and inflation in five countries

Inflation Rate	Growth Rate	
	High (above 4.5%)	Low (below 4.0%)
High (above 8.0%)	Japan France	United Kingdom
Low (below 7.0%)		West Germany United States

SOURCE: See Appendix.

dustry. The peasantry could be held in place even as its economic and social positions were destroyed.

The sectoral shift in the use of labor accounts for only a portion of the gain in output, however. As Edward Dennison has argued, the rest of the increase is associated with investment and technological advance.[14] We might try to distinguish analytically between a component of growth which results strictly from investment or technological advance and a component that can be attributed to sectoral shift, but sectoral shifts of labor were made possible by investment, which would have been less promising without the labor. The two were inseparable components of one economic process.

The political task a country confronts in trying to sustain growth has changed. The shift out of agriculture is no longer an integral part of growth in any advanced country. A generation ago, in the fast-growth nations, it was agriculture that had to be moved and modernized, but now such sectors as textiles and steel must be displaced or transformed. It may prove more difficult to assure "creative destruction" in industry than it was to displace the peasants and modernize agriculture in the postwar years. The central difference is that politically entrenched interests will have to be confronted directly rather than finessed. Several elements compose this new political challenge.

First, changes in industrial structure—the exit or merger of firms in

24

Table 1.9. Growth and inflation in five countries, 1978–1981

A. Inflation rate (percent) in five countries in 1981

Country	Inflation rate
France	13.4
United Kingdom	11.9
United States	10.2
West Germany	5.9
Japan	4.9

B. Average annual percentage increase in
domestic production (constant prices)

Country	Percentage increase
Japan	4.4
United States	2.5
West Germany	2.4
France	2.2
United Kingdom	0.9

C. Average annual percentage increase in
real consumer prices

Country	Percentage increase
United Kingdom	13.2
France	11.7
United States	10.7
Japan	5.1
West Germany	4.6

D. Pattern of growth and inflation in five countries, 1978–1981

Inflation Rate	Growth Rate		
	High (above 4.5%)	Intermediate (4.0 to 4.5%)	Low (below 4.0%)
High (above 8.0%)			United Kingdom United States France
Low (below 7.0%)		Japan	West Germany

SOURCE: See Appendix.

declining sectors and the reorganizations throughout industry—represent a challenge to the patterns of ownership which was avoided in the
process of agricultural modernization. Even medium-sized firms represent substantial numbers of jobs and their owners and managers have a
considerable political and social position in local communities. Thus,

25

there are a range of potential alliances between labor and capital, a variety of shared interests in resisting change.

Second, industrial workers are more highly organized and can take more varied and specific actions to protect themselves than could their agricultural counterparts. Their strategies will affect not simply their wages but also the organization of production, for industrial wage labor undoubtedly has more control of the shop floor and of changes in the pattern of work than its agricultural counterparts did. Moreover, the position of industrial labor is reinforced by a web of legal protections built up over recent years.

Third, and critically, the gap between returns from any two industrial sectors is likely to be less than the gap between agriculture and industry was a generation ago in the fast-growth nations. Whereas agriculture could be subsidized into political quiescence without eliminating the market incentives for it to move or modernize, the protections and subsidies required to appease political unrest in weakening industries may seriously dampen the marketplace incentives for adjustment.

These three problems are of long standing in the slow-growth countries, but in the fast-growth countries they present new political problems and policy dilemmas. Without the temporary advantage afforded by a large agricultural sector, the fast-growth countries, like their slower-growth partners, must now confront politically entrenched producer interests. They must find a new political settlement that allocates the costs of industrial adjustment without eliminating market signals and the market incentives for adjustment. At the same time, the rapid expansion of Japan, Germany, and France has itself sparked new political controversies over growth in Britain and the United States.

In 1950 Britain and the United States provided over half the value of world exports, whereas their fast-growth competitors—yet to get their booms underway—supplied only 21 percent. By 1977, however, the positions had been reversed. Japan, Germany, and France together provided 46 percent of world exports and the United States and Britain had slipped to roughly 25 percent. The slow growth of Britain and the United States brought considerable pressure to bear on their domestic industries. The collapse of the British auto industry during the 1970s was one of the most dramatic expressions of the changing competitive positions among the advanced countries.

It was inevitable that the disparity in wealth and industrial strength between the former world leaders and the rest of the advanced nations would be closed. Though rapid industrial catch-up and an accelerated shift out of agriculture accounted in part for the sharp difference in growth rates, the speed with which the gap was narrowed and the fact that Britain actually fell behind in the race for real and per capita income sparked difficult domestic debates. The pace of American and British growth rested on a series of national political settlements about economic arrangements and these settlements were now called into question. The governments of the two countries were organized to regulate or umpire their economies, not to take an active role in promoting industrial development. In Britain efforts to structure the state so it could play a leadership role in industrial affairs provoked sharp fights about the rights of business and the power of labor. Both Britain and the United States invested less and saved less than their competitors, and in both nations policies were suggested to raise those rates to rekindle growth. The proposals opened politically difficult distributional conflicts that split the broad consensus that economic priorities needed to be reoriented. Reorienting economic priorities in the face of new circumstances is a fundamental political challenge.

In all these advanced countries, the political task of managing adjustment is complicated by fears that even if growth resumed a full pace, new jobs in growth sectors may not be created as fast as workers are displaced in declining ones. Luddite fears that machines would destroy jobs and disrupt society have marked the entire course of industrialization. To observe that historically machines have permitted an expansion in production and employment which has more than offset short-term losses is not to deny that the surges and displacements have meant real and permanent losses to many of those directly affected. We do not, therefore, need to discover a long-run permanent shift in the employment capacity of the growth industries to conclude that the pattern of growth may itself generate unemployment. Indeed, the fears of enduring unemployment will fuel intense political efforts to protect existing jobs. A change in the employment content of production—jobs per unit of output—has occurred during a drop in overall economic activity. The downturn may have camouflaged the economic effects and political significance of this shift. Let us consider two such problems here.

First, the skill requirements of new jobs may not precisely fit the skills of the available labor pool, thus causing labor shortages and unemployment at the same time.[15] The problem created by changing patterns of world trade is not really the loss of jobs in any national economy but instead the problem of more difficult internal adjustment. Increases in manufactured exports by the advanced countries to less-developed-country markets have more than equaled the growth in imports. The Common Market (EEC), the United States, and Japan

27

increased their exports to less-developed countries from $36 billion in 1972 to $102 billion in 1976, while the trade balance in manufactures grew from $24 billion to $71 billion.[16] The adjustment problem, then, is the mismatch between the labor released from such traditional industries as textiles and the skill requirements of the new export sectors. "The level of qualifications and salaries in the menaced industries is inferior to those in the industries exporting to the Third World," explained a recent French government study.[17] The incentive to transfer is there, but the skills and the means may not be. Labor in these displaced sectors is relatively unskilled and immobile, and may in fact be pushed out of the labor market entirely.

There is a second problem. Between 1960 and 1970 there were three rapidly growing industries in Western Europe: chemicals, electrical machinery (which includes electronics and machine tools), and petroleum. Petroleum and oil products accounted for less than 1 percent of employment, so the changes there were of little import. Chemical output went up over 10 percent a year but produced only a 2.5 percent rise in employment. Electrical machinery did not have extraordinary productivity gains, but its share of employment rose substantially during the period. Together these growth industries increased their share of total output from 16.86 percent to 23.52 percent during the 1960s, but their contribution to employment rose only from 14.0 percent to 16.7 percent.[18] One might say either that the employment coverage of the new output was only 40 percent, or that the ratio of increased output to new jobs in the three sectors dropped from 83 percent to 70 percent. New production did not produce a proportionate number of jobs. The problems will worsen in the 1980s because advances in electronic microcircuitry have transformed the possibilities of automation into a technical reality. European labor groups note that German GNP increased 1.7 percent per annum between 1971 and 1975 while productivity rose 3.8 percent per annum. One would expect the result to be unemployment, and indeed unemployment did increase.[19] Still, the long-term employment consequences of microcircuitry cannot be specified at this time. There are conflicting trends and it is not clear which of them will have the dominant effect on employment. The number of office employees for a given unit of paperwork has declined, but the total volume of paperwork has expanded. Manufacturing productivity may go up with robotics, but factories must be reequipped to take advantage of that technology. A new product with linkages as extensive as microcircuits can generate a productive reorganization of the economy and of society as a whole. The economic problems become entangled, complicating the political task. We confront not a scenario of industrial doom but rather a period of troubled adjustment.

EVOLVING PRESSURES FOR ADJUSTMENT: SHIFTS IN INTERNATIONAL MARKETS

Increased oil prices and new conditions of international trade generate intense pressures for domestic industrial adjustments in all of the advanced countries. The shifts required today are certainly different from and arguably more difficult than those that took place during the expansion of the 1950s and 1960s. The employment issues just noted are only part of the story. The growth decades were characterized by declining commodity prices, an expansion of intrasectoral trade among the advanced countries, and a shift in the fast-growth countries from low-productivity agriculture into industry. In those years, firms adapted and resources shifted in order to capture the *rewards* of market opportunities. In the present epoch, adjustment and investment are necessary to offset market *penalties*. (The penalties affect all producers and are thus system characteristics.) Industrial changes are required to return to a revised version of the status quo. For the firm, there is a profound difference between responding to price signals that represent penalties for failure to change, and responding to price signals that offer rewards for success. Penalties undermine the existing cash flow and profit margins upon which company responses are based. When commodity prices or energy prices were falling, adjustment to the new price structure brought an increase in profits or profit margins. Substituting cheap oil for coal meant lower heating and production costs. Assuming for the moment that final product prices are fixed, we see that the rise in oil prices requires substitutes or energy-saving investments to reestablish profit margins. Increased oil prices that threaten to cut profit margins are the motivation for energy-saving investments, but again these investments will be made at the cost of diminished profits or profit prospects. The firm thus faces the need to raise capital for investment and finds it difficult to maintain cash flow. To repeat, under "penalty" conditions much of investment does not serve to increase either output or the market value of output. The penalty for that investment is the reduction of both profits and cash flows. If prices are raised, the process of course becomes inflationary. Productivity increases, the universal solvent for economic conflicts in the postwar years, have thus become more difficult to achieve.

29

Let us consider here two changes in the pattern of trade which, along with the employment issues, have altered the adjustment problem: (1) the need to export in order to pay for an increased energy bill and (2) the trade conditions that emphasize the potential real losses of exchange—the circumstances in which international trade looks like a zero-sum game rather than the more appealing game of mutual gains from exchange that we have been accustomed to expect.

The Oil Problem

OPEC's increased oil revenues and the oil tax have changed the composition of demand. The advanced countries have to produce a new mix of goods for new markets and each country's industry must change what it sells in response to this new demand mix. Increased prices for imported oil have transferred income from the consumers of goods and services in the advanced nations to the governments of the oil-producing nations. What concerns us here is the real transfer of resources, not the nominal monetary shift. The real transfer is reduced by any inflation in the oil-importing country which is not compensated for by further oil-price increases. When inflation in the advanced countries is not met by further oil-price hikes, it reduces the volume of goods and services transferred in exchange for oil by reducing the real value of any monetary price for oil. How, we must ask, is that new mix of goods determined and in what way does it differ from the previous mix?

OPEC countries can either invest or spend their oil profits. The money they spend shifts demand from the consumers in the advanced countries to the governments of the OPEC countries. For the moment, however, let us follow the flow of funds they invest. This money can be placed in real assets, such as corporate holdings or real estate, or in financial assets, such as bank deposits. The massive investment of OPEC money in financial assets creates that we call the "petrodollar recycling problem." In essence, this money must be put to real uses—lent to some final borrower who employs the funds to purchase something—and the international financial markets have become the device for such shifts. Part of these funds is lent back to large corporate or state borrowers in the advanced countries. Another part is lent to cover the trade deficits of non-oil-importing, less-developed countries, or to promote the development of the richer less-developed countries or the countries of the Eastern bloc.

The tendency, in sum, is to transfer purchasing power from the consumers of the advanced countries toward state and corporate borrowers, who spend a higher percentage of the funds on investment and use a different mix of goods. The nature of final demand is changed in the process. To cover their oil bill, the advanced countries must sell to the OPEC countries, or to the less-developed countries and the corporations that have borrowed OPEC dollars from international markets. The shift in demand is away from consumer goods toward intermediary goods and often turn-key plants, as when the Saudis or Soviets contract for the purchase of an entire plant. For the developed countries, therefore, the task is, as the French would say, "to redeploy" resources into those export sectors. Clearly, those countries that succeed will have more buoyant economies and those that do not will be more vulnerable to external pressures.

What quantities are really involved? The oil bill for the advanced countries is depicted in Table 1.10. The increments in the oil bill from year to year represent the annual pressure to shift resources toward export uses in order to pay for the oil.[20]

Other problems evidently resulted from the oil-price hikes. The most widely discussed is the need to assure that consumers in the advanced countries relinquish their income to pay for the oil and permit the real transfers to take place. The oil-price increase, as is often emphasized, represents a real decline in living standards to the extent of the added amount needed to pay for oil. If the OPEC oil bill is passed from one part of a national economy to another (or from one group to another), with each refusing to pay it by hiking price or wage demands, adjustment translates into inflation. A relative decline in income is in fact only one instance of a more general problem. The oil-price increases can reverberate across a country's economy only to be consolidated as inflation rather than as a change in relative prices and incomes.

It is now almost a decade since the first great oil-price shock occurred. The continuing high price for oil undoubtedly narrows the room for economic maneuver, meaning, for example, that every domestic boom is likely to translate into dramatically higher energy import costs. The increased demand for oil then pushes energy prices still higher. Yet the great political and economic dislocation that was feared has not materialized. Arab money has been recycled, resources in the advanced countries have been shifted to pay for exports, production structures have been adjusted to use less energy as its cost has risen, and the changes in real income caused by the OPEC oil "tax" have with difficulty been achieved. Certainly, the strains are evident. Many of the less-developed oil-importing countries continue to accumulate debt to buy oil, and in the advanced countries inflation still reflects in part an unwillingness to accept the decline in living standards that the oil-price

Table 1.10. Oil imports as percent of GNP for five countries, 1965–1975

Year	United States	Japan	France	West Germany	United Kingdom
1965	0.2	1.2	1.1	0.9	1.2
1967	0.2	1.5	1.3	1.1	1.4
1969	0.2	1.3	1.2	1.2	1.5
1971	0.2	1.2	1.2	1.1	1.6
1973	0.4	1.5	1.4	1.0	1.8
1975	1.3	3.8	3.0	1.9	3.6

SOURCE: *World Trade Annual* (New York: United Nations Statistical Office, for appropriate years).

hikes imply. Yet high energy costs have become part of a new normalcy—an unsettled and tenuous normalcy that promises continued stress and crisis, but a normalcy nonetheless. The oil crisis, however, may have hidden the real long-term risk inherent in our recent trade conflicts.

The Trade Problem

Pressures for industrial adjustment are also generated by changes in the dynamics of international trade which have left it a rougher and less congenial sport than it once was. In the 1960s it was thought that production costs and production structures in the various advanced countries were converging and that the expansion of trade would therefore lead to greater specialization.[21] Consequently, it appeared that international trade could grow without precipitating massive dislocations of workers and firms, that the domestic political costs of expanded trade were low. In the machine-tool industry, for example, Germany would capture a large share of the market for some tools, while the United States would become increasingly dominant in other areas of the market. Expanded exchange would lead to increased company specialization and produce higher incomes for both trading nations. There would be only winners in the trade game; the general welfare would increase for all. After the self-defeating era of protection between the world wars, this new faith was an exhilarating discovery.

There are indeed real gains to be achieved through trade and they are evident in the increasing contribution that free trade has made to growth and welfare in the advanced countries during the postwar years. Yet there are circumstances in which international trade produces real losers as well, cases in which the immediate gains from exchange are outweighed by their long-term effects on a nation's economy. These purely competitive trade conditions have become more important in the last decade and have contributed to adjustment problems in the advanced countries. One theme of our discussion is to explain how governments shape the outcomes in these fundamentally competitive trade situations, thereby altering the evolving pattern of comparative advantage.

If national policy can affect a nation's comparative advantage, then trade conflicts are to some extent battles over which countries will have accelerated rates of development. Two changes in world trade have made this point clearer in recent years. The first is the entrance of producers from the newly industrializing countries into the markets of the advanced nations. The congenial trade world proposed to us in past years depended upon converging production costs and specialization within sectors—not upon diverging production structures, which imply that labor and firms are displaced from entire segments of production. The newly industrializing nations were initially able to enter advanced country markets because of their radically lower labor costs. The sharp difference in production structures between the advanced and the newly industrializing countries means that trade between them poses the threat of displacement to advanced-country producers that make standardized goods with standard technologies and high-wage labor. The second and more important trade change is rooted in the nature of the competition between the firms in the advanced countries, which can lead to the emergence of a few dominant producers in crucial sectors. Government policies can intensify this competition in important ways. Strategies of rapid industrial "catch-up," such as those employed by Japan, may work equally well as strategies for pulling ahead. The common question raised both by advanced-country competition and by imports from the developing countries is how to accommodate newcomers—whether countries or firms—in traditional marketplaces. After examining these two elements of the new trade game, we shall consider how received trade theory leads us to underestimate the seriousness of the trade conflicts we are witnessing.

First, manufactured exports from the less-developed countries, and particularly from a small number that have come to be called newly industrializing countries, have become important in the markets of the advanced countries. Production from these new competitors forces adjustments in the advanced-country industries, creating a set of trade-impacted sectors. Equally critical, competition between the advanced countries is squeezed into a narrower range of businesses, presumably intensifying the competition in each. Each advanced OECD (Organisation for Economic Cooperation and Development) country will want to succeed in high value-added businesses where labor is not a critical part of competitive position. Moreover, in standard products with easily transferable production technologies, the countries with surpluses of cheap labor have long-run advantages. Conscious efforts to exploit those advantages as a development strategy can serve only to shorten product life cycles—that is, to shorten the time between the moment when an innovation gives a country a comparative advantage and the moment when countries with inexpensive labor will begin to export the good back to the market of the innovator.

Between 1970 and 1980 manufactured exports from the less-developed countries grew some ten times, reaching a total of $44 billion. By 1985, their manufactured exports to the OECD countries will grow to between $100 and $145 billion, according to Bank of International Reconstruction and Development (BIRD) estimates. In global terms, the imports are not dramatic, representing between 1 and 2 percent of total manufactures.[22] Moreover, the aggregate costs of such imports are usually paid for by increased exports from the advanced countries to the burgeoning markets in the newly industrializing countries. For example, imported textiles are made with exported textile machinery. The overall importance of trade with the newly industrializing countries is small in comparison with trade inside the OECD, but the present trend is clear and should not be underestimated. In 1970 only 5 percent of OECD manufactured imports came from developing countries. By 1980 the share had risen to almost 11 percent.[23] Furthermore, these countries offer the most rapidly growing markets.

At least until 1980, manufacturing in the less-developed countries was focused in a few sectors and, consequently, the impact on the advanced countries was also concentrated, the greatest impact being in textiles, clothing, and electronics and electrical machinery.[24] It is not unreasonable to assume, however, that the new producers will enter an increasing number of sectors, with steel likely to join the list soon. Cheap labor has existed for a long time; what we are observing is the growing capacity of government and business in a number of countries (the most successful of which have limited populations) to use this labor productively. The nature of the problem would of course assume different dimensions if large countries such as India or China begin to implement export-led strategies.[25] It is an open question how many developing countries will be able to follow the lead of these first exporters among the newly industrializing countries. The answer depends in part on the ability of developing countries to mobilize and organize manufacturing resources. It also depends on the willingness of the advanced countries to maintain open markets—a willingness that we can assume will decline as the number of would-be exporters grows.

The second trade problem is the more serious. It involves competition between companies from the several advanced countries, a competition abetted by governments concerned with jobs and trade flows. In one view government interventions simply serve to slow down the changes required by the market, to distort the most efficient use of resources given the international pattern of advantage, or to subsidize users at home or abroad. Government interventions, however, involve two quite different efforts. On the one hand, governments are indeed trying to prop up firms that are losing in international competition, using outright subsidies to maintain jobs where necessary. Subsidies to steel producers in the spring of 1981 were estimated by the *Economist* to average $27 per ton in France and nearly $100 per ton in Britain.[26] On the other hand, governments are hoping to create advantages for their firms in international markets, to help them reach a market position they can defend without subsidies. Certainly Japan accomplished this aim directly with its shipbuilding and steel policies and it did the same thing indirectly in the auto industry through market closure and financial promotion. In these cases of directed promotion, the stakes were not long-term subsidies but a change in the international pattern of comparative advantage. If this pattern cannot be taken as given but is constantly being created by the efforts, separate and joined, of governments and firms, then trade competition does not simply maximize common welfare. Rather, it establishes the relative position of different countries in the ever-changing system of international comparative advantage and division of labor.

To understand the potential government role in shaping the pattern of advantage, let us begin by distinguishing businesses according to which component of their operations most critically affects their competitive position. Among these components we might list raw materials costs, labor costs, distribution costs, research-and-development costs, and the operation of complex production systems. If we assumed that labor and raw materials costs reflected national characteristics, we might assume that some countries would have a trade advantage in industries in which these costs were low. But there are dangers in assuming that the costs of either materials or labor are fixed so that trade automatically reveals an advantage. Cheap raw materials are now largely a product of investment in recovery and transportation systems, and the mere location of the material reserves may matter less than in previous eras. Since the postwar shipping revolution, delivered cost and geographic proximity to coal and iron for steel producing have become quite different matters. More generally, a firm that finds itself at a disadvantage because one of its costs is above that of its competitors—say, its cost for raw materials or labor—will try to overcome the disadvantage by making investments in distribution, in production structures and machinery, or in product design. Thus, for example, the parts of the American textile industry which have survived the import onslaught have begun to reduce labor content in production.

Let us focus for a moment, though, on businesses in which research and development and the operation of complex production systems are critical. In capital-intensive production sectors such as steel and shipbuilding, productivity has been at the center of competition, whereas product advances have been the key in high-technology industry. This distinction can be somewhat deceptive, however. In consumer electronics, product advances into solid-state technology allowed the Japanese simultaneously to enter the small-set end of the television market and to make production advances that improved reliability and lowered costs. As a result, they were able to move up market and to squeeze out the American producers. A firm's initial advantage in product development or in the operation of complex production systems may be reinforced by a dominant market share. In a number of businesses substantial competitive advantage is accorded to firms with dominant market shares or with rapidly expanding volumes. If a firm with a dominant market share expands production rapidly, it can frequently drive production costs down. Part of the productivity gains will result from economies of scale and part will come from what have been loosely called learning-curve effects. In essence, neither the competitive positions of firms in crucial sectors nor the comparative advantages of the advanced countries will be fixed. Both can be created by the strategies of firms and by government policies.

Let us assume that one country protects its domestic markets in rapidly expanding industries in which production costs decline with volume because of scale economies and learning-curve effects. A domestic firm will be able to exploit this protected market to drive its costs down and then enter competitive export markets. In Chapter 5 we shall see how the Japanese consciously exploited closed markets and rapid domestic expansion to generate internationally competitive firms. Let us consider some examples. Rapid expansion in Japanese domestic demand has undoubtedly contributed to the jumps in productivity of the steel, shipbuilding, and automobile sectors. In automobiles, for example, Japanese production jumped from 1.3 percent of world passenger cars in 1960 (160,000 units) to 18.1 percent in 1975 (4.5 million) and in 1980.[27] Japanese exports during this same period grew to reach

45 percent of production. Japan has not been alone. France and Germany have also benefited from domestic expansion in auto consumption. The high-productivity firms exporting from expanding domestic markets became threats to employment and output in other countries. A close look at diverging productivity between Japan and the other advanced countries in motorcycles, steel, and television sets should convince even the skeptical that the changing trade flows reflect real changes in advantage. The French and American difficulties in steel emphasize that expanded output and government-based modernization do not in themselves assure competitive productivity. Expansion creates a set of opportunities, but these opportunities may not be used equally well by all companies. The benefits of rapid expansion depend on the choices about technology and production organization made by individual firms.

When new and more efficient producers enter the market, the real issue is which countries will be competitive in which industries. Not all industries are equivalent. Some, such as automobiles, are massive employers situated at the core of a series of related industries. Some of the British problems in steel, for example, must be attributed to the competitive decline of its auto industry. Other industries, such as integrated circuits, may shape both product and production technology in an entire national economy. Thus, pools of high-wage jobs and the pace and direction of national industrial development may well be at stake in trade competition. If not all industries are equal, and if governments can create advantage, then trade competition can be seen as a struggle between different paths of economic development or a fight for post position in the economic race.

Traditional trade theory tends to hide the constantly shifting and positively created character of advantage.*[28] In so doing, it hides both the real stakes in many trade conflicts and the role that government plays in plotting the course of national industrial development. According to the modern theory of international trade, free trade encourages countries to export in sectors in which they have a comparative advantage and to import in sectors in which they have a comparative disadvantage. Comparative advantage is usually assumed to depend on relative factor proportions or availabilities, under the assumption that all countries have access to the same production technology and differ

*This section is in large part excerpted from an article written by Laura Tyson and myself, "Making Policy for American Industry in International Competition." The views here relate only tangentially to the debate on the international division of labor, which implies a greater technical inevitability to the process by which industries will be redistributed to alter our economic geography.

merely in their endowments of factors of production. The traditional theory, according to both its Hecksher-Ohlin and Ricardian versions, posits the existence of mutual gains from free trade accruing "to national trading partners."* Even the country with an absolute disadvantage—a higher domestic cost of production for all traded commodities—gains from free trade by importing those goods in which its absolute disadvantage is least. Not surprisingly, then, discussions based on these premises are likely to take a dim view of government policy that is intended to alleviate the difficulties of domestic industries in international trade. Interference with the market, it is thought, can only distort the pattern of free trade; the difficulties of specific industries can be eased only at the expense of national gains.

Traditional trade theory, however, is powerless to deal with questions that do not fit its static orientation and its assumption of perfect competition. As soon as technological evolution and market imperfections are allowed to enter the picture, both the theoretical models and the implied policy prescriptions of traditional theory become confused. The static nature of trade theory is reflected in the assumptions of fixed technology and fixed factor endowments which are components of both Ricardian and Hecksher-Ohlin theory. For example, the Hecksher-Ohlin theory assumes a given standard production technology to which all countries have access, and also assumes given amounts of factor endowments in each country. Under these assumptions, the theory posits that trade will lead to increasing specialization among trading partners as factor prices, and hence production costs of traded goods, converge. The theory treats the determinants of factor endowments as exogenous and overlooks the important fact that technologies are not the same in all nations producing the same goods. As a consequence, critically important policy issues fall outside the scope of theoretical analysis.

The influence of government policies on the dynamics of comparative advantage over time becomes clear when one allows for the possibility of differing production technologies in different countries. This influence

---

*The modern variant of comparative advantage theory, referred to in the economics literature as the Hecksher-Ohlin theory, assumes the existence of two or more factors of production (starting with labor and capital) and argues that countries will tend to export goods embodying their relatively more abundant factors and to import goods embodying their relatively more scarce factors. Ricardian trade theory, in contrast, explains comparative advantage in terms of a single key factor of production, usually labor, although in more recent usage it has been used to explain trade based on natural resource endowment as well. In Ricardian theory, the precise pattern of specialization in production and trade depends on comparative costs measured in terms of the factor of production in question.

is clearly apparent in the impact that government policies have on the gradual accumulation of physical and human capital. Such policies can steadily turn a temporary competitive disadvantage in capital- or education-intensive industries into a comparative advantage. In short, national comparative advantage is in part the product of national policies over time. There are only a few industrial sectors in which comparative advantage is given in the form of fixed natural-resource endowment. In most sectors, comparative advantage rests on relative capital endowments, and these are the result of accumulated investment.

The role of national policies in the process of creating comparative advantage is forcefully demonstrated in the case of Japan, where policymakers consciously approached industry policy with the notion of creating advantage and with a view of dynamic change. To understand the economic transition they have engineered, it is first necessary to distinguish between the notions of comparative advantage and competitive advantage. Comparative advantage refers to the relative export strength of a particular sector compared to other sectors in that same economy and it is usually measured after adjusting for the effect of government policies that distort the supposedly autonomous workings of the market. For the purposes of our discussion, competitive advantage refers to the relative export strength of the firms of one country compared to the firms of *other* countries selling in the same sector in international markets. According to this interpretation, the competitive advantage enjoyed by the firms of a particular country in a particular sector may be the result of that country's absolute advantage in that sector. In contrast to the usual notion of absolute advantage, however, the notion of competitive advantage allows for the presence of economic policies that help or hinder the international performances of different firms. Thus the competitive advantage of the firms of a particular country in a particular market may be the result of a real absolute advantage or it may be the result of a policy-induced and hence distorted absolute advantage. Policy-induced advantage can accumulate over time into real absolute advantage, however, as when abundant capital and protection allowed the investment in steel development which made Japanese producers preeminent.

Whether competitive advantage is real or policy induced, the competitive dynamics of industry form the link between static and dynamic comparative advantage. Over time, shifts in competitive advantage for particular firms in particular industries can accumulate into a change in national comparative advantage. We must understand that comparative advantage rests on the accumulation of investments, and that a long-term strategy can slowly alter a country's comparative advantage

39

by altering its investment stock. The main point, again, is that accumulated investment, whether in physical infrastructure or the infrastructure of related markets and firms, is crucial to determining both competitive advantage at the moment and comparative advantage over time. In a wide range of industrial sectors, a nation creates its own comparative advantage by the efforts of industries and government to establish competitive advantage in the market. Where the eroding competitive position of individual firms unravels a web of domestic infrastructure, the outcome can be a change in comparative advantage. This is especially true in industries dominated by a few large firms. Although there may be no comparative disadvantage underlying the initial competitive difficulties of a particular firm, these difficulties can have a cumulative effect that leads to a national disadvantage. The costs of recapturing a lost market share will rise if the infrastructure, in the form of suppliers and distribution networks, is undermined. The collapse of suppliers, for example, may affect the industry's collective ability to sustain its technological position. As this discussion suggests, in advanced industrial economies comparative advantage—a concept much in vogue and loosely used—is to be understood as the cumulative effect of firm capacities and government policy choices and not simply as the effect of resource endowments in capital and labor.

Although the determinants of change in competitive advantage have been largely overlooked in most models of international trade, they have been the focus of at least one branch of trade theory—namely the product-cycle theory.[29] Product-cycle theory focuses on the role of technology and innovation in the dynamics of trade. Developed in the 1960s to explain changes in the pattern of U.S. trade, it states that trade in manufactured goods typically follows a pattern in which the country that introduces a product first becomes a net exporter of it, but then loses its position when the manufacture of that product becomes standardized and moves to countries that have a comparative advantage in the factor intensities required by the standard technology. In the period before technology becomes standardized, the innovating country enjoys the benefits of imperfect competition which accrue to a single seller. If increasing returns to scale exist, these benefits may persist for some time before competitors are able to enter the critical role of innovation in the product-cycle theory, and given the apparent links between innovation and the process of both physical and human capital accumulation, the countries that pursue investment policies in both arenas are likely to be those which are product innovators and which earn the resultant rents. Moreover, in addition to investment policies, a variety of national policies—from tax policies on capital income to depreciation policies to support for research and development—may influence the pace of technological change and thus affect a nation's competitive advantage in high-technology industries. In simpler terms, policy can clearly affect the number and variety of products in which a country initiates the product cycle.

Policy will also affect the pattern of trade which each product cycle produces. How long one country can hold an advantage in the production of a particular good—or conversely, how quickly a follower producer can catch up—is not determined by some inevitable economic process. Markets can be manipulated, and imperfections created, to influence these outcomes. In these dynamic conditions there are no automatic mutual gains from exchange.

Consider, first, potential imperfections resulting from production economies of scale. Significant competitive advantages may be gained by the firms of a particular country if their home market is protected and they are allowed to develop a scale large enough to capture cost advantages. Under these protected conditions, a greater portion of market demand will appear stable to domestic producers. Greater market predictability should lead them to standardize and automate production more rapidly, with an eye to capturing maximum scale economies, because the risk of being stuck with unneeded capacity will be reduced.

Second, learning-curve economies, like production economies of scale, can be the source of competitive advantage in imperfect markets. In the presence of learning-curve economies, rapidly changing final products (such as integrated circuits), quick market entry, and an initially dominant position may provide the producer with a market advantage during a long phase of the product's life cycle. Or, more ominously for those who follow the leader, early entry may provide advantage through a long phase of an industry's development. Thus, as production volumes increase, costs decline because of modifications in product and process technology. This argument applies most powerfully to the rapidly expanding advanced technology industries. Once again, in sectors where learning-curve economies are likely to be significant, government policy can play an important role in stimulating or hindering their realization in domestic firms and hence in affecting the competitive advantages of these firms in international markets.

The conclusion of this argument, again, is that comparative advantage is a dynamic concept whose pattern can be altered over time by government policies. Politics will shape market demand as well as the technologies of product and production. Of course, while government may help a few firms gain competitive advantage within several industries or segments of them, this does not mean that the country will have a competitive advantage in all of them or that it will use up the economic breathing space of its partners. A single country may lose its competitive advantage over a wide range of industries, however, and there is a risk that the sectors in which it loses will be high-employment industries whose competitive decline will have a significant aggregate on development and trade. Clearly, this is the stake in autos and steel. The real danger is that a country may lose comparative advantage not simply in a single business or even in a range of businesses, but rather in a type of business. Thus it is not simply that the Japanese achieved advantages in color televisions or in automobiles and motorcycles. Rather they developed skills in the volume production of standard or commodity items which can be applied to many businesses. Mass production stands at the core of the manufacturing sector of all advanced countries. Once a country has lost comparative advantage in a type of business, it may turn onto a slower growth path than its partner. Conversely, a country may lever itself onto a fast route. Japan, for example, can be said to have gained an advantage in industries in which high-volume standardized production yields quality and cost advantages. In modern mass-production sectors, comparative advantage hinges not simply on wage rates but on the operational control of complex systems that reduce unit labor costs substantially. The Japanese, by comparison with American producers, for example, have stripped the labor content out of a wide range of products. One could argue that the Japanese government strategy of controlled competition and targeted consumer booms contributes to this advantage. Nevertheless, the advantages created are real.

Instead of intervening to create or maintain comparative advantage, however, governments often act simply to subsidize uncompetitive production. In order to explore this practice we need some means of distinguishing among the myriad individual choices that government makes about industry. We must distinguish three kinds of changes in the condition of industry—growth, transition, and decline—each of which presents different competitive problems for firms and different policy choices for governments. In each case we ask the same question: Is there a strategy for governments and firms which will allow the companies to remain competitive in international markets? If there is no competitive strategy, or if the political or budgetary price is too high to reach a stable competitive position, then subsidy and protection are the only alternatives to decline. If there are competitive strategies, then knowledge of the kind of change which confronts industry can help to illuminate the political and policy choices.

In a growth sector, rapid increases in demand are accompanied by a quick evolution in the product and in its production or distribution arrangements. Maintaining absolute levels of output is easy in a growing market. The important problem for a firm is maintaining market share, cash, organization, and technology in order to stay abreast of the evolution of the industry. For a government, the problem may be to assure the growth of national production so that imports do not capture the expanding demand and weaken the position of national firms. Not all growth industries are equally significant, and we must distinguish therefore between those with extensive linkages to the rest of the economy, which are consequently of substantial national importance, and those which have limited attachments to (or importance for) other sectors.[30] The breakfast food and cosmetics industry are clearly unlinked industries, whereas the semiconductor sector and the auto industry have linkages so thick that their expansion can transform a whole economy and their decline can endanger it. The linked sectors are of greatest interest to governments, either because their significance is recognized early or because their extensive influence creates the need for new economic infrastructure. Finally, we must distinguish between growth sectors that are catching up in technology and importance with those in other countries and sectors that are genuinely new. Catch-up allows the government to identify both the importance of a sector and the appropriate technologies; the maps to the future are available in the industrial histories of one's competitors. Governments have the greatest stake in the newest growth-linked industry.

Some industries—or rather some product segments—are in decline. A declining segment is one in which there are no possible significant changes in product or process by which firms can regain competitive position, and one in which demand for the industry as a whole is stagnant. Some input into production or distribution may yield a cost advantage that causes a domestic firm to be underpriced by foreign firms or allows a domestic substitute to invade the market. Thus, for example, the primary competitive advantage of the newly industrializing countries is cheap labor in industries that have stable product and production characteristics. In such labor-intensive industries, a rundown in production or an exit from the market is the firm's only alternative to protection. The political problem here is lost labor and lost production. The industry as a whole faces common problems, and little besides subsidy or protection will help to resolve them.

There are only a few sectors in which decline in the face of foreign competitors or domestically produced substitutes is inevitable. Indeed, a loss in production or employment is more often the result of an inability to keep up with industry evolution or to weather changes in what goods are produced and how. Most losses are the result of marketplace defeat, not of decline caused by differential factor costs. Indeed, even when an industry appears headed for doom, it can sometimes revive if given enough time. The American textile industry had been dwindling for several years in the face of cheap labor imports, but in 1979 it suddenly began to export. Its resurgence is so broad that it cannot be explained simply by the availability of low-cost oil.[31] Rather, new company structures and new production technologies have made the renewal possible.

An industry in transition is a mature industry undergoing basic changes in its products or production processes. Its industrial structure is stable and patterns of competition have been entrenched as the result of accumulated experience. During periods of transition, changes in the characteristics of product demand or in the most efficient production system occur, and these changes alter the patterns of competition.

We may usefully distinguish between two types of transition. *Static transition* involves a return to the status quo ante in terms of industry structure. That is, there may be a sudden and abrupt market change—such as a shift in the product demanded, or in the production process, or in the level of demand—but no long-run change in the profile of a successful firm or in the industrial organization of the sector. Thus, the American auto industry has been rocked by business-cycle demand losses and the importation of small foreign cars, but it remains an oligopoly in which success depends on relatively similar corporate abilities. The only question is which firms will compose that oligopoly and what portion of the market will be supplied by American-assembled cars and American-produced components. A *dynamic transition* involves deeper and more basic changes in the organization of the typical firm and in the structure of the industry. Changes must involve more than production or product characteristics. Thus, for example, the emergence of artificial fibers transformed the textile industry. In apparel, the entrance of cheap-labor producers made some product lines uncompetitive; it also favored larger firms that could use foreign sources in certain lines, spread risks across products, expand marketing, and automate more of their production—options that often proved to be interdependent. In advanced countries, the market share of the large integrated steel firms is expected to decline, whereas that of the minimills and specialty steel firms will grow. In all three cases (textiles, apparel, and steel) the profile of a successful firm and the structure of the industry have changed. Within an industry, such change involves the emergence of new firms, the reorientation or death of old ones, and either a loss of labor or a change in work skills. Dynamic transition

44

produces both winners and losers in an industry, and the critical political issue is whose needs policy will serve. An industry in which there are corporate moves that could lead to transformation rather than decline may stick to its old ways if the firms that dominate the industry politically (or politically well-positioned labor groups) stand to lose from the changes essential to market success.

Thus, whether an industry survives a transition period or slips until decline is irreversible depends on both company choices and government policy. Though the buggy-whip industry was undoubtedly doomed as soon as the auto industry established itself, there are only a few sectors in which decline is inevitable. Whether an industry is defined as being in decline or in transition is a political determination that cannot be made by simple marketplace measurement, but the political definition will shape the actual market outcome.

Import figures understate the political significance of these trade issues. They do not show the domestic changes required to combat the import threat, changes and adjustments that would not take place or would occur much more slowly in the absence of these trade flows. For example, despite the rapid jump in clothing imports, major segments of the clothing industry in each of the advanced countries remain competitive. To remain competitive without protection, however, they have had to alter the organization of production and labor, technology, marketing, and patterns of subcontracting. Even if we were able to quantify the portions of the textile-apparel industry which have attempted significant reorganization in order to resist imports, we would still understate the political significance of these trade changes. In economic terms, we might ask what the direct and indirect trade balance and employment consequences were. Or more broadly, we might ask what investments and changes in the industry's structure were provoked by trade.

Politically, we must ask a different question. What portion of a nation's output is produced in industries that face serious adjustment problems? We must treat the textile-apparel industry, for example, as a political unit in order to identify the scope of the political forces at work, since the industry tends to act as a unit. We can count up the politically active segments of a nation's industrial base whose politics are trade influenced. Thus, we may wish to consider steel, textiles-apparel, consumer electronics, footwear, and automobiles together in order to get a measure of the full political impact of trade-threatened industries. There are great dangers in attempting to analyze the political dynamics of these industries as a single unit, however, because their aggregation .obscures the competitive dynamics within the industry. Still, such an aggregation may be a reasonable way to establish the potential scope of political resistance to adjustment.

In sum, two aspects of the evolving trade pressures for adjustment need to be emphasized. The advanced countries are experiencing more than simply short-term pressures on a set of vital industrial sectors. In many ways the very nature of the trade problem is new. The industrializing countries represent new competitors in traditional industries and they are forcing painful adjustments on their richer trade partners. More generally, they are accelerating the process by which new products and production processes are standardized; that is, they are speeding up the cycle by which advantage based on an innovation gives way to advantage based on labor costs. The sale of turn-key plants to developing countries captures this process vividly. The advanced countries *sell a custom product*, in this case an entire factory ready to start producing. They most often are paid *with the standardized products* made in those same plants. Buy-back financing arrangements for a turn-key factory create a direct link for the advanced nations between export of custom production and imports of standard products.

At the same time, there is no space for a multitude of competitive producers in many of the sectors in which the advanced countries compete between themselves. Some countries will end up without an aircraft, computer, or auto industry, whereas others, such as France or Japan, will try to enter them all. The pattern of comparative advantage which emerges will be shaped by government policies—both aggregate and sector policies. Governments will attempt to assist their industries to maintain advantage in sectors that are in transition and to create advantage in those which are growth-linked. Just as not all industrial structures or corporate organizations have proved equally effective, so some governments will demonstrate a greater capacity to assist industry in its struggle for advantage. Government policies are of course only part of the story; adjustment occurs within the firm, and corporate capacity for adjustment is clearly the first component of the process of industrial change. Yet the differing political capacities of governments to resist demands for protection or subsidy, and their different technical capacities to promote advantage, will also prove to be an element in the economic competition between nations.

INTERNATIONAL DIMENSIONS OF DOMESTIC ADJUSTMENT

National economic adjustment is not entirely a domestic political problem. An alternative to domestic adjustment is to transfer the adjustment problems to one's trade partners. A nation's ability to manipulate its relations to the international economy as a means of containing its domestic problems is constrained by political arrangements between states. In the Great Depression, the downward spiral of exchange devaluations and trade restrictions which accompanied and accelerated the decline of activity demonstrated that the transfer of adjustment problems was essentially a game of hot potato which burned everyone's fingers. The question of how to maintain an open-trade system, or at least one in which competing efforts at self-protection did not spell mutual destruction, pushed itself forward. These concerns spawned such institutions as GATT and the International Monetary Fund (IMF). The question here is not which system characteristics lead to a stable or open regime, or how and when regimes change. Rather, the question is when the fluctuating set of rules and procedures will complicate national adjustment problems, pressing for or delaying domestic adjustment. It is well understood that in the postwar years, the fast-growth countries (Japan, Germany, and France) were able to fix their currency values to promote export expansion into increasingly open international markets. Despite France's occasional efforts to shape the system, the three booming economies accepted the international structure and maneuvered within it. In the 1980s the game of hot potato makes the domestic tasks of industrial change all the harder.

Three circumstances are different now. First, trade imbalances express themselves not only as monetary issues but also as direct conflicts over the volume and composition of trade. Second, the trade conflicts cannot be resolved simply by making agreements about the *procedures* of trade—tariffs, quotas, and even nontariff restrictions; the conflicts are increasingly about *outcomes* and can be resolved only by additional agreements about the total volume and product mix of trade. Third, the United States is no longer able to determine unilaterally the structure of the trade, to provide either a stable monetary system or a passively open market for the other advanced countries. Even as domestic pressures to play international hot potato grow, trade agreements have sought to ban industry policies that simply defer or transfer adjustment problems. These agreements have been fragile bulwarks against beggar-thy-neighbor trade wars.

At the international level domestic industrial adjustment is a problem of industrial oversupply and competition for export markets. The export problem has been discussed earlier: the oil bill must be paid, and paid by exports. As a group, the advanced countries must sell in the OPEC and less-developed-country markets. The ability to adjust domestically is in part the ability to sell in these third markets. Politically, this adjustment is a matter of finding export promotion policies that are acceptable to companies and governments. The American objection to French use of below-market financing to gain an effective competitive edge is an example of the conflicts that have arisen over promotion policies.

The changed pattern of trade competition expresses itself politically in "industrial oversupply."[32] The sharp drops in employment and production which oversupply brings to some countries focus attention on the disruptions and dislocations of trade. In the Great Depression the term "industrial oversupply" referred to the manufacturing capacity that the collapse in demand made redundant. Recession-induced drops in demand are only one source of the present problem, however. The emergency of manufacturing capacity in the developing countries and the realignments between the advanced countries also produces oversupply. The challenge is now to manage the shift in the relative economic strength of the advanced countries and to accommodate the entry of new countries into the international marketplace for traditional products. As new competitive production comes on line, oversupply will result unless the losers—high-cost or low-quality producers—exit. The home governments of the losing firms have resisted the decline of their segments of the industries, just as the governments of the winners have often tried to accelerate the market shifts.

The nature of the political problem that stems from oversupply depends on the source of the excess capacity. We have mentioned three such sources in this chapter: (1) decline in demand, (2) diverging production costs, which can result from either competition from new industrializers or a shifting in productivity as part of competition between existing producers, and (3) government policy that either resists the decline of uncompetitive industries or speeds the expansion of successful sectors. All three are represented in real-world trade situations. Since 1974 effective steel capacity has risen by better than 10 percent while production has dropped substantially.[33] Production has fallen the most sharply in Japan and the Common Market, where capacity has increased the most because governments have sought to improve competitiveness by modernizing capacity. In the French and British cases, the governments until recently have resisted the option of shutting down outmoded facilities and reducing labor even while building new facilities. At the same time, the growth of steel production in newly industrializing countries has meant a loss in export markets.

The several sources of oversupply intertwine, but they call for quite different policy resolutions. First, declining demand calls for a division of the remaining markets among existing producers, each of whom is tempted to gain marginal revenue by operating high-cost plant at full capacity and selling the marginal production at below-average cost in someone else's market. The Davignon Steel Plan is intended to avoid such counterproductive tactics in Europe. Diverging production costs pose still knottier issues. They make it harder to negotiate a resolution of shifting positions in the market, whether those shifts result from the entrance of newcomers or a readjustment of position. Why should the winners concede at the bargaining table what they can win in the market? Foreign competitors will restrain themselves "voluntarily" only if they can be denied access to their export markets by trade barriers or subsidies to domestic producers. Trade policies and government domestic policies are used to win delays or to block the need for change altogether. Ironically, the only really vulnerable targets in the lot of players, and most probably the least significant market force, are the newly industrializing countries. The advanced countries will find it difficult to close off from each other, but they may resist the newcomers through collective action.

The troubles lie not in our technical understanding of the problems of oversupply but in the political task of resolving them. Whereas domestically the problem of oversupply is one of allocating the costs of industrial change to different groups, internationally it is a settlement of the costs of change that will be borne by each country. The difficulty is that the problem of oversupply—which in effect comes to mean trade conflicts about who produces what for which markets—is not susceptible to solution by the general negotiation of rules of trade. Market rules are stable under two conditions: first, when all actors are content that the process of open market competition produces outcomes that are in some broad sense acceptable, and second, when the losers are unable to interfere. At present, the trade outcomes themselves are challenged, a situation that calls into question open market competition as the process for settling political outcomes. Consequently, we are starting to see a set of sector-specific trade arrangements aimed at constructing generally acceptable outcomes. These specialized trade arrangements can be found in the form of such multilateral trade bargains as the multifiber arrangements, as well as in the private cartel arrangements tolerated by governments and producers which we now find in the steel oligopoly. The danger of specialized settlements is that a series of exceptions will undermine the will to maintain open trade, rather than simply accommodating specific domestic interests that are obstacles to general trade agreements. Thus, rather than the American textile and apparel industries being a protectionist exception, they may

49

become the cornerstone of a protectionist coalition. One may make so many exceptions that the exceptions become the rule. The policy challenge is to develop institutions and rules to deal with the exceptions.

Western governments, then, are no longer simply producing exports and determining the terms of entry into their own markets; they are now directly negotiating the trade outcomes. The international market space to accomplish domestic adjustment thus becomes the subject of negotiations between governments. Domestic adjustment becomes visibly entangled with international bargaining. The advanced countries have begun to settle the volumes and prices of exchange in particular goods, either by organizing the marketplace among themselves or by negotiating particular deals with other countries. Oversupply resulting in specialized trade regimes like the multifiber agreement is one source of pressure for negotiated trade outcomes. State trading is another.

State trading—direct dealing between governments—is not new, but one can claim that its volume has increased sharply. Although the precise quantities are not clear, several basic changes in the international market support this conclusion. First, in developing countries, many of which have only recently gained sovereignty, the state has taken the lead in sponsoring or organizing growth, or at least has played an expanded role. Political sovereignty and late development breed state traders.[34] Second, some of these developing-country governments have sharply expanded the investment funds available to them. Some, such as OPEC, have done this through trade, whereas others, such as Brazil, have done it by borrowing. Third, trade with the centrally planned East European economies has expanded substantially, adding to the layer of state exchange surrounding the chief Western economies. From 1969 to 1974 such trade expanded twenty times and in 1980 it constituted 6 percent of total world trade. Finally, there is the arms trade conducted between governments. Aggregate figures can be somewhat misleading, since exports to the Eastern bloc countries are concentrated in a limited number of sectors. For example, the Boston Consulting Group contends that in machinery exports the share going to developing countries, Eastern Europe, the USSR, and China is crucial and steadily growing (see Table 1.11). Sales in these countries are often contracted between governments even when the government itself is not the final user. In sum, the industrial countries, the core of the Western liberal economy, have now been surrounded by a set of state trades in Eastern Europe, OPEC, and the developing countries.

Increasingly, then, trade outcomes are the result of political bargaining. Negotiated settlements about outcomes make transparent the po-

Table 1.11. Machinery exports to developing countries, Eastern Europe, the USSR, and China as percentage of total machinery exports

Country	1966	1976	Increase
West Germany	22	33	11
United States	33	42	8
France	34	49	15

SOURCE: Boston Consulting Group, *A Framework for Swedish Industrial Policy*, vol. 1 (Boston Consulting Group, November 1978), p. 43.

litical element in trade relations and reveal more clearly the winners and losers. Some of the advanced countries that have the opportunities for intervention in domestic industry, such as Japan and France, may have advantages conducting trade deals with other governments. Government-to-government dealings or government influenced purchases may shape the outcomes in such sectors as telecommunications and aircraft.

Reaching these negotiated settlements—forced by state trading, the multiple sources of oversupply, and new entrants—will be increasingly difficult because of the shifting role of the United States in the international economy. Indeed, the capacity of the U.S. executive to exert trade leadership independently of domestic interest groups is now limited. If the United States is unable to contain its own lurking protectionist coalitions, the nature of choices will be changed for all its partners. America's postwar predominance allowed it to shape the international trading system, but within that structure other countries were able to pursue their own national economic purposes with considerable freedom from international restraint. The Japanese, the Germans, and often the French could until 1971 systematically undervalue their currencies without fear of American countermoves. Americans tolerated and even encouraged the formation of the EEC and the expansion of Japanese exports to America. The rules tended to reflect the American view of economic relations and to express American preferences, but the benefits were not at all one-way. Since America's international positions did not have to be shaped by short-term economic goals, considerable room for maneuver was left to others.[35] U.S. security objectives also helped to shape economic policy. New participants in the trading system were viewed as potential members of the Western security axis. This attitude was evident in U.S. policy toward Japan and Europe, and a generation later sectoral negotiations with smaller countries such as Hong Kong, Taiwan, Korea, and Singapore demonstrated similar concerns.

The intertwining of domestic and international policy goals in the United States in recent years has made it behave more like a normal power, and has forced a constant stream of international negotiations about the very rules of the monetary and trade games. The events of August 1971, when the dollar was cut loose from gold, were a statement that the United States had begun to shape its international policy to achieve domestic objectives. The domestic economic measures of November 1978 and October 1979 were a stronger message, a statement that indeed the United States would have to adjust its domestic economy to sustain its currency. In twenty years the United States has moved from supporting an international system, to manipulating that system in pursuit of its medium-term economic goals, to adjusting its domestic policies to international constraints as any other power does.[36] The greater intertwining of domestic adjustment and international regime construction has resulted from the decline of American hegemony and the end of the insulation of American markets from events abroad. Outcomes in both the domestic adjustment process and the international arena are consequently less determinate. Negotiation has become more difficult at a time when it is more necessary. Both domestic and international industrial politics are in flux, and each involves political bargains that depend on the other. As a result, everyone has less room for political maneuver in economic affairs.

CONCLUSION

The difficulties facing the advanced countries in the 1980s cannot be understood simply by considering the aggregate features of their economies. We must break each national economy into its industrial components and understand the adjustments they must make if the economy is to continue to grow in a rapidly changing world. In the present era it is more difficult to make the changes in the micro-components of economic growth—what is produced and how—than it was during the boom years of the postwar expansion. The reorientation of production toward exports in order to pay for oil, the adaptation to higher energy costs, the rationalization and reorganization that are necessary in the face of low-wage imports, and the rise of intense competition in the advanced sectors—all are forcing companies to scramble to avoid serious losses. The situation is very different from that which existed during the boom years, when industrial development was induced and eased by the lure of higher profits implicit in declining commodity prices, expanding trade, and rising incomes. In short, whereas a generation ago firms made adjustments in order to reap additional profits, today they often do so to avoid losses.

The present problem is at its core a political problem, even though there are certainly serious technical puzzles to be resolved. Even under the best of circumstances, the reorientation and reorganization of the economy inevitably entails social dislocations and political conflicts. In the 1980s, however, the political problems of industrial adjustment have changed as well. In the fast-growth countries postwar expansion was linked to a structural shift of labor out of agriculture, a transformation that is now complete. Consequently, these countries (France, Japan, and Germany in this study) must now displace powerful and entrenched industrial interests in order to accomplish the sectoral shifts and reorganization of production essential to continued growth. In the more mature and traditionally slower-growth economies, Britain and the United States, a relative decline in industrial strength gives a special urgency to the debate over the policies, political deals, and institutional arrangements that underlie their economies. In order to force an abrupt acceleration of growth, they must undertake basic changes in such politically central policies as taxes, thereby raising difficult distributional questions that have for years been closed or clouded. Finally, the stable international economy assured by America's postwar predominance has given way to a turbulent and often chaotic period which makes domestic economic management more difficult for all countries.

Different government adjustment strategies may have different long-term impacts on the relative economic strength of the several advanced countries. As governments attempt to create and maintain comparative advantage by policies that promote public and private investment, we must alter the way in which we interpret international trade conflicts. Although the gains from free trade are genuine and have been important, the struggle for dominance in many crucial industries involves real winners and losers. Government policies affect the outcomes of these competitive fights. The advanced countries are negotiating not only the processes and procedures of trade, but the outcomes as well. We must ask whether there are distinctive political and technical capacities that give some governments an advantage in the competitive management of adjustment.

This first chapter has presented the adjustment tasks the advanced countries confront and outlined the consequences of the policies they choose. The argument that follows considers how governments fit into the process of industrial change. It attempts to account for the national variation in the roles government plays in industrial markets. That variation, as we shall discover, depends on the relationship of a number of elements—political coalition, administrative structure, and the industrial tasks that confront the country. This discussion focuses on the system of money and credit. It considers how the structure of the financial system, the channels through which money and credit are allocated to competing uses, affects both corporate strategy and public policies for adjustment. Throughout the book the central proposition is that in advanced industrial countries the structure of the domestic financial systems helped shape the politics of industrial change in the postwar years. Financial systems influence both the leadership that state bureaucracies can exercise in the industrial economy and the nature of the conflicts about which goals governments should pursue.

The next chapter elaborates the tie between financial structures and the political and policy responses of government in the advanced countries to the task of adjusting their economies to the shifting conditions of the postwar years. The third and fourth chapters examine the politics of industry and economic growth in France and Britain, focusing on the effects that their very different financial systems have had on government policies and on the political conflicts that accompanied industrial change. The fifth chapter generalizes the argument in a succinct review of the American, West German, and Japanese experiences. The final chapter evaluates the argument linking variations in the financial system to the particularities of national political conflicts about industrial change and considers the relation of this variable to other elements of the political economy.

CHAPTER TWO

Finance and the
Politics of Industry

THE ARGUMENT

There are three distinct types of financial systems, each of which
has different consequences for the political ties between banks, industry, and finance, as well as different implications for the process by
which industrial change occurs. The three types are: (1) a system
based on capital markets with resources allocated by prices established
in competitive markets, (2) a credit-based system with critical prices
administered by government, and (3) a credit-based system dominated
by financial institutions. To distinguish between these three systems
we focus on the process by which savings are transformed into investments and then allocated among competing users. Our emphasis is on
the structural arrangements—the relations between the several markets and institutions through which funds flow—which shape this process in each country. Variations in macroeconomic policy as such do
not concern us, for the administrative and political strategies used to
alter the balance between consumption and investment are, in our
view, more likely to reflect the structure of the existing financial system than to be forces for reshaping it. Similarly, we do not address
the contention that certain financial systems are more amenable than
others to policy manipulations that favor saving.[1] We are concerned,
however, with the techniques by which governments pursue macroeconomic objectives, such as the control of the money supply or interest rates because these techniques help establish the routes by which
savings are transformed and allocated to competing investors and are
therefore part of the financial structure. For example, substantial national debt means constant governmental intervention in the bond

market to raise funds. Similarly, money-supply targets, much in vogue these days, can be pursued indirectly through interest rates or directly through quantitative limits on the lending of each financial institution.

This book focuses exclusively on domestic issues, not because I see the dramatic changes in the international monetary and banking systems as unimportant, but because I agree with Peter Kenen and Laura Tyson that one can isolate the dominant domestic structural elements that determine the domestic ramifications of an international economic development.[2] They have argued that though an international economic disturbance may be common to all countries, the structure of domestic institutions determines how the external disturbance is translated into a domestic disturbance in particular national economy. Moreover, the significance of these domestic institutions is not reduced by international developments that make countries more sensitive to changes that occur abroad. It is commonly argued that the increasingly elaborate international financial markets that link national economies ever more closely make it more difficult for governments to pursue autonomous economic policies. Domestic economic aggregates, such as the money supply and the interest rate, are more sensitive to developments in international markets than to government policy instruments. In this book, however, we are concerned with how resources are allocated through domestic financial channels, not with how economic aggregates are controlled. Thus, unless international developments undermine these differences in the domestic channels through which finance is obtained, the structure of the national financial system will be an autonomous influence on the political relations between business and government. In short, international financial developments that put common pressures on all countries have distinct national consequences that depend on the structure of the national financial system. Those consequences vary systematically with the type of domestic financial system.

In a given country the political implications of marketplace arrangements in the financial system can be understood by answering three quesions:

1. Does one or several financial institutions exert discretionary power over financial flows, that is, influence who uses funds on what terms?

2. Is market power used selectively and intentionally to affect the decisions of firms or the organization of an industry? (The alternative is that any market power is used simply to achieve financial gain rather than to influence industrial behavior.)

3. Can government employ the financial system or institutions as an instrument in its dealings with the industrial economy? (It can do this

either by discriminating between firms or sectors in granting access to funds or by creating financial packages that can be used to bargain with companies.)

At issue is the ability of government to influence company choices through the medium of the financial system. It is a premise of this book that the answers to these questions lie in the structure of the financial system; that is, in the several types of financial markets and in the relative size and the detailed operations of those markets. To adopt for a moment a different language, the different market structures determine whether financial institutions exercise influence over companies through the mechanism of exit or through that of voice.[3] Influence through exit means that if you object to price or service you take your business elsewhere. Influence through voice means that you remain a client but lobby the management for changes. In capital market–based systems with elaborate secondary markets, entrance to and exit from different financial holdings are quite simple processes. The accumulation of the entrance and exit choices affects the price of different financial assets and thus the desirability of those assets and the allocation of funds between them. In credit-based systems with fewer arrangements for an easy exit, financial institutions are obliged to remain loyal to their customers. They will consequently use their position to make their voices heard in the affairs of client companies. In a credit-based financial system with administered prices, the voice of government will be heard along with that of the financial institutions; in a credit-based, bank-dominated system, the financial institutions will more often speak on their own.

We shall take a closer look at the detailed operations of the national financial systems when we consider the cases of individual countries. The discussion that follows is intended only to justify analytically the existence of the three types of financial systems mentioned above.

Financing Industry

Financial systems serve to transform savings into investment and to allocate those funds among competing users.[4] In this chapter we will consider the types of markets that serve to perform this transformation and the way prices are set in those markets. Our central concern is to demonstrate how the company sector of the economy is financed.

The vocabulary of finance often adds mystery and confusion to the subject. To provide some basic vocabulary, we must distinguish, first, between financial agents and financial intermediaries and, second, between bank and non-bank financial institutions. Financial institutions, grouped into markets by the type of service they provide, stand between the savers and investors, serving either as agent-brokers or as intermediaries in shifting the funds. In common parlance, broker and intermediary mean roughly the same thing, but in the specialized language of finance they represent quite different activities. Individual savers may give their money directly to final users, as when they buy a new stock or bond issue. In that case, the saver transforms his savings directly into investment and the financial institution merely facilitates the contact between the saver and the buyer of money. The financier may take a fee for his efforts, but he is an agent-broker, not a borrower or a lender; he is acting as a go-between. To give a simple example, if I personally lend money to my uncle's company, then he and I have transformed my savings into investment. As the company grows, my uncle may decide to seek a wider circle of investors. He may issue either shares or bonds to attract their savings. He may engage a broker to put him in contact with the investors, but the basic link is still directly between saver and investor.

Alternatively, a financial institution may hold money on deposit in the form of investments by savers, insurance payments, or borrowings from other institutions. When these funds are passed to the final user, the financial institution has acted—in the language of finance—as an intermediary. It has, acting on its own behalf, taken money from savers and lent it to users. "Financial intermediaries obviate the need for each group of savers to seek out and choose among the wide variety of capital users, and conversely for each group of capital users to seek out and choose among the wide variety of savers."[5] The institution profits from the margin between what the funds cost it and the price it can demand from the user. Thus, for example, when I put my money in a savings or a checking account, I am putting it in a bank or investment fund. Those institutions then place the money with the final users of *their* choosing; they stand between me, the saver, and the user. They act as intermediaries in transforming savings into investments. Although I have not given my money to my uncle, he may still get money from me by an indirect route. The financial institution may buy my uncle's stocks or bonds or it may make him a loan. The stock represents equity in my uncle's company, of which the institution has now become a part owner. Bonds represent a kind of arm's-length loan, a loan without close supervision. Clearly, bonds will be issued only by the best credit risks and only for their long-term investment purposes. For other firms there are bank loans, shorter-term grants of credit directly supervised by the lending institution. In both cases, however, the financial institution has become an intermediary, and its activities are those of intermediation. (There are, of course, a multitude of services that financial institutions perform, such as brokering bills of sale to give producers funds before their customers pay and operating exchange markets to give international producers a guarantee as to the value of a deal. But for our purposes this broad distinction between agent and intermediary will suffice.) An agent-broker is a go-between who makes a profit for fees charged to the principals in a transaction. An intermediary, by contrast, buys and sells financial assets. For example, it buys deposits from savers with interest on savings accounts and then sells loans to users at a higher rate of interest. Its profit comes from the margin between the cost of its funds and the price at which it can sell them.

The second important distinction is between a non-bank financial institution and a bank. This distinction, though often blurred in practice, is quite simple in principle: a bank creates money and a non-bank financial institution does not. A non-bank financial institution invests money that it collects either in exchange for a service it performs or by borrowing. Thus insurance companies collect funds in exchange for the service of protecting their clients against specified risks. Investment companies collect money to perform the service of managing those funds to the profit of their clients. Lastly, a long-term lending institution may obtain funds by borrowing them in the bond or money markets. However they obtain the funds, the amount of money a non-bank financial institution invests equals the amount it has collected or borrowed.

A bank is different. It takes in deposits and lends out more money than it takes in, creating money in the process. A bank may take in a deposit of $100, but if it maintains a reserve of 20 percent it will lend out $500. It is a simple process and John K. Galbraith is right to say that for something so important, a greater mystery would be only decent.[6] Any institution that creates money is "bank-like."[7] Thus a savings and loan association is like a bank, even though its operations have been restricted. The reserves against which bank loans are made serve two purposes. First, they are a prudent protection, a guarantee that claims will not exceed the funds on hand. In the ordinary course of business there will be periods of heavy withdrawal—for rural banks, the planting season is such a period—that strain reserves. Second, reserves provide a means by which government can regulate the amount of money banks lend. Government increases in reserve ratios force a reduction in total bank lending. One bank may find additional reserves to maintain its existing loans, but it must get them somewhere else in the financial markets. Thus, government manipulation of reserve ratios will affect the volume of lending in the system as a whole.

All three types of financial systems have agents and intermediaries as well as bank and non-bank financial institutions. What makes the financial systems different is the relative importance of two types of financial markets; capital markets and loan markets. Capital markets and loan markets are alternative sources of funds for all companies. A third market, the money market, is a source of short-term funds for large firms and financial institutions.

In capital markets the financial assets sold are securities with more than one year to maturity. The principal "goods" are corporate stocks and bonds, mortgages, and government securities, each sold within a primary or secondary submarket. New issues of stocks, bonds, and the like are considered the primary capital market, for they signify the creation of new investment funds and their allocation to specific uses. Most of the buying and selling of capital-market assets, however, takes place in secondary markets. These markets, such as the stock market in the United States and the *bourse* in France, permit the exchange of financial assets. They do not create new investments but instead shift the ownership of existing financial assets. The secondary market permits initial investors to dispose of their investments in order either to take profits or to adjust their portfolio of holdings. Thus it permits long-term investments to be made without the investor tying his money up for the life of the bond—or in perpetuity in the case of stocks. Secondary markets also establish a price for financial assets issued by different companies and governments, thereby setting the terms on which additional money can be raised. James Stone has deftly described the theoretical assumption that capital markets establish a price for the financial assets of companies: "The market accomplishes its job through the assignment of prices. When it does its job correctly it juggles stock prices up and down in such a manner that every available dollar of new investment is channeled to that proposed project with the highest rate of return. Simplicity is the market's virtue."[8]

Elaborate secondary capital markets, some argue, are needed to attract initial investment in new securities issues. They propose that a large number of buyers and sellers of existing capital assets, as well as the institutions that link them (which together constitute a developed secondary market) are a prerequisite for active primary markets. The large secondary market solves particular problems. For example, a large number of buyers and sellers means that any seller is likely to find a buyer and, consequently, that routine price fluctuations are apt to be less extreme than they would be in a small market. Small secondary markets, then, could be thought to expose investors to a risk of market fluctuations, but at first glance, the French case would seem to disprove this argument. Although there is a limited secondary market in France, the primary market has raised substantial new investment in recent years. On closer inspection, however, we see that the French system has some special features. First, much of the new investment is money directed from parapublic lending institutions to parapublic firms. Thus the new investments are implicitly directed and insured by the government. Second, government management of price fluctuations in the secondary market creates a stability not normally possible with a narrow or limited market. The French case suggests, then, that a managed market may substitute for an elaborate and extensive secondary market as a means to attract investment in new securities issues.

Loan markets are an alternative of sorts to capital markets. We are concerned here with the market for business loans, not with consumer and home finance, which compete with companies for available funds. Business loans can be made either by banks that draw their funds from deposits or by specialized lending institutions that draw their funds from the bond side of the equity market or from the money market. Company lending can be divided roughly into short-term and medium- to long-term loans. In all countries short-term loans are commonly used to finance stocks, carry outstanding billings, and the like. Such loans are in principle self-liquidating; for example, when stocks are sold the money lent to buy the stocks is paid back. Medium- and long-term lending is more significant in Japan, France, and Germany than in the United States and Britain. Very simply, where capital markets emerged to finance industrial development, bank lending has been traditionally limited to short-term purposes. Where the capital markets were neither adequate nor reliable sources of development funds, banks or specialized institutions filled the gap with loans.

The third type of market is a money market. Though not central to this story, let us examine it quickly. In this market, credit instruments with maturities of less than one year are traded. The retail market for money is the branch deposit system for savings and checking accounts with which we are all familiar. The wholesale market is an institutional interfirm or interbank market. Most activity in these wholesale markets is conducted by intermediaries. Institutions may borrow money in these markets, lending it to final users, or they may place excess funds as investments with still other institutions. The money market allows institutions to nourish their short-term needs for cash and to invest excess funds without affecting their liquidity.

Thus far we have focused on the supply of investment funds and the forms these funds can take. Let us consider for a moment the problem of the demand for funds or, more precisely, the form in which a company will choose to seek those funds. The choice of instrument for obtaining outside funds will depend on the price of money in different forms, the company's own preference for debt or equity, and the market's preference for the balance between debt investment and equity investment in the company. If it has a long-term project, it will not want money to be withdrawn halfway through the project and will therefore sell either equity (a share of the company), or a bond (an arm's-length, long-term loan). If the company needs money in the short run to pay its suppliers while waiting for payment itself it will borrow from the bank. This, at any rate, is the story as British and often American textbooks tell it. Long-term money comes from capital markets and short-term money comes from bank loans.

What happens, however, if a company wants to invest in a new factory and cannot sell stock or issue bonds? If the firm is small it may not be sufficiently well known to attract anonymous investors. Or perhaps there are not many investors prepared to buy anyone's bonds and stock that year; most of them may be small and thus inclined to put their money into deposit institutions or banks. In this case, the firm may try to borrow money from the bank or deposit institutions on a long-term basis.

Long-term borrowing, however, is quite different from a short-term loan relationship. For the borrower it means a long-term relationship with an institution that undoubtedly will want to interfere in his business as a condition for permitting the continued use of its money. For the bank as well, the problems of long-term lending are qualitatively different. Any loan is a gamble on the future solvency of the client, but a long-term loan involves a new kind of risk. Obviously, a long-term loan on the business of the client cannot in reality be secured by any physical assets. Moreover, a bank gets the bulk of the money it uses from funds deposited for a short term at the going interest rate. If it lends a firm money for five years, during that period, the depositers may withdraw their funds at which point the bank's reserves drop and it must reduce its loans: in an extreme case it might not be able to pay claims presented to it. Another, potentially more serious problem may occur should interest rates change in unexpected ways. If the short-term rates go down and the bank has lent long, its margin of profit increases, but if the rates go up, its profit margins are cut or it loses money. To encourage the transformation of short-term savings into long-term lending, governments have often absorbed part of this risk of interest-rate fluctuation. As we shall see, this policy provides a lever for government to direct the flow of funds toward ends of its own choosing.

Long-term borrowing from banks or institutions exchanges the impersonal arm's-length dealings of capital markets for the personal institutional ties of banks or lending institutions. Indeed, the greater a corporation's dependence on debt as a basic element in its business strategy, the greater the influence of those institutions that provide it with credit. Many French and Japanese companies operate with a very high debt-to-equity ratio; that is, they use a high proportion of borrowed money. Such arrangements can permit a high return on capital because the company has less of its own money invested, but heavy debt can also make companies vulnerable to economic downturns. Very simply, debt represents fixed charges that must be repaid, regardless of business conditions, whereas returns to investors can be restrained by not declaring a stock dividend. One would predict, therefore, that in countries where companies operate with heavy debt firms will periodically find themselves extremely vulnerable to and dependent upon their banks and their governments. Companies tend to turn to bank financing when the growth rates they choose to pursue exceed the capital they can obtain from retained earnings and securities issues. This is why credit-based systems tend to be tied to late and rapid growth; investigation will show that in late-developing countries the state has helped to organize the provision of financial resources.

A system in which capital markets are the central means of corporate finance is thus very different from one in which loans or credits predominate. A financial system based on capital markets is weighted toward exit as a means of exercising influence. There is a tendency for banks to specialize in short-term lending rather than longer-term loans and to stay clear of the capital markets, leaving other financial institutions to specialize in capital-market operations. Relations between financial institutions and companies rest primarily on an arm's-length capital-market basis or on limited short-term lending arrangements. Where there are well-developed secondary markets for securities investment, financial institutions tend to manage portfolios of stocks, spreading their risks across companies rather than investing in the future of specific companies that they nurture through hard times. The often decried emphasis on stock-market values characteristic of American and British companies leads to a short-term focus on dividends and on capital return and is thus part of this same pattern. Even though large investment institutions have come to dominate capital markets in the United States and Britain, they have not changed the arm's-length bias of the two systems. The elaborate secondary markets allow investors an exit route.

Loan-based systems of corporate finance are of necessity premised on the exercise of influence by voice. Since such systems have more restricted capital markets and, in particular, a limited secondary capital market, it is harder for financial institutions to treat equity investments simply as a matter of financial portfolio balance. In a limited secondary market they may not be able to dispose of equity holdings without affecting the price of the stock. Exit is not easy and, as a result, these institutions are pressed into close monitoring of management and the exercise of voice. Limited secondary markets and the long-term loans characteristic of this system reinforce each other, militating toward intimacy between financial institutions and the companies whose equity they own and to whom they lend. Also, there is less institutional specialization. Indeed, the German "universal" banks, preeminent players in all financial markets, contrast sharply with the more specialized banks of the Anglo-American system. For "universal" banks equity investments and loans are alternative means of providing corporate finance.

The distinction between a capital-market system, with its emphasis on influence by exit, and a credit-based system, with its emphasis on influence by voice, can be observed in the lending and investment policies of financial institutions. The different relations between business and banks are defined by the criteria institutions use in deciding whether to grant loans and in determining how to deal with companies in trouble and with "bad" loans. In deciding whether to grant a loan, a bank can either assess risk on the basis of historic performances and securable assets or make that assessment on the basis of future prospects and projected cash flows. To pose the distinction at its most extreme: application of the first criterion makes a financier into a pawnbroker who takes company assets as security (which, as we shall see, is how American bankers often view their English cousins); application of the second criterion makes the investor a venture capitalist, betting on corporate futures and taking an equity position in a company as part of his stake (on a large scale this has often been the role of the German universal banks). The treatment of "bad" loans is a second criterion for defining the relations between businesses and banks. When faced with a business loan that is in default, a bank can either sell the company's assets or help the company work its way out of trouble, trading out of the situation by reorganizing the management and corporate strategy of the company in difficulty. Again, the pawnbroker simply sells out or exits from his position, whereas the venture capitalist has from the beginning intended to exercise his voice in the form of management advice as a means of protecting his investment position.

The existence of these two different systems is evident in a comparison of the French and American security markets (see Table 2.1). France has a credit-based system in which security, or capital, markets are of secondary importance. In America, the capital markets are crucial to corporate finance, one corollary of which is the great importance of investing institutions. Individual savings are funneled through investing institutions into capital markets to a greater extent in the United States. Finally, in France long-term credit institutions with limited deposit bases (note the liabilities) lend extensively to companies (note the claims). They funnel funds from savings institutions into loans.

We next distinguish financial systems by the way prices are set in the three types of financial markets—capital markets, loan markets, and money markets. The textbook notion of financial markets is that prices are set by the efforts of lenders to get the highest return (given their tolerance for risk) and the efforts of users to get the cheapest money for their different projects. In this perfect market, savers are offered a variety of investment options tailored to meet individual preferences for the balance between risk and return; users of money can choose between many sources of funds offered on terms suited to their different purposes. The flow of funds through different institutions and the price for borrowing money (interest rates) shift with the mixes of supply and demand for different instruments. In that sense stock and bond markets and bank loans represent different ways of doing the same thing. Both the suppliers and the users of funds are price takers, not price setters: neither has the ability to determine the prices by the volumes of funds placed or taken up. Thus unfettered markets are one possible mechanism for setting prices.

Not all markets are perfect, however; financial institutions may exert market power and shape the terms on which money is bought and sold. An institution may be dominant in a single financial market; that is, it may have power over prices in the bond or stock market but not in the bank lending market. Or one institution may have a position of influence in several different markets, thereby influencing prices in all markets and the movement of money through the financial system as a whole. For example, the French Caisse des Dépôts et Consignations, a public depository, has a powerful position in the bond and stock market as well as in the wholesale money market. The German universal banks are able to take positions in all types of markets, even though no single bank is dominant in any one of them. Thus institution-dominated markets are a second potential mechanism for setting prices. Efforts by buyers and sellers to

65

Table 2.1. Credit-based and capital market–based financial systems: the examples of France and United States, end 1975

Country	Securities markets as percent of Gross Domestic Product		Share (in claims and liabilities) with nonfinancial sector (percent)					
			Investing institutions			Long-term credit institutions		
	Bonds	Equities	Liabilities	Claims		Liabilities	Claims	
France	16	11	11.3	9.3		8.2	32.9	
United States	57	45	32.3	31.2		5.5	7.9	

NOTE: Liabilities represent deposits; claims indicate loans.
SOURCE: Figures taken from Appendixes 1A to 9A, Dimitri Vittas, ed., *Banking Systems Abroad* (London: Inter-Bank Research Organisation, 1978).

strike the best deal still determine prices and flows, but some players have the power to dominate the markets and influence prices.

Market power arguably has different consequences in capital market–based and lending-based financial systems. In capital market–based systems, concentration of financial institutions within any given financial market need not in itself overturn the arm's-length character of the system because easy exit is still possible.* Since most bank lending is short term, market power over the prices of loans does not automatically translate into an ability to manipulate company choices through access to a loan window. As long as banks are kept out of capital markets, investment institutions that have never had intimate ties to company management will tend to maintain a portfolio approach to investment. Market concentration that means that a few institutions control most of the business in a sector may bias prices and allow a few investors to determine allocation priorities, but whatever problems concentration may pose, it does not automatically imply detailed influence in corporate management. In fact, although institutional investors have come to dominate securities markets in Britain and the United States, the concentration is not so great that single institutions are able to shape those markets systematically. In a lending-based system that already rests on institutional ties, a financial institution's market power translates more directly into influence on its clients. This is not, of course, to imply that financiers and bankers in America and Britain have no influence in corporate affairs, but rather to point out that their influence is different from that of their Japanese, German, and French counterparts. Yet we must not overdraw the argument that the channels of finance structure power relations in the economy. In the United States, for example, legal limits on banking power are critical to the structure of the financial markets.

A third possible mechanism is that government will simply establish prices in these several markets. Prices, even if administratively set, can serve as devices that help allocate goods and services. That is, if prices are not free to move in response to the supply or the demand for funds, the result will undoubtedly be disequilibrium—an imbalance of supply and demand. Low prices (interest) may encourage more users but discourage savers, thus reducing supply. If supplies of funds are short, some additional mechanism will be required to discriminate among users who collectively demand more money than is available at a given interest rate. Controlled prices imply some administrative mech-

---

*Concentration is a technical economic measure of the organization of an industry. A highly concentrated industry is one in which a few firms control a substantial portion of production (or of purchases).

anism that chooses whose demands will be met, thus allocating resources. It is important to point out that administered pricing in essential markets may be very difficult to dismantle; the attempt to move from an administered price to a free price may create market disorder and political resistance.

In short, the different pricing mechanisms create three different types of institutional ties between finance and industry. Allocation of funds by price in perfect markets is thoroughly impersonal. Allocation of funds in markets dominated by financial actors gives those with market power the ability to make discretionary choices about whom to lend to and on what terms; thus discretion will more quickly translate into influence inside corporations. Lastly, where prices are administratively set by government, the likelihood is disequilibrium in which the supply and demand for money is balanced by administrative discretion. The crucial issue is who exercises the discretion when markets are in disequilibrium.

The final step in this brief sketch of financial systems is to consider the various ways in which governments operate in financial markets. First and most obviously, governments manage the creation of money to achieve either interest rate or money-supply targets. These objectives are pursued through arm's-length techniques, such as manipulating the level of reserves a bank must hold, or through more direct means, such as establishing quantitative limits on what each bank can lend. Second, governments manage and regulate financial systems to assure overall stability and the solvency of the individual institutions. To this end, central banks serve as lenders of last resort to assure that temporary mismatches of funds or illiquidity in the system does not set off a crisis. In Britain and the United States the central bank's role is essentially to act as a marginal stabilizer, whereas in France and Japan the central bank facilitates the creation of money by providing extensive access to their own funds and thus influence the allocation of funds. (For our initial discussion it does not matter whether the central bank, which has the most immediate responsibility, is actually under the thumb of the government, as in France, or independent, as in Germany and the United States.) Third, in managing the financial system governments may establish rules that implicitly favor one type of institution over another. Such biases may amount to subsidies to certain borrowers or lenders: if the biases are imposed by rules concerned not with resource allocation but with the conditions of competition—as, for example, in the rules governing savings and loan associations in the United States— then the logic that markets set prices will not be altered.

Fourth, the government is a substantial borrower and lender in many markets. In countries with a substantial national debt, such as the

United States and Britain, government securities are an important part of both the bond market and the money market. In countries where either the government or public agencies collect savings, these same institutions may be substantial lenders. This is the case in France, where specialized deposit institutions collect 30 percent of the nation's savings and then place them in bond or money markets. Fifth, the government may help banks manage the risks of transforming short-term borrowing into long-term loans. One device is to rediscount long-term financial paper at the central bank—in other words, to permit certain types of long-term loans to be converted into liquid assets, thereby reducing the bank's risk in borrowing short and lending long. When such a device is used, the government can influence the availability of credit to different users by choosing to favor loans to certain industries or firms.

It may seem difficult to distinguish between governments in terms of how they operate in financial markets, since, to one degree or another, all governments do all these things—manage the money supply, manage the stability of the system, borrow and lend, set interest rates, and facilitate bank lending. In fact, however, we can make such distinctions by asking two related questions. First, does a government place its emphasis on managing the aggregates of the system, such as the money supply, or does it attempt to manipulate the allocation of resources? Second, does it attempt to achieve its objectives—both aggregate and specific—by direct quantitative administration or by market manipulation?

In sum, then, national financial systems vary in three ways. The first dimension is the importance of different markets in shifting resources from savings to investment. Here we distinguish fundamentally between capital market–based systems and credit-based systems. The second dimension is the way prices are set in these markets. We have seen that the possibilities are competitive prices, institution-dominated prices, and government-fixed prices. The third dimension is the roles played by government in the financial system. Within the third dimension, national systems may be distinguished by whether government gives priority to controlling monetary aggregates or to allocating resources between competing uses, and whether it pursues either of those goals administratively or by manipulating market conditions. These three dimensions serve to distinguish three types of financial systems.

Three Models of Finance

The three financial models outlined here highlight the relationship between specific features of a financial system and political outcomes.[9]

Although the details of a particular financial system do not match any one of these three models precisely, its important structural characteristics must. We do not attempt to demonstrate that these are the only possible systems. There do, however, appear to be a limited number of possible arrangements, certainly empirically and perhaps theoretically. The role of government, the significant markets, the mechanisms by which prices are fixed, and the links between finance and industry seem interconnected. Each grouping forms a system. The logic of eliminating possibilities simply is not worth the effort since all we really need to do is establish that the systems are distinct from each other in politically significant ways.

The first model is a capital market–based system in which security issues—stocks and bonds—are the predominant source of long-term industrial funds. In such a system the central function of bank lending is to serve short-term purposes. In each distinct market prices are set in plausibly competitive conditions, a situation that implies a wide variety of capital and money-market instruments and a large number of specialized financial institutions. As a result, the saver and the investor meet across the divide of competitive markets, most often with the help of intermediary institutions. Since there is an active stock and bond market in which firms can raise long-term funds, they do not need to pass through the commercial banks to reach the capital markets and are not dependent on bank credit for long-term projects. The opposite side of this proposition is that, whether by historical circumstances or legal prohibition, financial institutions do not act as owner-managers and do not hold substantial shares of the stock of any particular firms. In such a system the central bank is concerned primarily with the control of monetary aggregates, be they money supply figures or interest rates. Only secondarily, if at all, is it concerned with the allocation of resources between competing uses. Though it may seek to control critical aggregates or a few central prices, it leaves the rest of the prices and aggregates to move on their own. The central bank and the commercial banks stand at arm's length from each other and neither the volume nor the allocation of bank lending is directly determined by the central bank. The central bank may act as a lender of last resort but it does so only in a very limited way. When the central bank does intervene in a capital market–based system, it does so by buying and selling to bring about market conditions that produce the outcomes it favors; it does not attempt to impose these conditions by administrative fiat. *This model places banks, firms, and governments in distinct spheres from which they venture forth to meet as autonomous bargaining partners.*

The market arrangements described by this first model tend to limit both the influence of financial institutions on (nonfinancial) firms and the influence of governments on the details of the lending activities of banks. They certainly limit government capacity to direct flows through capital markets, with two distinct consequences: first, government will not have natural handles in the market system by which it can selectively influence the allocation decisions of financial institutions; second, financial institutions will not routinely have influence inside corporations. Government intervention in corporate affairs will require specific legislative authorization and will operate outside routine market operations. Consequently, individual interventions by government may be broadly opposed by the financial community, not only because of the objectives of any specific intervention but also because of the threat that interventionist policies pose to the integrity of market arrangements. The market principle, as much as any particular purpose of government, is at issue in the political efforts to gain specific authorization for government action in industrial or financial affairs. Britain and the United States fit this first model.

The second model is a credit-based system in which market interrelations are dominated by government-administered prices. The stock and bond market is not easily accessible to private borrowers, though it is often used by the government as a means of raising money for its projects. Given the weakness of the capital markets, firms must turn to lending institutions, both specialized lenders and banks, for the funds they need. Indeed, banks may serve as crucial access routes to the capital market and general purpose banks may end up owning or voting much of the stock of important companies. Credit is at the core of the system of corporate finance, however, and the banking system's ability to extend industrial credit is therefore critical. Government chooses to underpin bank lending and to facilitate money creation. Finally, government sets the prices in important markets in order to shape the economy's priorities. Since prices are administratively fixed there is an inherent tendency for markets to be in disequilibrium; that is, at the established prices there are too many borrowers or lenders. The balance *must* then be achieved by administrative action that discriminates in favor of some users and against others. Some administrative rule must be substituted for the free play of prices in the market. The issue in this system is not whether government intervenes to affect the allocation of financial resources; the question is who controls the process and how.

To summarize the second model, credit extended by institutions becomes a linchpin in the system of industrial finance and government is drawn in to bolster the system and to make the administrative choices about allocation. It appears that government's role is to compensate for weaknesses in an existing private financial system. Historically, the state intervenes to accomplish particular purposes and the resulting financial structure institutionalizes its discretionary influence in the financial market. The political implication is that the state's entanglement with industry becomes part and parcel of the financial system. *The borderline between public and private blurs, not simply because of political arrangements, but because of the very structure of the financial markets.* The arrangements between bureaucracy and finance which blur this borderline can occur in widely different state structures. Thus, for example, the Italian financial system is more similar to the French than to any other, but the discretion it generates is diffused among warring factions in the Italian polity, whereas in the French system discretion is concentrated in the hands of the central executive.

The third model is also a credit-based system, but one in which a limited number of financial institutions dominate the system without themselves being dependent on state assistance. Markets, not administrative actions, determine prices, but the movement of prices in the markets reflects this concentration of financial power. Evidence comparing German and British stock exchange operations, for example, convincingly demonstrates that banks exercise market power over price movements in Germany but not in Britain.[10] In this model the state pursues aggregate instead of allocative objectives, and it does so through market operations instead of administrative techniques. As a result, the financial institutions have influence in the affairs of companies through their market power in lending and their domination of access to securities markets. *Government does not have the apparatus to dictate allocative choices to the financial institutions and consequently it has no independent instruments in the financial system with which to influence companies. Banks, however, can serve as policy allies for government, on terms negotiated between the government and finance.*

Both the second and third models are solutions to late development, whereas the first is tied to an earlier industrial transformation. The market differences themselves become important elements, though, in shaping the responses of all countries to their present economic problems.

The position taken here is that the three models are distinguished by structural differences and that the relations that describe the operation of the system—the differing importance of securities and lending markets, the mechanisms that establish prices, and the objectives and techniques of government management—are fundamentally distinct in each model. An alternative argument holds that one general model of a "financial system" can be used to predict the behavior of any national case, that one need only vary the quantities in the markets of each system to make predictions for any particular case. Formalizing the issue, we can say that the choice is between (1) a set of models, each of which rests on a different set of equations that expresses the behavior of each financial system, and (2) a single set of equations in which we vary the quantities in each national case to predict system outcomes. The existing literature is not much help in testing the proposition that there are several structurally distinct financial systems. There is an extensive institutional literature, but it focuses on the peculiarities of each system's institutions, not on the distinctions in the workings of their financial markets. Another body of literature assumes that a common financial model is adequate and does not test the converse. Some writings that produce evidence of structural differences do not ask the questions that could define those differences. Jacques Melitz's recent study of exchange-rate systems, however, offers strong support for the structural line argued here.[11]

Melitz claims that in general economists have had great success in using identical structural equations to describe the different national markets. He contends that commodity markets as well as production, consumption, and investment functions are quite similar. He is even willing to accept that wage and price equations are similar in different national cases, once one allows for variations in the openness of national economies. He takes a different position about finance, however. Though his central concern is money-supply issues rather than industrial finance, his argument directly supports the analysis offered here. Melitz distinguishes two models in his analysis, categorizing Japan and France as one type and the United States and Britain as a second. (The German case, which is the basis of our third model, is not discussed.) Melitz argues: "It is not surprising, therefore, that many efforts could be made to use a uniform model of the money-supply process for all nations, typically patterned after the United States. I believe, nonetheless, that such efforts are in vain. History and policy condition financial structures more than industrial ones. Whatever the reason, financial environments differ internationally in critical ways."[12]

In the United States and Great Britain the capital markets are very large, corporations rely heavily upon these markets for finance, and the commercial banks face major competition at home from other financial intermediaries. In the cases of France and Japan, however, the commercial banks dominate financing on the capital market and face virtually no competition at home from other financial institutions. Consequently, any analysis of the United States or Great Britain must emphasize the bond market, whose role is perhaps as large as or larger than that of the market for commercial bank loans. Indeed, in Great Britain the government's ability to finance deficits through bond issues is probably the most important element in the money-supply process. In the cases of France and Japan, however, any model of the money-supply process which does not put primary emphasis on the market for commercial bank credit will be misleading. At least in France, the bond market can virtually be ignored.

To cite another basic point of contrast: British commercial banks cannot borrow directly from the central bank; U.S. banks can do so to a small, but significant extent; and French and Japanese banks can do so to an enormous extent. If we omit the extreme case of Great Britain and compare the United States with France and Japan, we still find that the appropriate treatment of borrowed reserves in these cases is not the same. In the United States, borrowed reserves can be viewed essentially as a portfolio choice made by bankers according to opportunity costs. In France and Japan, however, borrowed reserves are so basic to bank operations that their level cannot be dissociated from the aggregate quantity of bank credit. That is, reserves borrowed from the central bank must be seen as a percentage of the total credit distribution. Finally, in France, for example, the central bank has only a limited portfolio of capital-market assets, such as government bonds. Thus, any references to open market operations in which the government. influences interest rates by buying and selling its own financial paper cannot even make sense. Melitz summarizes the issue well:

> My view then is that to use an identical schema in order to model the money-supply process in the United States, Great Britain, France, and other nations, is simply to indulge in all sorts of fiction, fictions which are important enough to defeat the very purpose of the modelling of the money-supply process. . . . It becomes impossible, subsequently, to infer the relationship between policy instruments and the quantity of money. Essential money scenarios and their consequences cannot be worked out. Even if a U.S. set of structural equations provided excellent econometric estimates for France, the estimates still would have no value, since we could not interpret the equations in accordance with the hypotheses; hence we could not base any explanations or policy conclusions upon the estimates.[13]

In short, the crux of Melitz's argument is that structural variations have quite different consequences for economic outcomes. For example, similar levels of demand for money do not result in similar prices or money-supply figures in different models. The same logic holds for our problem. That is, structural differences strengthen the case that political actors must adapt their strategies for managing the economy to the constraints imposed by their particular national financial system.

The State as Economic Player

We have distinguished three financial models. Let us pursue a bit further the political and policy implications of different financial arrangements, focusing on the distinctive possibility for state action implicit in the credit-based, administered-price system. We begin by distinguishing several different roles that government may play in the industrial economy.

As suggested earlier, the government can be an economic regulator, an economic administrator, or an economic player.[14] As a *regulator,* it is an umpire refereeing the behavior of others in the hope that if they follow a particular set of rules, a certain set of outcomes will occur. Controls on mergers and on securities issues are examples of such rules. As an *administrator,* the government executes certain operations based on a specific assignment or task, applying particular decision criteria and following set procedures. As a *player,* it pursues specific outcomes on a case-by-case basis, assembling packages of incentives which can be used to persuade or coerce. It discriminates among firms and applies administrative rules and regulations to accomplish particular objectives. All governments have discretion over the application of rules and regulations but only a few of them use discretion systematically to initiate and shape particular industrial outcomes. American antitrust legislation is intended to assure a "competitive" market, but it does not provide the government with a means of forcing particular companies to undertake government defined industrial objectives. By contrast, the Japanese ability to control selectively the flow of goods, capital, and technology allows government to influence the affairs of particular firms and the structure of sectors.

To be a player in the market a government bureaucracy must be able to make its administrative or regulatory decisions contingent on particular actions taken by the firms it administers or regulates. Those actions may have little relation to the general authority on which the bureaucracy's power rests. For example, the Japanese Ministry of International Trade and Industry (MITI) monitored technology imports to strengthen the nation's bargaining power and reduce the purchase price of those technologies. Since it could deny access to needed know-how, it could also influence investment and organization decisions, and in trade negotiations it was even able to force "voluntary" export restraints. Finally, some policies may require the coordination of diverse bits of discretion spread throughout the bureaucracy. The ability to discriminate, to make decisions contingent on actions often unrelated to the particular choice at hand, and to coordinate policies depends upon the internal organization of the bureaucracy and the channels of its outside influence as well as the ideologies of the bureaucrats themselves.

The concept of the state as marketplace player is quite distinct from the concept of public ownership. The distinction between public and private ownership does not identify the degree of control the government executive will have on a corporation's affairs. In a study of U.S. public utilities, for example, Marc Roberts found that internal organization, recruitment and promotion policies, and the need for outside capital, rather than any characteristic of ownership, accounted for differences in company behavior.[15] If the state is a passive stockholder, a public coupon clipper, its influence in public corporations may be minimal. It may find itself a regulator or an administrator, with a relationship to public companies that is similar to its relationship to private companies. The right to appoint top management may provide moments when the government can exert its influence, but the case of Enrico Mattei and the Italian Energy Corporation suggests that state-appointed managers may in fact become autonomous power brokers.[16] For our purposes, the impact of nationalization depends on the character of the relations between the state and public companies. The problem of control and direction remains after nationalization, even if the means used to control public enterprise may be a bit different from the means used to control the private firm.

The central argument of this book is that discretion in the provision of industrial finance—in the selective allocation of credit—is necessary for the state to enter continuously into the industrial life of private companies and to influence their strategies in the way that a rival or partner would. Even with public companies, the financial instruments for selectively allocating credit provide government a refined set of tools to supplement the appointment of management or the imposition of broadly defined government policy directives. Selective credit allocation is the single discretion necessary to all state-led industrial strategies.

There are two reasons why credit allocation is a particularly effective instrument of industrial policy. First, credit allocation is critical in industrial policy simply because specific business decisions are hard to control or influence through administrative or regulatory rules. Those same decisions may, however, be influenced by negotiation in which the payment for services rendered is unambiguously calculated in monetary terms. Discretionary influence in industrial finance permits the government to deal within the framework of business decisions and to affect the balance sheet directly. It becomes a player in the market. Second, credit allocation is a universal tool, one that eliminates the need to find specific authority to influence specific decisions or to control an agency that has formal authority over a specific policy instrument. It should be noted that taxation is not as flexible as credit allocation. Taxes can be used to target categories of action but they are difficult to manipulate toward specific industrial ends. Unless the principles of rational administration are violated, taxes cannot be bargained. Moreover, taxes operate to increase profits from gross earnings; they tend to follow rather than to lead new activities.

The universality of finance enables a single agency to exert influence across a range of issues without having to develop regulatory or administrative apparatus for each specific case. When discretionary control over finance derives from the operation of the financial system itself rather than from a specifically created and specialized agency, there are several bureaucratic consequences. First, this multipurpose policy tool is outside the direct control of the legislature. Funds are obtained by manipulating the economy's financial flows not by making budgetary allocations. Second, that control is likely to be in the hands of the minister of finance or the central bank. Discretionary control of the flow of industrial credit in the financial system can thus give economic ministries with general responsibilities a tool to form alliances with an ever-changing combination of industrial sectors and government agencies that represent industrial interests. This special glue for coordinating industrial policy is most likely to belong to the ministry that is best able to assemble bits of policy for changing objectives and that is most insulated against specific pressures from industrial constituents. As we shall see, in the French case control of finance facilitated a victory by those who sought to promote the development of French industry.

The player state must possess or control institutions that provide it with discretion in the affairs of firms and with financial discretion in particular. Unless it has direct influence in the allocation of credit by the financial system, it must either make the financial institutions its allies or confront them as political opponents to its interventionist strategies. Any government can provide funds to the sectors or companies it wants to support. The question is how public its efforts to do so become and how much special authority the particular intervention demands. (In the United States the Lockheed case involved a large-scale bailout linking government and banks, but it provoked wide-spread political opposition, chiefly because it required special legislation.) If, as a routine matter, the selective provision of finance can be used as an instrument of policy, the government can continuously intervene in industrial affairs as a private bargaining party without special authority.

Market Structures and State Capacities

We have argued thus far that the arrangement of financial markets, like the structure of the state administrative apparatus, affects the "capacity" of social groups and the political executive to act in pursuit of their goals. In considering the effect of the marketplace, we have viewed the financial market as a system—as the aggregate of its pieces. Structural arguments are commonplace in politics, and the subfield of economics known as industrial organization explores market structures as constraints on the behavior of the firm.[17] Here we are concerned to determine how market structures act as constraints on politics. The structural approach holds that a structure creates an enduring set of penalties and rewards that mold action independent of the motivation or purposes of the actors. The constraints of the situation or the channels of action determine which choices are expensive and which are cheap. A structural approach makes several types of claims.

First, within a particular financial market structure there will be regularity in the *form* of policy, in how policy is formulated and implemented, whatever the objectives. In the case of France, therefore, one might suggest that although the instruments of a centralized state are put to quite different ends by the Left and the Right, there are common elements in their approaches to policy and government simply because they face the same institutional constraints and options. A related proposition is that since financial market structure limits the repertoire of policy strategies, a particular government is apt to find some problems more intractable than others. This statement presumes, of course, that there is a limited number of ways of attacking certain problems and that some structures simply preclude finding workable solutions to particular problems. I have shown in *Political Strategies for Industrial Order* (Berkeley, 1977) how very similar policies succeeded in some French industries but not in others. Although the policies looked very much alike, the outcomes were different because the required solutions varied. In the cases where the French accomplished some reasonable version of their original purposes, the solutions required by the problem matched the policies that were applied. The structural argument suggests that particular institutional structures that create or conversely circumscribe capacities for state action will establish patterns of distinctive national competence and weakness.

Second, because structure constrains strategy, those who pursue new economic goals or try new approaches to policy must often reform or rearrange economic institutions and the links between them and the state. If new strategies or new problems require expanded capacities, it may be necessary to make structural changes in the economy. The required institutional reforms involve much more than redesigning organizations to achieve greater effectiveness, however. Since the arrangements between and within organizations establish positions of privilege, reform means dislodging incumbents from their strongholds. When these incumbents represent specific groups in the society, as they often do, "institutional reform" entails a political change in the social balance of power; it becomes a political conflict. To reform the banking system, for example, is to change the possibilities for financial institutions to lend or invest, and thus the possibilities for financiers to profit. Since it is often possible to foresee which groups will benefit and which will suffer, the politics of institutional change can take a very predictable form. In such a case, the structure will not simply set down regularities in policy but will create predictable kinds of political battles. The *how* of policy and politics will affect *who* will be allies and enemies, as well as the tactics used in their fights. The economic structure does not "create" politics, but by delimiting some of the possible issues and alliances, it can establish the channels through which political fights flow.

Implicit in this discussion is a simple model in which different institutional structures respond differently to the same stimulus. The argument is more complex than this model suggests, however. Stated somewhat differently, the problem is to assess the relation between policy content and policy form, not just that between structure and outcome. For example, one might hypothesize that national differences in industrial policy exist because the purposes that societies wish to achieve are different. Next, one might hypothesize that even when those purposes are the same, they will be achieved differently and with different degrees of success because structures differ. Finally, and more powerfully, one might hypothesize that the purposes pursued as well as the strategies chosen are affected by the relative costs of achieving different goals. The structural argument suggests that the form of policymaking affects the purposes pursued; structure affects not only outcome but also the goals themselves. Simply stated, what is attempted and achieved is affected by how it must be done.

To summarize, this argument makes two claims about the influence of financial systems on politics. First, the structure of the national financial system affects the capacity of the national political executive to intervene in the industrial economy. Second, since the financial system is a constraint on action and an influence on the power relations in the economy, it is an element shaping the arena for industrial and economic politics. National variations in the arena for industrial politics, then, help account for differences in the nature of the conflicts and alliances that emerge. This second claim is quite limited and should not be exaggerated. It contends only that financial systems are an intervening variable or a parameter in the political equation.

TESTING the ARGUMENT

The three models of financial system imply different degrees and different forms of executive discretion in industrial affairs. In the first model, the capital market–based system with allocation by competitive price, government aspirations to intervene at either the sectoral or the firm level are blocked or, at the very least, any interventionist efforts provoke public political controversy. In the second model—a credit-based, price-administered financial system—executive discretion in the allocation of credit, the discretion required for interventionist or promotional strategies, is extensive. In the third model—a credit-based financial system dominated by large institutions with influence in industry—banks can act as allies of the government in an industrial crisis but government discrimination between sectors is not automatically provided; the government gains discretion at second hand, exercising it through a negotiated partnership with coequals.

Two hypotheses, suggested by this argument, are explored in this book. The first is that credit-based financial systems with state-administered prices will facilitate intervention and ease the political problems of mustering support for state-led industrial promotion. In a state-administered financial system, in fact, the bureaucracy can hardly avoid exercising specific influence in credit allocation. Executive action based on discretion in financial markets is less subject to public scrutiny or political interference than intervention based on any administrative allocation or legislative program would be. Governmental mechanisms for exerting discretion in the allocation of the money flow through financial markets, even when their influence is exercised only on the margins, establish a private executive instrument of public intervention.

The second hypothesis is that in a system characterized by financial allocation according to market-established prices, an elaborated capital market, and limited industrial dependence on long-term debts, the state will encounter financial institutions as rivals defending the existing organization of the financial system and will confront financial markets as barriers to state influence in industry. The struggle to establish interventionist instruments or state-led industrial promotion can easily degenerate into a conflict over the sanctity of markets.

We take two approaches to the problem of testing these hypotheses. The first approach is to argue from case studies of France and Britain, examples that permit us to consider in historical detail how the structure of the financial system shaped political conflict about industrial change. The second approach adds the Japanese, German, and American experiences to those of France and Britain and correlates more formally the financial system and the process of industrial adjustment.

Interventionist Policies in Britain and France: A First Test

The British and French efforts to adjust to a changed world economy support the line of argument developed here: their different experiences with interventionist strategies cannot be explained without considering the role of their different financial systems.

The French system of intervention rests on its state-dominated, credit-based financial system with administered prices. Credit is allocated as much by quantity and administrative rule as by price. Indeed, the financial system embodies so much discretion that the state bureaucrats are virtually obliged to exercise it. These financial arrangements affect not only the form that policy takes—that is, how the state achieves its purposes—but also significantly influence the character and the outcomes of political conflicts about the purposes of state intervention. Institutional arrangements contain political biases that favor some groups and penalize others, and their influence as intervening variables of parameters in the political battles can be analyzed. Financial weapons were crucial in the postwar fight to alter the relation of the state bureaucracy to the business community. The Trésor in the Ministry of Finance was the bureaucratic stronghold that gave those fighting for economic modernization the leverage they needed to win their battle against traditional industrialists. The reforms the modernizers made in the financial system consolidated their power and strengthened the policy instruments they could devise in the years that followed. The reformed financial system became for the state executive both an instrument of economic policy and a device for constructing specific political alliances. The financial system served to amplify the political resources of those favoring rapid industrialization and it later influenced the fight between the modern, growth-oriented alliance and the traditional preservationist segment of industry.

In the British case the financial system, with its elaborate securities market that allocates resources by price, proved an obstacle to a government effort in the 1960s to establish an interventionist apparatus to promote industrial adjustment and redevelopment. State bureaucrats and politicians had to go around the private financial system in order to use money grants as a means of industrial intervention. The financial system's autonomy from the executive also influenced the character of postwar Labour party economic strategies and the nature of the government's response to Britain's declining industrial position. Despite Labour's hope of reforming capitalism, the government had neither the instruments to do so nor a conception of how to manipulate the industrial economy. Physical controls, which proved unworkable, were seen as the only alternative to a reluctant endorsement of the market system. Even nationalization did not alter the fundamentally arm's-length relations between government and the now-public companies. As a result, the first postwar Labour government led the return to a neoliberal economic normalcy. The need to construct new institutions that paralleled or challenged the private financial system contributed to a conflict over the distribution of gain from industrial growth. This distributional conflict in turn undermined a common desire for more rapid growth and gave the appearance of pluralistic paralysis. The lack of a state capacity to exert industrial leadership and the character of the fights required to create such a capacity shaped the political terms in which economic decline was confronted.

The British political battle rested in part on the effort to imitate the French style of indicative planning and intervention. Could the British government have developed promotional policies that would not have challenged the institutional underpinnings of the nation's economy? Were its tactics of intervention what made financial structure seem so important a barrier? Could one argue that other, less troublesome strategies for exerting industrial leadership could have been found? The German case, we shall argue later, does not provide a counterexample—state promotion of industry by arm's-length leadership—because the structure and direction of German industry required virtually no change during the boom. If we cannot prove that the British *had* to attempt interventionist policies, we can certainly argue that there were both political and technical constraints on the range of policies the British state could choose. Only when the tension of failed development becomes great enough will political pressures suffice to break the institutional arrangements born of the political fights that accompanied past growth. If the old structures fail, then a new political victory must occur to imbue the new institutions with direction and purpose. The arrangements in the British financial market made it all the harder for either Conservatives or Labour to achieve that political victory.

Such historical reconstructions have the advantage of highlighting the role of a favored explanation—here, the role of finance—but that very advantage also points up the limited utility of case analysis. There is a risk that the reconstruction will overplay the importance of the favored explanation and underplay that of its competitors. Certainly the case-study approach does not permit any means of weighing competing explanations. Put more baldly, historical reconstruction allows the author to order facts at will, perhaps making a plausible case but hardly permitting a test for the argument. We shall confront this limitation by widening our focus and adopting a different technique in our second approach.

The Politics of Industrial Adjustment in Five Countries: A Second Test

The politics of industrial adjustment provides a second device for exploring the political consequences of different financial market structures. The French-British cases do not require much formal comparison. The financial systems in the two countries are demonstrably different and our historical reconstruction illuminates their impact on industrial politics. It is easier to demonstrate how a credit-based financial system facilitated state policy in France than to demonstrate how, indirectly, a capital market–based system undermined state industrial leadership in Britain. In the French case, we can demonstrate that finance was used to implement policy, whether or not an alternative technique was possible. In other words, we can show that one interventionist state used financial instruments as a principal mechanism of policy, demonstrating the policy problems such a choice resolved and the political advantages it offered. What our case study cannot show is that an interventionist or promotional state *must* use such mechanisms, and that any other approach will founder politically or technically. The contention that British financial institutions acted as a limit on state action requires a more complicated line of argument. Here we must contend that the conflict that occurred resulted at least in part from efforts to lift the limits on state action.

A single case, or even two, cannot demonstrate the generality of the argument that financial markets structure the terms of the politics of industry. Accordingly, in Chapter 5 we shall present three more cases: Japan, Germany, and the United States. With the resulting set of five countries we shall try to establish a correlation between the type of financial system and the approach to adjustment. This larger enables us can also more effectively to isolate the financial system from other characteristics of the countries. Though the number of cases is still too small to do more than simply reinforce the argument emerging here, its plausibility can be greatly strengthened by expanding the set.

A government's various policies for industry, if taken as a set, represent a political settlement among different social groups and sectors about the terms of industrial change. The issues in that settlement are not only the immediate economic gains and losses from market changes, but also positions of power and privilege in the market and in policy-making. For example, industrial management may in fact make higher wage payments in order to gain or to maintain control over the organization of production. Union leaders may accept wage restraint in exchange for policy influence. The United Auto Workers did just that when they accepted a position on Chrysler's Board of Directors in exchange for wage restraint; so did the British unions in the later 1970s when they accepted influence in policymaking as part of a government strategy of income policies. The political decision to press firms to adjust price signals in order to preserve jobs or maintain production, is ultimately a decision about who will pay for the costs of industrial change, about who will gain and who will be protected.

To explain the techniques of state policy and the political settlement that policy embodies, we must first ask: (1) who predominates in politics, those seeking opportunity and profit in market changes or those seeking insulation from the market; and (2) does the dominant group require government support or aid for its plans, and what help is the state capable of providing. Any attempt to answer these questions must consider both the formation of the "secondary majorities" that influence policy in a particular sector and the inclinations of the governing coalitions that constrain the outcomes in the individual policy arenas. Since we have argued that industrial change takes place at the level of the firm, we will begin with the formation of "secondary majorities" in industry. Initially, we might posit that the political objectives in a particular sector, the types of conflicts, and the pattern of policy which emerges reflect the ability to use finance in a selective way.

To proceed systematically we need a more explicit statement of the outcome to be explained—the process of industrial adjustment. The analytic problem is not so much what weight should be attributed to markets, institutions, or political actors as explanations of policy; the essential problem is how they interrelate. Our task is to fit finance into an interpretation of the state's capacity for managing industrial adjustment.

The Process of Adjustment: The Outcome to Be Explained

We shall first view the problem of industrial adjustment from the top, from the vantage of the political executive and its capacities for action. Then we shall start again from the bottom, considering the problem from the vantage of the firm, to explore what the state may be asked to do and how the direction of policy is determined. We shall conclude this analysis by proposing that there are three model solutions to the political-technical problems of adjustment, each tied to a different arrangement in the financial system. Each model turns on capacities for action and mechanisms for determining the direction of policy.

The Political Executive's View of the Economy.

As it views the industrial economy, the political executive has four options:

1. to stay out of the market, letting price signals drive industrial change

2. to protect existing economic organization by limiting foreign access to its market and subsidizing declining firms and sectors

3. to compensate the losers in the processes of change, bribing them not to interfere

4. to intervene to promote or shape industrial change.

The executive's choice depends in part on its administrative capacities. The first three choices—hands-off liberalism, arm's-length preservationism, and compensation—do not require specialized administrative machinery or unique state capacities. A hands-off policy may involve a bit of compensation or subsidy to the losers but there is no need to organize market outcomes. Industrial preservationism can be achieved either by subsidy or by protection, since both act to mute market signals and relieve the need for change. Subsidy usually requires a direct budget outlay and protection can provoke international repercussions, but neither instrument is inherently complex to administer and in neither case does the government need its own view of how industry should develop. It will accept either the "view" of the market or the position forced on it by political pressure from the industry.

Purposive industrial intervention is much more difficult to implement both technically and politically. To promote or shape industrial change, a government must be able to do three things:

1. have its own view of where industry should be going, which should emerge from its own definition of public purposes and its own interpretation of industry dynamics

2. mobilize and allocate resources in pursuit of the outcomes defined by its view

3. link domestic and foreign economic policy.

A policy of positive promotion means that the state must help generate cash for investment, maintain cash flow for corporate health, promote markets to assure demand, and provide development funds. In sum, intervention to promote competitive development or to protect specific industries requires special and specific technical abilities—the capacities of the "player state" which we discussed earlier. When the state acts as a player it does more than umpire competition to assure that the market works properly, and it must do more than simply administer specific rules and regulations. To be a player, it must specify the objectives it seeks and assemble bits of policy to press toward its goals. To pursue specific industrial outcomes on a continuing and systematic basis, the state must have the capacity for discretion and discrimination. A state strategy of purposive development requires a distinct set of capacities, of which the capacity for action is only the first.

How a government establishes the *purposes* of its policy, the next question, is intertwined with its administrative capacity to act in industrial affairs. A first possibility is that the choice between policies that accept market outcomes and support price-driven change, those that seek to mute the market to preserve existing arrangements, and those that try to promote and direct, will be set by the market options of the firms in that industry. This hypothesis would suggest that an industry or firm in decline might turn to government for protection; that one in ascent might seek government support for its expanding efforts; and that a mature and profitable sector with stable markets and a solid competitive position might simply want the government out of its hair. Though this assessment is plausible as far as it goes, competitive position alone cannot account for national differences in the political strategies adopted by industry or in industry's demands on government. If production is declining, it is not inevitable that the industry will seek protection. Thus, the textile industry is seen as a declining sector in all the advanced countries but its political strategy and marketplace fate have differed from nation to nation. Governments have resolved differently the issue of which portion of the textile industry to protect from decline. In part, their choices have depended upon which firms have had the capacity to adjust to market competition by changing product and production. German firms have displayed greater capacity to adjust than French firms, which is one reason why the French government has had a greater concern with preserving employment and with preserving the traditional organization of production. In France natural fiber manufacturers (cotton and wool producers) sought protection from foreign imports, but they also won protection from *domestic* producers of artificial fibers. In Britain, modern capital-intensive and integrated firms have emerged in the face of cheap Commonwealth imports. By contrast, expanding steel and shipbuilding industries in Japan have been aided in their development by the state, whereas until recently prosperous German firms sought to keep all governments out of the steel industry. It must be emphasized that part of the differences in sectoral outcomes in different countries derives from relative corporate capacities. The firms that compose the several national industries are not the same—not in size, not in management strategy or ideology, and not in the resources available to them. Consequently they will need different things from government.

The Company Executive's View of the Economy.

A firm faced with changed market conditions can adopt one of three basic strategies. The first choice is to *exit* from its previous set of market activities, as when the United States Steel Corporation began to invest in unrelated industries instead of investing in the new steel plant and equipment required to keep it competitive in steel itself. The choice of exit may result from mistaken judgments or from acquiescence to ineluctable market forces. In exiting from one industry or product segment, a company may choose to enter another, taking a position of producer and directly accomplishing the intersectoral shift of capital adjustment involved. Alternatively, it may simply invest funds in purely financial assets and become a corporate rentier, allowing the financial system to accomplish the transfer of capital resources. Firms may exit from an existing activity without seeking protection if they have some alternative use for their resources, but organized labor will rarely exit voluntarily without some compensation. For an industry in decline, it is likely that some firms will have to exit and certainly some of the labor force will have to do so as well.

The second available strategy is for the firm to try to remain competitive within its industry by *adapting or adjusting* to the new market conditions. The corporate decision will depend on the changed elements in the competitive equation and the capacities of the firms in question. The adaptation may take the form of *new products*, such as IBM's development of a copier, or the improvement of existing products. The distinction is a slippery one. The integrated circuit and later the microprocessor were fundamental innovations in electronics components. They made possible both the improvement of a range of existing products from autos to telephone-answering machines as well as such completely new products as the personal computer. The company's adaptation may also take the form of *process innovation* aimed at controlling production costs and thus lowering selling price or increasing profit margins. Process innovation, however, may mean job losses or a reorganization of work and a change in the labor-skill mix. Product and process adjustment are not easily separated. The process advantage of silicon microtechnology allowed Japanese producers to reduce the labor content of television manufacture dramatically while increasing the quality of the product offered. They had entered the American market with small television sets made possible by solid-state technology, a product technology that permitted production advantages. It is also important to note that when the American television firms were driven from the market for color television, their ability to enter the next round of product competition, and thus their long-run competitiveness, was fundamentally compromised. Product and process changes are both company tactics, but the strategic choices of which they are a part must be defined differently.

The redesign of the American automobile to meet demands for higher gas mileage and greater product reliability is a *defensive* effort by American auto companies to hold onto their current market share. IBM's computer series, the 1401, was an *offensive* effort intended to undermine the competitive position of its opponents. Offensive moves are intended to expand a market share or weaken an opponent, whereas defensive moves are intended to retain a market share or to respond to an opponent's initiative. Process and product adaptations are tactics in these strategies. These adjustment strategies may involve changes in the organization of the firm, such as divisionalization, or changes in the institutional environment in which the firm operates, such as a merger.

The firm's third strategic choice is to mute the market conditions that are forcing change through a mix of approaches that range from protection against external competition and government subsidy to private conciliation with domestic rivals in the form of cartel. This third strategy aims to preserve the existing industrial organization and its terms of competition.

Since the firm may seek government assistance in any of these three strategies, we can usefully distinguish between the price governments pay to facilitate adjustment and the costs they incur by resisting decline, though the techniques of policy will be the same in each case. We can label payments to increase market incentives for adjustment as "transfer costs" and payments to maintain production that would not otherwise survive in market competition as "subsidies." Politically, of course, payments for adjustment blur into subsidies. Unless government intervention produces internationally competitive firms, it will tend to preserve ailing enterprise and government policy will degenerate from promotion into protection.

The weight of industry's demands on government will be greater if the sector speaks with a single voice. Each industry sector consists of many distinct segments, however, and within each segment the individual firms may have made different strategy choices. The politically articulated interests of the sector cannot in any simple way be derived from the market position of the industry or any of its segments. Its political interests must be understood as the product of a conflict *within* the industry about the appropriate market and political strategies.

The Transformation of Political Demands into Public Policy.

The political demands made by a firm or by an industry are obviously not processed into government policy automatically. If an industrial sector could capture and dominate the government agency that directly affects it, government policies might closely reflect the demands made by the strongest supplicants. Private capture of segments of the public policy machinery is certainly more typical of the United States than it is of France or Britain, for the U.S. bureaucracy is more open to direct private influence and each policy arena is more securely insulated from others. Even in the United States, however, the needs of one sector often have to be balanced against the demands of other industries. If, on behalf of American agriculture, the U.S. government insists that Japan open its market to American rice and oranges, it may have to limit demands that Japan open its markets to American electronic products. American demands that the Japanese restrict auto exports limit the American ability to insist that the Japanese change interfirm arrangements in integrated circuit production. Consequently, whatever the needs or wishes of industry, we must look outside the industry to find an explanation for the policies finally adopted. Each industry might capture a component of the bureaucracy which speaks on its behalf and even provides for part of its policy needs. But there will be issues, such as trade, in which the needs of sectors are directly competitive and cannot be met simultaneously.

We must take this analysis further. If the state simply reproduced the demands of the strongest social groups or the winning political coalitions, the government would simply reflect the political balance in the society and policies for a given sector of the economy would be settled by political competition within that sector or between sectors. In fact, however, government has powerful means of shaping the demands made upon it and the political executive can thus play an active role in determining the outcomes of the several conflicts. It can extend resources to the groups it favors—everything from privileged policy access and the right to administer state policy to selective access to credit. The technical capacity to pursue specific industrial objectives, discussed above, is also the basis of a capacity to shape the political terms of industrial change. The state can be as active in shaping the political competitions as it is in molding the marketplace.[18] Therefore, the political outcomes within each sector depend on state policy as much as they shape it.

To understand which sectoral demands prevail and the form they finally take, we must turn to the character of the coalitions that govern. If national coalitions are to delimit the range of policy across a set of sectors, policies must constrain choices within each sector or many of the same actors must be involved in the decisions in each industry. The consequence is that we cannot simply add up the expressed market needs of the different sectoral components of a coalition to discover the orientation of policy, any more than we could add up the position of different firms in a sector to discover its policy demands. Different coalitions presumably imply different policies and hence different industrial strategies for adjustment in several advanced nations, but these coalitions are not mechanical reflections of the economy. We can conclude from this discussion that mounting pressures in particular sectors will produce a national resistance to adjustment or growth only if they alter the composition of the governing coalition and the producer alliances on which industry routinely depends. Mancur Olson's proposal that we simply count up interest groups to estimate impediments to growth is both a futile and a pointless task.[19]

Struggles to formulate state policy for industry and the economy are, finally, struggles about how to allocate the costs and profits from industrial change. Unless there is a political settlement that distributes the gain and pain of growth, the distributional struggle will undermine the consensus to pursue growth. The question of the state's capacities to shape the political and marketplace outcomes in specific sectors and the question of the actual purposes it pursues join together here. The political settlement can simply be *left to the market* with the state giving some small compensation to those who complain the loudest. U.S. trade adjustment assistance to workers and communities damaged by imports fits this notion. The state may *impose* a distribution by consciously manipulating the market or the distributional outcome can be explicitly *negotiated* among the producer groups involved. Clearly, these are not exclusive alternatives: most negotiations contain some degree of threatened coercion and those who would coerce may employ negotiation from a position of strength as their vehicle. Nonetheless, each country may establish a different mechanism for achieving a settlement that embodies different combinations of markets, compensation, state-imposed distribution, and negotiation.

The politics of adjustment thus has three parts: (1) state capacities to act in the economy, which sets the range of possible policy strategies, (2) a political settlement that distributes the gains from change and in so doing establishes which market pressures will be resisted, and (3) a political process by which that distributional settlement is reached.

Three Models of Adjustment

Even this cursory review of the technical and political roles of the state in industrial change suggests three models of the adjustment process. Each model embodies technical capacities for state action in industry, a political settlement allocating the costs of industrial change, and a political process by which the settlement is reached. The role of the financial system in each model of industrial change is different. The three models of change are: (1) state led, (2) company led, and (3) tripartite negotiated.

In the state-led model of development, the government bureaucracy attempts to orient the adjustment of the economy by explicitly influencing the position of particular sectors, even of individual companies, and by imposing the solutions on the weakest groups in the polity. The state seeks to select the terms on which sectors and companies confront the market, either by explicitly providing resources to favored groups or by creating conditions that will force the recalcitrant to adjust. The state is an economic player, usually pursuing some form of development. The aggressive promotion of industrial modernization which we find in Japan is not the only state-led possibility. A different balance emerged in France, where change was more contained. Finance acts as an instrument of such efforts, permitting bureaucrats to intervene in the affairs of particular firms and to allocate capital between competing uses. A state-led adjustment process politicizes and centralizes the process of industrial change. Those excluded from the circle of the favored are evident and can plausibly blame their plight more on political weakness than on economic failure. Consequently, the government-imposed balance of the costs and gains of change rests on the continued ability of the executive and the political winners to exclude the losing groups from policymaking.

In the company-led model of industrial change, the basic choices are made by individual firms without outside interference, leaving the workers or communities who are displaced or damaged to fend for themselves or to seek compensation from the government. In this model the state does regulate and compensate but, fundamentally, the costs and gains of change are allocated through the market. Above all, the government does not have a view of the long-run development of the economy and of industry. The financial system is the vehicle that allocates resources among competing uses. Its autonomy from government isolates the government from the workings of the industrial economy.

The tripartite-bargaining strategy involves an explicit and continuing negotiation of the terms of industrial change by the predominant social partners. The bargaining base of the several partners rests both in the organization of the policy and in the organization of the market. In his study of the Netherlands, Arend Lijphart shows that bargains are explicitly worked out by elite representatives of the several political groupings, which incorporate the producer groups.[20] The organization of politics creates the basis of negotiation. The Swedish case, by contrast, is an instance in which labor market organization creates the basis of the national bargain.[21] In the German case, as we are so often told, finance plays a role in resolving the particulars of corporate crisis, with banks playing an almost parapublic role. The Swedish and German cases suggest that a powerful position in one market—labor, capital, or goods—provides the basis for entering into political bargains about the operations of other markets. In this third system of adjustment, financial institutions operate as potential government allies as a base for limited social bargaining.

Each of these ideal types suggests a basic political approach to resolving the controversies that accompany adjustment. The particular capacities of business and the organizational purposes of labor account for the specific thrust of policy within each model. Peter Katzenstein, in his interesting discussion of adjustment in small states, focuses on the capacities of business and the purposes of labor. He considers variation within the bargained-adjustment model and seeks to account for the several national outcomes within his set of small states.[22] Because the small states must remain open to the international market, their exports must be competitive abroad. Their domestic political arrangements force them to bargain over the allocation of the burdens of change. Given these constraints on policy, the nature and strength of business and labor *do* become the central issues in accounting for the particulars of policy. The small states represent only one type of adjustment, however. Since the countries we are considering present a wider variety of political approaches to adjustment and a greater range of market problems, we have focused on a prior step, establishing the several models of adjustment and differentiating the market problems they confront. Having distinguished these approaches to adjustment, we will later speculate on how variations in the position of business or labor affect the success of adjustment and the distribution and gain from it.

If we fit our countries to the three ideal types, we find that Japan and France can readily be categorized as state-led promotional types whereas the United States is a company-led regulatory type. Germany has many characteristics of the tripartite-bargaining type, in which there are often specific deals between finance, labor, government, and industry, but no overall explicit bargain. Sweden, whose centralized labor bargaining system has been so well depicted by Andrew Martin, is perhaps a better example of the bargained model.[23] Britain represents a case of failure to make any particular choice about an approach to adjustment: the political and industrial power of labor in that country has made it impossible to move without the unions' support, but the unions are not organized for the task of making detailed corporatist bargains and the companies are not prepared to accept them in that role. The tradition of private and often public company autonomy from government and finance lends the British case characteristics of company-led adjustment, whereas the state's effort to take the initiative is reminiscent of state-led adjustment.

Finance and Adjustment: The Hypothesis

Each of the three models of financial system has implications for the government's capacities to intervene in the market and for the types of political conflicts which emerge when the executive does act in the industrial economy. The proposition here is that each type of financial system is one of the defining components of a specific model of the process of adjustment. The financial marketplace, not just the arrangements of politics, sets the arena for the fights that accompany industrial change. Let us express the logic of the tie between the types of financial systems and adjustment processes in three propositions (see Chart 2.1). First, a credit-based, price-administered financial system is an instrument of state intervention which blurs the lines in the market between public and private sectors; it is part and parcel of a state-led model of adjustment. Second, financial systems with extensive and efficient capi-

Chart 2.1. Financial systems and the adjustment process

Country	Financial system	Predicted adjustment	Actual adjustment
France Japan	credit-based, price-administered	state-led	state-led
West Germany	credit-based, institution-dominated	tripartite-negotiated	tripartite-negotiated
Great Britain United States	capital market–based	company-led	unclear (Britain) company-led (U.S.)

tal markets both limit the channels of state action and generate opposition to intervention; they create institutional circumstances favorable to company-led adjustment. Third, institution-led or bank-dominated capital markets create the conditions for negotiated adjustment.

The evidence to be presented in the case studies supports the hypothesis that types of financial systems are correlated to models of the adjustment process. With their credit-based, price-administered financial systems, France and Japan should have state-led adjustment processes. The United States and Britain, which have capital market–based systems with competitively determined prices, should have company-led growth. Germany, with an institution-dominated, credit-based system, should have elements of negotiation in the processes of change. Only the British case does not fit the predictions of this hypothesis, for reasons that should become clear. The reader will simply have to accept the country categorization developed in this preview, since the text that follows is a justification and interpretation of the schema. In the final chapter three alternative explanations of the relations between business and government are developed and evaluated: explanations built around the balance of political forces, the economic situations confronting a country which determine the choices open to its governments, and the structure of the state bureaucracy.

Since the proposition that the financial system structures the politics of industry can be denied, it can also be tested. In a theoretical argument that links the structure of finance to the process of adjustment, the proposed linkages can be examined by considering first the financial system and then the process of adjustment. A skeptic might argue that if the structure of finance is constructed by state bureaucrats, either to facilitate state strategies of intervention (as in France) or to prevent links between finance and industry (as in the United States), then the variations in the financial system and the process of adjustment would have common political origins. There would be correlation but no causation; financial structures would be derivative of politics and not a real and independent influence on the politics of adjustment. The British and French case studies are crucial to our evaluation of this argument. When British bureaucrats confronted an entrenched market financial system, they were *not* able to turn it to their purposes of modernization. In France, conversely, the character of the financial system presented the political modernizers with valuable weapons.*

*We should acknowledge at the outset that this kind of analysis faces a "measurement" problem. To establish the plausibility of a relation between finance and the politics of adjustment, we have developed categories that distinguish types of finance and adjustment. Our national cases have then been assigned to these categories. In the case of the financial system, there are systemic characteristics (though not quantities) which enable us to assign a particular system to a specific category. In the case of the adjustment process, we depend on a qualitative characterization of the industrial politics of each country. This problem of measurement cannot be resolved within the scope of this study. Detailed and comparable evidence over a wide-enough range of industries to permit a formal five-nation comparison simply does not exist. Though a range of sector cases in these countries has been examined in the research presented here, any formal measures of them would simply represent a glorification of a still qualitative judgment. Only a detailed set of comparable sector studies—a book for each country—could truly permit a more explicit measure. It is therefore open to judgment whether the national cases examined here, based on evidence presented later in this text or available to others, fit the proposed characterization of adjustment. At issue is the existence of distinct national adjustment processes. We can alter the categories and still sustain the original argument. We cannot contend that all national adjustments proceed in similar fashion without abandoning this enterprise. In sum, the effort to correlate characteristics of finance, state structure, and economic situation to the national adjustment process provides evidence that is consistent with our proposition that financial systems structure the politics of industrial change. In fact the evidence points to the significance of the British and French cases, and makes their historical reconstruction of more general significance.

Part II

THE EVIDENCE

CHAPTER THREE

The Interventionist Temptation:
The French Case

To alter industrial structures it is often necessary to enter into the structures themselves.
—Pierre Moussa, French banker, in *Revue des deux mondes,*
October 1976.

This chapter contends that French strategies of state-led development and industrial intervention have depended on the selective allocation of credit made possible by the credit-based, price-administered financial system. The arrangements of administration and politics in France did not in themselves create the distinctive state capacities that allowed successive governments an extensive place in industrial life, nor did administrative discretion, long a tradition in the French bureaucracy, suffice to give direction to a modern economy. The argument that interventionist capacities rest as much on financial as on administrative arrangements is developed by analyzing the structure of the French financial system in order to understand the possibilities for government action it creates. Three political struggles crucial to the postwar economic growth of France, struggles in which the outcome was affected by government action, are then considered.

The first of these struggles was the Planning Commission's fight for political survival in the late 1940s. The outcome turned not only on the balance of political forces in the society at the time of the Planning Commission's creation but also on the commission's ability to win bureaucratic contests by selectively recruiting business allies through discretionary allocations of capital. The interventionist apparatus was indeed latent in the French system and had been used for narrow and specific projects in the past, but its application to an economy-wide modernization effort was very much the product of this postwar fight over the organization and the purposes of the state.[1]

99

The second conflict pitted the traditional elites of France's rural and small-town past against the forces that favored promoting industrial development. In response to this conflict, the state pursued competing and seemingly contradictory purposes—fostering growth while simultaneously containing its political consequences. Resorting to arrangements of the financial system that enabled it to target financial flows to specific uses, the government was able to subsidize groups that resisted change while thereby strengthening the market forces that favored growth. In short, it can be said that the government devised a policy mix that primed the growth engine and force-fed it high octane fuel while at the same time stepping on the brakes.

Third, there was a series of conflicts which represented a struggle to force French firms to adjust to competition and international markets. The state intervened to assist the transformation of once insular French firms into modern corporations. The specific industry policies, many of which were badly mistaken, must be measured against the political tasks of keeping French industry alive while it changed and adjusted. In the postwar years French governments walked a tightrope to modernization: the financial system was their balancing rod for that crossing.

THE POLITICS OF DEVELOPMENT

At the end of the Second World War French industry was composed primarily of small to medium-sized companies that had been insulated from foreign competition for decades. Both the economy and the society remained predominantly rural in character. In the next twenty-five years, however, a radical transformation was completed: France emerged as an industrial economy with firms that were dependent on foreign sales and able to compete with imports in their home markets. After a series of troubled mergers and reorganizations, the structure of French industry came to resemble that of its foreign competitors. The giant, centrally controlled corporation whose management is increasingly divorced from its ownership became a commonplace in the advanced sectors.

The changes wrought by economic development irrevocably altered French society. Frenchmen earned their livings in new ways and spent their lives in dramatically different circumstances than had their grandparents.

Elements of traditional France of course survived, but peasants and small businessmen discovered that their positions were radically different. Larger farmers became rich and smaller peasants found their marginal position less and less tenable; along with agricultural workers, they moved to the cities in increasing numbers. Much of the small-scale business that had been a part of French life for so long survived in a protected preserve, walled off from competition by special rules and tax laws. Yet many small firms found themselves serving the advanced industrial sectors as part of a shock absorber against economic fluctuation, and small distributors proved unable to exclude from their markets entirely the supermarket and the department store that symbolized the new order.

The dislocations caused by this transformation produced intense political turmoil. Workers and middle-class students demonstrated their political reaction to their changed circumstances most dramatically in the events of May 1968, but the most enduring expression of their response was certainly the Socialist party's reemergence and rise to power. At the same time, traditional France stubbornly resisted its demise, the uprisings led by Poujade in the 1950s and the movement headed by Royer in the 1970s being only the most explosive reminders that it would not pass away quietly. These movements indicated the potential for a coalition, much like those that appeared during the Third Republic, which would actively fight against growth and derail the industrial advance.

The postwar economic transformation was not, then, a preordained market process to which politics was a sideshow.[2] Rather, the policies of the political executive were essential, in two distinct ways, to sustaining growth throughout the postwar period. One set of state policies served to contain the political opposition of the traditionalists who resisted the marketplace developments that were slowly displacing them. A second set of state policies served as instruments for directly promoting and organizing the forces of change in the economy. Subsidized privilege to encourage change was consequently set against subsidized protection to preserve existing social and economic relations. Whether by intent or by fortune—and we will argue that the result was in large part intentional—France reached a political balance that dissolved or contained the traditionalist coalition against growth without eliminating the market differentials needed to generate the transfers of investment and resources that growth requires.[3] These two kinds of policies were evident in each important phase of development—in reconstruction, in the boom years, and in the present era of strained adjustment. These political strategies to support industrial development depended on selective instruments of intervention, which were themselves shaped by the structure of the French financial system.

While the financial system is a marketplace for money—which is to say that its internal workings follow the economic logic of markets—it also acts as an institution that delimits the actions of different groups and thus has a clearly political function as well. Thus, political-economic analysis must find a way to remain true to the economic analysis of market phenomena while at the same time interpreting political behavior. In this book we treat financial markets as we might treat political institutions. Institutional arrangements for government administration, politics, and the marketplace can affect the content of policy and the politics of industry through three mechanisms. First, they can affect the political definition of a group's *interests* by establishing presumptions about what it must do to get what it wants. Second, by affecting the issues on which different groups can coalesce, institutions can establish both the nature of those groups and the possible political *alliances between them*. Third, they can determine what an alliance or group can obtain from any political victory by constraining that group's *capacity* to act, by setting the range of policies a government can conduct.

The French experience offers a wealth of insight into the role that institutions play in shaping politics. Indeed, it was Alexis de Tocqueville's central insight that institutions influence the nature of conflicts between social groups and the content of the policies that emerge.[4] In de Tocqueville's view, the character of French sociopolitical institutions made equality and liberty conflicting goals. He argued that liberty could be guaranteed only if there were intermediary institutions between the central state and the individual—institutions that served both as buffers against the state and as instruments that communities could use to resolve local problems. On this basis, de Tocqueville held that the revolutionary state's destruction of such institutions in the name of equality was in fact the destruction of the foundations of liberty. Destroying intermediary institutions not only limited the capacity of citizens to act locally but also exposed them to the whims of a central bureaucracy. From another point of view, however, the centralized state becomes not the enemy but the very instrument of liberty. In prerevolutionary France, after all, the institutions of local politics were also institutions of social inequality which promoted the subjugation of peasants and the power of landlords. By destroying these institutions in the name of equality, then, the revolutionary state can be said to have furthered the cause of liberty. Since political efforts to replace these old institutions also threatened to establish springboards for local opposition to the new more centralized regime, local autonomy came to suggest counterrevolution and the fragmentation of the French political community. Whether we associate liberty with local government or with the central state, the general point remains: institutions have played a major role in shaping politics. As Peter Gourevitch argues in observing the Gaullists, the pattern has been universal in French politics: when in opposition support decentralization as a means of establishing a foothold in power; once in power use the instruments of the centralized state to hold on and exclude challenges.[5] (Perhaps the most radical proposals of the present · socialist government are those to decentralize the system of administration.)

The establishment of the Fifth Republic in 1958 provides a more recent example of how institutional evolution can alter patterns of political behavior. The Fifth Republic's institutions increased the powers of the president and checked the powers of parliament. This strengthened executive, combined with a bureaucracy reformed during the Fourth Republic, altered the channels of interest-group influence and consequently changed the type of policy alliances that could be built. Narrow interests presented their positions individually and in technical terms, instead of collectively in the more general political terms of broadly based interest-alliances. This pattern facilitated specific deals in which the state could pursue its own purposes by exploiting conflicts and divisions within sectors of the economy.

It is obvious, then, that institutions affect both the form and the content of politics and that political interests and political objectives are shaped by the institutional context in which they are defined. The influence of the French system of state administration on contemporary policy has been extensively argued, and the bureaucratic base of the French executive's ability to intervene selectively in the economy has been well documented.[6] The administration has been at least partially insulated against direct outside interference from pressure groups or parliament. It has been staffed at the top by a set of bureaucrats recruited from special schools—bureaucrats who can use their autonomy to develop an interpretation of the public interest which is more than the sum of particular pressures, or different from it. The considerable discretion embedded in French administrative practice makes it possible for the bureaucracy to pursue its objectives by discriminating in favor of some groups and against others.

The ability to exert industrial leadership rests as much on the organization of the system of finance and its relation to the government bureaucracy as it does on the nature of the administrative structure, however. A developmental state in a modern economy requires more than an interventionist bureaucracy or a political balance that permits aggressive modernization; it also demands a marketplace for finance organized to give the political executive an instrument of discretion and hierarchical control in the economy. Executive influence in the financial system makes it simpler for political leaders and senior bureaucrats to direct the flow of funds and credits in a relatively private fashion. In the French case particular agencies and specific policy instruments have been popularly identified as the locus of intervention. Some observers concluded that the demise of the Planning Commission and the relative decline in the importance of the Fund for Economic and Social Development (FDES) in the 1970s indicated that the interventionist state was withering away in the era of Giscardian liberalism. But because the state's interventionist capacity emerges in part from the organization of the financial system, new interventionist bureaucracies and policy tools can be bred with ease, as has indeed been the case in the recent industrial crisis.

This chapter argues that the continuity in the form of French industrial economic policy results from the use of the financial system as the vital instrument of state intervention. It also contends that this continuity in form is more than simply a matter of national style, and that it has an influence on the content of policy. The ways in which groups achieve their aims affect who gets what; the structure of finance amplifies the power of a relatively small group of bureaucrats and political leaders to shape the direction of the economy. In developing this argument we will consider three separate political issues: (1) the political fight to establish the Planning Commission and shift the emphasis of French economic policy; (2) the effort to subsidize traditional France while assuring investment in modern industry; and (3) the intervention that helped force French industry out of its industrial dark ages and into a competitive international economy, as well as the interventions now being made to assist its adjustment to strained international conditions. Throughout we will pay close attention to the organization of the financial system and the instruments it offers to the political executive. We begin with the fight to establish the Plan.

CONSTRUCTING THE INTERVENTIONIST APPARATUS

Despite the conventional image of French industrial intervention as an alliance of big business and the state, the emergence of the Planning Commission and the active use of interventionist instruments to promote industrial expansion were by no means inevitable.[7] The interventionist state was not the product of some ingrained national character,

of an ideology of etatism, or of a historical tradition of close involvement in the economy. Nor did the reorientation occur, as some suggest,
simply because new men gave fresh purpose to the French economy in
the late 1940s.[8] Instead, the shift occurred because new purposes were
embedded in old institutions and the relations between state institutions and those of the economy were altered. Existing institutions were
reformed and some new institutions, such as the École Nationale
d'Administration, were established. This institutional reorientation was
not simply an administrative reform; rather, it represented an explicit
political victory that shifted the relative positions of business leadership
and state bureaucrats.

The Second World War proved a watershed in the evolution of
French politics. Participation in the collaborationist Vichy government
discredited parts of the political center and right that had dominated
France for generations. The resistance movement, which inherited
power in France after the armistice, was led by Charles de Gaulle, a
nationalist from the Right, but as a government it included heavy representation from the Left. The prewar pattern of stalemated centrist
politics was broken, if only for a moment, and new possibilities opened.
There emerged new parties that represented a mix of interests different from those that had predominated before the war. Before the
routine of squabbling centrist parties reasserted itself, the relations between business and the state had begun to change.

Although the disruptions of the war had opened the way for the
reorientation of the state's role in the economy, the shift in state
policy still required a battle within the bureaucracy. The bureaucratic
fight for economic modernization began at the nadir of business influence in modern French politics (the result of business collaboration
with the Vichy regime) and at the peak of a tide of labor influence
that had been building during the years of wartime resistance. But the
outcome of this conflict within the administration was by no means a
direct result of the outcome of the struggle for control of government
itself. Had the moment been lost—had traditional politics taken hold
before the institutional changes of administration and finance had
been achieved—the economic forces that resisted the transformation
would have been better situated politically to influence policy. The
course of postwar growth might have looked very different.

The technical rearrangements within the administration were engineered by a small elite committed to economic modernization. These
institutional innovations reinforced the capacity of the core bureaucracies—particularly the Ministry of Finance—to intervene in industrial
affairs selectively and on their own initiative and to reorient the use of

economic resources according to their own priorities. In these postwar years the influence of the Ministry of Finance was extended beyond the budget to include the economy's financial system. The Trésor in the Ministry of Finance, for example, is said to have changed from being a bank for the government into being a bank for the economy.

In these early years the fight for economic modernization swirled around the creation of the Planning Commission. The Plan, as it became known, represented a clear political initiative to use reformed administrative machinery to force changes in French industry.[9] It was initiated with support from labor, survived despite the resistance of business, and then evolved into a mechanism for collaboration between business and the state. Its political struggle and the technical tasks of economic management were intertwined. If, as Jean Monnet suggested, the basic task was to change behavior by disseminating a few basic ideas widely, then public relations was supplemented with a good deal of arm-twisting.[10] Selective control of access to industrial credit was an essential weapon in the Plan's fight for political survival and in its technical handling of its actual economic responsibilities.

Two components of that postwar contest concern us here. The first is the role of the selective control of credit in the political struggle to create the Plan and to win the Trésor's eventual commitment to the project of modernizing the French economy. The second was the reform of the financial institutions themselves to give the state greater influence over the allocation of credit in the economy. The financial system, as we shall see, was first a stake in the fight to make modernization an objective of state policy, and later (in its revamped form) an instrument for the modernizers in the continuing struggle for economic development.

Initially, the political position of the Planners was very fragile. Nothing about the governing tripartite coalition dictated their victory and the major policy reorientation it brought. As a result, the Planners encouraged widespread participation in the development of the Plan both to legitimate their efforts and to create the political resources needed for the series of struggles with their bureaucratic and business opponents. Labor's support, which was used to force the hand of business in the modernization committees in which sectoral work was undertaken, was probably crucial to the survival of the Plan in its early years.[11] At the same time, however, the Planners shied away from direct conflict with the business community and sought to prove that they were committed to profits, markets, and the private sector. Direct clashes with the rest of the bureaucracy were also avoided. The control that other agencies exercised over the incentives and coercive powers of administration which the Plan employed was seldom challenged directly.[12] The plan intruded on, but did not occupy, the bureaucratic terrain of other agencies; it never attempted to replace other ministries or to displace their powers. Even more important was the fact that Monnet did not attempt to link planning to existing administrative controls of the economy. Such controls allocated specific quantities of materials in this period of real scarcity. He recognized that business opposition to the direct allocation of resources by bureaucrats would mount and that such resistance could undermine the planning effort itself.[13] He also realized that direct physical control would require the Plan to gain dominant influence in the host of physical planning departments in the various agencies, as well as in the diverse trade associations to which state powers had been delegated. Since such an effort would either require a massive bureaucracy or spread a small one too thin, the planners sought to operate by controlling the allocation of credit (the opposite of the choice made by their British counterparts in the same years). Operating through credits, the Planners did not need to capture as wide a range of power or to influence as diverse a group of authorities in order to make their weight felt in the economy. With "finance" as their chosen weapon, they needed only one bureaucratic ally, the Ministry of Finance. This alliance would not be easy to construct, but it limited the administrative terrain that had to be captured and simplified the bureaucratic political problem.

Interestingly, while the Planners sought official labor union representation as a political resource to legitimate their efforts, they worked with individual private businessmen to devise and implement their industrial strategies. Official business organizations were intentionally avoided, because the Planners feared they might be constrained by traditional business attitudes and policy commitments.[14] By choice, then, the Plan was somewhat insulated from the detailed pressures exerted by economic interest groups; this was an explicit political gamble that left possible opponents outside the policy apparatus. Those who were adversely affected by policy or who felt powerless because they were not involved in the choices could then mobilize against the Plan. State alliances with individual components of the business community proved to be a central feature of French postwar intervention. The ability of state bureaucrats to control access to investment funds, or to allocate the funds themselves, facilitated these selective alliances.

By the late 1940s the modernizers had lost an ally and gained an opponent, and the first Plan was thus implemented in a political setting very different from the one in which it had been formulated.[15] The CGT, the trade union dominated by the Communist party, withdrew from the French Plan in opposition to the U.S. Marshall Plan. In addition, organized business, which had never massively supported the Plan, was now encouraged by a changed political environment to express its opposition to state intervention.[16] The resistance coalition had cracked and left-wing influence in the government had dwindled, reducing the threat of nationalization and other challenges to business and leaving companies freer to flex their political muscles. In fact, the opposition of organized business to this new state planning venture is not surprising. The major business associations that had been excluded from the formulation of the Plan were dominated by the small and medium-sized businesses, the businesses that had the most to lose from the active promotion of efficiency and modernization. The state was aiming for the first time at the elimination of "unproductive" firms, and those "unproductive" firms were an important constituency of organized business associations. Business opponents of planning had allies within the government and out, for both the budget side of the Ministry of Finance and the financial community were opposed to the costs of the Plan's commitments.[17] Had the Planners lost the financial instrument—influence over the allocation of industrial credit—they would have been isolated and probably defeated, leaving the traditional client-based ministries who controlled the programs that allocated resources directly as the agents of any industrial policy. The balance of state versus business initiative would have been different from that in the United States in any case, but the prevalent image of the autonomous state struggling to force development would not have emerged.

In the many specific policy battles in which the stakes were the survival or adjustment of less productive firms, the Planner-modernizers pursued their objectives through the control of finance, whereas the business groups and their bureaucratic allies countered by using their control of the instruments of physical planning. The Planners' original decision to pursue their aims through finance proved useful, for with this single instrument they were able to confront varied opponents on different political terrains. Not surprisingly, the main beneficiaries of the investment allocations were their business allies. The Planners forged close ties with the steel association, for example, which received the largest single share of public investment in the private sector (16 percent).[18] The steel, electrical equipment, shipbuilding, and petroleum industries—all beneficiaries of the Plan largesse—proved invaluable allies in the commission's successful fight to restore modernization credits at the beginning of the Korean War.[19] Even in these sectors, however, business cooperation with the implementation of the Plan was by no means complete, and the Planners relied on competition between firms in a particular sector to accomplish their objectives, taking funds away from one company and giving them to others. For example, when the Wendel steel groups refused to install a continuous strip mill, the modernization funds set aside for this purpose were instead made available to the firms grouped in the Usinor combine.[20]

The Marshall Plan helped solidify the link between the Plan and the Trésor, an alliance that in turn strengthened the modernizers in their hold over the instruments of finance.[21] Monnet and his entourage had convinced the Americans that Marshall funds should be invested to increase supply (this being the best means of controlling inflation), but in fact the Plan was concerned mainly with expanding supply for its own sake rather than with controlling inflation. The impression that the Plan had close American ties was reinforced when one of Monnet's assistants became head of the European Marshall Plan Administration. This impression proved useful, helping the Plan win influence over the use of Marshall funds even though their formal administration remained in the hands of the Trésor. The joint management of these funds, as noted above, served to commit the Trésor to the task of modernization and gave a lasting financial cast to French industrial intervention.

The alliance with the Trésor was made all the more important by a series of postwar reforms that expanded the government's influence in the financial markets. These reforms completed a process begun under the Popular Front government and continued during the Vichy period—a process that reversed the state's historic dependence on the financial sector and slowly turned finance into an instrument of state policy.*[22] The public or parapublic institutions that became so important after the Second World War had emerged in piecemeal fashion during the preceding century and a half. Though they differed as to whether they were banks or specialized financial institutions, pools of deposits or lending institutions, primarily public or basically private, they were all sponsored by the state to do things that the underdeveloped banking system could not or would not undertake. They were intended as much to lessen the government's dependence on the purely private financial sector as to undertake specific tasks. Perhaps

*Historically, the financial sector in France had developed to finance the state and serve its purposes. This role expanded in the latter part of the nineteenth century when successive governments sought to finance the infrastructure for large-scale industrialization. It was then that the first joint-stock banking establishments appeared. The private segment of finance remained quite autonomous of direct government control even though the state had been the initial and often the primary client.

the most dramatic example, the Caisse Nationale des Marchés de l'État, was initiated as a mechanism to finance the public works projects of the Popular Front government when the private sector resisted.

A system for the effective regulation of the banking sector was also emerging before the Second World War.[23] In the interwar years the Bank of France was transformed from a private commercial bank dominated by its two hundred largest shareholders (though it had the functions of a central bank) into a publicly controlled central bank. The politics of the reversal are clear. As a commercial operation, the Bank of France competed with the rest of the private banking system. With its refusal in 1926 to rediscount short-term treasury notes—in essence, a refusal to accept government debt as a negotiable instrument—it became a policy rival to government as well. Its challenge to the autonomy of government economic policy created widespread support for reform, both in the financial community and in government. The left-based Popular Front replaced the bank's Council of Regents (its largest shareholders) with a government-appointed General Council, thereby establishing state control over the regulation of the financial system. At the same time, the Bank of France became more active in the money market, gaining the capacity to affect both the quantity of money and the rates of interest. Legislation permitting a money-market role for the central bank was passed by a conservative government after the demise of the Popular Front. These reforms in the role of the Bank of France were not simply a repudiation of private capitalism; within both the banking sector and the government there was pressure for more effective financial regulation.

At the end of the war the expansion of state power in the financial system took three forms, each suggesting a separate impetus for change: nationalization, which emerged from the Left; expanded regulation for bank stability and macroeconomic control, which was a concern shared by government and finance; and the establishment of mechanisms for selective credit allocation, which was important to the modernizers in the bureaucracy.

The nationalization of the Bank of France—the first step in the postwar reforms—simply codified the developments of the interwar period. Nationalization of the commercial banks, however, was vehemently opposed by the banking sector and by the nonsocialist elements in the consultative assembly. The Left prevailed but the opposition limited the range of the takeovers. Nationalization wrought little change in the internal operations of banks, however. They retained their identities and continued to compete with each other and with the remaining private banks. When the radical thrust of the first postwar reforms subsided, the bank managements began to assert their autonomy from the government. "In 1947–1948, for example, the nationalized banks refused to finance the investment plans of nationalized industries until sufficient pressure was brought to bear by the Ministry of Finance through the intervention of the Trésor and a state guarantee of such loans."[24] This autonomy should not be exaggerated, however. In a crunch, the state could impose its will directly and it could always use indirect mechanisms of regulation and control to supplement its direct means of influencing the allocation of credit. As time passed, the banks retained their autonomy but became government allies in the overall project of development.

The second element of expanded state power, the framework for government regulation of banking practices and control of credit policies, was inherited in large part from the Vichy regime. That wartime government had established a permanent banking committee, which was in fact an experiment in self-regulation, and a banking control commission that for the first time accorded wide regulatory and investigative power to the government. The postwar reforms simply shifted power more firmly into the hands of the government. The self-regulating banking committee of the Vichy years was replaced by a National Credit Council (Conseil National du Crédit) composed of diverse interests. The council's power was limited and the Bank of France and the banking control commission actually did the substantive work. The council did serve as a link between government and the banking community and between the agencies and the parapublic banking institutions.

The third extension of state power in the financial system was the establishment of mechanisms to influence the allocation of credit. These new structures served not only to create discretion for the government but also to draw the commercial banks into closer ties with their industrial clients. At the beginning of this period the deposit banks were short-term commercial lenders rather than industrial lenders, whereas the *banques d'affaires,* with more limited funds, had closer industrial links. The rediscounting devices introduced by government served two functions: (1) they reduced bank risk and encouraged longer-term industrial lending and (2) they served as a forced education in helping banks learn to assess and judge term loans on their own. Rediscounting required a signature from a parapublic institution—such as the Crédit National—and in a literal sense this offered the banks training in loan evaluation. In response to their expanding industrial business, the banks developed their own internal capacity in the form of a loan evaluation system and industrial lending groups.

Ironically, both the Plan, which was to become an instrument of private relations between state and business, and the reorganized financial system, which was to facilitate this relationship, took root during a period when leftist and labor influence was strong and that of business weak. The modernizers, a political-bureaucratic alliance symbolized by the alliance between Monnet and Robert Schuman, tended to concentrate their power in the Plan and the Trésor. The traditional ministries, which had closer ties to their client groups, were sidestepped. One must not interpret this development as a fragmentation of the state, a loss of purpose and direction.[25] It was instead part of a political struggle to redefine the purposes of the bureaucracy, a struggle in which one side made its camp around the state-financial system.

THE FINANCIAL STRUCTURE OF AN INTERVENTIONIST STATE

The significance of the alliance between the Trésor and the Plan and the importance of the Trésor's commitment to the goal of development can be understood only by examining the financial system in some detail. This section depicts the financial system as it existed at the time of the Mitterand victory in May 1981 in an effort to clarify the significance of financial arrangements for current government economic policies.[26] Since it is the structure of the financial system, rather than the issue of ownership, which defines the options open to government, the nationalizations carried out in 1982 have not fundamentally altered the system. We shall return to our narrative of the politics of industrial adjustment after this review of the financial system.

A brief sketch of the institutional relations between finance, government, and business serves to introduce the "players" and enables us to identify the political significance of these financial arrangements. The crux of our argument is that these institutional ties derive from the operation and organization of the markets for finance. We must therefore consider how the financial marketplace creates and sustains these institutional arrangements. It is not the quantities but the relations between markets that deserve attention.

How does the system look to a senior bureaucrat in the economic ministries who is interested in intervening in the economy without provoking a public political debate? He must consider both which discretionary instruments of intervention are available and the obstacles that might prevent their use. Our political bureaucrat gains leverage in industry through finance in three ways: (1) through his influence over funds that are collected and allocated by governmental or parapublic financial institutions; (2) by the discretionary leverage he can exert over the relative attractiveness of different loans made by private and public institutions; and (3) through the funds he can control by establishing alliances for specific purposes with financial institutions. The executive looks out on a set of institutions. What does he see?

The French financial system can be viewed as a set of concentric circles with the economic bureaucracies at its core. Those core bureaucracies include the Ministry of Finance, which controls government funds and the broad lines of economic policy; the Ministry of Industry, which monitors the primary communication lines to the business community; and the Bank of France, which is the direct agent of financial regulation and administration. (The Planning Commission, once a vital player inside the bureaucracy, was diminished in power and importance during the 1970s but still provides a forum in which industry and government can meet and coordinate their actions. Whether it will regain influence under the Socialists is not evident at this writing.) At the very center of the core are the Trésor in the Ministry of Finance and the National Credit Council.

The first of the circles surrounding this core comprises the parapublic financial institutions—such as the Crédit National, the Crédit Agricole, and the Crédit Hôtelier—which supply long-term credit. Also part of this group is the Caisse des Dépôts, a crucial intermediary and a source of funds for the money and bond market. Although formally independent of the government, these institutions are called on to advise on government policy and often to execute policy decisions. The second or outer circle contains the banks, both public and private, which must be divided into commercial banks and *banques d'affaires*. Although these banks are more directly influenced in their daily decisions by government wishes than, say, their British counterparts, their predominant ties are to their clients.

Finally, outside the financial circles there is the world of business and industry. It must be broken down into small and medium-sized business and large-scale business. Larger business must itself be divided into state-controlled, bank-controlled, management-controlled, and family-controlled companies. The links between finance, government, and industry are different for each type of business. It is important to note that family-owned firms, which are seemingly more resistant to bank and government influence, do not comprise only small and middle-sized companies. Indeed, of the two hundred largest firms in France, nearly forty are still in family hands (majority control) and another sixty appear to be dominated by the owning family. Forty more are foreign multinationals and thus also outside this state-bank network altogether. Equally important, the Suez Bank group is said to be more independent of government maneuverings than the other big banking group, Paribas. The influence of the banks in French industry is thus uneven, varying not only from industry to industry but also among the firms of a single industry.[27]

The agencies in the core of the system directly influence the choices made by the parapublic institutions in the first circle, and those financial institutions in the first circle can in turn influence the decisions of the banking system. The arrangement is not strictly hierarchical. Inner circles do not have automatic authority over outer circles and the particulars are not settled by command, yet the structural intertwining that emanates from a strong center opens the way to deals and alliances. The critical point is that the political executive, acting through the Trésor, can influence—but not dictate—credit allocation. Its routine management of the financial system gives it discretion over the flow of funds.

Let us examine the pieces of this structure, keeping an eye on the players that provide the capacity for the selective intervention characteristic of the "player" state. Since we are concerned with the purposes that government can accomplish in the economy, we begin our discussion with the Trésor.

The Trésor is the sanctuary inside the temple of the Ministry of Finance, the economic apex in a centralized state. The significance of the Trésor cannot be overemphasized and, indeed, many observers consider it unique among the world's finance agencies. As one senior French businessman who began his career at the Trésor remarked:

> You live with a profound belief that France is the center of the world, that Paris is the center of France, and that the Trésor is the center of Paris. . . . The Trésor's influence and prestige extend into every part of France. It represents the State inside the three largest banks: Crédit Lyonnais, Banque Nationale de Paris, and Société Générale. It also has a viselike grip on the finances of the French public sector, one of the biggest in the West, and on government subsidies.[28]

The Trésor is not simply a bank for the state but an instrument for intervention in the public sector and the private industrial sector. One senior financial official at a public company remarked, "We can't do anything in the financial markets without the Trésor's approval."[29]

A remarkable range of policy responsibilities concentrate here, including a concern with money supply, bank regulation, and control of government loans or grants to industry. The Trésor manages the finances of the central government, but it has used that power to manipulate the national economy as well. Government departments account for a substantial portion of total investment and the Trésor exerts power over investments made by the public entities.[30] Moreover, the Trésor is itself a financial intermediary, intervening in the economy with loans and transfer facilities. The Trésor has three basic divisions: International, Money and Finance, and Investments and Participations. In general, macro-monetary policy and financial regulation are handled in the Money and Finance division. The Investments and Participations division directs the more detailed activities of the Ministry of Finance in the economy. One segment of the Investments and Participations division deals with foreign investment by French firms, a second segment with the finances of public sector firms, a third with the activities of the specialized lending institutions (discussed later), and a fourth with a range of interministerial committees concerned with managing declining firms and promoting expanding ones. We shall consider these specialized divisions as we proceed. What is distinctive about them is that they depend as much on bank alliances and subsidized loans as on budgetary funds to achieve their purposes.

The Trésor's extensive power derives from its position as the bureaucratic agent and voice of the minister of finance.[31] Its influence and authority rest on the minister's willingness to exercise the power that, at least formally, is his. The Trésor is the point at which the pinnacle of the French state bureaucracy joins the administered character of the financial marketplace. The elite positions of the French bureaucracy are staffed by the graduates of two schools: École Nationale d'Administration (ENA) and the École Polytechnique (Polytechnique). The top graduates of those schools enter the so-called Grands Corps, which are a cross between gentlemen's clubs and restrictive unions. One set of corps is technical-engineering in character and dominates ministries occupied with energy and infrastructure. The second group is the administrative corps involved with the operation of the state itself. The most prestigious and powerful of these corps is the Inspection de Finance, which is filled by the top five or six graduates of ENA. It is an exaggeration to say that the Trésor is run by the Inspection, though the director and much of the staff are drawn from the Inspection's top rank. In sum, then, the Trésor operates the levers of a financial market in which vital price relations are set by administration; it operates with the full prestige of the elite of the elite bureaucrats and with all the power of the Ministry of Finance.

The core staff of the Trésor is tiny—a mere one hundred or so—and even its ranking officials are young, often in their forties. Quite evidently, then, it operates through a set of intermediaries; its ability to exert its power is limited as much by the constraints of time and staff as by the autonomy, pressure, or resistance of its go-betweens. Since the heads of these intermediaries are often former Trésor officials, the authority of the Trésor is balanced by the experience of those in other public positions. The Trésor can set basic policy lines and when drawn into the fray it can put great force behind specific policies. Trésor opposition alone can suffice to block initiatives or force their adjudication at the ministerial level. Clearly, however, the Trésor does not decide alone nor does it always formulate its own policies. It is instead most often the point of decision, the focus of much of the action in economic affairs. At one time the power of the Planning Commission lay in its privileged voice—amounting almost to a veto power—in the Trésor's industrial decisions, a power it hoarded and used on focused purposes. Today the Plan is not consulted regularly. In economic and industrial matters it is thus vital to know who proposes to and disposes for the Trésor.

Perhaps the most significant case in which the Trésor decides and others implement is in its relation to the Bank of France. There is a widely held view that the Bank of France simply executes policy decisions made at the Trésor—that it lacks the political muscle to be more than the Trésor's agent. Observers think that the Trésor would win in an outright contest with the bank, but this view is difficult to substantiate. The hierarchy of the National Credit Council, which regulates the financial system, provides a symbolic indication of the relation between the two institutions: the minister of finance is the chairman of the council and the governor of the Bank of France is its deputy chairman. The director of the Trésor summarized the position succinctly: "We establish the lines of policy. . . . The banks know we are better informed than they are because we draw up the government's financial and monetary policy months in advance. After all, we are at the center of three markets: money, bonds, and foreign exchange."[32] This last remark is the most revealing. The Trésor's place in the system of financial markets creates its political leverage and gives it a unique character.

Much attention is directed to the Trésor's best-known instrument for direct economic intervention, the Fund for Economic and Social Development (FDES). This interministerial committee is divided into more than a dozen subcommittees that cover most sectors of the economy and most kinds of publicly supported infrastructures, such as ports and housing. During the period of close state management of the economy, the *dirigiste* years of the capital shortage, the FDES was the channel through which the government financed reconstruction. In 1972 the total funds the government allocated in this fashion dropped to 500 million francs, but in the recession year of 1974 the money poured into industry rose to 2.2 billion francs.[33] (By contrast with the Trésor, the Ministry of Industry disposes directly of perhaps a little more than one-tenth of the total government reconstruction budget.) These funds—which are drawn from the state budget, not from the financial system—give the Trésor a bargaining chip and a weapon in dealings with private firms, public institutions, and the bureaucratic rivals, yet these budget funds are only one piece in the mosaic of its financial power.

A circle of specialized lending and parapublic banking institutions surrounds the core bureaucracies. Created by the government or dominated by it (many of them are staffed by officials drawn from the Ministry of Finance), they are influential both because of the funds they lend and because of their role in government financial operations, which includes rediscounting commercial loans. Taken together, the parapublic institutions lend about one-third of all credit extended in the French system. They are considered specialized institutions because they do not draw funds directly from deposits made by savers. Rather, they borrow money from other financial institutions, including government agencies that collect deposits and channel them into these long-term institutions. There are many such institutions, each with its own function and history (Chart 3.1 offers a list of the set of such institutions), but we shall examine only three of them here: the Crédit National, the Crédit Agricole, and the Caisse de Dépôts.

For industrial finance, the Crédit National is the most critical of these parapublic banking intermediaries. It is a private company, quoted on the stock exchange, and its purpose is to encourage, in collaboration with the government and the banks, the growth of industry. Not a bank itself, but rather a lending institution, it depends on borrowings in the money markets to obtain its funds. Immediately after the Second World War, when capital was extremely short, the Crédit National was a primary source, along with the Trésor, of industrial finance; it thus became a major element in the *dirigiste* system. Ordinary bank lending has since become the foundation of medium-term lending and the relative importance of the Crédit National and the system of parapublic institutions as a whole has declined. Nonetheless, the Crédit National engaged 7,289 million francs in 1975.[34]

Crédit National funds can be lent directly to industry or used to guarantee the loans or liquidity risks of banks that advance medium- or long-term funds to industry. The sums the Crédit National can influence are therefore much greater than the sums it engages on its own account in the form of loans. In addition, it manages and supervises funds that the government lends or grants to companies. In particular, funds from the FDES are often administered by the Crédit National, as

Chart 3.1. Major long-term credit institutions in France

This chart lists the more prominent institutions and government agencies that have been classified in this study as long-term credit institutions. It is not exhaustive and does not attempt to indicate the relative importance of particular institutions.

	Main financial activities
Public agencies and institutions	
Fonds de Développement Économique et Social (Economic and Social Development Fund)	Industrial finance
Caisse des Dépôts et Consignations (Deposits and Consignments Fund)	Finance for public authorities and institutions
Caisse des Prêts aux Organismes d'HLM (Social Housing Loans Fund)	Housing finance
Caisse d'Aide à l'Équipement des Collectivités Locales (Local Authority Investment Assistance Fund)	Local authority finance
Banque Française de Commerce Extérieur (French Foreign Trade Bank)	Export finance
Caisse Nationale de Crédit Agricole (National Agricultural Credit Bank)	Agricultural finance
Caisse Nationale des Marchés de l'État (National Fund for Public Contracts)	Guarantees for public works and small firms
Semi-public institutions	
Crédit National (National Credit Bank)	Industrial finance
Crédit Foncier (Mortgage Credit Bank)	Mortgage credit
Comptoir des Entrepreneurs (Building Contractors Finance Office)	Construction finance
Caisse Centrale de Crédit Hôtelier, Industriel et Commercial (Central Fund for Hotel, Industrial and Commercial Credit)	Finance for small and medium-sized firms
Institutions owned by consortia	
Sociétés de Développement Régional (Regional Development Corporations)	Finance for regional development
Institut de Développement Industriel (Industrial Development Institute)	Venture capital
Sociétés de Caution Mutuelle (Mutual Guarantee Societies)	Guarantees for small firms
Long-term credit banks	
Banques de Crédit à Long et Moyen Terme (Medium- and Long-Term Credit Banks) Mainly subsidiaries of large banks, sometimes jointly with major equipment manufacturers (FINEXTEL, CODETEL, etc.)	Term finance and leasing

SOURCE: Dimitri Vittas, ed., *Banking Systems Abroad* (London: Inter-Bank Research Organisation, 1978), pp. 133–134.

are investments made by the Caisse des Dépôts. Both on its own account and on that of the state, the Crédit National is deeply entangled in the life of industry and finance. Though it is trusted by industry, the Crédit National is essentially an arm of the government, which it serves as an instrument for defining industrial policy, a means of mobilizing financial support, and a meeting ground on which to implement policies. Its ties are mostly to the Trésor, but how extensively it is consulted in the actual formation of government policy is not clear. Even within the Crédit National and the Trésor opinions are divided, and actual cases are hard to observe.

The Caisse des Dépôts et Consignations is the repository for funds that flow in from the several public savings networks, a pool of $100 billion. Table 3.1 suggests the importance of the public savings banks in the overall financial system and the importance of the Caisse in the distribution of funds in the economy.[35] It is important to note the percentage of loans and claims made by the Caisse, but since it places other funds with long-term credit institutions, this figure understates its influence. The long-term lending institutions draw only one quarter of their funds from depositors, drawing the rest from the money markets nourished by the Caisse. In 1978 the Caisse held approximately $4 billion in loans and nearly $20 billion in securities as well. It is devoted primarily to the financing of public infrastructure, such as housing and roads, and supports the activities of local government in particular. In 1975 nearly 3 billion francs were available to the specialized financial institutions, such as Crédit National. Another 2.5 billion francs were lent or granted to nationalized industry, particularly in the energy and transport sectors. Finally, about 222 billion francs were provided to industry through the purchase of shares or bonds.[36] Thus, publicly collected savings reinforce this network of financial intermediaries that may borrow funds in money markets. The ability to allocate savings collected through public agencies provides a second point of government influence in the flow of funds: the Caisse has administrative discretion not only over final lending decisions but also over which intermediary institutions will have funds to make loans, and over the conditions in the bond and money markets from which lending institutions draw funds.

With assets greater than those of the Bank of America, the Crédit Agricole, the last of the parapublic institutions examined here, is often considered the largest bank in the world.[37] In fact, however, this odd administrative arrangement born of the insulation of the French agricultural community and the historic weakness of the French financial system is not really a bank at all. It was the absence of any extensive

Table 3.1. Shares of loans and other claims on the non-financial sector in France, end 1975

	French francs (in billions)	Percent of total shares	Growth factor 1965–1975
Central bank (4.1%)			
1. Bank of France	56.6	4.1	1.7
Deposit-taking institutions (48.3%)			
2. National banks	243.4	17.5	4.5
3. Other deposit banks	157.6	11.3	4.5
4. Investment banks	26.0	1.9	4.5
5. Popular banks	34.9	2.5	5.6
6. Agricultural credit banks	177.5	12.8	6.2
7. Mutual credit banks	18.3	1.3	n.a.
8. National savings bank	—	—	—
9. Ordinary savings banks	13.9	1.0	n.a.
10. Postal Giro	—	—	—
Long-term credit institutions (32.9%)			
11. Long-term credit banks	8.9	0.6	
12. Foreign Trade Bank	12.0	0.9	10.3
13. Crédit National	25.6	1.8	3.8
14. Crédit Foncier	52.7	3.8	2.7
15. Caisse des Dépôts et Consignations	222.0	15.0	4.2
16. Social Housing Loans Fund	74.2	5.3	n.a.
17. Other special credit institutions	11.5	0.8	n.a.
18. Public Treasury (and FDES)	51.0	3.7	1.2
Investing institutions (9.3%)			
19. Insurance companies	97.9	7.1	5.1
20. Mutual funds (SICAVs)	25.0	1.8	22.1
21. Common investment funds	6.0	0.4	n.a.
Other financial institutions (5.4%)			
22. Cooperative credit institutions	14.4	1.0	4.5
23. Finance companies	53.4	3.9	7.5
24. Regional development corporations	7.1	0.5	n.a.
	1389.9	100.0	4.2

SOURCES: Lines 2, 3, 4, 11, and 23 from Banking Control Commission, Annual Report, 1975; line 19 from rough estimate from various sources; lines 20–21 from Stock Market Operations Commission, Annual Report, 1975; all other lines from National Credit Council, Annual Report and Appendixes, 1975 (Annexe 19); all in Dimitri Vittas, ed., *Banking Systems Abroad* (London: Inter-Bank Research Organisation, 1978), p. 129.

rural banking system at the end of the nineteenth century which prompted the emergence of a series of local cooperative associations known collectively as the Crédit Agricole. At the center of the system is the Caisse Nationale of the Crédit Agricole (CNCA). The local branches drew the funds of the peasantry into financial institutions and provided a source of credit for rural producers, thereby mobilizing the resources of rural France for the development of rural France. The Crédit Agricole has been accorded innumerable privileges, in return for which its lending activities are restricted to rural or small-town France and to agricultural industries.

Rural France has progressively produced more savings than investment opportunities. The Crédit Agricole draws in a substantial portion of these savings because of its special privileges, yet it cannot lend outside a restricted rural and small-town arena. The creation of a central agency that pools the funds of the local cooperatives is a means of channeling the savings to uses outside of agriculture. The funds collected by the central bank of the Crédit Agricole are in excess of 100 billion francs, 40 percent of which end up in the money markets while the rest are channeled directly to particular institutions for fund lending.

The Crédit Agricole has traditionally reported not to the Bank of France but directly to the Trésor, which thus has institutional influence over the disposition of this enormous pool of funds. It does not need to interfere with the ordinary activities of this institution; any occasional project of importance to the government can simply be dealt with in one or another specialized arrangement. At least one Crédit Agricole subsidiary with several billion dollars in assets was created, according to its own officials, simply to respond to specialized requests for lending that the government might make.

Finally, we come to the banks, the outer circle of government financial influence on the economy. The three major deposit banks—the Banque Nationale de Paris, the Société Générale, and the Crédit Lyonnais—are publicly owned and appear to be receptive to government influence in particular deals, or at least open to playing a role in government industrial policies. All observers contend, however, that in their day-to-day operations they function essentially as private banks. The other networks of deposit banks are now controlled by the two major *banques d'affaires,* Paribas and Suez. These two investment banks have long had substantial equity positions in industry, and one Paribas official has concluded that his bank in fact ran its own industrial policy in several sectors. The bank itself has admitted its dependence on government policy and good will and its readiness to act as a state ally in policy. Paribas followed state policy because its maneuvers require state acquiescence and funds from the nationalized banks. Moreover, Paribas is run by a group of former civil servants who have direct ties to the Ministry of Finance. One ranking Paribas official neatly summed the situtation up: "The state is everywhere; nothing is possible without the state."[38] The state also exerts its muscle in banking through a web of subsidized and privileged credits. Their volume is immense. In 1979, for example, 25 percent of all loans to firms (nonfinancial and nonconstruction) were made at privileged rates; over 55 percent of all loans for exports were made at subsidized rates.[39]

The political executive, therefore, has at its disposal an intricate array of instruments with which to intervene in the economy or in a particular industry. As a result, the director of the Trésor can actually make policy that is intended to shift resources between sectors and even between firms. Jacques Melitz has aptly summarized this power:

> The most relevant question for recent years then is whether the authorities have succeeded in reallocating resources in accordance with their designs. Once again, I see no reason for any major skepticism. The French system is well conceived to help in launching an airbus or to restructure an ailing industry in accordance with a clearly laid plan. The funds are always there and they can be made available quickly. The subsidized loan is also a frequent form of assistance. When newspaper headlines blare forth a government agreement to undertake some multi-billion franc project in a sector of French industry (public or private), this may sound like an embrace of Keynesian principles of pump priming: but the typical connotation is a decision to accord a public loan for that amount. The additional cost to the Trésor, then, is at the most the interest rate subsidy on the loan or a small fraction of the sum in the headline.[40]

It is hard to capture the flavor of these combined operations. One element, of course, is simply the practice of favoring some sectors, or at least assuring that those sectors receive funds—a practice that requires adjusting the broad terms of access to capital markets. The more detailed interventions seem to have a style all their own. Two statements, one by a banker and one by a government official, evoke the atmosphere remarkably well. The Trésor official remarked: "We don't ask all the time, but if we do make a request for assistance in a particular project it would be difficult for anyone to refuse." The chief financial officer of a major institution put it similarly: "Of course they can't ask on a daily basis, but if they do we can't refuse."[41] In short, the Trésor can assemble pools of funds for specific projects when the need arises.

The executive's power in this financial system derives not from some administrative arrangement that establishes these exceptional institutional ties between banking and government but from the inner workings of the markets for finance. We must go beyond this institutional outline to consider the working of the financial system. The critical issue is the relation between several types of markets. The French system of finance is credit based; that is, most external financing of private companies is arranged through borrowing from financial institutions rather than through the independent sale of securities. The market for bank loans (and loans from parapublic lenders) is maintained by government intervention. The result is the intimate set of ties between government, financial institutions, and firms which we described above. At this point it is useful to examine the system's workings one step at a time.

The French securities market (stocks and bonds) is small by international standards. Indeed, as a proportion of the gross domestic product it is smaller than the securities market of any other advanced country (see Table 3.2). Its total size has been estimated as equal to that of the oil sector alone on the London securities market. Within this securities market, bonds have played a much more important role than stocks.[42] Public issues dominate the bond market, but only a minor proportion is made up of Trésor debt (5 to 10 percent in recent years).[43] Since the bulk of the public bonds are issued by national firms, such as the railways and electrical companies, and by the specialized parapublic lending institutions that have no deposit base, it appears that the bond side of the securities market is even less significant for private companies than the aggregate numbers suggest. The securities market funds primarily nationalized firms and state favorites.

Prices in the bond market—that is, the level and structure of interest rates—are set by the Trésor.[44] Its decisions are implemented on a daily basis by the market intervention of the Caisse des Dépôts et Consignations, which is the source of 16 percent of the total of loans and similar claims in the economy. With the price—the interest on bonds—set by Trésor decision, the private sector then selects the volume of bonds it will attempt to buy. Since the prices have been kept low in order to promote industrial expansion, demand for bond financing is always greater than the available supply of funds. Administratively set prices cannot move to balance supply and demand, and some other means must therefore be used to allocate the available money. The result is a "queue on the borrowing side of the market."[45] Those standing in the queue line up are as follows: (1) the Trésor itself, which in fact can control the positions of the others; (2) the parapublic financial institutions and companies under Trésor tutelage; (3) the national firms in the semicompetitive sector; and (4) the private firms. Though direct

Table 3.2 Domestic securities as a proportion of Gross Domestic Product, 1975 (percent)

Country	Bonds[a]	Equities[b]
France	16	11
West Germany	30	13
Japan	41	29
United States	57	45
United Kingdom	43	41

[a]Nominal value of bonds outstanding.
[b]Market value of listed equities.
SOURCE: Dimitri Vittas, ed., *Banking Systems Abroad* (London: Inter-Bank Research Organisation, 1978), p. 30.

government control of the bond calendar was relaxed recently, none of our interviewees suggested that this change had altered the pattern of access.

Although the market in equities is limited overall, new stock issues raised substantial sums in the late 1970s. Indeed, in some years more money was raised on the French markets than in the London markets. This seeming anomaly provides a clear view of the dynamics of the French system. Ordinarily, the existence of a limited secondary market—the market where stocks are exchanged after their initial issue—makes for sharp swings in price. Price in thin markets (those with few buyers and sellers) is responsive to the sale of relatively limited volumes and allows for market manipulation as well. The French secondary markets would therefore appear hazardous for small investors, and it is not irrational caution but normal prudence that historically has pushed small savers toward more secure short-term deposits. Insurance companies and pension funds, which are important institutional investors in the British-American system, are not primary because of the extensive state social security system. As a consequence, the major banks and state institutions are the large and dominant players in these security markets. They are able to overcome the weakness of the market by their ability to organize, distribute, and buy substantial quantities of new issues for their own portfolios. The crucial result, however, is that in raising funds on the securities market a firm does not escape the influence of the major financial institutions—particularly the banks—and the government.

The limited importance of the securities market for corporate finance means that firms must seek external funds as loans from banks or parabanks. To understand the system of industrial lending, we must first distinguish the banks from the parapublic or specialized lending institutions. The banking system is itself highly concentrated, with only five major commercial banks. As noted earlier, three of these are the nationalized banks and two are private bank networks, which are themselves attached to the *banques d'affaires,* Paribas and Suez. These investment banks (Paribas and Suez) are intimately tied to industry, having substantial equity positions. (The nature of the *banques d'affaires* will be examined more closely in Chapter 4.) Since the legal boundary between deposit and investment banks was largely washed away by 1970, the deposit banks are now able to own equity in companies and the investment banks can accept deposits.[46] This development has given the investment banks cheaper money and increased the links between deposit banks and industry clients. Overall, the ties between finance and industry have been strengthened.

Alongside the banks is a set of specialized financial institutions, each one of which participates in the transformation of savings into investment. For example, when California depositors put money in a Bank of America checking account, the bank uses their deposits to make loans to farmers, businessmen, and consumers. In France, the institutions that collect short-term deposits do not always lend them to final users; the two functions are not combined under one roof but allocated to separate organizations. Funds collected by the deposit organization are lent to credit institutions, particularly long-term credit institutions, which in turn lend the funds to final users. This procedure creates a second step in the process of transforming savings into investment. In Britain and the United States the bank is the single intermediary between the saver and the final user. France (along with Italy) does not share this bank-centered financial system. The special deposit-taking institutions—everything from the postal savings bank and the Crédit Agricole to the major national banks—collect a substantial proportion of the economy's savings. The specialized character of these institutions is suggested by the small proportion of deposits that they lend directly to final users. These deposits flow to the specialized lending institutions, which control nearly a third of the funds that the financial system provides to the economy (see Tables 3.3 and 3.4).

As we have noted, such quantitative measures understate the significance of the specialized financial institutions. These institutions also play a role in determining which bank loans will be eligible for the various government subsidies and privileges that make them more attractive to the commercial banks. The additional step from saver to borrower, performed by the second intermediary in France, allows the government to stand between the savings and the investment institu-

Table 3.3. Shares of long-term credit institutions in liabilities and claims with the non-financial sector, end 1975 (percent)

Country	Liabilities	Claims
West Germany	12.8	23.5
France	8.2	32.9
Italy	9.1	29.9
Japan	11.0	22.8
United States	5.5	7.9
United Kingdom	4.9	21.4

NOTE: Liabilities represent deposits; claims indicate loans.

SOURCE: Dimitri Vittas, ed., *Banking Systems Abroad* (London: Inter-Bank Research Organisation, 1978), p. 22.

tions and thus to influence the allocation of funds. The relations between the multiplicity of institutions and the markets, many of which are government-sponsored, are set by administrative arrangement, not by the free play of prices in markets. Again, Melitz summarizes these relationships succinctly:

In this system there are evidently three major interest rates: one in the money market, one on bank credit, and one on bonds. Two of these rates are controlled, one is free, and the relation of the free one to the other two is the key to the entire structure of interest rates in France. If the Bank of France raises its rate of intervention on the money market (as best measured by the "taux de l'argent au jour le jour," and not the very sluggish official discount rate), the banks will raise their lending rate (as best measured by the rate on overdrafts, "le taux des découverts"). One result then will be to lengthen the queue on the bond market—that is, this result would follow unless the authorities avoided it by similarly increasing the interest rate on bonds. They will typically take this complementary action since their usual reason for increasing the official rate of intervention on the money market is to protect the franc.[47]

We have distinguished between banks and specialized lending institutions. A second distinction must now be made between a privileged sector in which the prices of money and access to funds are selectively manipulated and a market that is not directly manipulated. The boundary between the two sectors is not clear, and indeed the directly manipulated sector powerfully influences the way the uncontrolled sector operates. Since market operations and administered operations take

Table 3.4. Shares of different types of financial institution in liabilities and claims with the non-financial sector, end 1975

Country	Central bank		Deposit-taking institutions[a]		Long-term credit institutions		Investing institutions		Other financial institutions	
	A	B	A	B	A	B	A	B	A	B
France	8.3	4.1	71.7	48.3	8.2	32.9	11.3	9.3	0.5	5.4
Japan	4.3	4.1	68.7	58.1	11.0	22.8	16.0	15.0	—	—
West Germany	5.4	2.3	61.5	60.1	12.8	23.5	20.0	13.0	0.3	1.1
United States	4.2	4.2	57.3	51.8	5.5	7.9	32.3	31.2	0.7	4.9
United Kingdom	3.9	5.2	51.5	48.4	4.9	21.4	39.5	24.4	0.2	0.6

A indicates percentages of shares of deposits and other liabilities.
B indicates percentages of shares of loans and other claims.
[a]Including public-sector agencies, such as the National Loans Fund in the United Kingdom.
SOURCE: Dimitri Vittas, ed., *Banking Systems Abroad* (London: Inter-Bank Research Organisation, 1978), p. 5.

place within the same institutions, we cannot label one set of institutions as the administered or privileged market and another as the nonprivileged market. The administered sector works in three ways: through intermediaries such as the Crédit National, which have as part of their task the financing of specialized activities; by preferential terms of refinancing and by subsidies accorded to loans through commercial banks; and through exemptions from credit ceilings. The first two mechanisms should be clear from the previous discussion. The third—exemptions from credit ceilings—requires that we examine both the operation of the nonprivileged market for company loans and the management of the money supply.

The nonprivileged market for company loans—that is the market in which government does not selectively manipulate access or price by subsidy or some technique of rediscounting—is not a truly free market either. It is hemmed in by administered flows that substantially dictate the workings of the nonadministered segment. The keys here are the money market, which links institutions with an excess of funds to those with an excess of demand, and the market in bank loans. The price in that money market, the interest rate, is set by the Bank of France. Since the marginal cost of funds to a bank is fixed, only the volume of lending remains to be determined. Since the price is fixed, competing demands by would-be borrowers cannot be determined. Since the price is fixed, competing demands by would-be borrowers cannot be settled by auction. Nor can the supply be increased by paying savers more, because that price too is fixed. When the economy booms demand will increase because more borrowers will pay the fixed price. "This elasticity of supply . . . means that demand is a powerful influence on volume. If the demand for bank credit rises the result is primarily to raise the quantity of bank credit rather than the price."[48] There are two possibilities in this situation. First, supply and demand will be balanced by some administrative criteria or by discretionary executive acts that determine which would-be borrowers will get their loans. In that case, we want to understand the system of discretion. Second, all demands may be met. In that case, we must locate the source of the money, used to fund the loans. Presumably a fixed price means a fixed supply of loanable funds. The answer is that both the volume of loans and their allocation are shaped by administrative discretion.[49]

The exercise of administrative discretion in the allocation of loans in the nonprivileged market is tied to the system of controlling the money supply. Indeed, Donald Hodgman, writing in the 1960s, argued that the French arrangements were more effectively used to manipulate the direction of investment flows than to maintain a handle on monetary aggregates.[50] The administrative vehicles are varied. At one time a system of rediscounting bank loans was a basis of government discretion. More recently ceilings on the amounts a bank can loan, regardless of its total deposits or reserves, have been the basic device for controlling monetary aggregates. When a bank pushes beyond allotted limits, the price at which it can refinance the loans by borrowing funds from the central bank is prohibitive and additional lending is thus constricted. Exceptions to these credit ceilings are granted for favored loans, however, *a practice that amounts to a mechanism for allowing specific increases in the money supply to be targeted for particular purposes.* Better still, it assures that whatever the other demands for money, those of vital or favored enterprises will still be met; favored projects will not be driven out of the market either by interest rates or by a restricted availability of funds. This system of aggregate management has an implicit bias: it sacrifices control of quantity for influence over the direction of flows. Over time, however, a variety of mechanisms for exerting greater technical control of quantity have evolved and the number of exceptions has been reduced. The important point is that the capacity for controlling the direction of money flows by administrative decision is built into the French system of regulation and is available to government whenever needed. Equally important, this capacity is tied to the processes by which prices are set and lending volumes determined.

The scope of selective influence that the government exercises over access to money and the price at which it is available is quite remarkable. One analyst from a major central bank described the system of intervention in France as "unheard of in other West European countries."[51] A recent Bank of France publication reported that in 1979 43 percent of all credits to the economy in France were made with some kind of privilege or subsidy and that 25 percent of corporate lending was subsidized directly.[52] The extent of intervention in fact has provoked a real irony. In the last fifteen years the French government has moved to eliminate its detailed intervention in the markets and thus clear away portions of these specialized circuits. Though this would seem a liberal move, leaving more room for the play of the market, it may in fact have strengthened the state's hand in the economy. The same central bank observer noted: "Around 1950–60 the controlled sector became so complex that it was impossible to judge the real effects on the economy of the large number of partial measures or to coordinate these rationally. For this reason return to the machinery of the market, corrected as necessary by the unconcealed measures such as interest rate subsidies paid out of the budget, seemed paradoxically to be the way in which official action could be made more effective."[53] Thus, it is not contradictory that officials of the Mitterand government, which seeks greater control over industry, have expressed real interest in "liberal" measures prepared in the Trésor but never implemented during the Giscard years.

The political consequence of administered prices and quantitative controls on the money supply is that government and the banks have endless opportunities to exercise discretion in the allocation of credit. Since the demand for investment funds is inherently in excess of the supply available at the administratively established prices, some other criteria *must* be adopted. The entangled set of privileges and administrative decisions has two implications. First, the government *must* make choices about who receives funds. Intervention is a necessity, which gives government leverage on the allocation decisions of all actors in the system. Second, undoing the interventionist arrangement requires either releasing control of the *supply* of lending (and thus of the money supply in general) or replacing the fundamentals of the entire financial system. There have been efforts to reform the system of capital markets and thus reduce the dependence of firms on lending by financial institutions. The government of Giscard d'Estaing sought means to push the capital markets out of the nineteenth into the twentieth century. The strategy was to make both the stock and bond market more attractive to small savers and to provide wider access to the bond market. The Loi Monory, which provides tax credits for the first 5000 francs added to a stock portfolio and thereby raises the effective rate of return on such investments to over 30 percent, makes stock purchases remarkably attractive. Whether these changes would have altered the basic character of the financial system remains unclear, but the initiative remains entirely with the government. This observer frankly doubts that the system will change in its central characteristics, even if the Socialist government of 1981 pursues this initiative.

In essence, the French financial system is a credit-based system with administered pricing. In many of the markets the system of matching supply and demand is controlled by quantitative management rather than by freely moving market prices. The financial system provides the central executive with several instruments for influencing the development of the economy. First, there are funds for direct loans and grants made by the Trésor. Second, the parapublic and long-term credit agencies provide information to the government and serve as allies in negotiating with industry, besides serving directly as instruments of government policy for allocating credit. Third, the banks themselves have substantial equity and loan stakes in industry and thus represent another set of government allies. Fourth, the many privileged circuits and the use of controlled interest rates build administrative control into the heart of the system. Finally, the system for controlling the money supply gives the executive tools for controlling who uses the funds.

Of course, administrative discretion need not be used to achieve specific objectives of the central political executive; in other words, the financial system in itself does not make a player state. How the possibilities are used depends on the character of the bureaucracy, its relations to various groups in the society, and the political balance. Thus, the financial systems of France, Japan, and Italy have important similarities; the differences in the way they are used depend upon the relation of the bureaucracy to the political system in each country. There are three structural characteristics of the French bureaucratic system which in recent years have permitted the coordinated use of these financial potentials. First, there is an elite civil service whose ranking bureaucrats are a definable caste of elite administrators, recruited through Polytechnique and ENA. The careers of this elite are bound together through the privileged position provided by the institutions of the Grands Corps. This small group has an enduring interest in maintaining the role of the state bureaucracy in the French system.[54] Second, since the creation of the Fifth Republic in 1958 the political executive as a whole has been independent of detailed monitoring or control by the legislature. The parliament had more influence over the composition and direction of the government during the Third and Fourth Republics, and the instability of cabinets pressed the bureaucracy to function as the guarantor of continuity in policy. Third, the ministerial cabinet system—which draws elite bureaucrats, political advisers, and some outside experts into a staff for each minister—provides a means for the political master to supervise and control his bureaucracy.

This portrait of finance and bureaucracy, however, tends to overstate the purposive control that ranking bureaucrats or political executives exercise over the disposal of funds, because it does not focus on the complex political struggles that determine final allocation. A tension always exists between the purposes pursued by the upper levels of the administration or the government and the positions defended by the particular financial institutions and the constituencies that have benefited from specific privileges and preferential access to funds. Indeed, since de Tocqueville a host of writers have depicted the French state as paralyzed by internal rivalries and rigid routines that fragment the hierarchy and wall off different administrations. Michel Crozier has developed this image into a formal model, and more recently Alain Peyrefitte, a minister of justice, has used it as a general explanation of French difficulties.[55] The portrait of purposive control drawn in some of my own writings would seem to contradict this image of paralysis. Let us assume for the sake of argument that the two images capture different elements of the whole and ask which characteristics lead to paralysis and which to effective action.

In *Political Strategies for Industrial Order* I examined interventions in which the strategies adopted were similar but the outcomes quite different.[56] My analysis suggested that it was differences in what must be done, rather than how people went about doing it, which accounted most simply for variations in outcome. We might, using this approach, distinguish between the purposive and the paralytic portraits, viewing them as two aspects of one system. The centralized state can then be seen as both an instrument of action and a target for those who would defend existing privileges.

Energy policy provides an example of the French state exerting real control. Twice the French state has shifted the base of the economy, once from coal to oil and once from oil toward nuclear power. It did so by imposing on the society choices made inside government. Central policymakers cannot pay attention to everything, however, and only a limited number of issues can be resolved by the continuing intervention of top-ranking bureaucrats or politicians. But when the success of policy depends on choices that these central executives can make by themselves, or on choices made by alliances that they dominate, the purposive side of policy will prevail. Mobilizing money is a task the central administration does well and one that is crucial to energy policy; the policy choices can be made and implemented entirely within the state system. In energy policy, therefore, the purposive side predominates.

By contrast, education and social welfare policies suggest that the French government is a lumbering giant unable to be redirected or halted. In these sectors reform requires dismantling privilege and uprooting the position of the civil servants who conduct policy. Routine is embedded in the state bureaucracy. The groups whose privileges are threatened are clearly defined and often readily mobilized. Moreover, the centralized state is an easy target against which they can direct attempts to defend their privileges. The entrenched routine of the centralized bureaucracy itself becomes an obstacle to any change in the direction of the policy.

The clear implication is that we must avoid such generalizations as "strong state," "weak state," and "centralized society." We must instead examine the relations between institutional arrangements and government policy choices on the one hand and the formation of political interests on the other. These factors will differ within various sectors of a society according to the nature of the problem and the character of the groups involved.

FINANCING GROWTH IN A TRADITIONAL ECONOMY

In the political fights that shaped the postwar development of France, the financial system functioned not only as a technical set of economic arrangements that provided finance to industry but also as a weapon to be used and a prize to be captured. We have argued that French industry emerged from the war with a tradition of restriction and protection and found itself in an economy short of capital and materials. The problem was not only to reconstruct but to modernize French industry and economic life. Since business was shattered by the war and at any rate ill suited to taking the initiative, the state bureaucracy exerted its leadership. Significantly, a handful of men, including ranking government officials, sought to reform the postwar bureaucracy and later the role of the state in the economy.[57]

Postwar policy was not simply the consequence of a tradition of state initiative and involvement in industry, nor was it brought about by the institutional and ideological heritage. Instead, an explicit political victory turned state involvement in the economy toward new purposes. Changes in the organization and function of the critical institutions made that redirection possible. The bureaucracy refined its instruments for selective intervention in industry and public and parapublic financial institutions discussed above were set in operation or reformed, thereby permitting the bureaucracy to generate and allocate investment capital. These institutions remained the central state's agents in industry throughout the postwar period, enabling it to coordinate choices in different ministries and to intervene selectively in specific sectors and firms. As a result, the very relationships between the components of the economy were changed. Political will was translated into institutional reality to accomplish economic purposes, industrial leadership was exerted by a state able to act as an economic player.

The most enduring of those institutional innovations has been in the state-dominated financial sector. Though the Planning Commission has received much publicity and attention, the Plan did not control government resources. Rather, it was the Trésor that provided the muscle and the apparatus needed to push and manipulate the economy. Under the direction of François Bloch-Lainé and seemingly very much by his choice, the Trésor began to serve the purposes of the Plan.[58]

The creation of the Plan was only the first battle in a long war for industrial development. It is not necessary to tell the full story of the "campaign" here, but we do want to demonstrate that the instruments of finance which the government dominated were vital if not indispensable to its outcome.

Finance as a Weapon in the Political Fight for Growth

The postwar boom in the world economy combined with the fact of prewar French industrial backwardness to create powerful market incentives to move resources into industry and consolidate them into internationally competitive firms. Indeed, some have argued that the whole of the French expansion can be explained primarily by the growth of market incentives and that government policies in fact slowed the working of the market.[59] Yet studies show that the domination of politics by fundamentally antimarket forces—the coalition of rural and small-town interests which for many years governed through such agents as the Radical party—resulted in the suppression of market forces.[60] These peasants and small businessmen, as well as the larger companies that survived because of restrictive practices, had an interest in controlling the market to assure their continued existence. At the end of the Second World War the same groups were still preeminent in French society. Moreover, the business associations after the war were dominated by small firms, and parliament was dominated by small-town and rural interests. The political defeat of traditional France and the rapid industrial growth which that defeat allowed were certainly not inevitable. Why weren't market forces simply suppressed again? Indeed, the political victory that paved the road to French industrial expansion was not simple, cheap, or ever really complete. As noted in the beginning of this chapter, government executives bent on promoting expansion had to find a way to meet the demands of traditional France without eroding the market return on new uses of resources which was required to assure investment in competitive industry.

Two sets of political tactics led to the political victory of industrial modernization and development. The first set of tactics immobilized those economic interests which had the most to lose from a rapid development and might therefore have restricted the pace of development. These groups were bought off and trapped politically. The political and institutional innovations of the Fifth Republic, evidently designed to strengthen the executive generally and not to fight any particular battle (economic or otherwise), best exemplify this set of tactics. The second set of tactics actively supported the creation of market pressures that would compel firms to adjust. The creation of the Common Mar-

ket exemplifies this second tactic. The combination of tactics created a
pincer, to use Stephen Cohen's term, which held traditional groups in
place while the economic ground beneath them was cut away.[61] The
pincer emerged not so much as a conscious strategy but as the government's response to conflicting imperatives. In many cases, however (as
in the establishment of the Common Agricultural Policy of the Common Market), a conscious price was paid to traditional France to buy its
acquiescence to policies that in the long run could only erode its political and economic positions further. Establishing this pincer required
four actions: (1) the insulation of government economic policymaking
from direct parliamentary and pressure-group influence; (2) the establishment of a broad nationalist conservative coalition; (3) the establishment of the Common Market; and (4) the arrangement of subsidies
that made the government appear responsive to the demands of all
groups while still assuring the investment needs of the modernizing
sectors.

The financial system permitted a sleight of hand which helped the
government to establish this pincer. It expanded the resources the
government could distribute while clouding their precise disposition,
thereby permitting the executive to support the growth sectors without *overtly* withholding subsidies or funds from the traditional economy. The government might have adopted "To each his subsidy" as
its motto, but in the end the system favored growth. The structure of
incentives which set the flows of funds in the financial sector was
based predominantly on executive choice, rather than on the discretion of parliament. As a result, specific executive choices were
shielded from public debate and it was difficult for anyone to do the
sums necessary to a serious assessment of the balance of policy. The
ambiguity of numbers also complicates our task, making it very hard
to demonstrate quantitatively the impact of the financial system on the
politics of development; the evidence offered is necessarily indirect
and suggestive.

Let us look at the four components of the pincer. The proponents of
growth were concentrated in the most centralized institutions of the
state, whereas the traditionalists were entrenched in the parliament and
in the arena of local politics. At the beginning of the Fourth Republic
and again in the Fifth Republic, purely political reform had transferred
power to the executive at the expense of the legislature, thereby
strengthening the positions of the modernizers. Yet it would be quite
wrong to imagine that there was a pitched battle between a modern
center and a traditional periphery. At each turn those who captured
the center sought to stabilize their position by establishing alliances with

the economic notables of traditional France. A pitched battle, which the modernizers might well have lost, was probably avoided because French agriculture could be modernized without sharp changes in land ownership. Farm productivity could be increased by mechanization. Later, as the economy changed and larger, internationally competitive firms emerged, the government groups found stronger support for a politics of growth. Nonetheless, the centralized bureaucracy was home base for those who sought to promote development, and the political insulation of that bureaucracy allowed the modernizers to chart a course that did not by any means reflect the immediate interests of the then dominant producer groups.[62]

The pincer's second component, put in place by de Gaulle in the 1958 coup that brought him to power, was a nationalist conservative coalition. The need to elect a president encouraged this conservative unification but it also produced a polarization of politics. The party composition of that coalition has shifted since the heyday of de Gaulle's personal appeal, but the initial need for a broadly based coalition to support a powerful executive has remained. As a consequence, parliamentary channels of influence dwindled in importance after 1958 and interest groups that had no influence with the executive were isolated. In one sense, then, small business and agriculture were trapped inside a conservative majority, but in another sense they held the fate of that conservative alliance in their hands.[63] Certainly the concentration of power in the executive limited the influence of locally based groups between elections. As industrialization proceeded, between elections rural France became the work force of an industrial nation: the left reorganized itself around the revitalized Socialist party; and the charismatic appeal of de Gaulle waned. Conservative victories came to depend more and more on the votes of economic marginals in traditional France, the very groups that a strategy of development was supposedly committed to transform or displace.[64] As a result, no one won a clear-cut victory. Traditional small businesses were protected inside the economy by social laws and rules that compensated for their inefficiency. Agriculture was massively subsidized, and although the number of marginal farms declined, the number of medium-sized and larger farms remained stable and even grew. Yet, despite the protections, the relative social, economic, and political position of traditional France eroded. To quote Stephen Cohen, "Once-powerful social groups were held in line politically so that they could not dismantle the growth machine. This was possible in part because who represented the peasants, the colons, all the elements of traditional France, better than de Gaulle? Who did more to destroy them? . . . It was a pincer. Gaullism kept the powerful but vulnerable forces of the French past politically impotent, while the market displaced them."[65]

The third component of the pincer was a foreign economic policy that served to force competition within the domestic market and to undermine the restrictive self-regulating arrangements of traditional French business. The establishment of the Coal and Steel Community and the subsequent creation of the Common Market were critical political victories for economic growth; but, like the creation of the Plan before them, neither was accomplished easily. The first effort to create cross-national competition as a means of undermining the traditionalists of French business, the 1947 Italian-French Customs Union, was defeated in parliament.[66] The passage of the Coal and Steel treaty in 1952 was thus a political reversal of position. Those who supported the Coal and Steel Community did so in part as a means of keeping broader European integration alive. The steel producers opposed it virulently, however, fearing it would be a means of extending public control over their sector, and the nationalized coal industry also opposed it, though less noisily. The official French business association was also against the treaty, but steel users, at Monnet's initiative, were organized to support it and to nullify the producers. In the end, however, business opposition could not be translated into political power and the treaty was ratified.[67] The ratification of the treaty that created the Common Market involved a similar mix of economic conflict and foreign policy purpose.[68]

These two treaties burst the insulation of the French economy and forced firms to compete, first in European and later in world markets. The presence of outside competitors made it harder for French firms to arrange markets, that is, to set prices or production by agreement. Whereas firms had once sought protection and state certification of private arrangements to control domestic markets, they now had to seek assistance for competitive adjustment. The modernizers had created market forces that could push the economy in the direction they favored.

The concrete payoffs by government to specific groups were the fourth component of the pincer. They served to buy the acquiescence of some groups in rural and traditional France to the evolution of the economy and to encourage firms in expanding sectors to speed the workings of the market. The Common Market, for example, brought with it the Common Agricultural Policy, which in practice meant a German subsidy of French farmers. This subsidy in effect expanded the state-budgeted funds that could be spent to maintain incomes and consequently helped the government keep the social peace in the agricultural sectors without removing funds from other development purposes. For the purposes of our discussion, it makes little difference whether such subsidies indicated the state's strategic anticipation of political opposition or its concessions to pluralistic democracy; the cries for financial help had to be met, and the only question was how to meet them.

The financial system thus permitted the growth industries to be nurtured without *visibly* starving the traditional sectors. While visible monetary benefits were given to both advancing and declining sectors, the market and inflation were left to shift the resources.

Inflation as a Political Tactic in Promoting Growth

Charles Maier has shown that satisfying the monetary demands of all groups and letting the resulting inflation determine the relative value of these money assets is an old trick in French politics. He demonstrates how the French middle classes, after both the First and Second World Wars, "revealed a tendency to accept the indirect taxation of inflation rather than the direct levies needed to avoid it."[69] Unable to tax for the funds it required, the government had simply printed the money. Although the proposition cannot be conclusively demonstrated here, I would suggest that the government again tolerated a controlled inflation, with predictable consequences, in its general management of the postwar economy.

Let us assume a case in which all demands for investment funds in the economy are met, if necessary by having government create the funds. To encourage growth, interest rates are kept low and the supply of money is expanded with the extra funds targeted to investment. If the resulting sum of consumption and investment exceeds existing goods and services, then, in a quick and crude view, inflation will result. The inflation may buy the capacity for expanded supply, if in fact the excess money has been directly channeled into investment. In such a controlled inflation, the sectors in which profits and productivity are expanding rapidly will gain and the more stagnant sectors will lose position. In other words, creating money for investment might be thought to assure both a steady increase in supply and an inflation that erodes the relative position of declining sectors.

The French financial system, as we have described it, is best understood as a set of administrative arrangements within which several markets are permitted to work under control. It is not a single market into which the government introduces distortions. One can exaggerate and suggest that the financial system is one of arranged flows. The exact

biases in the system are nearly impossible to unravel, for the government as well as for scholars, but several systemic elements provide
important evidence that the system has been used as I have suggested.
These elements are all drawn from the earlier discussion of the financial system. First, interest rates have been set to encourage investment
and savings and to discourage consumption. Second, the basic financial
innovations since the war have assured the more modern sectors of the
economy funds for growth and have encouraged banks to lend to them
for investment purposes. At the same time, some of the financial channels—such as the Crédit Agricole and the Crédit Hôtelier—have favored the traditional sectors. Third, quantitative control of the money
supply and central bank refunding of bank loans have been used to
target money-supply increases to specific users. Fourth, the French
government has assigned highest priority to promoting growth rather
than to controlling the money supply. Its financial system has been a
powerful instrument in the conflicting purposes of maintaining growth
and preserving political stability. It has also made it appear that political choices were merely market outcomes.

As we have demonstrated, the senior French financial bureaucrats
can expand the money supply and target the increment to specific uses
of their own choosing. This capacity, I am arguing, was employed as a
political tool in a manner that produced inflation. (In fact, French
growth has been accompanied by high inflation throughout the postwar years. The comparison with other advanced countries is explored
in Chapter 2.) In the postwar period government faced a set of political
demands to protect traditional sectors against marketplace pressures
but it recognized that growth sectors would be slowed if they were
starved of funds. The selective manipulation of the state-dominated
financial system by the government to reconcile competing demands
for money without slowing growth or provoking intense political conflict can produce inflation in two ways. Both involve increasing the
money supply, but the inflationary outcome occurs in a different way
in each case. Both processes were almost certainly at work in France
during the last decades.

The point of the analysis that follows should be stated boldly at the
beginning. French governments sought to avoid direct political conflict between modernizing and traditional economic forces by using
the administrative discretion embodied in the financial system. To use
the financial system as a political balance rod on the tightrope across
the chasm between an agricultural and a fully industrial society, the
governments had to tolerate inflation. Stopping the inflation provoked by the use of a state-dominated financial system to promote

growth would certainly have created political battles that no government was willing or indeed able to engage. Inflation thus served to dissolve political conflict by disguising the nature of government choices.

The first mechanism is straightforward. Recall that the French government has used quantitative management of lending to regulate the financial system. It set prices of money at a rate at which demand would exceed supply and then allocated the available supply. The lending quotas or ceilings allocated to different institutions were lifted and still are lifted for uses favored by government policy. In essence a money-supply target would be fixed and the lending ceilings for the various institutions set to reach that target. Loans that favored users that pushed the volume of lending through the ceiling thus had the direct effect of expanding the money supply beyond the initial target. This additional money supply could be expected to translate in part into additional goods and services and in part into higher prices. The precise outcome would depend on the exact circumstances. This administrative technique could serve to defuse political conflict because traditional borrowers would not have to be denied directly the funds they sought. The existing pie of lending would not be carved up into smaller pieces to make a place for the new users. Rather, the lending pie would be expanded by making additional funds available to the favored ones. We would expect the traditional users to consume the initial lending allotment. In this fashion banks could maximize their lending, profits, and growth. Assuring funds to politically privileged sectors by exceeding ceilings inevitably required that the control of the money supply be quite loose. At least in the beginning the Planners were willing to tolerate inflation caused by excess demand, as long as tolerating excess demand assured productive investment. The French officials were unable or unwilling to control price levels by restricting demand on money, if in doing so they would have restricted growth or produced unmanageable social conflicts.

There is a second and subtler line of argument linking selective manipulation of money and credit to inflation.[70] It begins by acknowledging the intense political conflicts over growth which resulted as French farmers and traditional businessmen struggled to survive. Most discussions of inflation assume balanced growth or even a steady-state economy. They do not examine how sectoral changes, in which industries displace one another or in which declining firms and obsolescent technologies limit productivity, contribute to inflation. They may consider the macrocosm of growth, but not the microeconomic process of adjustments in what is produced and how. We shall first elaborate the demand-shift theory of inflation, and then return to the place of finance in this application of theory.[71]

To begin with, how can the process of industrial change contain the seeds of inflation, and why should political efforts to resist or speed up adjustment add to potential inflationary pressure? Though the economic literature asserts that restrictions on economic flexibility and mobility can simultaneously produce slower growth and an increase in inflationary pressures, we lack both the empirical data and the accepted techniques needed to explore this premise. Here we shall trace the outlines of a generally agreed-upon argument.

Growth involves change and adjustment, the shifting of resources from one sector to another or the more productive use of resources within a particular sector. Those who would benefit from these changes may seek government help in organizing and implementing adjustment and those threatened by them may seek government protection. We must therefore distinguish between the price a government may pay to facilitate adjustment and the costs it may incur by resisting the decline of mature industries.

The notion of a "transfer cost" can be used to express the price of adjustment. Adjustment requires that entrepreneurs risk investments and that existing workers change employment or new workers be brought into the market. Marginal improvements in returns on capital or in wage rates are not likely to provide adequate incentives for transfer in the face of entrepreneurial risk and the costs of changing jobs. Consequently, substantial payments will be required to induce businessmen and workers to enter new industries. The transfer cost, then, is the sum of payments necessary to induce the entrepreneur to assume the risk—and to convince the worker to accept the dislocation—of entering a new sector.

The market will provide incentives for adjustment if the transfer premium—the gain from entering the new sector—is larger than the transfer costs. Even so, the process of buying resource shifts may be inflationary. The theory of demand-shift inflation explains how a rapid and sizable change in the demand composition of an economy that is close to full employment can produce inflation without an increase in aggregate demand. In essence, the expanding industry may have to raise wages to attract labor and other inputs. It may be able to absorb those wage increases without raising prices because of productivity gains. But if labor (or capital) in the declining industries wins wage increases to keep pace with the gains of its expanding counterparts, the increases may be passed on in the form of higher prices. In that event, prices will increase in all sectors.

As long as the expanding sector is able to stay one round ahead in the bidding war, it should continue to attract labor, but the price of transfer is bid up in each round, continuing an inflationary process as long as the shift of resources continues. Thus, the greater the political ability of labor and business to defend existing wage differentials and profits in the face of deteriorating markets or increasing competition, the higher the transfer costs will be. In a segmented labor market or an economy crisscrossed with subsidies, the same results might be expected at less than full employment.

Subsidies express the direct costs of resisting decline of output or employment in uncompetitive industries. The techniques are varied, but all subsidies seek to maintain production that might not otherwise survive in market competition or to transfer income to labor and capital in a favored sector. A subsidy, as we shall use the term, is a government-effected transfer of resources to a firm which is intended to reduce the cost of production and distribution, to supplement profits, or to make up for losses incurred. It is not a payment for specific goods or services, although the price of government purchases or sales to a firm may contain subsidy payments. Direct payments by government are not the only form of subsidy, however. Such restrictions as trade barriers, which allow the protected firms to extract additional income from the market, are also subsidies. Institutional arrangements and laws, such as those that protect workers against dismissal or that guarantee a market share for particular companies, retard adjustment and permit the retention of incomes that otherwise would be lost. Taken together, these payments, arrangements, and laws represent supply rigidities that discourage the more efficient use of resources. They directly affect the costs of adjustment. Clearly they dampen the market incentives to move resources from a subsidized declining sector to an unsubsidized expanding one.

A government may provide subsidies to permit individuals and firms to resist market pressures. The government may still want to capture the collective economic gain that a transfer of resource represents. There may, nonetheless, be social gains from a sectoral shift of resources. If the government wishes it can force adjustment by paying part of the transfer costs, in effect offering a kind of countersubsidy in pursuit of growth to reassert (or even strengthen) market incentives. The government might then be seen as reestablishing or widening the differential that would exist without subsidies or comparative wage deals, encouraging businessmen to make the choices that a set of distortion-free market signals would suggest. Subsidy is therefore overcome by subsidy in order to assure adjustment.

The competitive bidding for shifting resources takes place at even higher price levels if some of the bidders are in subsidized sectors. The bidding is amplified further if both declining and growing sectors are subsidized. Increased wages in the growing sector, for example, represent an effort to create a differential between sectors sufficient to move resources. If the protected groups are able to maintain their relative position, the gains won in the growing sector will produce higher costs throughout the economy. If the transfers are to continue, the growing sector will once again have to outbid its competitors for resources, reassert a wide differential by raising wages, and start the process over again. If the protected groups are unable to keep pace, inflation then serves to reduce their relative position and depresses their wages in relation to those in expanding sectors. If workers in the less productive sectors are able to win wage increases that keep pace with the inflation—so that, essentially, prices are not flexible downward even in relative terms— inflation will continue as long as transfer takes place. In this fashion adjustment could build a constant level of inflation into the economy.

Thus, it is not simply that a manipulation of the money supply provokes a demand or generates price increases. To provide everyone with money (thereby increasing the money supply) while giving favored users privileged rates is to facilitate an inflationary process of bidding for resources by the growing sectors. In their study of French inflation Salin and Lane concluded that rigidities in the French economy—an unwillingness to adjust—contributed in important ways to the postwar inflationary bias. The argument developed here simply contends that the ability to subsidize these restrictive practices while at the same time financing the expansion of growth sectors was made possible by the arrangements of the financial system—arrangements that allowed resources to be targeted without particular regard to market criteria.

An inflation tied to industrial expansion—either directly, by money-supply increases made to finance investment and give subsidies to traditional sectors, or indirectly, by the competitive bidding of a demand-shift inflation—will inevitably alter the real returns of uncompetitive traditional sectors and expanding modern industrial ones. Over time inflation can reduce the real value of the nominal level of protection and subsidy accorded to declining sectors. Inflation—whether conscious strategy or the unintended but tolerated outcome of myriad tactical choices—silently facilitated an erosion of the position of traditional France which would not have been attempted by more open means. It has become a truism that inflation is a product of social conflict or even a weapon in social struggles.

The preceding analysis has simply suggested the conflicts and the techniques behind the postwar French inflation. Whether or not this financial strategy was tied directly to that inflation in the fashion argued here, the more basic proposition still holds: the extensive discretion over flows of funds in the French economy allowed the executive to pursue two contradictory purposes in growth and social order. Finance is thus linked to the first of the state's two economic roles, clearing away the political underbrush so that markets can work.

INTERVENTION AND THE TRANSFORMATION OF
FRENCH INDUSTRY

The expensive effort to maintain an uneasy balance between economic development and political order has also been evident in the policies pursued in particular industrial sectors. In our discussion of industrial intervention we need to consider (1) whether finance was in fact a crucial element of interventionist policy in industry, and (2) whether the use of finance as a government instrument of intervention affected the policy outcomes in industrial sectors.

The condition of French industry at the end of the Second World War determined the technical problems that intervention by the executive had to address. These problems ran deeper than the need to reconstruct war damage or the temporary lack of funds to do so. Industry was simply not structured to facilitate expansion and modernization. Its organization encouraged firms to resist adjustments to changed conditions and to defend narrowly defined market positions.[72] Small and medium-sized firms dominated industry; French companies were smaller than those in other industrial economies, in terms of total assets. Consumer production had long been rooted in regional and local markets that permitted the survival of small firms and plants. The dominance of small producers was reinforced by the cartel arrangements they employed to manage the market. The goal of the cartels "was either to adjust the utilization of capacity to demand and stabilize prices, as was generally the case in the 1880s and even earlier, or to divide domestic markets and fix prices and production quotas in order to maintain a steady stream of investment in the new industrial sectors."[73] Controlling the market limited the need for smaller firms to change or grow, of course; and even the larger firms were small by international standards.[74] In 1910 the leading electrical equipment and chemical manufacturers in France were both between one-tenth and one-twentieth the size of selected German and British counterparts, and the situation had not changed entirely by the end of the First World War.[75] Big business was state-oriented because most of the large firms were in heavy industries of concern to the government. Heavy industry required large amounts of capital, and vague networks of firms were established to solve the problems of raising those funds in primitive capital-market conditions. The close ties with government and finance which resulted served to stabilize demand, limit competition, and slow diversification.

When the large firms did diversify to new sectors, there was little central control in the rather loose amalgams they created. Size did not improve the ability of firms to adjust to changes in markets, nor did it promote greater efficiency. In the United States operating efficiency was the objective of multidivisional organization. In France the domination of "groups" indicated a continuing preference "for indirect rather than direct control over operations" and for combination as a means of controlling markets and meeting financial needs. "These arranged markets tended to block the emergence of larger more efficient corporations. The elimination of restrictions, if it could have been done, raised the spectre of an industrial implosion and social chaos."[76] It was feared that if an uncontrolled market were to force rapid and abrupt changes on firms, the social consequences would be politically disruptive. This fear served to justify the restrictions on competition.

By the end of the 1970s the largest French firms had begun to resemble more closely modern corporations of the American type. There is no reason to assume, however, that today's more efficient, centrally managed, and multidivisional French companies would have emerged automatically from the cartels and holding companies of the late 1940s. The weight of the evidence leads this observer to conclude that in competitive conditions, without state support, many French firms would have lost their own domestic markets to imports long before they had adjusted to international competition. The central political executive manipulated foreign competition to generate pressure for domestic economic modernization, but since the capacity of French firms to adjust was limited, the pressure itself had to be modulated. Certainly an erosion of the nation's productive apparatus would not have been tolerated. The situation was the opposite of the Japanese case, in which intense domestic competition and external protection were combined to create a high-growth system. It is not possible (though some authors have tried) to contrast French intervention and its consequences with outcomes that *might* have been produced by competitive firms operating in free markets.[77] The struggle was *to create* the markets and competitive firms themselves.

Since the development of large-scale industry occurred later and was more complex and discontinuous in France than in other countries, the management of that transformation became part of the job of postwar French economic policy. Each effort at modernization undermined elements of the old structure, but the damaged groups retained the power to insist on aid and subsidy. When less than competitive solutions to one set of industrial difficulties were tolerated, of course, problems remained for the next round of adjustment.

The French government has intervened continuously in the affairs of public and private companies since the Second World War. Before the war it was primarily an industrial arbitrator, attempting to balance competing claims in order to maintain social order, but since 1945 it has more often had to act as an entrepreneur, organizing and promoting industry. The pattern of entrepreneurial intervention has remained quite constant over the years. Whether the task has been to restructure industries in difficulty, to promote the French position in oil, or to support programs in electronics, alliances between bureaucrats, financiers, and businessmen have played an important role.[78] What made such alliances possible was not simply a system of cronyisms, but rather the nature of the marketplace ties between government, finance, and corporations. Confronted with firms that required extensive financing, the state found that its ability to amass great quantities of capital or to involve bankers who would undertake that task was crucial to the formation of these coalitions. In a sense, a government concerned with expansion elbowed in on restrictive cartels in its efforts to resolve the finance problem.

There have been three waves of industrial intervention in France: the postwar reconstruction; the era of consolidation sparked by the Common Market (which was also the heyday of the grandiose Gaullist project); and the current interventions to facilitate adjustment to a changed world economy. Although the tactics of intervention look similar across all three periods, the problems to be resolved, the purposes of the government, and the institutions at the center of the fray differed from one period to the next. Let us look at each period in turn.

In the first period, the capacity for continuous selective government intervention was, as we have seen, created to assist in reconstruction and modernization. In that first phase intervention became associated with the notion of planning. After the war there was a desperate need for investment to rebuild and begin anew but since the financial market could not be relied on for financing these investments, the state assumed the responsibility.[79] Part of the money invested was taken from budgetary allocations and passed through the FDES, part was invested by the long-term credit institutions directly lending money to final users, and part came as bank loans facilitated by a system of central bank rediscounting which was intended to remove the liquidity fears of deposit banks and to encourage long-term commercial lending. But the government did more than expand the volume of investment funds. It also used its discretion in finance to give priority to "key" sectors, particularly iron, steel, and cement—all of which were needed for building. Thus the period of reconstruction (1946 to the early 1950s) was characterized by selective policies that encouraged particular sectors, often through the promotion of specific companies. At the same time, the system of rediscounting served to "train" the commercial banks, previously focused on short-term lending, in the art of industrial finance. The state allocated capital and implanted growth-oriented attitudes in the leadership of the financial system.[80] As the capacity of firms to make investments from retained earnings grew, the de facto central administration of investment decisions evaporated. That is, the state could no longer deny or block projects that could be financed by company profits, even if it considered them to be of secondary importance. It could, of course, still advance the projects it favored by assigning them priority in the allocation of credits.

The second wave of intervention can be dated from 1958, the year of de Gaulle's second ascension to power and France's entry into the Common Market. The interventionist capacity was used to implement an industrial strategy of political grandeur which comprised such great projects as the Concorde airliner, a color television system, and the creation of "national champion" firms—firms whose fate was thought to be identical with that of the nation. Many of these projects involved enormous wastes of money and deeply damaging misdirections of industrial effort. Too often, they provided the external trappings of industrial might without creating an underpinning of companies able to continue competitive development on their own.[81]

More than symbolic politics was at stake during this era, however. The formation of the Common Market and the threat of German manufactures had created competitive pressures and a competitive mood in the French market. The financial system supported rapid expansion with administratively maintained low interest rates for investment and industry—rates so low that in real terms they were often negative.[82] Indeed, as noted before, the entire system of long-term credit institutions built up in France and reinforced after the war biased the banking system toward industrial investment and away from consumer lending. This continued development was slowly effecting a reorganization of French industry; the web of medium-sized plants was being consolidated into a network of large-scale, hierarchical, modern corporations.

The pace of mergers between the largest companies accelerated in the late 1950s, reflecting growing concentration throughout the economy.[83] In sectors of greatest concern to the government, an effort was made to force the creation of national champion firms on a scale suitable for international competition. The existence of more concentrated sectors, of course, made it easier for the government to conduct selective policies; government executives could negotiate on an ongoing basis with several dominant firms. Though Table 3.5 quantifies the transition to large-scale industry, it conceals the internal chaos in many of the so-called multidivisional firms—chaos that left them more nearly resembling the financial holding companies typical of France than the multidivisional companies they claimed to imitate. The larger firms created by mergers were often hodgepodge without effective central control. In steel, for example, the government had forced waves of concentrations but rational internal management was never effectively established.[84] A small firm grown large by internal expansion can establish coherent lines of authority as it grows, but when a dominant firm absorbs a lesser one there are often organizational problems, and combinations of peers are the most difficult of all. When the mergers were arranged to accommodate specific government pressures, as was often the case, these organization problems were made all the worse.

Many firms stumbled during this period of transition, only to be picked up by the government. The outcomes of intervention, to put the best light on government policy, represented the limits to which traditional business structures could be stretched, the extent of public and private understanding of the terms of international competition, and the political constraints on dislocations of rapid growth. The elite, technically trained bureaucrats—the technocrats—had no clear idea of how a modern corporation competing in international markets ought to be managed. As a result, they indiscriminately encouraged business-state links that were appropriate for government procurement but that were ill-suited to help firms competing in international markets. They also insisted on products that were better fitted to the choices of mature firms with established markets than to the needs of the new and often weak entrants to international competition. I have described elsewhere the circumstances in which the pattern of French intervention was successful.[85] What is important in this discussion is that the state, despite the range of errors, kept alive lines of industrial development and

Table 3.5. Distribution of the 100 largest corporations in France, 1950–1970 (size of corporations measured in sales values)

Type	1950	1960	1970
	Product lines		
Single	42	28	16
Dominant	21	27	32
Diversified (related)	33	40	42
Diversified (unrelated)	4	5	10
	Organizational structure		
Functional	50	32	14
Functional-holding company	24	29	12
Pure-holding company	20	18	12
Multidivisional	6	21	54

SOURCES: G. P. Dyas and H. T. Thanheiser, *The Emerging European Enterprise: Strategy and Structure in French and German Industry* (London, 1976); F. Roure, *Etude typologique financière des holdings pures françaises: Analyse des holdings americaines* (Paris, 1975), vol. 4. The research underlying this table was largely conducted by Gareth Pooleyn Dyas during the time I was working in France. At the time, I felt that he overstated the degree of coherence in the companies that I was also familiar with.

segments of industry that might otherwise have collapsed in the face of competition. In electronics and steel, for example, it seems clear that without state intervention several major firms would simply have died before they adjusted.

After a few years it became painfully evident that many of the technocratic errors were costly misdirections of resources. As a result, the bureaucrats came to have less confidence in their prescience and began to realize that their intervention often produced new troubles without resolving the old ones. The second wave of French interventions had thus begun to ebb when the international oil crisis struck in 1973.

The third phase of French state policy can be dated from the beginning of Giscard's presidency in 1974. The shift, of course, was not simply political, but was forced by the crunch of higher costs and drooping demands that narrowed the room for policy maneuver. The rhetoric of the Giscard years claimed that new policies altered the underlying relations between government and the economy, establishing a new and more liberal economic order in France. Though the reality belies these sweeping claims, certain important changes did take place.

The state's close and detailed direction of the economy in the reconstruction years ended in the 1950s and has dwindled since then. The two great economic projects of the postwar years had been completed, or at least were well in hand, by the beginning of Giscard's presidency: the shift from agriculture to industry was largely accomplished, and industrial reorganization had been achieved. As the postwar capital shortage gave way to expansion, company dependence on government investment waned, the internal capacity for raising money grew and more autonomous capital markets could be tapped. This increase in corporate financial autonomy was reflected in the budget as a percent of gross domestic product, which fell from a high of 31.8 percent in 1953 to 21.4 percent in 1972.[86] It is not that spending declined, but that the economy expanded. Yet since 1972 every downturn or crisis has shown that though the technical tasks have changed and the political problem is fundamentally different, the state presence remains. The selective hand of the state is evident in the current problem of forcing resources out of long-protected and subsidized sectors and into more competitive industrial sectors.

In France, the pendulum between liberalism and intervention swings in an arc different from the one to be observed in the British and American experiences. During postwar reconstruction, when attention was focused on a few critical sectors, the inner core of the system predominated: the Trésor was the source of money, the Plan the origin of advice, and the Crédit National the most important of the agencies that instructed the banks in medium-term industrial lending. The Trésor, with the advice of the Plan, even decided who would have access to the private capital markets. The focus on a few vital sectors, which restricted the number of choices, permitted the handful of men in the Trésor and the Plan to make decisions of wide-ranging industrial importance.

Since the early reconstruction years, day-to-day industrial choices have moved beyond the two outer circles of financial institutions, the parapublic lending institutions and the banks. This shift in the location of activity from center to periphery (one of the elements of Giscardian "liberalism") signified not a decline in state influence but a transformation of its purposes and means. The decline in Trésor loans to the economy—often cited as a proof of liberalization, a lessening of state influence—is more indicative of a shift from core to periphery within the state system. Moreover, a focus on the aggregate of loans hides the changes in the state's purposes and the means it has used. Between 1959 and 1972 the volume of loans declined 36 percent, but the actual funds for uses other than agriculture and housing increased by 134 percent. The reason is simple: the percentage of funds in the Trésor budget allocated to agriculture and housing combined dropped from 53.5 to 2.2 percent.[87] Moreover, since a portion of these Trésor funds is used to subsidize lending by financial intermediation, the total volume of funds affected by state discretionary choice is dramatically understated by these figures. An increase in lending from the parapublic lending institutions accompanied the decline in Trésor loans. Several forms of aid were passed along as subsidies or privileged lending conditions. These more indirect forms of aid were "more evenly divided among the sectors than were subsidies and treasury loans . . . so that the state came to exercise real influence over more and more sectors and firms."[88] In sum, decisions made in the core of the economic administration are not implemented through direct administration as often as they once were; instead, they are more often executed through a web of alliances which molds individual purposes to a common end.

Another thrust of so-called Giscardian liberalism consisted of policies to strengthen firms as agents of change in competitive markets.[89] Yet, looking beneath the rhetoric, one sees that strengthening the firms did not mean eliminating the state's influence. Certainly one purpose for ending price controls in 1975 was to raise the profit margins of companies that had become overly dependent on debt to finance investment. But in many sectors price controls represented a system of state-regulated price-fixing. Thus, the decision to abandon price controls could be seen as a government-abetted attack on private collusion, rather than as an attempt to eliminate purposive state intervention. The collusion and price-fixing often continued, in some cases enforced by suppliers.

Similarly, the emphasis on making French firms compete in international markets signaled a shift away from limited technological and production priorities as the criteria for government policy, but it did not indicate an end to government promotional efforts. In the monetary and financial field an attempt was made to strengthen private securities markets as a means of lessening corporate dependence on state-dominated financial institutions, undoubtedly a liberal effort. At the same time, however, mechanisms of money-supply control have depended on strict controls of the quantities of money lent by specific institutions, with exceptions granted for specified purposes. All in all, France has one of the most statist and administrative arrangements to be found among the Western economies. Giscardian "liberalism" did not disengage the state from specific interventions but only shifted the priorities and techniques of state policy. Of course with the Socialist victory a more direct role has been assigned to the state.

FINANCE AND INTERVENTION IN THE ERA OF
GISCARDIAN LIBERALISM

Restructuring the French economy to meet the new imperatives of the international economy is the positive project to which the interventionist apparatus has now been turned. Whereas the postwar effort sought to expand the productive capacity of industry, this new effort seeks victory for French firms in international competition. In retrospect, the 1960s can be seen as an intermediate period in which the government attempted to apply the techniques of expanding production, developed a decade earlier, to the new problems of establishing competitive firms. In some sectors this strategy was successful; in others it was a disaster. Many of the difficulties—the Concorde and the computer fiasco—resulted from the mismatch between market requirements and government policy. After a period of retrenchment, the techniques have been rearranged for the 1980s.

Restructuring has three parts: withdrawal from declining sectors, entrance into growth sectors, and the promotion of exports.[90] The first part, "shifting out," is "intellectually easy but politically difficult"; that is, though it is easy to identify low productivity sectors, it is not easy to shut them down.[91] The second part, "shifting in," should be politically easy but has proved intellectually difficult. There are few objections to new and higher-paying jobs. But which are the sectors of the future? Several are evident already, but the French feel that entry is blocked by American and Japanese domination of the high-technology industries, particularly electronics. Their fears are well founded. Although France is the fourth largest exporter in the world, it absorbs increasing deficits in trade with the United States, Japan, and Germany. Finally, French restructuring must be export-oriented so that the new industries and the reorganized older ones can pay the costs of imported fuels. The weight of the oil bill presses heavily because the very rapid rundown of the coal industry has left the French dependent on imported energy and nuclear power. The industrial restructuring, both the move out of declining labor-intensive sectors and the move into higher value-added activities, is hobbled by the halfway modernization of French industry since the 1950s. France is now paying for the political compromises that for over two generations subsidized traditional producers in the name of social peace.

Part of the state's "shifting out" policy in the late 1970s appeared relatively easy. The disasters of Gaullist industrial policy, such as the Concorde project and the state-created computer company, could either be allowed to die or be reorganized.[92] Foreign workers could be sent home and, in fact, between 1974 and 1977 some 350,000 workers did leave—about one-third of the workers then unemployed in France.[93] The most serious problems were never confronted, however. Most of the new employment created during the decades of economic expansion was in the service sectors—health, education, and banking, to name a few.[94] To increase productivity in these sectors would now require a fundamental reorganization of the service institutions themselves, but health and education are state administrations and reorganization of the administration may be the most difficult of all tasks in France. (Banking, incidentally, is itself a highly unionized semi-administration.)

Consequently, the government paid most attention to the lame-duck firms, the companies that could not support themselves in the competitive markets. Indeed, from the late 1960s through the election of 1978 the central thrust of the state's industrial policy was to assist firms in difficulty. The elements of that policy are quite familiar in both purpose and execution. Economic crisis forced bankruptcies, which gave the state leverage to reorganize the sectors and firms in difficulty. The objective of state-promoted corporate reorganization was that losers should be reorganized when possible—and merged or retired when necessary—but that the public should be protected from the consequences of company failure. This general goal does not constitute a prescription for actual policy, of course, since reorganizing companies and protecting the public often conflict in practice. During the period when the French left and the right were relatively evenly balanced, government policy emphasized maintaining employment rather than attempting to force competitive reorganization. With the political collapse of the left in the election of 1978, however, the government initiated tougher policies toward troubled firms and sectors which did displace management and employment. The government did not view labor as a serious threat to its plans to allow many firms to close and to shrink employment in others. As it turned out, this underestimation of the threat from the left was a rather serious political mistake.

The central instrument used by the French state to rescue potential survivors and to save usable industrial "material" has been the CIASI (Interministerial Committee for Management of the Industrial Structure). CIASI does not act as a conglomerate manager with active holdings in firms. Instead, it promises state funds in order to encourage owners and their bankers to develop and implement a rescue or merger plan. The largest cases are handled by the ministers in the central government, whereas smaller problems are handled by representatives of the ministries at the local level. The CIASI does more than "buy" participation, however; it arranges collaboration. The negotiations about who should put money into which projects are conducted within a financial family in which the ranking state bureaucrats are the elders. (We have previously quoted both a bureaucrat and banker to the effect that the state could have what it wanted, if it insisted, in the form of bank support for projects it initiated.) The negotiations themselves hinge on the system of finance and would be impossible without it. This case-by-case treatment of industrial affairs—into which the CIASI put a billion francs of state budget money but mobilized for its efforts another eight billion francs in private funds—reveals the essence of the "player" state.[95]

The cases of the textile and steel industries clearly display the problems of getting out of traditional sectors. They show how the compromises of earlier years have led to current problems and exhibit the changing tactics of government intervention. In both cases, the place of finance is evident. Let us begin with the textile industry.

For more than twenty years after the Second World War, French policy sought to preserve a textile industry that was composed of small firms using outdated labor-intensive production strategies. While the industry worldwide was being revolutionized by the development of artificial fibers and the emergence of exports based on the cheap labor of the developing countries, the French government fostered a nonintegrated textile industry that was unique among highly industrialized countries. It sought to protect the small traditional producers, who provided 14 percent of the nation's industrial jobs at the end of the war and were diffused through the small towns of several regions.[96] The continuing importance of small firms in the French textile industry is best established by looking at other European economies. In 1962 the average number of employees in a textile firm in France was 24, whereas in Germany it was 46 and in the Netherlands, where integration occurred early, it was 111.[97] The policies intended to preserve the industry simply ossified it and made it all the more vulnerable to the real revolution taking place beyond France's borders.

Three lines of policy were important in the attempt to maintain this structure. First, labor costs had to be kept down because small firms could not make the capital investments necessary to shift away from labor-intensive production strategies. But low wages could be sustained only if a rural and docile textile labor force were maintained, and this required massive government assistance.[98] Foreign workers were channeled into rural firms, and there is some evidence that the government blocked the development of new plants whose higher wages would have started a competition for workers.[99] During slack times the government directly subsidized wages to prevent layoffs, reducing unit labor costs for these essentially cyclical businesses. Second, the state gave the primary manufacturer of artificial fiber a monopoly position in the supply of rayon, thus keeping that firm out of the textile business. The government thus limited the expansion of the advancing segment of the industry and presumably dampened the traditional firms' need to adapt to new technology and product. Third, state policy sought to protect the domestic market and promote colonial markets.[100] Even after the Common Market was established, with supposedly uniform external tariffs and no internal tariffs, import penetration in French textiles and clothing was dramatically lower than elsewhere in the EEC.[101] This situation resulted in part from the indirect protection of subsidy but it was also a consequence of a multitude of restrictions and obstacles to the entry of goods.[102]

The policy mechanisms changed over the years, with the government taking a more direct role in determining the evolution of the industry and the fate of particular firms. The first wave of intervention came in the 1950s, when small business was still dominant in the councils of French industry and when a parliamentary regime magnified their political influence. The government delegated to an industry association the administration of programs designed largely by the industry itself, to serve the needs of small producers.[103] This program was funded by a tax on textile sales and was fitted into a broader program of managing reconversion and permitting orderly decline which the association had established. The fund "was managed exclusively by the Syndicat Général de l'Industrie Cotonnière Française, which used these [monies] to preserve the small scale nature of the textile industry."[104] The program was aimed at buying up outdated production equipment, both to close down uncompetitive firms and to provide funds for modernization. The central assumption was that new equipment would make the small producers more productive.

The second wave of intervention, which occurred in the 1960s, sought modernization through the mechanism of merger. As the textile producers declined in economic importance and the small producers lost influence within the trade associations, policy was increasingly made to serve the needs of bigger companies. Employment in the industry had already dropped from 692,000 in 1951 to 542,000 in 1961 and some concentration had occurred during the same period.[105] The larger firms now became the allies of government. Undoubtedly the shift in government policy was also tied to the bureaucracy's greater independence from parliament, which resulted from the Gaullist governmental reorganization. What is not clear in the several available accounts is whether the government actively sought out the larger firms or whether they exerted pressure that shifted the orientation of government policy. The programs of support were still administered by a trade association, the Union de l'Industrie Textile (UIT), but government policy was now explicit: the funds would be used to encourage concentration, reinvestment in textiles could be funded only as part of a merger movement.[106] This line was enforced by a government review of all cases and by the exercise of government influence over the association representatives who allocated the funds. Though this fund did press for concentration and though it represented a third of the total funds invested in the cotton sector, other programs still preserved the smaller producers. Policies that sustained a cheap labor market provided disproportionate aid to small firms that had no other options; the division of the market by fiber type was still in place and protection still helped to close out imports. Moreover, many of the mergers were primarily financial in character and served to keep old plants in operation.

The third wave of intervention, in which the government bureaucracy itself finally made and implemented policies, has sought to respond to the downturn in demand and to the pressure from cheap-labor producers in the newly industrializing countries. The boom in Third World textile exports has made it essential that the French establish a core of integrated, capital-intensive producers (virtually reversing the industry structure) in order to maintain their market position. In the United States producers responded to Third World exporters by investing in more capital-intensive production; they changed their product and cost position and began to export to Europe, which was strong evidence that a competitive industry could be established in the advanced countries even if employment were sharply reduced. The French problem was that their textile industry was still composed of small and vulnerable companies at the time when the world economic slowdown of the 1970s began to place greater pressures on all textile firms. Employment, which had been declining at a rate of just over 2.2 percent in the 1950s and 1960s, began to drop at a rate of 4.2 percent in the first part of the 1970s.[107] An effort was made to limit imports by negotiation or unilateral action, and indeed imports still represent a dramatically lower percentage of consumption and production in France than in other European countries. Not all the pressures could be kept out, however, and domestic policy also had to change.

In the 1970s textile policies became more aggressively interventionist and were reminiscent of tactics previously used in more strategic sectors.[108] Tactics for ailing firms were now formulated by the core bureaucracies and parapublic financial institutions, or by alliances between them and banks. The shift is best exemplified by the CIASI, which determined at an interministerial level how best to rearrange the affairs of private companies and then sought private monies to carry out its plans. Its best-known intervention in textiles was the detailed rearranging of the affairs of the Boussac textile empire; it decided not only how to liquidate the holdings but also what losses Boussac's private fortune would bear.

In sum, the efforts in the 1950s and 1960s to preserve economic order and social peace in the textile-producing regions left an uncompetitive industry that was ill equipped to adapt rapidly to the changing market pressures. The French have consequently been advocates of continued protection and orderly adjustment in the textile and apparel sectors, in contrast to the Germans and the Dutch, who have sought to force the industry to adjust. The degree of protection and subsidy is evident from an examination of employment and production indexes. Employment in the textile industry dropped more slowly in France than anywhere else in Europe.[109] At the same time, French textile production dropped sharply, indicating a general decline in labor productivity. The same pattern appears in the apparel sector. During the present crisis the economic ministries have managed government intervention more directly. The technocrats established mechanisms to intervene directly in firms and push aside trade association intermediaries. And when they intervened directly, their instruments were drawn from their influence in finance.

The story of French steel parallels that of textiles. The partial adjustments of the 1950s and 1960s proved inadequate to the pressures of extended slowdown in the 1970s. As the need for rapidly forced industry change has grown, there has been a shift away from intervention through trade association intermediaries toward direct government involvement in the details of firm management. The first interventions in steel, as in textiles, involved largely horizontal mergers that brought a multitude of plants under holding-company umbrellas and left family control intact.[110] In the present world economic crisis, loose associations of companies and plants have given way to tighter, more centralized management and a tougher internal rationalization. Again, finance proved to be a crucial mechanism of government influence in the industry.

For many years the state could stand as an intermediary between the national and the international market, cutting off the domestic economy from the world. Steel demand and supply were in relative balance worldwide, and the European market was a relatively stable oligopoly under public management.[111] Any effort to invade French markets on a long-term basis would have involved heavy capital investment in new plants and a willingness to accept heavy losses if the French government chose to deflect a steel invasion by subsidizing national firms extensively. Thus, although the French were high-cost producers, the government could hope to restructure the industry within a protected and a stable market.[112] At each crisis in the industry, the government could step in to force a reorganization of the companies. Many of those crises, it is said, were provoked by price controls; but the price controls were the almost inevitable results of extreme inefficiency and state protection of a stable oligopoly. In a sense, the price controls cushioned the rest of the economy against the consequences of inefficient steel production. Squeezed profit margins were caused not so much by price controls as by high costs.

As part of its effort to force the steel industry into a competitive mold, the government in the 1970s promoted massive new seaside facilities that were to incorporate the latest in production technology.[113] Since these facilities demanded firms large enough to finance their construction and operate them successfully, there was pressure for a continued consolidation of firms. An alliance between finance, industry, and government to finance the investments required for the consolidation was molded in a series of semi-contractual deals that established a pattern for state-business dealings in other sectors.

The steel trade association was always an important spokesman in bargaining with government about policies toward steel and continued to be an important agent in raising capital for the industry. The government's use of its influence in the capital markets to piece together this alliance became evident in the painful culmination of these efforts. The French were just bringing their new steel capacity on line when the downturn in worldwide economic activity came in 1974–1975. Though the first parts of the southern complex and the last elements of the northern complex were beginning production, older and completely inefficient plants were being kept open in order to pressure employment.[114] Average costs in the industry were coming down, but not as rapidly as they could have if the older plants had been closed. In 1976 the French required, on the average, 50 percent more man-hours of labor per ton of steel than the Germans, though the most efficient French plants were competitive.[115] Such halfway solutions had been expensive but manageable when the demand for steel was still rising and when a stable European producers' oligopoly existed, but they were no longer plausible once the market collapsed. Until 1975 there was a relative balance worldwide between increasing demand and the capacity of new facilities coming on line. Before 1974 over 90 percent of effective capacity worldwide was being used.[116] When demand fell, however, expansion plans begun before 1974 were not quickly scrapped and a substantial oversupply was created in French markets. Prices fell some 30 percent by 1977, while wages and other costs increased by an equivalent amount.[117] The strain on old management structures and sheltered but inefficient production was enormous. Between 1974 and 1977 the French steel industry added 14 billion francs to its debt (about 3 billion dollars). In 1977 alone, the industry's sales were 34.2 billion francs, whereas its debt was 38 billion francs—an appalling situation. Its net losses exceeded 6 billion francs in that year, the third successive year of losses.[118] The productivity picture was even worse. To produce an output roughly five times that of the French, the Japanese used only twice as many workers.

After the elections of 1978 and the "implosion of the left," the game in steel changed dramatically. The first government intervention in 1977 had been of the old style, a financial rescue plan of loans from the FDES in exchange for industry commitments to close plants and shed labor. This measure was only a stopgap, and in September of the following year the executive quite literally took matters into its own hands. The financial problems were confronted by turning outstanding debt into participatory loans, "non-interest-bearing debentures which in principle will be repaid when the industry recovers from the current crisis."[119] Most of the money owed to both the banks and the government was handled in this manner. A part of the debt was "converted into capital in three new financial holding companies controlling the three steel groups."[120] The chairman of each holding company was to be nominated by the old creditors (now stockholders), not by former shareholders. The former shareholders now had holdings in a subordinate set of companies, but they had a minority share there also. The government took direct responsibility for paying off the small investors by establishing a special fund to be managed by the Caisse des Dépôts et Consignations. As a result of these changes, roughly two-thirds of the steel industry's equity is now in the hands of the government or of government-controlled financial institutions. Perhaps the most dramatic shift was the appointment of the chairmen of the new operating companies; in one case, the government simply displaced existing family management and appointed an *inspecteur de finance* who had once headed the Crédit Agricole. This massive financial reorganization was handled entirely as an executive matter and involved very limited budgetary funds. The operation was managed by leverage inside the financial system.

Interestingly, in both steel and textiles government policy involved more detailed intervention during the late 1970s than ever before. Liberalism might do for routine matters, but in a crisis the strong arm of the state was needed.

"Shifting in," the second part of the policy of industrial restructuring, seemingly received little formal attention for a number of years. Indeed, according to one view, adjustment was to be left to the market and the firms should simply redeploy themselves.[121] Recently the new Plan (number eight) has listed six priority sectors to which state efforts should be directed. (Political pressure, ironically, has forced innovation in textiles to be added to the list.) The Trésor, in recent years a better indicator than the Plan of where policy is going, has organized special interministerial committees to promote these priority sectors. These committees are arranged along the lines of the CIASI, the body set up to handle declining firms. In principle, they will use small chunks of budget money to mobilize larger sums of funds in the financial system.[122]

Though it is unclear whether these committees represent new money or simply involve a relabeling of previously budgeted funds, a new emphasis is evident. From one point of view, rhetoric has simply caught up with reality. There have long been substantial promotional policies for the growth sectors in which the state has had serious interests—aircraft, telecommunications, and energy. Even in the automobile sector, where the profitability of the major companies immunized them against government influence for a number of years, the selective hand of the state, using its financial fingers, has become apparent. In the merger between Citroen and Peugeot, the state assembled a kind of dowry—a very substantial loan—to sweeten the marriage and ease the early years.[123] In the automobile components sector, which remains fragmented, the government has stepped in to force a series of mergers around major companies. This rationalization was undertaken entirely at government initiative, when bureaucrats and auto executives alike began to understand that part of the Japanese cost advantage in auto production lay in the organization of their components sector. The presence of a few dominant components firms makes possible a larger volume of production and facilitates investment in production development.

From a second point of view, the technocracy is asserting that despite the problems of earlier years it can successfully play a more aggressive role in the adjustment of private firms to changed international markets.[124] The interventions of the 1980s were qualitatively different from those of the 1960s, which had produced a parade of competitive disasters. The earlier strategy was to insulate the market with protection and subsidies, creating a preserve within which high-technology industries could then be bred. The intent was less to make sure that competitive French firms would emerge on international markets than to force products of French design on those markets. The French, however, simply could not control markets in electronics, which were changing character every few years, and they could not impose unprofitable aircraft such as the Concorde on foreign buyers. The strategy of designing a product before considering what buyers want does not work in competitive markets. The present policy intends to reverse the priorities and general emphasis of the 1960s. The aim now is to help establish commercially viable firms to take up defensible market positions. At least in principle, policy success is to be judged in terms of commercial viability, rather than in terms of intermediary technological or production criteria.

Let us take electronics as a case in point to see the shift in emphasis.[125] That industry divides roughly into three final-product segments: (1) computers; (2) professional equipment such as radars and the hardware for television production and telecommunications; and (3) consumer electronics. Behind these product segments lies the components industry. Most developments in the electronics industry rest on innovation in integrated-circuit components and the competition in all three segments moves with cycles of product innovation, though in somewhat different ways. Two strategies are open in competitive world markets in all three final-product segments. For standard products that become commodity items, firms really require world-market scale to reach unit costs that permit them to sell competitively and keep up with the rapidly evolving technology. The larger volumes implied by world-market scale permit a company to drive down production costs and to spread the relatively fixed research and development costs. The only alternative strategy is to specialize in market niches where volume is not so critical, or to start a generation of products and then abandon it when price competition becomes intense. Generally speaking, the French in the 1960s attempted to compete in the most profitable product lines of foreign firms because these products were prestigious. But the French electronics companies simply could not keep pace in computers or semiconductor components, critical elements of the industry. Despite a variety of mechanisms to insulate national markets or to use state influence to sell television and telecommunications systems abroad, the industry could not be protected against foreign competition. Nor could the firms adjust rapidly enough to become potent competitors. As in steel and textiles, a series of troubled mergers occurred, but under more intensely competitive circumstances. With even less time to adjust, the resulting hodgepodge organization had more immediate and more damaging consequences in electronics.

By the late 1970s a new policy had emerged which aimed at using the French base as a springboard into international markets. One clear case was the effort to turn a middle-weight multinational, Honeywell-Bull, into an instrument of French policy. The repackaging of computer holdings that extricated the government from its state-sponsored fiasco and drew Honeywell-Bull into its net was similar in form to the other reorganizations we have discussed. Telecommunications policy provides a second illustration of the new approach. Here the strategy is to use a vast expansion of the telephone system as a procurement base on which to rebuild the French integrated-circuit industry and open up new types of consumer markets. A mix of state procurement, finance, and budget subsidy underlies this new effort, which is at least plausible as a strategy. The aim is to use state power to help firms in these innovation-centered sectors ride market forces rather than resist them.

Finally, the export problem, the third component of a restructuring policy, has been receiving serious attention all along. The French are heavily dependent on imported oil and the full array of interventionist arrangements has been devoted to the task of expanding exports in order to pay for it. The most obvious effort has been the aggressive financing of exports and export investment to provide effective subsidies. This policy is a nominal violation of international trade rules, but the French are renowned for their effective use of functional subsidies in trade competition.[126] These financial tools have not been used simply to serve the export-financing needs of industry, but have been employed to open new markets. For example, the Crédit Agricole has spearheaded a drive to promote exports in the food industry, which ranks behind only construction and public works in importance within the economy. Crédit Agricole, in its reconstructed role, is not simply financing exports but is offering support "when needed in the form of syndicated loans to countries interested in buying farm equipment and food processing plants."[127] Technip, a state-owned company, plays a similar role in the construction industry. One of the world's largest construction firms, it serves as an instrument in state-to-state negotiations, serving the industrial vehicle through which private contracts are channeled. Its financial structure and public status permit it to take a loose view of profits as return on invested capital and constitutes a subsidy that helps French manufacturers fulfill construction contracts. Technip harvests contracts that provide export outlets for French companies. Certainly the most direct financial effort by the state has been in the export of large-scale capital equipment, such as communication systems, airplanes, and armaments. These various manipulations of financial instruments for the aggressive promotion of French trade positions depend on the direction taken by the government in operating the financial system.[128]

This review of French adjustment strategies suggests that whenever direct selective actions are found, a financial instrument can be identified as a vital element of policy.

THE NEW GROWTH EQUATION

Before we return to our main theme, finance, let us put the current industrial difficulties of France into political perspective. Managing this latest adjustment to changed patterns of international trade and extended economic slowdown has posed new political-technical problems. During the first two waves of state intervention, there were three main technical problems. The first was to encourage industrial expansion by keeping interest rates for investment below market rates and assuring that the supply of funds for investment was not a limitation on the economy's ability to grow. The second was to intervene in industrial affairs to encourage the modernization of both the capital stock and the organization of firms, ultimately absorbing in the public purse or diffusing to the community at large the costs of slowly building hierarchical management structures through mergers of small- and medium-sized firms interlinked by negotiated agreement. The third problem was to modernize agriculture, because a more efficient agriculture would simultaneously release labor to industry and provide productivity gains. By the 1980s there was little more to be wrung from the earlier sources of growth. The rapid shift out of agriculture was over and the modernization of the management and structure of French industry was under way. Resources must now be shifted out of low productivity industrial uses into firms and sectors that can make better use of them, while production in existing sectors is reorganized to meet intense international competition. At the same time that old activities are closed down, it is necessary to find new ones that can support the high wages demanded by workers in all advanced countries. But for once, the French can no longer follow the more advanced countries; they have used up the advantages of backwardness and are now obliged to invent their own future.

The changed process of growth fundamentally alters the political problems. In the past, the agricultural and other traditional groups could be subsidized to maintain political order even as they were being displaced; the political problem was how to modulate the pace of change while stoking the industrial engines to pull the growth train. A patchwork industrial structure that accommodated politically powerful but uncompetitive firms with hodgepodge organizations, as well as inflation, was the price paid to avoid direct confrontation with groups being displaced. But such confrontations can no longer be avoided and the government has forced the closing or reorganization of large firms with visible and concentrated pools of workers. Perhaps the most dramatic instance was the abrupt dismissal of forty thousand men in the steel industry work force, an action that provoked demonstrations in Paris.

It is not simply that confrontation has replaced finesse as the dominant mode of industrial politics, for the groups to be confronted have changed and their political position is different from that of their predecessors. The agricultural and small business classes have simply been maintained in their hothouse, in the hope that in a changed market they will somehow become exporters. Leaving these groups alone represents productivity gains foregone. Indirectly, this approach denies resources to expanding sectors or raises the price at which they must buy those resources; but it does not directly interfere with the development of the rest of the economy.

Arguably, it is labor's changed political position that has altered the political equation of adjustment. In the old equation it would seem that labor was the candidate to be squeezed, to make the sacrifices required by growth. Whereas agriculture and traditional business had to be supported and expanding modern business required subsidies for investment, labor was weak—weak in the market, in policy, and in politics. The three components of the union movement—Communist (CGT), noncommunist but radical (CFDT), and moderate (FO)—often competed for members within the same factories, thus weakening any one component's ability to establish the strong plant-level bargaining units required to support extended industrial action. The legal rules that structure labor-industry bargaining also served to weaken efforts to establish a stable system for collective negotiation. As a result, protest politics became the means commonly used to improve one union's position against another's and to force the government to take a hand in wage settlements. Certainly the labor movement has won political victories, particularly in moments of crisis. Any gains could dissipate in the routine negotiations where labor is handicapped by law and its own divisions. Consequently labor has often sought formal rules that could be monitored and enforced, even by a less than sympathetic government. The result is an elaborate system of formal arrangements which protects jobs and raises the costs of layoffs. Compared with Germany, for example, the labor system in France remains extremely rigid. In comparisons of matched factories, it has been found that the blue-collar organization in French firms is marked by a more rigid internal hierarchy and a greater inequality of salaries than one finds in German firms.[129]

Union access to policymaking was limited by mutual choice of government and labor. The CGT, for example, withdrew from the Planning Commission in 1947 and labor was kept out of policymaking by the Conservatives. Organized labor's limited ability to influence policy reflected itself when the events of May 1968—a student uprising joined by widespread spontaneous worker strikes—produced substantial wage increases as part of a return to order. Though the level of political turmoil was significant and remarkable, the pattern of industrial conflict was not new: after a long erosion of labor's real income during which worker demands had not been effectively represented by the unions or satisfied in ordinary bargaining, a wave of strikes produced a wage jump.[130] These gains in real income were lost by a currency devaluation the next year, however, a devaluation quite specifically intended to reestablish the competitive edge lost by firms when wage costs rose. By contrast, Michele Salvati contends that Italian labor was able to block similar government devaluation strategies in the wake of its wage gains in the "hot Autumn" of 1969. The difference in the strength of the political left in the two countries accounts for the difference in outcomes. The Italian Communist party was a burgeoning threat to the conservative hold on government, and a decline in standards of living might have increased its appeal and the militancy of the workers. In France, the Communist party and the left were not a threat and there was little likelihood of a repeated wave of strikes.[131]

The political challenge posed by French labor changed when the reformed Socialist party—its voter appeal considerably broadened—formed a working alliance with the Communist party. Suddenly the left coalition was an alternative government and the purely political costs of simply refusing labor's demands were substantially increased. There is little evidence that the French unions were more powerful as bargaining agents in 1980 than they had been a decade ago, and indeed labor markets had softened with the increase in unemployment. Yet wages kept up with prices in the 1970s; in fact, real incomes continued to grow despite a steadily rising unemployment rate.[132] At one point unemployment benefits were raised to 90 percent of salary for a year. If there were any doubt that the government was trying to purchase the quiescence of *employed* workers, it came after the elections of 1978. With the faltering of the left alliance and the squabbling between the parties and between the unions which ensued, the government moved quickly to force industrial reorganization that meant cuts in the work force. In the case of steel, the program went ahead with only minor changes, despite the massive protest march in Paris.

Rising wage rates inevitably put pressure on labor-intensive sectors with low productivity and on capital-intensive industries operating with excess labor. As wages rise so too does the cost that the government incurs in order to ensure the survival of such firms and to maintain excess labor. This cost takes the form of subsidies, higher domestic living costs, and foreign resentment of French protection or subsidized exports. Since restructuring cannot be avoided and since it involves large-scale labor displacement, political confrontation becomes likely. The French system has the technical capacities to provide selective assistance for industrial transition and transformation, but when such assistance produces clearly visible winners and losers, the purpose and operation of the system become more controversial. The political genius of the postwar French system of finance was its ability to obscure the disposition of resources and to transform the public management of financial flows into a private executive matter. In addition, for a decade from 1958 until 1969 de Gaulle gave the transformation of society and economy a political meaning that included and attracted even those being displaced by the changes. Perhaps the greatest failure of Giscardian economic management was that the strategy of industrial adjustment was not embedded in a project that gave political legitimacy and general meaning to individual policies. Policies that indeed represented a technical necessity appeared to be arranged for the benefit of a limited part of the French community; selectivity came to be seen as abuse and corruption. Giscard demonstrated the political limits of technocracy.

Though the Socialists cannot elude these same economic problems, their political choices are different because their constituencies are different. They must mollify if not satisfy a labor constituency that anticipates gains, not greater pain, from the left's political victory. The political challenge to the left is to make the unavoidable industrial change acceptable to its own constituency without alienating the industrial and managerial community, which in the end—whatever the nominal forms of ownership—must actually organize the process of industrial change. The real drama of the socialist strategy will come, not in the policy of nationalization (which simply extends existing arrangements), but in the choice of whether and how to reform the highly politicized structure of labor relations.

The socialist strategy is evidently a separate story. The only question that should concern us at the end of this analysis is whether the changes they are making represent a continuation of the financial and business arrangements we have analyzed or whether the epoch of nationalizations marks that true break in French political economy which the Socialists hope for and the conservatives fear. Our analysis suggests that the relations between business and the state depend fundamentally on the structure of the state bureaucracy and the financial system on the one hand and on the purposes to which government wishes to put its influences in business affairs on the other. Given this pattern, the nationalizations undertaken by the Socialists should not fundamentally alter the technical ties between big business and the state. In financial matters ownership will matter less than the channels through which funds flow from savers to investors. Though there have been some proposals to alter these channels, the suggestions are contradictory. Indeed, the government is likely to discover it possesses the instruments necessary to conduct a strategy of aggressive industrial development even without the extensive nationalizations completed in 1982.

If nationalizations have not altered the technical relations between big business and the state, they have undoubtedly changed the politics of the situation. The big business segment of the French private business community has in one swoop been eliminated. With the particular interests of the large capitalists eliminated by amputation, the state should, in principle, be able to pursue its vision of the general interest. But, company autonomy may be found to depend more on financial conditions than on ownerships. Thus Renault, which has been profitable and served as an instrument of state development policy, has retained considerable autonomy, while the major steel companies, and even firms such as Thomson CSF which have had market or financial problems, have been the subjects of detailed government intervention.

Ironically, the elimination of the political influence of the "big" capitalists may simply recreate the situation in which the community of small- and medium-sized firms are politically dominant. These firms have been the traditional enemies of government development policies. Private interests may become synonymous with small business interests, as they were in the years just after the Second World War, and what remains of the private sector can be expected to resist industrial readjustment projects in particular and state initiative in general. In this case, the price of eliminating the influence of big capital will have been the reestablishment of the influence of the petite bourgeoisie. In any case, the selectivity of the financial system will also take on a new political meaning, but it will not be eliminated.

FINANCE IN THE FRENCH POLITICAL ECONOMY

The central proposition of this chapter has been that the interventionist strategies of development pursued by the French bureaucracy and executive would not have been possible without the capacity for action created by the financial system. A credit-based, price-administered financial system made possible administrative influence and often discretion in the allocation of capital. We have examined the opportunities for executive discretion in capital-resource allocations which are inherent in the operations of the French financial system. We have explored the institutional ties between government, finance, and industry, and have argued that those institutional links depend on the organization of the markets for capital. The capacity for political and economic action embodied in executive discretion over credit flows was important to the outcomes of three political battles central to the postwar development of French industry.

First, finance was an important instrument in the Planning Commission's early struggle to survive. It was not simply that the Plan's technical economic objectives were assured by allocating capital to privileged uses in a credit-short economy. Rather, its political survival depended on this centralized financial tool. The victory of the Plan, in fact, changed the relations between government and business in France. A state-fostered development strategy was perhaps latent in prewar arrangements, and certainly there had been extensive interventions, yet a strategy of development and the government capacity to implement it were postwar creations. These new business-state relationships were evident in the twin roles that the state now played in the economy: on the one hand, it assured that the market provided incentives and resources for industrial modernization and, on the other hand, it actually managed the reorganization of industrial structure in specific sectors and firms.

In the second political battle state policy facilitated the workings of market forces by preventing groups damaged by economic modernization from using politics to halt the growth machine, while at the same time assuring investment funds to segments of the economy whose expansion was essential for development. The selective apparatus and the mechanisms of quantitative control of financial-institution lending allowed the state bureaucracy to pursue these seemingly contradictory ends aggressively.

Third, the state served as crutch and prod in the transformation of French industry away from an insular world in which small-scale production and intercompany connections slowed change toward an international marketplace in which a more modern industry composed of hierarchically managed giant corporations could compete with its counterparts. Again, finance was crucial in shaping the state bureaucracy's capacity to intervene in industrial affairs.

The state-dominated financial system gave those supporting economic modernization a privately held instrument with which to pursue their goals. Since the financial system is administratively controlled, its biases are the prerogatives of the bureaucrats who regulate the system. Whether the executive took the lead and imposed its own objectives, operated through intermediaries and alliances, or simply biased the access to funds in the economy, this set of financial arrangements maximized executive influence and constricted the opportunities of others to participate in the formulation of critical policies. A small elite group could shift the policy priorities of government precisely because that group did not need to capture an extended administrative terrain or amass specific legislative support to accomplish its purposes. Its tactics could remain hidden in the shadowy world of finance.

CHAPTER FOUR

The Unsettling Agenda: The British Case

This chapter considers the efforts of the British government in the postwar years to reverse the nation's long decline from industrial preeminence. In its attempts to promote economic development by exercising industrial leadership, the government confronted substantial institutional constraints. The organization of both the financial system and the state's economic administration—constructed in years when Britain was an industrial pioneer with a preeminent position in international markets—limited government's ability to intervene systematically and purposefully in industry affairs to promote industrial redevelopment. The government's struggle to build and reform institutions that would serve interventionist purposes opened up conflicts about the distribution of gains from growth and about the place of businessmen, bureaucrats, union leaders, and financiers in the governance of the economy. In part as a consequence, the seemingly technical question of how to promote industry became a political struggle within the elite over who would govern the process. The broader battle about whether and how to conduct a promotional policy to reverse industrial decline shattered an underlying consensus about the need to give new priority to industrial growth. The will to modernize the economy was therefore dissipated in a struggle about who would gain and who would lose from development.[1] The financial system enters the story as a source of constraints on state action and as a source of political conflict when the government attempted to lift those contraints. Before turning to this story, we must first set the context in which the fight for industrial redevelopment occurred.

ECONOMIC DECLINE AND POLITICAL CONFLICT

Britain's industrial decline has been underway for a century, and whatever its causes, the difficulties are now deeply rooted. Britain's slow growth relative to that of its industrial competitors is simply the most aggregate symptom of the trouble (for the comparison of growth rates see the Tables in Chapter 1). For years Britain has been losing international market share across the whole range of industrial sectors primarily because of the weakness of her competitive position within each sector. The kinds of industries in which British firms are represented cannot account for her relative decline in the period up to 1974.[2] Britain did make the shift from cotton production into motor cars; the difficulty is that the automobile industry itself has collapsed.[3]

British productivity gains in industrial production offer another indication of the general weakness of British industry. The gap between British and German productivity growth in the postwar years is evident.[4] Studies of the differential productivity rates discount the effect of shifts between sectors. Though the gap can be attributed to differences in capital intensity, the same technologies and sometimes the same production system is used less effectively in Britain. After nearly a decade of 1 percent productivity increases, British productivity rose in 1979 and 1980.[5] Unfortunately, the rise in productivity was accompanied by a steep fall in output and employment. Further evidence of the declining quality and technological position of British industry comes from a comparison of the unit value of German and French exports with the unit value of British exports. In most sectors, Germany and France are exporting higher-value goods than Britain is.[6] In the mechanical engineering sector—a good indicator of the competitiveness of an economy because it includes a range of manufacturing businesses in which management of complex production and design problems is critical—this decline has been clearly documented over fifteen years.[7]

This general weakness means that in order to sustain growth Britain must do more than simply move out of low productivity sectors into high productivity ones; it must also make basic changes in the structure of its industries and the organization of companies. Unfortunately, sectoral shifts and the reorganization of production are tied together in a way that proves troublesome for Britain. The adoption of new technologies that will increase productivity has been associated with the shift of resources between sectors. Rapid technological modernization is facilitated by rapid expansion that allows firms to adopt the newest production methods and products. Historically, however, such rapid industrial expansion has depended upon the movement of labor out of agriculture and into industry, at low wages. (One of Britain's more eminent economists, Nicholas Kaldor, has contended that a "rapid deployment of labor away from agriculture employment is necessary for high growth.")[8] In Britain, of course, that shift ended long ago. Whatever the validity of the proposition that the exit of labor from agriculture is linked to high growth rates (and the evidence is at least consistent with it, as Chapter 2 suggests), Britain must now both displace and reorganize entrenched industrial groups. Without rapid expansion, both the shifts and the reorganization are more difficult. Without the shifts and reorganization, rapid expansion will not occur. Thus, Britain's economic difficulties will not be solved by a few adjustments of the economic dials or the presence of a steady hand at the monetary helm.

In the 1950s Britain slowly discovered that it was losing ground to its European trade rivals, that it was not sharing equally in the boom that was propelling France and Germany. This discovery was driven home by a nasty economic trap: every economic expansion drew in imports more rapidly than it expanded exports.[9] The resulting trade imbalance put the pound sterling under pressure, bringing fears of a devaluation. Devaluation was considered unacceptable because of fears that it would endanger both sterling's role as a reserve currency and the City of London's position as a financial clearinghouse. Trade barriers were ruled out as a policy choice—or rather, they were never considered—and bouts of deflation seemed the only alternative. But deflation could only aggravate the problems of the manufacturers because shrinking demand would lead to lower profits and investments. Continuing deflation did interfere with the readjustment of British industry to changed world market conditions. In order to escape from the trade trap that would periodically force the choice between deflation and devaluation, Britain had to find some other way to revive its industry.

The postwar growth debate began when, in 1961, Harold Macmillan's Conservative government created the National Economic Development Council (NEDC) to promote the competitive development of British industry. The NEDC was less a program than a statement of political concern abut the supply side of the British economy, and a suggestion that fiddling with the levels of demand management was not sufficient to assure continued economic prosperity. The formation of the NEDC at last put the problem of industrial decline on the already crowded agenda that had set political discourse since the war. Since the British still viewed themselves as a rich and powerful nation, the economic agenda had been focused on issues of distribution rather than problems of production. The recognition that one must develop policies to confront an industrial decline thus necessitated the reversal of some deeply ingrained perspectives.

One distributional debate concerned Britain's role in the world. It expressed itself in battles over defense budgets and about the place of sterling in the international economy. In 1956 the Suez crisis forced a reevaluation of Britain's pretense at remaining a global political power, but Britain's monetary role in the world economy was not settled for another ten years. The political parties shared responsibility for the continued refusal to devaluate, which they saw as a defense of sterling. It is hard to exaggerate the devastating consequences of the overvalued currency on British industry. Imports appeared more attractive and exports less so, the exact opposite of the situations in Germany and Japan, where the currency was systematically undervalued. Protected or semiprotected Commonwealth markets seemed to provide relief, but these politically created markets may have created longer-term difficulties. Though there are no systematic studies that demonstrate the effect on British firms of their long-time focus first on the colonies and then on the Commonwealth, the anecdotal evidence strongly suggests that the isolated markets distorted the product mix and production structures of British companies, in turn weakening their position in competitive markets. To return to the main point, an overvalued currency encouraged imports, made British firms' existing positions in foreign markets vulnerable to competition, and made new markets harder to enter. British industry, in essence, operated under a handicap of high prices—an interpretation consistent with the evidence that British exports lost market share in all markets and in all industries. The NEDC symbolized a change in domestic priorities, but the continuing commitment to sterling's reserve role in the international monetary system epitomized the enduring desire to maintain Britain's world role, even at the expense of its domestic economy. Sterling was finally devalued not by a political battle in which the interests defending the reserve role of sterling were defeated, but rather when the pound weakened so badly that no set of policies could maintain it as a secure trading and investment currency.

At home, the distributional debate was over shares of consumption. For example, an agreement to build the welfare state had been reached during the war, and the only debate concerned specific principles and purposes. Since the British took the wealth of the nation as a given, they paid little attention to the effects various welfare policies had on the system of production or on the possibilities for growth. Indeed, just as a debate on how to speed growth opened in the late 1950s, public expenditures, particularly spending for local services, began to grow

174

steadily as a percentage of national income. These expenditures grew until the mid-1970s,[10] and only then was there a broad debate over the consequences of public expenditure for investment and production. Although savings and investment in Britain are far lower than in the faster-growing economies, the political argument seldom focused directly on who should save and how investment might be expanded. There was amorphous support for redevelopment, but no real debate—let alone agreement—on the issue of who would lead and profit from growth.

For many years a steady increase in British living standards hid the importance of the production problems from popular view. For example, increased real income helped maintain labor peace through the postwar years. Since relatively slow growth (an economy expanding less rapidly than its trading partners) is not clearly and directly linked to unemployment or inflation, it does not provoke immediate public concerns. It is the immediate unemployment and inflation issues that motivate the public. Only in the late 1960s, when inflation and taxes slowed down the yearly increase in real take-home pay, did an era of labor unrest begin, and even then the political focus was still on distribution.[11] Prior policy commitments that restricted growth were not reconsidered. As a result, Macmillan's push for growth through investment was hemmed in by policies that allocated resources to England's international position or to domestic consumption.

Debates about power and position in the economy proved to be the real stumbling block to the revival of the British economy. Behind the often technical arguments lay the political problem of defining the privileges and positions of labor and management in modern Britain. Much more than the share of production taken by these different social groups was at stake: their influence in the making of government policy and their rights to internal self-governance also hung in the balance. The difficulty was that these political issues could not be settled. Whether in the political arena or in industry, a negotiated "settlement" of the distributional terms of economic change required cooperation between producer groups, but no basis for such cooperation could be established. Each side was simply too strong to be beaten or displaced and, consequently, neither side was ever strong enough to impose a radical shift of policy for an extended period.

It is not enough to argue that producer groups had a policy veto and that corporate paralysis ensued as a result.[12] Rather we need to know why a collaboration of producer partners did not emerge. For example, although Swedish politics are labor-dominated, a deal was struck which allowed private management considerable autonomy during a long period of political rule by labor. Even in Germany, where first the Christian Democrats and then the Social Democrats governed, a greater collaboration between labor and management was achieved. Two paralyzing fights prevented a similar collaboration in Britain: the fight to define the state's role in the economy, and the fight over labor's role in the factory and in politics. Let us first consider the labor issues briefly. It will set the stage for the central story in this discussion, the evolution of the relations between business and the state.

In Britain, distributional issues, which inevitably divide labor and management, completely obscured the common stake in industrial expansion and corporate growth which can sometimes unite them. Labor's interests, for reasons we shall explore, lay in preserving the industrial status quo rather than in collaborating to create a new industrial future.[13] In public-policy terms, the "labor" problem has been defined as one of controlling wages for overall stability and limiting strikes that disrupt production, despite the fact that by international standards Britain was a country with few strikes until the late 1960s.[14] Conservative and Labour governments alike pursued these goals—wage controls and limits on strikes—by seeking legislation to alter union structure and practices.

From the beginning, British labor has tried to prevent the state from intervening in collective bargaining, fearing that government would enter the fray on the side of management. To the unions, then, legislative efforts to provide a more orderly pattern of wage bargaining threatened to erode their market and political positions. A century of court decisions had declared that unions were neither criminal nor civil conspiracies.[15] These negative victories gave no explicit definition of either union rights or union responsibilities and, as a result, the British trade union movement had emerged as an essentially self-governing unit, independent of the state bureaucracy. The organizational strength of the unions, their labor market position, and their political power have combined in such a way that a government has few obvious and widely accepted constraints with which to compel union compliance.[16] Their organizational strength also limits the value of any inducements the government might offer for union cooperation. The Conservative party has tended toward confrontation with the unions and the Labour party has edged toward direct collaboration, but neither has been able to alter substantially the rules of play in the labor market.[17]

Since the war the Labour party did negotiate with the unions a series of income agreements—formal wage-restraint arrangements. These agreements were strong evidence that the labor leadership would make trade-offs between short-term gains for its members and long-term public policy goals, and also that it would deliver on its promises of wage restraint by members. The leadership had to fight off charges that it had "sold" the socialist birthright for a pot of capitalist porridge. The limits of negotiated wage policy should not be attributed to a particular ideological obtuseness by the leadership of the British labor movement.

Both parties tried to create labor bargaining arrangements that would establish a more predictable economic environment for companies by limiting the use of strikes in wage negotiations and by controlling wage drift. Less attention was paid to how to involve labor in a negotiation about the terms of industrial change. In short, stabilization objectives—wages and strikes—were given priority over adjustment goals. Ironically, the very failure to confront the burden labor would bear in the process of change provoked labor to take a militant stand against change. Nowhere was this pattern clearer than in the coal mines.[18] The mining industry shrank in the late 1950s and the 1960s with the rise of oil as a main source of energy. The labor force fell from over 700,000 to less than 390,000 between 1957 and 1972, while the number of pits dropped from more than 800 to less than 300. This decrease in employment was brought about in collaboration with the unions, as Lord Elberforce's report on the industry explained in 1972.[19] One element in that arrangement was the substitution of a national system of day wages for a patchwork system of locally established piecework rates. Despite the collaboration of labor in the reorientation of the industry, the relative position of the miners in the national wage scale fell from third to twelfth, declining from a position well above average to one somewhat below average. Certainly as employment in mining dropped, the pool of unemployed labor would be expected to weaken labor's ability to win wage gains. Yet this was a powerful union with the capacity to close down the country. It was seemingly rewarded for its collaboration in adjustment by a decline in the economic position of its remaining members. No union leadership could contain a mass movement under such conditions. The Tory government's choice, when faced with labor militancy, was to confront the unions and attempt to make their power the main issue in a political struggle. The decision cost them an election.

The problems of establishing a basis of collaboration between labor and management have undoubtedly been complicated by the internal organization of the union movement. British labor has not been organized or motivated to serve as a partner in cooperative industrial strategies and industry has not sought such collaboration. The basic story is widely known. Politically unified and nominally centralized, British labor has been fragmented at the level of plant and firm. Shop-steward power has represented both an ideological and a practical threat from below to the more conservative central leadership. According to David Soskice and Lloyd Ulman, shop-floor power has grown dramatically, as reflected in the more extensive plant-level bargaining and the increasing number of official as opposed to unofficial strikes.[20] (Official strikes are those called and authorized by the union, whereas unofficial strikes are those begun without its approval. Since national unions have often sanctioned strikes begun at the lower levels, precise numbers are often misleading.) Soskice and Ulman argue that a Conservative government unwittingly promoted this decentralization in the 1950s when it in essence agreed to a hands-off policy on internal union organization in exchange for wage restraint. The fragmentation of union authority and decentralization of power produced a two-tier bargaining system for wage deals: the national unions moderated their demands and the plant became the focus of bargaining. Shop-steward power was, in this view, a direct result of the withdrawal of national unions from the frays in which the real incomes of workers were decided. Inevitably this withdrawal reduced the ability of national unions to pursue policies of long-term industrial adjustment.

The labor movement is also ideologically divided between the mass unions (such as the miners), which have promoted radical socialist projects, and the unions of skilled workers (such as the operators and repairmen), which have been more narrowly concerned with the wage differential and bargaining rights. The status of "skilled" workers is embedded in rules and privileges that must be defended. The positions of power held by skilled workers in the factory have been threatened by efforts to rationalize production, particularly by efforts to restructure mass production. The British craft-union tradition, which emphasizes workplace rights and shop-floor power, provided a guide to such workers in resisting industrial change.[21] The emergence of white-collar unions that have no direct stake in industrial change and growth has further complicated this problem of internal division. Consequently, the leadership of the Trade Union Council cannot negotiate policies that satisfy the entire membership and is pressed to defend particular interests, sometimes those small groups of workers who are attempting to control events on the shop floor. It would be difficult for British unions to negotiate an aggressive industrial adjustment or redeployment policy that entailed job loss and required the acquiescence of shop stewards in specific plants. The seemingly endless labor troubles of British Leyland revealed the difficulties of such negotiations. In sum, the system of labor relations, the organization of the union movement, and the character of political conflict all press toward labor strategies that defend the industrial status quo.

178

Turning from the struggle to define labor's role to the fight to determine what the state should or could do to promote the competitive adjustment of British industry, we see that this conflict too raised distributional issues and obscured the common concern with an expanded productive apparatus. The British political agenda was changing in the late 1950s and the idea of a "mixed economy" took on a new meaning in that reordered agenda. It no longer referred simply to an economy in which there were both public and private enterprises but also pointed to government efforts to accomplish public purposes by intervening in private industry. The NEDC, as suggested, was a first halting step toward the interventionist policies that would draw the government into detailed interaction with the affairs of specific sectors and individual companies in the 1960s and 1970s. After more than a decade of the effort and despite shifting party fortunes and the fluctuating premises and purposes of state policy, mechanisms have been established which facilitate selective and specific intervention in markets and even in particular private companies. "The achievements in institution building," as Stephen Blank notes, "were not negligible."[22] In the end, we will argue later, these institutions began to change the structure of arrangements between government and industry, subtly altering the limits on policy. There was certainly no revolution in the relations between public and private sectors, however. Indeed, in the end the traditional ministries reasserted their authority.

The attempt to expand state capacities for economic administration to accommodate new policy goals became a central political struggle in the 1960s. Looking at the outcomes of the effort obscures the enduring political importance of the fight itself. A consensus did exist that the state should act to promote growth, but there was controversy about how the state could best achieve this goal. Industrial intervention, for which these institutions were intended, was one means of using the state as an instrument of economic promotion. The political effort to create interventionist instruments ultimately shattered the underlying consensus that government should act to promote industrial revitalization.

"Coalition analysis," Peter Gourevitch writes, "enables us to see how the process of getting a policy adopted affected its content. . . . What must be illuminated is how specific interests use various weapons . . . fighting through certain institutions in order to achieve their goals. Each step in this chain can affect the final result. We seek to explain policy through the content of group interests and the effort to form alliances among them."[23] The institutional innovations or administrative reforms required to accomplish particular policies become part of the chain of coalition building. A set of interests that generally agree on policy purposes may not be able to form an alliance if the implementation of the policy entails innovations and reforms that challenge the institutional and market positions of particular interests. When the implementation of policies necessitates administrative reforms that threaten the relative power of social groups, then these reforms cease to be mere technical adjustments: they affect the policies sought and the political alliances that can be formed.

We begin by describing the conflict about the state role in the economy which erupted between the Labour and Conservative parties in the late 1950s—the time when they first confronted the problems of industrial decline. We then explain how the financial system and the bureaucracy constrained the policies that could be implemented and influenced both the political interests of the producer groups and their political strategies. Next, we shall examine the politics of intervention in the 1960s and 1970s, struggles which, despite the intensity of party rhetoric, produced new and accepted relations between banks, business, and the state. Finally, we shall consider whether the process of reforming these institutions affected the central task of industrial adjustment.

Our goal is to understand how dealings between business and the state were affected when their relationships were caught up in battles between and within political parties. Though we shall sketch these political fights, our intent is not to recount party history or institutional development. The purpose, instead, is to demonstrate how a partisan political issue that sprang from a change in institutional structure interfered with the reestablishment of stable relations between producers and resulted in unstable and changing lines of policy. The story is important to our general argument because the system of finance helped structure this fight.

REESTABLISHING A NEOLIBERAL NORMALCY

Two polar policy choices—nationalization and arm's-length neoliberalism—have shaped the political debate about the state's role in the British economy. These choices represent an intellectual dichotomy that has been sustained by conflicts between and within the major political parties. Despite the massive expansion of the state's actual involvement in industrial life and the ongoing links between government and industry which that expansion entailed, the debate is still argued in terms of a choice between opposites. The term "mixed economy" has been understood as connoting an economy that contains both public and private ownership—pressing forward the question of where the boundary ought to be drawn and underplaying the question of what constitutes appropriate government involvement with firms of either the private or the public sector.

The debate within each party has been subtler than these simple categories, or even the policy debate between the parties, would suggest. When in power the leadership of each party evolved centrist positions that often diverged from its official policy proposals and campaign rhetoric.[24] Once it returned to the opposition, however, its critique of its rival and its statement of platform again tended to be dominated by ideological considerations. In short, the diehards of the party in opposition clung to a rhetoric that sustained the polarization of the policy debate, whereas the leaders of the party in power tended to take a more pragmatic approach, adopting policies that represented a middle road between ideological extremes.[25] Throughout this debate, the relative positions of labor and business, both in politics and in the market, were as much at issue as were the specifics of policy. Nationalization and neoliberalism were code words for different political victories. The resulting policy framework made it harder to debate two key realities: the expanded role of the state in the economy and the importance of producer associations in the routine of government policy and corporate strategy. Despite the rhetorical division, the institutional framework of a neoliberal economy had been reestablished by the mid-1950s as the matrix of economic life.

The debate over economic decline was structured by the particular configuration of market operation and political position which this matrix yielded. After the war, policy reinforced an arm's-length relation between government and the private sector. These hands-off relations were replicated in many ways in the newly expanded public sector. The possibilities of constructing a positive role for the state in industrial development were barred by the institutional arrangements in the economy as much as they were obscured by political rhetoric. The key arrangements that reasserted this neoliberal normalcy were neither natural features of national character nor a continuation of political settlements made during the previous century of industrial development. They were a political creation achieved in the immediate postwar years.

Labour in Power

Nationalization and planning were the central components of Labour's postwar policy for industry. The party project involved a commitment to using the country's resources in the best interests of the nation (planning), and to assuring community control through the public ownership of the most important firms (nationalization).[26] The difficulty of translating this general goal into concrete policy proved to lie in the forms taken by planning and nationalization. Planning rested on administered resource allocation rather than on the manipulation of markets through prices or credit allocation.[27] As a result, the bureaucrat was set against the marketplace players rather than being allowed to pursue his own objectives as a player in the market. Nationalization became an end in itself, one that could be implemented without giving careful thought to how socialized enterprise could serve as an instrument of policy.[28] The result was an arm's-length arrangement in the public sector which left bureaucrats and public managers on opposite sides of a divide. Despite all the splits, debates, and changes of direction within the party, when abrupt elimination of administrative resource allocation (the bonfire of government controls as it was called then) ended the period of physical planning and the original schedule of nationalization was completed, the basic relationships of power and control in the economy remained unchanged.[29] The basic laissez-faire, arm's-length arrangements in the marketplace had not been altered. This outcome set the terms for the struggles over the state's role in the economy which were to follow. Let us look more closely first at planning and then at nationalization.

The problem facing the Labour government that took power after the war was to identify the characteristics of capitalism and decide how to replace them. All economies require coordination and coercion to operate; activities undertaken by one group must be linked to those of other groups and some means must be found to compel individuals to accept outcomes and activities they might not choose voluntarily. Markets and administration, both of which involve the negotiation and side payment that accompany any deal, may be seen as alternative means of accomplishing these two tasks. Indeed, the blend of pricing, administration, and bargaining is different for all economies. Planning implied finding a substitute for prices, which imply profits, as a means of allocating resources.[30] To the labor left, profits suggested exploitation; at the very least they represented capital's appropriation of a share of the product. The chain of implication that tied prices to profits to exploitation is long, but planning was seen as a socialist alternative to the class-based exploitation thought to be inherent in market capitalism.

The Labour government's peacetime planning was done through the machinery that the senior Labour leaders had helped to establish as members of the wartime coalition.[31] Two elements of the wartime relations between business and government proved important for later developments. First, no planning commission was established to set industrial priorities and objectives, principally because there were none. Such clear policy objectives as there were existed at a general, macroeconomic level. Morrison—a force in the cabinet, the Labour party, and the economic bureaucracy, as well as a principal architect of policy—wrote that the problem in the postwar years was not the lack of priorities but the conflicts between them. In the end, however, not resolving conflicts between priorities has the same effect as not setting priorities in the first place. When planning becomes administrative co-ordination, all the conflicting purposes of the society are expressed through the bureaucratic rivalries within the government.[32] Planning, as a cabinet activity, was thus openly political, with few means to make private executive choices or to shelter any long-term priorities from shifts in party fortunes. As a result, overall responsibility for the management of the economy was placed back in the Treasury.[33]

Second, planning was to a large extent a restrictive administrative allocation system for distributing scarce resources in the period of dislocation after the war. The period of most direct government controls was 1945–1947; in the period from 1947 until the Conservatives took power, the controls were much more limited. The inconveniences of rationing were never justified by some general Labour party strategy for the nation or the economy. Indeed, controls were in large measure implemented by businessmen from the sectors being administered.[34] This meant that withdrawal of business support could paralyze the planning system. As a result policymaking was immediately vulnerable to the decisions of businessmen, an odd position for a Labour government to find itself in. As Jacques Leurez observes, many thought that the main danger of wartime planning was not bureaucratic domination of society, but corporatism, the ceding of state functions to private groups.[35] When business support was withdrawn, the Labour government had no technical apparatus with which to sustain planning. Still, the shift from direct control was a victory for the Keynesian theory of the Labour party's "managers" over the socialist ideals of the Labour left. That victory smoothed the way for the Conservatives to establish a consensus in favor of demand-management policies.

As an alternative to administrative planning, the British might have turned the financial system to the ends of planners, allocating credit as a means of distributing resources, and created a trained cadre of bureaucrats prepared to use these instruments. Indeed, the French planners had turned to credit allocation precisely to avoid being trapped in existing bureaucratic commitments and trade-association arrangements. Instead, in Britain the prewar private banking system was left essentially intact and the administrative service essentially unreformed. The Bank of England was nationalized, but its senior leadership remained untouched.[36] A loan fund of 50 million pounds was established, but it was not part of the basic apparatus of the economic ministries. Actually, two parapublic financial institutions—the Industrial and Commercial Finance Corporation (ICFC), intended to meet the financial needs of small businessmen, and the Finance Corporation for Industry (FCI), intended to facilitate the reconstruction or reorganization of large and medium-sized firms—had been established by the Conservative government in 1945. Though Labour retained these financial institutions, it did nothing to bring them under direct ministerial control or to use them as instruments of policy. In the same period, a National Investment Council, which was composed of the leaders of the major financial institutions, including the chairman of the stock exchange and the governor of the Bank of England, was established but never became an instrument of policy. The government's basic financial concern was with the aggregate of investment, although to some extent it manipulated public-sector investment in order to influence private-sector allocation decisions. The decision to use Marshall Plan funds to repay the public debt, rather than to allocate them among preferred industrial objectives as the French did, has often been cited as evidence that the postwar Labour leadership basically wanted to reestablish the preexisting order as they imagined it.

The Labour government, then, adopted planning but eschewed one of the most powerful instruments of planning: credit allocation through the financial system. We are concerned here not with the economic merits of this technical decision but with the political reasons for ignoring the policy option. Labour was traditionally hostile to the financial sector (and to financiers) and unfamiliar with its operations. This hostility to financial policy instruments diminished in the party center and on the right during the period in which they held power, but the Labour government's leaders still lacked expertise in matters of finance and those civil servants who would serve Labour ministers lacked the experience with finance needed to manipulate the system. The basic questions—whom to appoint, what to ask them to do, and how to control their activities—must have seemed formidable obstacles to any policy of planning through the control of finance. At the same time, Labour must have seen the system of wartime administrative controls already in place as a means of outflanking "enemy" territory—the City of London—and thereby avoiding the need to control it.

Finally, the new Labour government probably lacked the power to enforce any decisions to nationalize or reorient the banking system. A capital strike or an international flight from sterling could have caused crippling problems in the war-strained economy. There was little reason for the government to assume it could muster support for broad radical reform, particularly because the party's leaders, who sat to the right of their backbench supporters, would not be apt to commit themselves to such a cause. The United States, with which Britain was negotiating postwar loan agreements, would also have opposed any assault on the bastions of private power. The U.S. government had already expressed concern at the extent of social spending and the size of possible budget deficits, and it applied strict conditions to its 1946 loan as well as to Marshall Plan funds. Indeed, the American connection may have helped to consolidate the Morrisonians' victory over the left, much as the IMF later helped Denis Healey and James Callaghan in their battle against Wedgewood Benn in 1976–1977.[37] These tactical considerations fitted well with the wartime experience, which had seen Labour's general policy line move from outright hostility to capitalism toward an acceptance of class cooperation. As a result, the British lost a platform of intervention and a means of redefining priorities and claiming power which they would have gained by drawing finance to the side of rapid growth—lost them, one might argue, because no one sought to pursue these new priorities with sufficient energy.

Nationalization was the second component of Labour's postwar policy for industry. Particularly in market economies, nationalization does not eliminate the problems inherent to government-company relations, but simply changes the terms in which that relationship is expressed. The negotiating positions of the two parties shift when the state bureaucracy and the government executive obtain a legitimate and permanent stake in corporate affairs, but the negotiations themselves continue.

Once the right to interfere has been established, the procedures and purposes of intervention become the central issues. During periods of crisis both public and private companies will turn to the government for assistance, but during routine periods both will attempt to preserve their autonomy and operate without interference. The choices taken by public companies operating in market economies therefore directly reflect market conditions. Such companies also confront a tension between pursuing commercial objectives, in which efficiency and effectiveness might be measured by profits, and pursuing social objectives, in which ordinary commercial criteria are relaxed and the market penalties for accommodating social purposes are made good from the public purse. If the public company pursues purely commercial objectives, it may not differ in any substantial way from a private one. If it pursues only social purposes, its efficiency may suffer or its administration may become the political instrument of a bureaucrat or politician. Moreover, its dependence on the public purse limits its management autonomy. When private firms are nationalized, the political executive must decide what administrative arrangements should be made to monitor public companies and press them into the service of government objectives. Since the purposes for the public sector were not defined when Labour held power after the war, the result during the years of Labour opposition was a fight within the party about whether public ownership should remain a part of party doctrine.[38]

By reproducing in the public sector the arm's-length arrangements that already existed in the private sector, the first wave of nationalization essentially avoided this problem of how to control public companies. Since Tory opposition to the first nationalizations was limited, the form of nationalization became the primary issue. The first industries to be nationalized—fuel, power, and transport—were all losing money, so opposition to their takeover was limited. What purposes these reorganized industries should serve, however, was a question that went unanswered. There was a notion that public purposes would at least in part replace private profits as the guides to company behavior, but little more was said.

The Morrisonian notion of the public corporation, expressed as a theory by William Robson,[39] was founded on the distinction between policy and management. Morrison, who as a minister in the Attlee government had the opportunity to implement on a wide scale what he had tried in the case of London transport, wrote that "the management of these industries can broadly be relied upon to get on with its work . . . the minister can let the people in charge carry on the work to be done."[40] He believed that the key was to choose the right man and then let him manage.[41] Unfortunately, the line between formulation and implementation of policy is a misleading one. Without a detailed understanding of the choices a corporation must make, the options it confronts in the market, and the range of means for responding, the policymaker cannot really determine his objectives or assess when one objective must be set aside in the interests of another. Lacking any real understanding of the situation, the policymaker will find his choices defined by others.

In order to develop a sound conception of their public firm's position in the market, ministers and bureaucrats require a system of reporting, monitoring, and evaluating performance and policy. The state's objectives are different from those of the corporation or the conglomerate but many of the administrative problems are the same. The state must develop means to become a player in the market, whether the companies it confronts are public or private. Though instruments for control and intervention in public enterprise have evolved in Britain, they did not exist in the first years after the war.[42] Since the initial nationalizations were not accompanied by shifts in administrative organization, they could not arm the state bureaucracy with the instruments it needed to intervene in industrial life. Even now, the initial Morrisonian arm's-length nationalizations haunt government efforts to control public companies.[43]

Conservative Neoliberalism

Conservatives returned to power in 1951 advocating the restoration of "free enterprise" while accepting the welfare state.[44] The term "butskellism" refers to the continuity in policy between Richard Butler, the Conservative chancellor of the exchequer, and Hugh Gaitskell, his Labour predecessor. Indeed, both men were Keynesians in their approach to macro-policy. The differences between the two parties were at the micro-level of sectoral and industrial policy. The Conservatives emphasized policies that reinforced the liberal arm's-length relation between business and the state.[45] Conservative policies created a distance between business and the state, and between finance and industry, leaving each component relatively autonomous. Concretely, Conservative policies meant abolishing the remaining administrative controls (particularly food rationing), rejecting planning that had become associated with the use of these direct controls, and denationalizing the steel industry. For the next decade economic policy debates focused on demand management.

The Conservative reassertion of neoliberal policies spiced with demand management was not simply a continuation of an enduring Conservative stance, but rather the result of an ongoing battle inside the party. In fact, many of the issues that arose in the late 1940s had already been debated by the Conservatives in the early 1920s. Working them out once more, this time in opposition to a Labour government, the Conservatives emerged with a set of policies which broke with the interventionist formula that had been brewing in the party during the interwar years.

Despite the free-trade and free-market ideology that had characterized British industrial preeminence in the last part of the nineteenth century, the downturn in the traditional export sectors after the First World War and during the Depression brought to Britain the same trend toward protection, cartelization, and rationalization (the elimination of excess capacity and the introduction of more efficient production) which appeared in other advanced countries. In the British case protection was linked with the idea of "imperial preference." Despite the fact that the Commonwealth provided only a quarter of British foreign trade, policymakers looked to a trade system in which United Kingdom industry exchanged manufactures for Commonwealth raw materials and foodstuffs.

During these years of depression the British government acted to organize trade and to assist export industries in their struggle to remain competitive (or at least alive). Though the burgeoning new industries grew on their own, there were subsidy programs for such sectors as shipbuilding—programs that were supplemented by overt intervention to direct the rationalization of production. In the case of the cotton textile sector, the then-private Bank of England took the initiative to reduce production by purchasing and scrapping surplus capacity. The government also helped industries to conclude international agreements that would control excess supply. Some industrialists supported these programs through a lobby called the Industrial Reorganization Committee.[46] They proposed that if a majority in the industry supported a scheme, the state ought to compel the minority to accept it. This proposition's most prominent supporter was Harold Macmillan, who pushed a resolution backing the program through the Conservative Party Conference in 1934.[47] Small producers and those who feared they would be displaced by the politically managed trimming of industry opposed this trend toward interventionism. Nigel Harris writes that the pressures from "free enterprise and from the 'reorganizers' found the government uneasily balanced between."[48] Yet through the 1930s the Conservative government seemed to lean increasingly toward intervention.

This party struggle was reproduced inside the major trade associations, where it took the form of a conflict between small and medium-sized companies. Tendencies toward government-led industrial reorganization were reinforced during the war, and this gave an edge to the medium-sized firms that were pressing for closer ties with government. The government was dependent on the trade associations to wage the war and the industrialists were dependent on government for the authority to police their industries. By the middle of the war some industrialists had in fact concluded that a politically managed industrial hierarchy would be the basis of the postwar economy.

The postwar Conservative espousal of free-market liberalism was, then, not an inevitable outcome of preexisting commitments to maintaining a separation of state and society. There existed an alternative economic strategy, one that was justified by the paternalistic rhetoric already fixed in conservative tradition. The shift toward neoliberalism took place between 1947 and 1949. If Jean Monnet had been the model for the Tories in 1947, Ludwig Erhard replaced him in 1949.[49] When the Conservatives returned to power they were more committed to liberal doctrine than at anytime since the 1920s, even though many of the original supporters of state intervention had now held cabinet office. The shift poses few puzzles. Labour had adopted the wartime planning system as its peacetime policy, leaving the Conservatives a choice: they could either attack the principle or the practice of planning. The public's growing opposition to direct controls suggested a popular predisposition to reject the system itself. The return to prosperity facilitated by the international expansion, the Korean War boom, and the long drop in the relative prices of commodities entrenched the liberal doctrine in conservative politics. The Conservatives had become economic liberals.

In sum, the separation of the state from the affairs of economic society was not a long-standing structural principle of the British political economic system but a consequence of recent political conflict. The failed Labour reforms and the Conservative conversion to economic liberalism laid the foundations of the postwar liberal economy—the system that would shape the political fight about how to cope with the problem of industrial decline.

THE BRITISH FINANCIAL SYSTEM AND THE STRUCTURAL BASIS OF NEOLIBERALISM

The postwar political choices reinforced the noninterventionist character of the British bureaucracy and financial system. The task here is to identify the market characteristics of the financial system and the organizational characteristics of the bureaucracy which proved to be obstacles to the introduction of interventionist policies. The movement toward state support for industrial rejuvenation was ambushed at the start by the need to make substantial rearrangements of the mechanisms for conducting business; until this task was completed, political leaders lacked the weapons needed to mount a political offensive to reorient the economy.

The Financial System

The British financial system grew up financing commerce and eventually became the self-governing center of the international monetary system. No system of long-term finance to promote industrial growth was established, because as Alexander Gerschenkron has contended, none was needed in this first and unique case of industrialization.[50] The result was a certain distance, a lack of direct involvement, between industry and finance on the one hand, and a lack of detailed government involvement in the affairs of finance and in the allocation of industrial credit on the other. Thus, when an interventionist policy thrust reemerged at the end of the 1950s, the financial system offered few natural handholds to those trying to implement an industrial policy.

The question here is what structural features produced this outcome—the distance and lack of involvement between finance, industry, and government. We must distinguish structural features—characteristic rules, procedures, and roles of the different institutions that are forced by the organization of the financial markets—from procedures that stem from the attitudes of bankers about "appropriate" behavior. Of course, individual attitudes about how to behave are entangled in the structure of choices, but the emphasis here is on the pattern of choices created by institutional and market arrangements. Let us first consider the relations between finance and industry.

The British financial system evokes the image of a complex and competitive market. Large numbers of investors and savers meet in the marketplace, where no small group of institutions can dominate. "London's position as a leading financial center has been based on the multiplicity and specialization of the financial intermediaries operating there."[51] Several of the markets, particularly the retail banking market, are in effect oligopolies. Yet in Britain, power in one financial market, such as bank lending, does not translate into power in other markets, such as the security or money markets. The result is that businesses seeking funds do not face a single set of capital suppliers who can exert power in their affairs. This situation contrasts sharply with the French system, in which lending relationships and bank stockholdings tend to establish enduring institutional ties between finance and industry. The British financial system can be characterized by its arm's-length relations, in which investors are buying financial assets for their portfolios.[52]

Several characteristics reveal the nature of the British system. First, the securities markets and investing institutions are at the heart of the system and are vastly more important than they are in France. One measure of the relative importance of the securities markets is the ratio of domestic securities to the Gross Domestic Product (GDP). Table 4.1 illustrates the contrast as of 1975. The securities markets, once the domain of individual investors, are increasingly dominated by pension funds, insurance companies, and unit trusts. Between 1963 and 1980

Table 4.1. Securities markets in France and the United Kingdom, end 1975

Country	Bonds as percent of GDP	Equities as percent of GDP
United Kingdom	43	41
France	16	11

SOURCE: Figures taken from Appendixes 1A to 9A of Dimitri Vittas, ed., *Banking Systems Abroad* (London, Inter-Bank Research Organisation, 1978).

the portion of securities held by individuals dropped from 54 to 37 percent, and by the year 2000 institutions are expected to expand their holdings to between 70 and 85 percent of the value of United Kingdom equities.[53] A few institutions holding major corporate stocks suddenly find themselves with the influence to affect both company policies and the resolution of industrial crises. British nonbank financial institutions nevertheless differ in major respects from the French *banques d'affaires* and the German general all-purpose banks, which also have large equity holdings. The newly powerful British institutions are accustomed to making arm's-length judgments about future stock prices; they do not have the expertise or inclination to become industrial counselors or advisers. So long as power in the form of equity is diffused among a restricted set of large financial institutions, no one institution will be dominant in any single company. Collectively they have power, and in most instances they must act collectively in order to exercise that power. The power of large institutions and banks in the British market thus remains more fragmented than it is on the Continent, although the changes now taking place may one day permit closer ties between finance and industry. The importance of these institutions can be seen in Table 4.2.

Despite concentration in the securities markets, the dominant investors in the securities markets do not control access to those markets, nor do they make loans. Conversely, the commercial banks do not invest in the securities markets. Corporate access to these markets is arranged by brokers, such as the merchant banks. Buyers of securities, arrangers of access to securities, and lenders represent three distinct groups. To oversimplify, savings institutions (such as insurance company pension funds) and investment companies, as well as individuals, buy securities. Merchant banks arrange the offerings and commercial banks lend the money for short-term needs. Financial institutions specialize in specific market activities.

Table 4.2. Share of investing institutions in liabilities and claims with the non-financial sector, end 1975 (percent)

Country	Liabilities	Claims
Germany	20.0	13.0
France	11.3	9.3
Italy	6.9	2.6
Japan	16.0	15.0
United States	32.3	31.2
United Kingdom	39.5	24.4

NOTE: Liabilities represent deposits; claims indicate loans.

SOURCE: Dimitri Vittas, ed., *Banking Systems Abroad* (London, Inter-Bank Research Organisation, 1978), p. 25.

Close relations between banks and firms are based on either long-term loans or shareholdings. Neither of these mechanisms ties British commercial banks to their clients. They are not substantial investors in corporate equity. When lending to companies, they have traditionally taken narrower and more short-term views of their clients than have their counterparts in other advanced countries.[54] The short-term view permits these banks to function without a detailed understanding of company situations or an ongoing concern with industrial management. The British banking system was never organized to finance industrial development and the old preference for short-term, arm's-length lending continues.[55] In the 1950s the president of the Institute of Bankers, who was also the vice-chairman of one of the major banks, contended that long-term lending was not the proper business of banks; their proper function was short-term lending. Despite an expansion of medium-term lending by British banks, only 15 to 20 percent of their loans to industry are term loans—that is, extended for more than one year.[56] In Germany and France, the figures are closer to 60 percent. Happily the differences are dramatic, because problems of definition and measurement mean that precise numbers are of dubious usefulness. One difficulty in making such comparisons is that many British short-term loans really amount to a renewable facility that creates long-term loans at short-term rates. These overdraft facilities may well provide medium-term money, but they maintain the more limited type of bank-company relations called for by short-term loans. The banks have provided term loans during periods of industrial crisis in the 1970s, but this policy was not part of their longer-term strategy and certainly was not a central characteristic of British industrial finance in the years we are considering. In all such studies, however, the numbers follow a consistent direction that suggests a bias toward short-term financing and away from longer-term industrial finance.[57]

A short-term bias in company loans is sometimes justified by the banks' need to be prudent in assuring a proper balance between short-term and long-term funds. The British banks, however, have not made any attempt to raise long-term money in the bond market, as a strategy of medium-term industrial finance would require. Larger British companies themselves have direct access to the bond market for long-term debt finance. Smaller firms are generally agreed to lack reliable sources of medium-term capital and plausibly could benefit from innovative financing arrangements. Comparative studies show that German banks borrow money in the bond market which they then lend to companies, and that French banks lend on to industry on the basis of short-term deposits.[58] The reason is not that German and French bankers are smarter and better risk-takers than British bankers, but that the structure of the financial systems constrains banks differently in each of the three countries.

The financial structure of British companies is also a measure of the nature of bank lending. British firms have not been heavily dependent on long-term debt that would allow outside financial influence in their affairs.[59] They have turned to bank credit during crises, both in the aftermath of the first oil price hikes and more recently during a deepening recession, but these cases and others like them are viewed as exceptions. Financial gearing is a measure of the ratio of equity to debt in nonfinancial companies. The ratio suggests dependence on outside debt finance but does not distinguish dependence on bank loans, which is an institutional relation, from bond indebtedness, which is not. Again, precise numbers prove little because so much in the ratios turns on accounting practice, which varies between countries. Such ratios have historically been lower in Britain than on the European continent or in Japan, however. The national ratio of internal funding and equity to fixed investment suggests the same thing. British companies finance expansion from savings and the sale of equity, not from credit.[60] In fact, German, Japanese, and French firms invest more than they save from profits and get the rest of their funds from borrowing.[61]

With an elaborate stock and bond market available for long-term financing in England, a prima facie case can be made that British bank lending ought to limit itself to short-term needs. The proper comparison for testing the notion that British banks have a peculiarly short-term bias is the banking system in the United States, whose structure is closer to that of the British system. In the United States the multiple functions of finance have been divided into separate institutions, which are coordinated by markets rather than combined into single institutions and coordinated by administrators. The New York commercial banks—the center of American banking activity—make 23 percent of their loans to business in the form of term advances; if the figures are meaningful, they suggest a marginally higher level of long-term lending in the United States than in Britain.[62] The American and British cases together suggest that in an economy with a strong securities market, the level of term lending by banks to nonfinancial firms will be lower than it is in countries that have weak securities markets. This suggests that the British relation between finance and industry is the product of a type of financial system, and that British banking attitudes, though more conservative and less innovative than American views, derive from that structure.

What matters here is that the traditional British banking view and the structure on which it rests affect the way the bank deals with its clients, putting distance between finance and industry. The British Treasury argued this position in hearings before the Committee to Review the Functioning of Financial Institutions headed by Harold Wilson in 1977:

> The government has the impression that in the U.K. there has been a tendency for financial institutions to maintain an arm's-length relationship with clients to a greater extent than in other countries. It can be argued that they would be better placed to meet industry's needs for capital effectively if their relations were closer and their understanding greater. . . . More generally, neither the institutions nor banks have sought on any scale to stimulate management performance by intervening in the companies' affairs, given the need for expertise and management time which would be involved.[63]

When making medium- or long-term loans, banks must assess a company's overall competitive position in its industry, looking beyond its short-term ability to repay a loan. Long-term loans are not self-liquidating, that is, they do not depend on the farmer's repaying the costs of planting when his crop goes to market or on an importer's repaying his borrowing as he sells off the stock he has purchased. The Association of American Banks in London also testified before the Wilson Committee. It made a distinction between a liquidation approach and the going-concern approach.[64] And while acknowledging that all banks use some elements of both approaches to evaluate the creditworthiness of borrowers, the committee concluded that the "former is the traditional basis of overdraft lending in U.K. clearing banks [deposit banks like our Bank of America] while the latter is the method preferred by the American banks, who lend mainly on a term basis."[65] The contrast made by the American banks is certainly self-serving, but it underlines the nature of British banking.

In sum, the distinction between long- and short-term lending is of great importance to the relations between finance and industry. Long-term loans must be repaid from future profits and therefore, as a minimum, the bank must make an assessment of the company's competitive future. Short-term loans can simply be secured against existing company assets. Long-term lending, to caricature the issue, is a matter for investment banks; short-term lending against secured assets is a matter for the pawnbroker. Different financial structures reflecting distinct origins may resolve similar problems in unique ways. The emphasis on short-term lending is not necessarily an economic flaw in the British financial system, but it does have political consequences. If companies are not dependent on outside funding, the financial system has no levers with which to influence them. The British financial system has evolved rapidly in the last two decades, but the changes have not altered the compartmentalization of financial and industrial worlds. The banking system has been an oligopoly and concentration in the purely British banking community increased. Mergers decreased the number of major British banks from eleven to four. At the same time, the American banks operating in England have grown to rival their British hosts in size and importance. Their rapid expansion was initially made in order to follow American companies abroad and to escape American regulation. Though the American banks have not sought to establish a chain of branches competing for deposits but have competed only for a portion of business, their banking practices have inevitably begun to seep into British banks. A change in banking and money supply regulations in 1971 also encouraged bank competition, further modernizing the traditional British practices.[66]

Another way of capturing the essence of the British system, and of identifying the kinds of reforms which would be necessary if the government were to use financial institutions or the financial system to help conduct industrial interventions, is to look at the banks themselves. The British merchant banks, to choose one example, have their homologues in the continental *banques d'affaires* and the American investment banks.[67] All three types are turned toward the long-term problems of companies, but their differences represent three different national relationships between industry and finance. The British merchant banks are at their core banks to finance commerce; they emerged in the last century as a place where for a fee a bill of exchange could be guaranteed and thus used to provide operating funds to a company. The American investment banks have traditionally provided advice and assistance to companies looking for money rather than supplying the required funds themselves. The French *banques d'affaires*, by contrast, are industrial banks concerned with the business of industrial companies; they take even more direct interests in firms by underwriting in their own names (or that of others for whom they act) a part of the capital issues of industrial companies.

Let us imagine three concentric circles. In the first circle are the American investment banks, which perform the two functions shared by all long-term banks: giving advice and assistance in placing surplus corporate funds and in obtaining additional funds when necessary; and structuring the overall financial position of a company and advising it in its negotiations with other companies, for example, during mergers or takeover. American investment banks are forbidden by law to engage in commercial bank credit operations, whereas important tasks such as raising capital for the private sector by equity issues are reserved to them. In the second circle are the British merchant banks, which are investment banks that also have a certain limited capacity to lend money and take deposits. Their depositors are for the most part large companies and a few wealthy individuals, in contrast to the mixture of large and small clients that deal with the commercial banks. This limited clientele means, however, that the merchant banks have a smaller amount of money to lend from their own deposits than do the commercial banks. Consequently they must finance credit operations with funds drawn from more expensive wholesale markets (such as domestic money markets and internal markets like the Eurocurrency market)—markets that are also available to their larger competitors. This situation places the merchant banks at a competitive disadvantage. In the third circle we find the *banque d'affaires*, a merchant bank that also manages an industrial portfolio. This merging of the activities of a bank and a holding company gives it a captive clientele for its services and a captive source of deposits. But the activities of holding company and merchant bank are more closely tied together than that. "A *banque d'affaires* is a bank that, in light of the restructuring of the national economy or the international economy, uses together its varied instruments that range from its own credits and the issues of stocks or bonds to actually taking a share in the capital in the companies."[68] Investing its own funds is seen as an act of confidence that can attract more outside money. During periods of crisis this can permit the bank to reorganize companies without a liquidation of assets. This is not to say that the banks directly manage companies, but rather that they supervise company interests and help guide them. These banks become directly involved in industrial reorganization. The former president of one such bank remarked that: "*To change the structure* [of companies and industry], *it is necessary oftentimes to enter into the structures.*"

The contrast between the *banques d'affaires* and the merchant banks is evident: "It is a characteristic of most merchant banks, especially British ones, that they flourish without much intervention in management and with no real machinery for investigating the performance of firms."[69] Obviously, the differences in the three types of financial systems are embedded in the process of industrialization. The *banque d'affaires* is the clear counterpart of the "player" or developmental state, whereas the merchant bank and the investment bank reflect a situation in which government has an arm's-length relation to the economy. Since the securities market and retained earnings are thought to provide long-term money and the banks are considered the proper source of short-term funding, industry and finance are left to occupy independent spheres.

Having sketched the nature of relations between finance and industry in Britain, let us examine the relation between the British government and the financial system. To begin with, the British government does not control channels of borrowing and lending which would facilitate the selective manipulation of credit allocation by the political executive. Handles available in other countries, particularly the parapublic banking institutions that are important in France, simply do not exist in England.[70] The public sector collects a very small percentage of the national savings; the recently established postal savings system, for example, represents less than one-tenth of 1 percent of national savings.[71] More important, such public institutions are rivals to the highly developed private banking system. Indeed, such institutions as Finance Corporation for Industry, Industrial and Commercial Finance Company, and Equity Capital for Industry were established as the Bank of England's response to outside pressure and were intended to preclude more extensive government intervention. The FCI and ICFC were formed in 1945 and the ECI was established in 1975. These financial institutions (FCI, ICFC, and ECI) are in fact collectively owned by the private financial institutions and the Bank of England.[72] The National Loans Board, which administers lending to nationalized companies, is an administrative rather than decision-making body. The limited significance of these long-term credit institutions is indicated by their share in the claims and liabilities of financial institutions with the nonfinance sector.[73]

When the British government does intervene in the financial markets, it generally acts through reserve requirements or open market operations, both of which preserve the market character of the system. That is, it affects the volume of bank lending either by imposing requirements on reserves the banks must hold or by buying or selling government issues in the market. These sales increase or decrease the liquidity in the system. The central bank announces the direction it expects interest rates to move and in anticipation other financial institutions act on those announcements. It is the Bank of England's ability to affect market conditions in ways that will move prices (interest rates) in the directions it chooses which gives those announcements such force.[74] When the bank does act, it does so through the discount market, which consists of a set of institutions specialized in buying, selling, and holding Treasury and commercial bills. These banks mobilize short-term funds that would otherwise stand unused and make them available to the government and to other banks. The discount market helps keep the banking system and the government as a whole in balance; it also acts as a buffer between the Bank of England and the commercial banks. Commercial banks buy and sell in the money market, dealing with the discount houses which in turn deal directly with the central bank.

Since 1971 the British have moved even further toward pure market mechanisms, attempting to discard the limited quantitative restrictions on bank lending imposed in the 1960s. The 1971 Competition and Credit Control Act was a forceful move toward arm's-length management of the system. Importantly, quantitative controls were never viewed as a central component of the system tied to government-imposed prices, but were considered an unfortunate deviation from market principles.

Many of the arrangements in the British system of monetary management result from an emphasis on managing the government debt, which was the fundamental task of the central bank from the end of the war until late in the 1970s. The *Radcliffe Report* of 1959 (the major government review of the financial system) considered debt management to be the bank's fundamental task.[75] This view implied that controlling the structure of interest rates was the central object of policy, since interest rates dictated the cost of debt. The *Radcliffe Report* was very explicit: "The authorities . . . have to regard the structure of interest rates *rather than the supply of money* as the centerpiece of the monetary mechanism. This does not mean that the supply of money is unimportant, but that its control is incidental to interest rate policy" (italics mine).[76] This emphasis meant, as Catherine Hill argues, that aggregate demand management was dominated by fiscal policy, because monetary policy was linked to financing public debt.[77] *Government could not effectively manipulate interest rates for industrial development because it was already manipulating them for purposes of financing the debt.* Jacques Melitz raises this practice to a principle, contending that in those countries with massive government debt, such as the United States and Britain, the problem of financing this debt becomes the focus of government financial intervention.[78] Recent Thatcherite reforms and an emphasis on government policy simply reaffirm the arm's-length principles. The money-supply aggregate becomes the dependent variable and interest rates are simply a result of market demand for money. Government debt management remains the crucial constraint.

Despite the market organization of government intervention, a series of qualitative interventions has taken place in the form of Bank of England directives about the proper composition of lending. Two aspects of these qualitative controls are important to us. First, "the directives do not specify a curtailment of the business of any particular bank or any particular customer, but only the whole of a class of business. A directive to [a bank] to restrict lending to Imperial Chemical industries would be considered most improper."[79] There is a "great reluctance to interfere in the business relationship between individual financial institutions and individual customers."[80] In other words, these interventions do not approach those of the French or Japanese in terms of administrative control or specificity. Second, while some of the directives to maintain lending to industry were linked to exemptions from ceilings on lending, most were aimed at restricting consumer spending.[81] These qualitative restrictions are enforced more by moral suasion than by direct administration. In fact, they amount to nothing more than an ad hoc resolution of temporary conflicts between interest-rate policy and particular economic needs. They are not envisioned as a means of conducting industry policy or organizing the financial markets.

The government executive's place in the financial system can be understood by looking at the Bank of England itself. The bank's existing responsibilities in that traditional system create both a technical and a political barrier against its being transformed into an instrument of government industrial intervention.

First, the bank has been responsible for managing Britain's international monetary position. At one time, of course, that role made it the central regulator of the international monetary system and a defender of the role of sterling as a reserve currency in international trade. The bank advocated maintaining a high value for sterling in terms of gold and supported the domestic economic policies that this position implied. Much has been written about how this stance led to over-valued British goods in international markets and provoked a series of domestic restrictions that took the heart out of any boom.[82] The collapse of sterling's value and the emergence of the Eurocurrency markets have relieved that particular tension between domestic and international goals. By dealing in everyone else's currency, London has been able to remain a preeminent financial entrepot, although the rise of the Eurocurrency system has made the British economy more vulnerable to outside events.[83] The earnings from the City of London's financial dealings are a significant contribution to the balance of payments, and maintaining the financial community as a service export sector is a legitimate and important concern of the government.[84] Although a combination of interventionist regulation in the domestic market and a less restrictive and less formal management of international financial operations might be technically possible, such a schizophrenic position would certainly be hard to sustain. The old tension between foreign and domestic financial concerns, expressed once in the fight over exchange rates, recreates itself as a tension over regulation in London markets. Moreover, there is a clear institutional bent toward the international and away from the domestic. Until recently the Bank of England had no industry policy group charged to consider the problems and needs of industry and to administer policies explicitly aimed at satisfying those needs. Such institutional biases can be changed, but not easily or immediately.[85]

Second, the Bank of England sees some conflict between its fundamental responsibilities in managing the money supply and any role it might play in rediscounting bank lending to industry, either to encourage long-term loans or to influence the direction of financial flows. (This system of rediscounting has been described in Chapter 3.) The problem could be managed, but at the price of controls more formal than either the bank or the system has been accustomed to. Management of the monetary aggregates—interest rates or money supply— dominates the bank's thinking.

Finally, and perhaps most important, the Bank of England has been a spokesman and a lobbyist for banking interests with the central government bureaucracy at the same time that it has been the government's central regulator. This role has deep roots in British history. In fact, whereas the elaborate financial markets originally emerged more to finance government than to finance industry or commerce, the Bank of England was one of the sites for the fight between the political capitalism of the Stuarts and the market capitalism of the Puritans.[86] The bank has worked to insulate financial institutions from central government control, which in practice has meant augmenting its own influence or promoting projects of its own as alternatives to government propositions. Although since its nationalization the bank is formally subordinate to the Treasury, there is a kind of arm's-length arrangement between them. Indeed, the bank has distinguished between its own business and matters in which it serves as agent of the Treasury. Its own affairs include fixing the bank rate and managing the money market and the exchange markets—responsibilities that, Samuel Brittan argues, are the best predictor of the bank's actual behavior.[87]

The important result is that Whitehall officials—the central bureaucracy—are not intimately acquainted with the financial sector leaders or with the operations of those financial markets. Indeed, the Bank of England's insulation of the financial sector from the government is directly tied to Whitehall's ignorance and separation. An expansion of government-directed lending, particularly if the direction were set in Whitehall and implemented by the banks, would involve the Bank of England in a politically determined industrial strategy—a profound reversal of its historical role. Particularly since it has not developed expertise in the area of industrial policy, its own autonomy would be undermined. The bank does not lend itself easily to service as an instrument of government policy for industry.

The Bureaucracy

The obstacles to industrial intervention are not restricted to the financial system. The institutional results of early industrialization affected the structure of government administration as well as that of financial institutions. As a result, a bureaucracy that was organized to conduct only arm's-length dealings has been the second obstacle to interventionist policies.

The responsibility for economic policy was located primarily in the Treasury and secondarily in the Bank of England. The economic innovations and reforms of the 1950s were an effort to create a capacity to generate macro-economic policy and to gain control of expenditure and expenditure planning to match the requirements of Keynesian policy.[88] Even as late as 1970 there was no policy division in the Treasury which had explicit responsibility for the effect of economic policy on industry. Importantly, there were no spokesmen for industry in the inner group of the core economic bureaucracies—nor were there any explicit instruments for selective intervention in industry.

The nature of the civil service and its relation to its political master, the government executive, buttress this bureaucratic-organizational bias against industrial intervention.[89] The British civil service has a virtual monopoly on policy formulation. No one else has the resources or access to translate general directions into detailed policy. The issue here is not whether the policy objectives of the ministers are subverted by a recalcitrant civil service. What matters is that ministers are dependent on the bureaucracy to give form and shape to their objectives and have few resources to manage or intervene in that process themselves.[90] With their attention diverted by cabinet, Parliament, and constituency, it is estimated that they are able to spend only fifteen hours a week on ministerial responsibilities. A minister's personal staff is limited to a political secretary, if that, whose own attention will also be divided among the minister's responsibilities. Also important is the fact that the ranking British bureaucrats reach their positions slowly; there is no system of "high flyers" as in France.[91] One oft-noted consequence of slow promotion is that civil servants tend to stay with their careers for a long time; since few move into the private sector, personal links between public and private sectors are not established.[92] The policy process, then, is dominated by bureaucrats long since socialized within the civil service. That administrative tradition has been reinforced by the recentralization of economic policy in the Treasury and has been directly tied to the arm's-length emphasis of policy.[93] As Thomas Balogh writes, "The unsuitability of the present organization of the British administration at the higher policy-making level is the principal explanation of the drift toward laissez-faire."[94]

Interventionist policies run against the training and traditions of the bureaucracy; indeed, an instinctive resistance to the selective use of state power seems built into the norms of British civil service. The principles of hands-off government have been embedded in a tradition of administrative law which enjoins bureaucrats from making selective decisions that discriminate against particular firms.[95] John Armstrong argues that this traditionalist role is also an unintended product of Oxbridge generalist training:

> Once an administrative elite socialized in accordance with the Oxbridge prescription was firmly established, the administrators themselves acquired an interest in perpetuating the noninterventionist role definition. An interventionist position would have revealed the specific inadequacies of their training, disrupted their corporate solidarity, and reduced their status in a general elite. Each element of their administrative setting (rural nostalgia, oral examinations, etc.) is defended because it is part of the system which perpetuates these interests. At the same time, rejection of the disturbing elements (e.g., an elite technical corps) prevents feedback which might alter the system.[96]

The case of North Sea oil provides a clear illustration of the mismatch between those traditions of noninterventionism and the requirements of interventionist policies. When compared with either Norwegian policy during the same years or with British policies in later years, the initial attempt to exploit this resource must simply be judged a failure. As a result of the approach taken to the oil, neither the British Treasury nor British industry realized the substantial benefits that were available.[97] The rights to exploitation were sold off for a song, taxes were avoided, and British industry was not drawn into producing equipment for the oil market. The central problem, according to the conclusions reached by a series of official investigations, was that British civil servants had neither an independent understanding of the oil field's potential nor a strategy for maximizing the state's gains in its bargains with private oil companies (which were primarily American). Lacking the technical skills or a source of advice internal to the bureaucracy, the civil servants had to depend on the information and views of the private oil firms. Policy was operated and conducted in an arm's-length administrative fashion through the agency of private oil companies. Government policymaking was viewed as a choice between options, but the definition of choices was seen as a technical matter. Consequently, the British government was left with only the semblance of control. When Labour came to power it established the British National Oil Company as its policy instrument, thereby creating a means of direct intervention in the industry.[98] The company provided the government with better information and a better bargaining position with the private companies; in short, it signaled the emergence of interventionist policies.

Though the North Sea oil case does suggest a Conservative commitment to limiting the extent of government intervention, particularly in profitable sectors, and illustrates the difficulties of intervening through the traditional state structure, it ought also to remind us that the British government often did involve itself actively in industrial affairs. Although the nationalized industries were not systematically manipulated for centrally determined ends during the years of Conservative neoliberalism, government was certainly conscious of the size of the public sector and the implications of its activities for private investment. Moreover, while there was a dramatic expansion of intervention in the private sector by governments of both parties in the 1960s, there were sectoral programs in the private sectors in the 1950s as well. Indeed, Clement Attlee's government had reorganized the private steel industry before changing its intent and nationalizing it. Part of the antipathy of business toward Attlee's government and nationalization stemmed from this Labour reversal, this turn away from collaboration with business toward public ownership, which business saw as a stab in the back. After they returned it to private hands, the Conservatives continued to monitor the industry. Other examples abound. The shipbuilding industry had been the subject of government attention for years, and during the laissez-faire 1950s it received substantial support. Faced with a bevy of small aeronautics firms toward the end of its decade in power, the Conservative government supported a forced rationalization of the industry, easing the transition with a contract for a new bomber. In 1959 the government urged the cotton producers to develop a plan to restructure their industry. The plan encouraged the scrapping of old equipment and investment in new machinery. It was predominantly financed by the government, though it involved a levy on the industry, but it was monitored by the trade association, the Cotton Board. The scrapping was relatively successful but reinvestment was more limited than anticipated and the government chose not to displace or force mergers of the small firms so characteristic of the industry.

The fact is that when industrial disruption provoked a crisis, the British government—despite its neoliberal tradition—did respond by attempting to ease the pain of adjustment or by trying to protect against the very need for such adjustment. One might argue, therefore, that when the pressure for assistance is strong enough or the government determination great enough, some means of carrying out an industrial intervention will be found. In that case, the apparatus for intervention, the chief concern of this book, is simply a minor detail. How, then, does the fact of extensive intervention in the midst of a neoliberal period, despite the traditional arm's-length apparatus, affect our argument? Is there less intervention in Britain than in such countries as France and Japan? Is it conducted differently, in ways that have substantive meaning for the type of outcome or the distribution of costs? Or is it simply done with less success? Such questions can be answered only by making a systematic comparison of the set of British and, say, French state interventions, or by comparing the development of policy across a broad range of industrial sectors. This process would involve far more than simply counting up actions; each action compared would require a separate research effort. What more limited evidence can be brought to bear on the matter?

Several characteristics of British intervention during the neoliberal years need special emphasis. First, intervention did not have developmental purposes but was conducted on a case-by-case basis. Although more activist governments have also taken a case-by-case approach, the British government differs in that it did not attempt to use intervention to reorient the economy. Equally important, actions that could now be taken under the auspices of a single piece of legislation, and through existing apparatus, required individual enabling legislation in the 1950s. This procedure certainly made debate more public and, by requiring that a separate coalition argue each case as a legitimate exception, it raised the political costs of each intervention. The French apparatus for intervening to save industrial lame ducks, discussed earlier, demonstrates that a general instrument has an administrative advantage over case-by-case legislation. The French apparatus was arranged to handle a wide variety of cases; the scope of the intervention and its economic significance would determine what level of the organization would treat the specific case. The most significant cases were submitted to an interministerial group, but even the concerns of relatively small firms could be addressed. The scope and the interventionist intent were certainly greater than anything existing today in the British government.

Second, it could be argued that the arrangements for intervention meant that the British government was more dependent on the business community for the formulation and implementation of its policies than was, say, the French government. In Britain it was necessary to act through trade associations because there was little interventionist apparatus and almost no bureaucratic inclination to intervene. As a result, the agencies conducting government policies were the bureaucracies most closely tied to the industry and most likely to reflect its views. No general monitoring body was in a position to comment on or object to plans developed in these agencies.

Third, as the North Sea oil case suggests, the existing apparatus definitely limited the effectiveness of policies. The fact that both parties decided to construct a new interventionist apparatus whenever they chose to expand the scope of intervention is strong evidence of an institutional constraint on policy.

An institutional normalcy, a standard set of arrangements, had emerged in the British economy by the end of the 1950s. According to that standard, financial, industrial, and political power existed in separate worlds: business was at arm's-length from finance and both distanced themselves from government. The state bureaucracy was manned by a professional civil service and headed by a political executive whose party base afforded it control of Parliament; as such, the government policymaking apparatus was protected against capture by elements of the society it governed. Indeed, with the nationalization of the Bank of England and its increasing integration into the government policy apparatus, the state bureaucracy's domination of the policy process was probably strengthened. Nonetheless, the state lacked eyes to follow events in industry (independently of its business informants) and hands to intervene in a specific and selective fashion. There was no point at which government could exert leadership in industry and no instruments to mount a coordinated or unified national effort to reverse industrial decline. In order for the state to conduct interventionist policies, its links with the economy would have to be reshaped to allow the state to become a marketplace player. A bit of anatomical restructuring was in order to provide eyes, hands, and a bit of economic instruction for the brain.

TOWARD AN INTERVENTIONIST STATE

In Britain, then, those who wished to use the state to spark industrial reorganization and development needed political and bureaucratic platforms—platforms well situated to influence policy but insulated from the short-term political repercussions of their actions. The necessary process of institutional construction allowed party conflict to intrude into the corporate arrangements that set the terms of competition and coordination in the economy. New policy instruments meant new structural relations between business, industry, and the state.

The general goal of more rapid growth was of course easy to agree upon. Growth and productivity, as Maier and others have argued, was the solvent of postwar conflict in the West.[99] Agreement on the policies that would realize these—the policies that would begin to make concrete the terms of change—proved much harder to achieve. Importantly, the strategy that would actually promote growth was not obvious. Unlike the French, the British could not draw maps of the future from the library of backwardness, for in Britain the problem was not how to move out of agriculture into industry or how to force competitiveness on protected industry. The problem was how to generate change within an entrenched industrial economy. Of course, the technical and the political aspects of the matter were intertwined; positions on what was wrong and how to correct it were linked to the advantages that specific groups might gain from particular strategies.

The most important issue, however, was whether the state could be used actively to promote industrial rejuvenation in a mixed economy. Let us quickly summarize the players and the course of the fight. The Conservatives disagreed over the role of the state. Some (loosely termed the left) claimed it could serve the purposes of industry; others (the right) thought it would only foul the workings of the market and strengthen the position of those who might challenge private enterprise. The policy choice, then, was whether to build a business-state alliance to address industrial problems or to make a commitment to increased profits as the sole basis of rejuvenation. Should matters be arranged à la Monnet, or at any rate in a British version of what French planning was about? Or should they be arranged in the style of Erhard, which meant stepping aside to let supposedly profit-hungry and aggressive business "get on with it"? The Erhard strategy meant promoting rejuvenation within the existing structure of business-state relations, whereas the Monnet options required institutional changes. The Conservatives were also divided on labor's role in policy and economy. They quarreled about whether labor should be dealt a role in policymaking and whether the state should involve itself as participant and arbiter in wage bargaining. For them, the unions often appeared an outright enemy, at best a sometimes partner. Only on the issue of sterling was there a consensus; the commitment to an international role for the currency, made at the end of the 1950s, was not in question.

The Conservative positions on these issues of state and labor have depended not only on opposition to Labour but also on which action has been victorious in the party's own leadership fights. Churchill, under whose leadership the neoliberal normalcy was established, gave way to Harold Macmillan. Macmillan had accepted a positive role for the state in the interwar years and he embraced this approach again when in power. Macmillan ceded to Lord Home, which brought no real change, and then leadership fell to Edward Heath. When in opposition, Heath took the party back to a neoliberalism defined in opposition to the Labour government's activist policies of industrial intervention. When in power, however, Heath turned back toward intervention but then lost the party leadership to Margaret Thatcher. Her campaign to reduce the state's involvement in the economy signified still another reversal.[100]

For Labour, policy choices have alternated between a managerial capitalism with social democratic overtones (sponsored by the party right) and a socialism implemented through an expanded public sector (the goal of the party left). The former policy was best represented by Harold Wilson's enduring commitment to sterling and James Callaghan's use of the International Monetary Fund to force a control of spending; the latter has now taken the form of the so-called alternative strategy, which proposes protection and an internal industrial readjustment implemented through nationalization. At the beginning of the 1960s the balance was weighted heavily against the Labour left, and indeed, Anthony Crossland and others proposed scrapping the party's commitment to extended nationalization. Yet, the left retained a capacity to define some party positions but had limited power in government. When in government, the managerial moderates were forced to tone down seemingly radical legislation proposed by the left (such as the National Enterprise Board) by giving it a moderate implementation; and some proposals, such as the 1976 proposal to nationalize the banking sector, were simply buried in study committees. Throughout the 1970s the parliamentary party leadership remained in the center, but the tone of the party rank and file was increasingly dictated by the left. After two decades of struggle, the left had the moderates on the defensive in terms of both policy initiatives and party power. Finally, in late 1980 the balance in the party shifted even more decisively to the left, provoking an effort to establish a new center party.

The Labour left's socialist tone throughout the period certainly frightened the business community, making it all the harder for Labour party leadership to pursue the rejuvenation of the private sector through state leadership and initiative. One M.P. caught this tension when he argued that the private sector should ignore his own party's rhetoric:

> The private companies whose investment decisions ultimately determine the rate of growth, and hence the ability of a Labour Government to satisfy its supporters' aspirations, are not staffed with experts on Labour history and sociology. They are apt—foolishly, no doubt, but not altogether incomprehensibly—to take the party's rhetoric at face value, and to believe that it really does have some deep moral objection to private ownership as such. They therefore view the advent of a Labour Government with unnecessary trepidation and take fewer risks with their shareholders' money than they would if a Labour Government were not in power. But since Labour Governments need to maintain business confidence just as much as Conservative Governments do, Labour Ministers cannot afford to let these misconceptions continue. In order to allay them, they have to bend over backwards to prove that, in spite of what they may have said in opposition, they do not intend any harm to the private sector at all. The net result is that Labour Governments display *more* tenderness towards the private sector than they would have to do if their policies were explicitly revisionist in the first place: that the National Enterprise Board, to take the most obvious recent example, will almost certainly have fewer teeth than it needs because, when the party was in opposition, attempts were made to give it far too many.[101]

It was difficult for Labour to establish confidence and trust in industry when its purposes required expanding the power of the state, and when one wing of the party proposed using that expanded power against business.

Though the current divisions within the two parties are not new, the weakness of the "managerial" center and the strength of the crusaders on the wings do mark a departure from the earlier pattern. Indeed, when Macmillan was in power and Labour was debating Clause Four of its platform, which committed the party to nationalizations, the centrist elements in each party were in the ascendant and the two parties were substantively close together. Now the left in Labour is ascendant and the prime minister is from the Conservative right. One might contend that the shift toward the wings resulted from each party's inability when in power to establish enduring institutional arrangements for growth policies, and from the threat posed by such constraints as bargaining restrictions on labor and the nationalization of business. The Labour left and the Conservative right each came to support policies anathema to the dominant producer constituency of the opposite party. The need to reform producer arrangements contributed to party conflict, and such conflicts in turn made it more difficult to establish workable arrangements at the producer level.

The need to reform finance and bureaucracy to carry out interventionist policies severely complicated the problem of determining the economic purposes such an interventionist apparatus would serve. In the broadest sense, would intervention serve to promote the redevelopment of private industry, or would it serve as a means of replacing private companies with public firms? If the Conservatives were to use the state to promote industrial redevelopment, they would have to challenge the principles of neoliberalism which had become the orthodoxy of the 1950s. Labour was willing to conduct such reforms, but because of its own left wing it was unable to commit itself unequivocally to a strategy of subsidizing and facilitating the renewal of private industry. Consequently, any reforms it undertook carried some element of threat to the private sector, which was thus pushed to oppose interventionist instruments that it might otherwise have created or used for its own ends.

Thus, policy paralysis and instability were not simply the results of the ability of organized producer groups to veto the policies they opposed, as Beer argues, or the inevitable product of two-party competition, as Stewart contends. They instead resulted from an inability to find terms on which to make a deal about the nature of state industrial intervention.[102] Since neither unions nor industry could in fact be beaten—that is, removed from electoral or policy influence for an extended period—a negotiated settlement was necessary. The terms in which the actors posed the issues themselves made it remarkably difficult to reach such a settlement; still, institutional change did occur.

Since the early 1960s, whichever party holds power has been pressed to pursue explicit industrial policies and to create the instruments for selective intervention that such policies require. The Tories have often moved reluctantly, abandoning arm's-length policies with regret in response to specific industrial problems, whereas Labour has pushed harder, in fact proposing active intervention as an alternative to nationalization. The new British capacity for selective intervention has three components. First, businessmen have been involved on a sector-by-sector basis in the definition of industry's needs and institutional means have been established to give weight to their views in the formulation of policy. Second, a set of instruments has been created which can generate the financial packages that permit the government to bargain with companies and industrial groups. Third, "parapublic" banking institutions have been established that can manage state-held firms and execute policy within industry. The skeleton of the apparatus seems to have survived the present Conservative "return" to market principles. Indeed, if the current Conservative intention of gaining administrative control over public-sector companies is successful, this Conservative government will have massively increased the real power of government to pursue detailed industrial objectives.

In the rest of this section we seek to display the new fabric of interventionist institutions and to understand how the conflict about establishing these institutions, which was primarily a party conflict, limited what the state could in fact accomplish. We shall, therefore, recount the political story of the battle over the state's role in the economy and describe the new institutional arrangements that establish the parameters of policy. At each step in the story, we shall consider efforts to expand the state's capacity to mobilize and allocate funds or to promote new strategies by business or labor. These efforts brought technical changes in institutions and markets. When those technical changes challenged the position of business, they became political issues. It is the tension between the reforms in institutional structure and market operation on the one hand, and the challenges to social and political position on the other, which troubled the effort to establish stable policies for industrial adjustment. It is important to note that with few exceptions the policies created channels of government intervention in industry that bypassed or rivaled existing private-sector financial mechanisms. There was no basic strategy for using existing private financial institutions as a technical arm or a political ally. In fact, the existing institutional structure, the market arrangements and the political position of the financial community, meant that private financial markets would be a barrier to intervention and that private financiers would oppose such policies.

The Conservatives

Planning, as we have seen, emerged as the Conservative response to the sterling crises (which provoked the infamous stop-go policies of the 1950s) and to inadequate industrial growth. Specifically, it was the sterling crisis of 1961 which initiated the turn toward planning symbolized by the government's decision to move the National Economic Development Council (NEDC) off the drawing boards. In deciding to implement the NEDC, the government sought to demonstrate that it had broken with the pattern of temporarily cooling off the economy for exchange-rate reasons and then firing it up again. Though the government had not abandoned the defense of sterling, it had come to question the cost of that effort.[103] More generally, though, the emergence of planning represented an effort to revise failed policies, one that emerged more as result of a leadership shift within the Conservative party than as a consequence of changed economic circumstances. In 1951 Churchill and his circle of advisers had felt close to the City of London; they rarely concerned themselves with industry and played on the divisions between the Federation of British Industry and the British Employers Conference when attempting to deal with Labour.[104] Macmillan appeared more receptive to industrial initiatives and his sponsorship of the NEDC was sparked at an annual meeting of the Federation of British Industry.[105]

The questions for the Conservatives in 1961 were what kind of planning apparatus should the NEDC be, whom should it involve, where should it be located, and what should it do? The choices they made produced a debating society and an internal lobbyist, a new hand at the table who was not dealt any cards or provided any chips. They chose not to alter any of the privileges of labor, business, or finance or to establish means of systematically manipulating any of the markets. They sought in round-table consensus a substitute for a governmental economic strategy. Suspicious of Treasury expertise, which had seemed to place the external value of the pound before domestic growth, they decided first of all to separate the NEDC from the Whitehall bureaucracy. The second choice was to include the Trade Unions Congress in these deliberations, in order to encourage labor to make the short-run accommodations needed to achieve long-run growth. Third, it was decided that the NEDC should concern itself with microeconomic policy issues and focus on the problems of key industries through its sectoral working parties (Economic Development Committees). Its reports were able to establish that if all bureaucracies concerned took the appropriate measures, a pattern of balanced growth was possible. What the

NEDC did not do was provide any assurance that such "appropriate measures" would be taken.* The process was therefore mainly a consensus-building activity involving business and the trade unions, rather than an effort by a government agency to develop or implement a new policy. The financial sector, it is important to note, was simply left outside the policy debate, which is to say that the question of how to mobilize national resources for industrial development was excluded. The discussion of industrial policy was truncated before it began.

The NEDC reflected the British image of French planning, which had captured the British imagination in the late 1950s. To the British the French system seemed able to establish targets and objectives, and through logic and encouragement to make expansionary choices—all without controls or direction. But hidden behind the rhetoric of planning was the fact that the French government was willing to discriminate selectively between sectors and firms using credit, purchases, and permissions. The Conservative leadership in Britain borrowed the rhetorical notion that indicative planning did not involve government interference with corporate prerogatives.[106] They ignored the reality that French planning was conservative coercion to build a new France.

Labour at the Helm

It was in fact Harold Wilson's Labour government that proposed in 1964 using state support and pressure to promote the competitive readjustment of British private industry—an innovation for a Labour party that, while in opposition, had still been quarreling about its stance on nationalization.

> Committed to the continued existence of a large private industrial ownership, the defense of the pound, and a measure of wage restraint, albeit combined with price control, the Labour Party of 1963 seemed already to have abandoned pretensions to the class struggle and adopted an ideology suitable to such an economy. . . . It had become an "integrative" party as a result of its own practice, imbued with a concern for national unity remarkably similar to that of the Conservatives under Macmillan or Baldwin.[107]

*More than a decade later, in the 1970s, a Labour government linked the deliberations of these NEDC sectoral working parties to specific Whitehall decisions allocating resources to industry and brought financial figures into the deliberations about industry policy. The NEDC business committees have become government-generated industrial lobbyists for programs worked out in conjunction with the government. These sectoral working parties provided both a government view of the industry apart from the existing representation arrangements in the Ministry of Industry, and a means of generating support for government programs. The decade of the 1970s saw the development of overtly interventionist policies.

The Labour party proposed, in essence, to accomplish *public purposes* through *private firms* rather than to extend the scope of the public sector. But the effort failed. It cannot plausibly be argued that the policies of the first Wilson government improved the position of British industry or left an array of policies and instruments that would assist a later government in a similar effort. The question is why Labour could not at least reform the government's system of intervening in industrial affairs. Was it an inevitable failure of a social democratic party, so tied to the existing system as to be unable to envision needed reforms or to muster support to accomplish them? Or was it a failure of nerve and leadership by a particular prime minister who made some very questionable technical judgments?

The position taken here is that existing institutional arrangements complicated and delayed the emergence of an interventionist apparatus and a consensus to employ it. Labour came to power in 1964 with a commitment to organizing a more effective use of national resources, to restructuring the industrial base. Today, conservative economists propose a free market as the best supply strategy. In the mid-1960s the same problems were thought to be structural and the solutions proposed were interventionist.[108] Labour was not able to embed its supply-side concern in enduring institutions or to frame the policy problem in a fashion that pressed for more competitive British industry.

The problem was that the Labour government had to immobilize or coopt groups and institutions that stood outside its natural constituencies, groups implanted in the very institutions it needed to reform. Labour's ship foundered on three rocks: (1) Wilson's defense of sterling, (2) the failure to tie the Treasury to new purposes of government, and (3) the challenge that selective intervention from newly founded institutions posed to the autonomy of the financial sector and industry. Wilson's refusal to permit even a debate about sterling and his willingness to scuttle his domestic policy objectives in what was to be a final defense of the currency force us to consider how the pound's international status became identified with the national interest.

A fully adequate and persuasive account is not available. Stephen Blank suggests that the leading politicians of both parties simply did not think the problem through; they simply accepted Britain's international leadership role and the place held by sterling in such a vision.[109] This interpretation sidesteps the problem of why pressures did not exist to force them to reconsider, and why a system of ideas did not emerge in which to couch the debate. In fact, the Labour party included an articulate opposition to support for sterling, which Wilson chose to ignore. Among the Conservatives, Macmillan was self-conscious enough to use the NEDC to establish what he hoped would be a political counterweight to the defense of sterling. In contrast to Blank, Frank Longstreth has contended that the support of sterling represented a victory of the City of London over industry.[110] Indeed, he argues that the financiers not only had their way but established a kind of hegemony in economic policy which allowed them to define the issue in their own terms. One can easily understand the defeat of the industrialists on the matter of sterling in the interwar years but the absence of a struggle is what is remarkable about the postwar era. Though this situation might be explained by the strength of the City or by the weakness of organized business, business interests may well have diverged less than they seemed to at any one moment. As a sterling-based protected trading area the empire provided something to both parties: to industry it gave a privileged market in which the overvaluation of currency was not critical, to the City it provided the base for the currency's international trading role. A substantial portion of the country's foreign trade was inside the sterling zone. Interests did not diverge so much on the value of currency as on the deflationary policies implemented to preserve its value. Still, this argument does not account for Wilson's willingness to act along policy lines that were advocated by the Bank and the Treasury inside the government and by the City outside it. At this point, further discussion is largely speculation about Wilson's vision of himself and of his political purposes. Defense of sterling was entangled with a variety of issues. For example, those in the Labour party who wished to debate the sterling matter also opposed Wilson on entry into the Common Market. Similarly, the reserve currency role that sterling continued to play was a part of Britain's arrangements with America. A debate on sterling would have had widespread reverberations. Only a clear vision of the prices being paid to defend sterling and of the benefits of a new policy might have made the political risks of that debate appear worthwhile.

The political story of Labour's failure can best be understood by exploring the creation of three institutions: the Department of Economic Affairs, the Industrial Reorganization Corporation, and the Ministry of Industry. Each of them represented an effort to expand the planning and interventionist capacity of the state of supplementing existing institutions or markets. Each effort at reform encountered entrenched opposition—from within the bureaucracy, finance, and industry—that was strong enough to block basic change.

The Department of Economic Affairs (DEA) was established as a counterweight and rival to the Treasury and came to symbolize the government's failure in economic policy—both its over-long defense of sterling and its inability to engage the central apparatus of government in an effort to promote industry. The Labour leadership believed that a growth strategy could not be accomplished through the Treasury as it was then constituted. The possibility of placing a planning unit inside the old Treasury apparatus had been considered and dismissed, largely because of fears that the unit's advocacy of an economic and industrial growth strategy would lose out to the Treasury's traditional concern with financial control. It was therefore decided that the new ideas and expertise must be nurtured in a new department, though the practical decision to implement the DEA is said to have been made in order to provide the number two man in the Labour party, George Brown, with a job to match his political stature.[111] The Treasury thus continued unreformed. No attempt was made to shift it away from its role as the controller of public spending toward a new role as bank to the economy, a concept that François Bloch-Lainé had developed in France. Dividing the responsibility for economic management so that the DEA dealt with the long term and the Treasury with the short term was also a crucial mistake. Long-run objectives involve short-run decisions, and the new department therefore represented a direct challenge to Treasury primacy in economic advice. Brown in fact intended to become minister of finance.[112] The original Labour party plan called for the DEA to control capital expenditure, leaving current spending to the Treasury. But Brown traded away any such right for the DEA on the eve of the election victory.[113] It certainly would have been difficult to implement if tried. The sharp differentiation in responsibility froze the Treasury in its short-run perspective.

The scope of the DEA's responsibilities was broad. It had four divisions: economic planning, sectoral planning, wage and price policy, and regional policy. The problem was that it had no resources with which to implement its purposes and was thus severely handicapped in its challenge to Treasury preeminence. The difficulty for the DEA was that while it had the power to propose, the Treasury retained the capacity to dispose. As Michael Shanks points out, the economic crises and the division of labor "reinforced Treasury's traditional weaknesses: a low concern for growth among economic priorities, a lack of knowledge of and interest in the working of industry (including the impact on industry of fiscal and monetary policies), and an overriding concern for the defense of sterling. Thus as the balance of power within Whitehall tilted away from the DEA and toward Treasury, the ill which labor in opposition had diagnosed and sought to cure became embedded deeper and deeper in the structure of government."[114]

Largely because George Brown's union background gave him an experience and credibility important to the government in conducting wage restraint policies, the DEA ended up with responsibility for implementing an income policy. With no resources to allocate, the DEA was not able to involve itself directly in corporate or sector strategy. Thus planning was reduced in substance to wage discipline. Industrial promotion and growth did not figure in the department's operation responsibility.

Too much weight has been given to the idea that union participation in planning institutions was an obstacle to British government intervention, particularly by those who are comparing the British and French experiences. In France, labor support was indeed crucial to establishing the Plan and the interventionist apparatus, but the fact of labor union participation in the British planning effort cannot plausibly be linked to the failure of industrial intervention strategies. More important were the intended purposes of the unions' participation. The Labour party would, of course, support union participation in planning. Both the party and the unions saw planning as a means of engaging unions in wage control. It was the necessity to give income policy "more teeth" to bolster sterling—to make labor sacrifices for what were in fact financial interests—which led to Brown's resignation, destroyed the plan, and finally brought about the disintegration of the DEA.

The plan's crucial weakness was that it started with a desired outcome and attempted to derive from that outcome the actions and activities that each component of the economy should undertake. It did not derive a collective objective from a negotiation and exploration of the possibilities in the several sectors and was thus disconnected from industrial reality. It was premised, furthermore, on expansionary policies—policies that were abruptly reversed when a sterling crisis resulted in massive devaluation. Whether this last defense of sterling was in fact a victory of the Treasury over the DEA, a last triumph of the City over industry, or simply a mistake in judgment by Wilson is not central here. Wilson's refusal to allow a systematic discussion of the possible consequences of devaluation meant there was no plan for turning devaluation to Britain's advantage, however, and made it more likely that market pressure for devaluation would be viewed as a dramatic defeat that must be resisted.[115] The death of the plan and George Brown's departure from DEA brought an end to this first experiment in implementing supply and growth policies through the central Whitehall apparatus.

The Industrial Reorganization Corporation (IRC) represented a challenge to the financial community similar to that which the DEA had posed for the Treasury.[116] Indeed, the IRC was spawned by the DEA in an effort to establish instruments of selective intervention in industrial affairs. The IRC finally emerged when the government's macroeconomic policies faltered and it chose to impose deflationary measures to support sterling. It was intended, like the NEDC before it, as a kind of formal commitment to industry in the face of policies that slowed growth. IRC was a parapublic financial institution with resources of 150 million pounds licensed to intervene in the market to promote the restructuring of British industry. Mergers, it was felt, would leave British firms stronger and more efficient in international markets. Greater size was thought to provide firms with the economies of scale, both in production and in research, needed to compete with the Americans. It was argued that a public instrument was necessary, first because the private capital markets would not respond to the potential of the mergers and second because the IRC could work with the monopolies commission to avoid unwarranted mergers while still encouraging needed ones.[117]

The IRC was intended to supplement, not to replace, market forces. It was intended to make a profit on its operations, justifying its decisions by market criteria. It would seek, however, to alter the outcomes that would occur naturally. Earlier public banking efforts—such as the ICFC and FFC—had been intended to fill gaps in properly functioning markets. The notion behind the IRC was that British finance was too passive and conservative. The public sector could give an adrenalin injection to the financial market by becoming an aggressive marketplace player. The IRC intervened in a series of industry-control fights, seeking its objectives by taking sides in takeover and merger battles, and in some cases by creating those battles. The pattern, according to one observer, was that the IRC supported the aggressive outsiders, the "thrusters," in their efforts to take control of major corporations or to prevent the effective domination or cartelization of British industries by more traditional businessmen accustomed to arranging matters by negotiation.[118] These newcomers were thought to be more comfortable with the IRC and willing to turn its access to the public till to their advantage. The analysis of the backgrounds and positions of those who supported the IRC and participated in it, as well as the sides the IRC took in specific fights, supports this view. The IRC was opposed by established business associations and by the Conservative party. Only certain segments of the business community could benefit from its selective policies. The parapublic bank that facilitated selective intervention thus also generated specific alliances between government and segments of the business community. Selective intervention and specific alliances were counterparts.

The IRC was overtly selective and interventionist but it was not part of a development or adjustment strategy. Indeed, the notion that the IRC was a kind of fuel-injection system for a sluggish economic engine meant that the political executive did not need to have an overview of the competitive place of British firms in world markets. It did not demand a decision on which industries were most likely to grow and could be developed to benefit the economy. There was never an intent to use the IRC, as the French used their interventionist instruments, to urge firms to move out of protected empire markets into competitive but expanding markets in the advanced countries.

The IRC was an odd sort of interventionist instrument for a socialist government. It is understandable that it should have been set up as a rival to existing financial markets. It is less clear why it should have been established as an independent body outside the government bureaucracy, or why its operations should have been dominated by a board of businessmen, described by Wilson as "what must have been the highest powered group of industrialists and financiers ever to sit round one table as co-directors."[119] But on further consideration these matters are not surprising after all. Where, without massive reform of the Whitehall machinery, could such a device have been placed *inside* the government? Furthermore, though the resources of the IRC were substantial, they were still limited in relation to its task. Though it had to make alliances with forces in the private sector in order to succeed this cannot explain the degree to which control was ceded to a business-dominated board. Business' dominant role is easier to understand when one remembers that, in the absence of an earlier history of intervention, government bureaucrats and Labour party officials lacked the expertise in industrial affairs needed to operate such a board. Probably, in the short run, such expertise could have been found only in the business community. The IRC was dismantled by the Conservatives in 1971, only to be resurrected by the next Labour government as the National Enterprise Board. We shall deal with that part of the story later in this section.

The one enduring institutional change introduced by the first Wilson government was the establishment of what is now the Department of Industry, which embodies and symbolizes the new interventionist tone of business-state relations in Britain. Government support for private competitive adjustment in industry was first expressed in the support for technological innovation extended by the Ministry of Technology (MinTech). That ministry's original functions were limited to research and development and the sponsorship of key industries, but after a slow start it expanded at the expense of other departments, in particular the DEA. It gained prestige and new functions after the July 1966 deflationary measures, which precipitated the resignation of its minister, Frank Cousins, and his replacement by Anthony Wedgewood Benn. Shipbuilding and engineering responsibilities were transferred to it from the Board of Trade. In early 1967 MinTech absorbed the Ministry of Aviation, and in July the Shipbuilding Industry Act gave Benn authority to form and support the Upper Clyde Shipbuilders. In 1969 it captured many responsibilities of the more laissez-faire Board of Trade, leaving the board with the task of providing services to industry and commerce, responsibility for a few service sectors, and regulation of exports, shipping, and civil aviation. In October 1969 MinTech was merged with the Ministry of Power and also assumed responsibility for the IRC; the NEDC went to the Cabinet Office, coordinated with the Treasury; and the DEA was disbanded. The Board of Trade and MinTech were merged in 1969 to form the Department of Trade and Industry. The change in label—from Board of Trade to Department of Industry—expresses the shift in emphasis and the move toward interventionism.

The Industry Expansion Act of 1968 gave the new department powers of intervention which went well beyond those of the IRC. The minister could make grants or loans available to particular firms when he was satisfied that they would improve the efficiency or profitability of an industry or would create, expand, or sustain productive capacity. The IRC had been obliged, as a parapublic bank, to make a commercial return on its overall operations but the new act made no such demands. Indeed, as Andrew Graham argues:

> This act was also virtually the only time during the whole period of the government when it was explicitly stated in relation to the private sector that the justification for the intervention was "*because of the divergence between national and private costs and benefits.*" This compares with the IRC which was *not* allowed to "support ventures which have no prospect of achieving eventual viability." And the view expressed by the Public Accounts Committee was "that bodies such as the SIB ... should be guided by strictly commercial principles"—a view with which the Ministry of Technology agreed. Looked at in this second way the Industrial Expansion Act was very much about objectives, not just about means.[120]

The interventionist seed first planted at the NEDC by the Conservatives was transplanted by Labour to DEA and finally took root at Industry. It had, though, taken the energies of the first Wilson government to establish the base of the interventionist apparatus. The political energies behind intervention were obscured by the institutional problem and the struggle against devaluation. No enduring vision of the state's role was formulated and no workable political alliance to support it was constructed. This initial effort would be challenged both by left-wing Labour and by the Conservatives.

The Tories Return

When the Conservatives led by Heath came to power in 1970, they were pledged to a disengagement of government from industry; they insisted that government must not go on propping up ailing industries but must instead create a more rigorous competitive climate in which less efficient firms would release their resources to more productive ones. Basically, the strategy was to make society behave more like an economics textbook's prescription for economic efficiency. The political strategy was simply to refuse intervention and let the social and political chips fall where they would. The intent, according to the minister of industry, was to avoid making "lame ducks of us all."[121] The irony to be explored here is that the Conservatives left office having established sweeping powers for government intervention in private industry, seemingly completing what Labour had begun.

The Conservative disengagement policy was implemented by John Davies, formerly head of the Confederation of British Industry. The IRC and the Prices and Incomes Board were dismantled and the role of the NEDC was cut back. However, the backbone of the policy—a strong stand on allowing lame ducks to die—collapsed with the crises of the Upper Clyde Shipbuilders and Rolls-Royce. The shipbuilders had been propped up with subsidies. When the firm collapsed at the withdrawal of support, the workers refused to behave like proper factors of production: they seized the yard rather than "redeploy" or be unemployed. The Rolls-Royce case saw inflation undermine the aircraft engine company and endanger the British position in this expanding sector. Recognizing the political costs of standing by and watching these failures were too high, the Conservatives established interventionist instruments as a political expedient, without elaborating any particular theory of intervention. Not surprisingly, the instruments therefore offered no real challenge to existing producer relations or to market mechanisms. Intervention was a political tactic to keep the peace, not an economic strategy for mobilizing national resources to redevelop British industry.

The 1972 Industry Act was the vehicle for Conservative intervention. It set up the sort of interventionist instruments that the Ministry of Industry needed in order to respond systematically to these crises. The act was a complete reversal of earlier policy; it gave the secretary of state for industry "sweeping powers to intervene in industry by providing any form of financial assistance to any industry or any firm in any case where he thought that this assistance would be of benefit to the economy of the U.K. or any part of it."[122] So sweeping were these powers that they proved more adequate to the needs of the interventionist-minded Labour government that took office in 1974.

Heath was able to execute the policy change by exercising his prerogatives as prime minister and by drawing on the personal loyalties of cabinet ministers. There was considerable opposition. Many Conservative M.P.s who could be classified as neoliberal were opposed to the bill. The number of restive members was greater still and was swelled by opposition from the Confederation of British Industry. This backbench rebellion included members who later backed Margaret Thatcher's bid for leadership.

Labour Tries Once More

Labour completed the construction of the interventionist apparatus when it returned to office in 1974. It was not clear whether its interventionist reforms were intended to use nationalization to alter class relations in Britain or to give support to private British industry. Once again, policies for industry promotion splintered over distributional issues.

One line of interventionist policy supported private industry. An Industrial Development Unit (IDU) was established in the Ministry of Industry and headed by a deputy secretary. It was intended to fund schemes that emerged from NEDC deliberations. The Treasury established for the first time "its own Industrial Policy department [and] for the first time the Whitehall machinery seemed to have geared itself to integrate economic and industrial policy in a meaningful and sensible way."[123] Officials in the Ministry of Industry reported that it was much easier to make their views heard and that they had substantive impact on policy. The IDU operated its own industry schemes, which were intended to revitalize particular sectors and to respond to demands from troubled firms. Its staff was drawn from the private sectors as well as from the civil service, and this infusion of bankers and accountants seemed to provide government with a new set of informal contacts. It was linked to industry through the traditional Ministry of Industry sectoral divisions, as well as through the NEDC, with its thirty sectoral working parties. These working parties were almost inevitably pressure groups for industry. In essence, the government had created its own lobbyists to make sure that industry would make the sort of demands government could meet.[124] Since there was a link between working-party deliberations and IDU sector schemes, it was hoped that the NEDC deliberations would produce a closer collaboration between firms and government. That is, it seemed important to convince industry that these deliberations could directly affect policy and produce actions immediately helpful to business.

Tax policy was the second interventionist vehicle that supported the private sector. In absolute terms, tax policies were more important than selectively administered funds. Companies were permitted to write off investment in plant and machines in a single year, and 54 percent of investment in industrial land. Furthermore, they were permitted to store up tax credits against future profits. The consequence, according to some observers, was that the effective rate of tax for many major companies fell nearly to zero.[125]

The second line of policy—one that contradicted the first—was the use of state power to extend the boundaries of public authority and increase the power of labor. Its constituent elements were the National Enterprise Board (NEB), charged with making planning agreements that would link the quids of government policy to the quos of company choice, and a proposal to nationalize banking. In effect a challenge by the left wing of the Labour party to the privileges of business, this policy inevitably undermined government efforts to build an alliance that would prop up its other policy of supporting private business. Though the NEB had its origins in the IRC, there were two important differences. First, the NEB was not an investment bank but a holding company, in essence providing the government a conglomerate through which it could manage its industrial holdings. Second, it was funded to the tune of £1000 million, with the intent of extending public ownership into profitable sectors.[126] Other governments have invested in advanced sectors without threatening the privileges of private enterprise, but as originally legislated the NEB was assigned the task of challenging the private business monopoly of the advanced sectors where growth could be expected. Though the NEB has made some investments in sectors such as semiconductors, most of its holdings have been in troubled sectors, such as automobiles. In several crises, the Hebert corporate failure for example, NEB provided a means by which private and public interests could combine to restructure rather than close a troubled firm.[127] By 1976 the Confederation of British Industry (CBI) had reconciled itself to the NEB, as had the Bank of England. In its 1976 policy statement, *Road to Recovery*, the CBI envisioned a more independent body with government shareholdings and the ability to provide temporary assistance to firms in financial trouble. The NEB has won a place in economic administration as an instrument of intervention in troubled or declining sectors, and stripped of its missionary functions it has survived the resurgence of free-market policies under the Thatcher government.

Planning agreements were the second prong of the challenge to private business power. It was thought that by striking particular deals with individual companies, resources could be provided for specific private commitments to particular public purposes. This plan was another attempt to imitate the French case, in which such arrangements were an important part of the approach to business both formally and informally.[128] In Britain, where by tradition bureaucrats inexperienced in industrial affairs dealt at arm's length with a business community that feared intrusions on its power, the agreements were viewed as shackles on companies that required flexibility in their markets. More important, the fact that labor unions were to be a party to these agreements posed a major threat to management prerogatives. Even though the planning agreements never became a central component of policy and labor union participation in the agreements was minimized, they contributed to the atmosphere in which the government's overall industrial policy came to be viewed as a challenge to private industry.

The most direct challenge to private business was the Labour left's proposal to nationalize financial institutions. Britain's industrial problems, the left claimed, resulted in part from the diversion of financial resources away from industry toward consumption, speculation, and overseas investment. Their proposed solution, the nationalization of the major financial institutions, carried in the Party Conference but was diverted when cabinet moderates led by Prime Minister James Callaghan called for a study. Neither the Wilson Committee's report nor the NEDC studies of financial and industrial sectors[129] provided any evidence that the banks or lending institutions had denied cash to industrialists starved for investment funds. These findings seemed to refute the left's proposition that funds diverted abroad would have financed British growth if invested at home. Indeed, during the worst years of the recent recession, when firms could not obtain funds in capital markets, the banks vastly expanded their lendings and helped firms survive.[130] Moreover, whatever the failures of the British system or the success of other national arrangements, there was no evidence that nationalization would solve its problems. The major French deposit banks were nationalized but, as in Japan, it was the way in which the financial system was managed that created a bias toward industrial investment. Such techniques could be implemented in Britain without public ownership.

The rhetoric with which the left argued for the nationalization of financial institutions—as a punishment and a cure for failure to provide resources to industry—obscured the more important issues. One such issue is whether the mutual assumptions of firms and financial institutions about proper financial practice have shaped the strategies of British firms in a way that has undermined their competitive position in international markets. To put the issue differently, were corporate financial strategies appropriate to an earlier era of international competition, and were they held in place by traditional assumptions about how to finance companies? If British corporate strategies differ from those of their foreign counterparts in ways that can reasonably be attributed to the means by which they obtain finance, then the organization and activities of the City of London might be said to affect the whole performance of British industry. The Boston Consulting Group, in its incisive studies of Japanese corporate strategies, demonstrates how Japan's particular financial system facilitates market-expanding strategies and thus provides evidence that different sets of financial assumptions and arrangements can affect corporate strategy.[131] If that assessment is correct, then one might ask whether restructuring the institutional arrangements of the financial market might make possible more competitive company strategies in Britain. Indeed, British firms do seem to have pursued short-term financial goals rather than long-term strategies that would assure them an enduring position of strength in the market. Confronted with companies operating under different strategic assumptions, the market position—and ultimately the financial position—of British firms could be eroded. This view is substantiated by abundant cases, for example, the experiences of Rover and Jaguar.

In Britain, quite unlike France, the debate never focused on this central technical problem of the relation between finance and industry strategy because the politics of the discussion forced the business sector into a defensive alliance against nationalization. The second hidden issue was how resources could best be mobilized toward industrial redevelopment. The issues debated were really those of social position and power, not those of economic strategy.

In sum, the Labour government of Wilson and Callaghan sought again to expand the interventionist apparatus. That effort provided a forum for a challenge to private enterprise from the left of the party, and it entangled the political issues of who should control business with the technical question of how state resources could be used to make British enterprise competitive in world markets, regardless of whether those enterprises were publicly or privately owned. The left did not have the power to upset the arrangements of social power, but its initiative, political presence, and rhetoric interfered with the creation of a business-state alliance for growth. Traditionally, intervention was seen as a threat, a Trojan horse, not simply a gift of aid. The Labour left's proposal of an alternative economic strategy—nationalization and protection—made the danger seem all the more real.

The Screw Turns Once More

In Britain the efforts to expand the interventionist capacity of the state simply drove the parties and producer groups apart, for each policy introduced to promote industry was also viewed as a challenge to the position of business and finance. Each political cycle has exacerbated the free-market-versus-nationalization dichotomy, leaving no intellectual or political space in which to build a strategy by which the state could nurture private enterprise. Events since the Conservative victory in 1979 simply suggest another turning of that same screw.[132]

The electoral failure of the moderate "late" policies of Edward Heath opened the way for Margaret Thatcher to lead the Conservatives to the right. Her policies have sought to reinforce the market character of the British economy by withdrawing the state from detailed involvement in the industrial economy and by promoting instead an improvement in the operation of the marketplaces for labor, capital, and goods. Though the strategy involved containing the power of labor, legislative initiatives to achieve that end have been limited by the cautious approach of the labor minister, James Prior. Rapidly rising unemployment has served to weaken labor's market position, but without real changes in the organization or purposes of the union movement any economic upturn can be expected to lead to renewed labor aggressiveness. The Thatcher strategy has also sought to adopt steady monetary targets aimed at a long-run reorientation, substituting them for the short-term management of demand known as Keynesian fine-tuning. The intent has been to reduce the level of government spending and borrowing in order to free resources for private sector expansion.

Whatever the merits of their economic logic, the Conservatives' ideological emphasis on the private sector has seemed at times to divert their attention from the real workings of the economy much as the Labour left's commitment to nationalization has obscured its view. For example, in all countries the expansion of the telecommunications sector is considered essential to the long-run development of the economy. In the United States, the powerful private companies are adequately nurtured by the capital markets. In Japan and France, catch-up efforts are primed by the national governments. In Britain, the tele-communications industry also faces profitable expansionary opportuni-ties, and as elsewhere, it must borrow to take advantage of them. Brit-ish telecommunications is a public industry, however. Its borrowings count as part of the public sector borrowing requirement, which the government is committed to control. As a result, its borrowing limits are strictly controlled and expansion is therefore constrained. This is more than a technical anomaly or a situation in which a government committed to expanding profitable business is ironically trapped into limiting growth. Asked about the matter in a private interview, a senior government spokesman, reinforced by his private adviser, contended that money spent in the public sector for *any* purpose was inherently less productive than money spent in the private sector for *any* purpose.

Despite Thatcher's dramatic effort to redirect policy, her govern-ment reveals important continuities with its Labour predecessors. The control of domestic credit was first introduced by the last Labour gov-ernment in response to IMF demands during the sterling crisis in 1976. Indeed, for two decades there has been a bipartisan trend toward con-trolling monetary aggregates rather than the structure of interest rates, a trend evident in the United States as well. Similarly, the Conservatives have not dismantled the interventionist apparatus so painfully con-structed by earlier governments, though they have used it for some-what more limited and different purposes.

The Thatcher initiatives, halfway through her term of office, have failed—both by the government's open admission and by most mea-sures by which that government would judge its own success. Even the basic objective of controlling money supply aggregates has not been achieved and efforts to halt their expansion have had damaging effects. Higher interest rates increased company borrowing as companies bor-rowed in desperate attempts to stay afloat, a development that for an extended period has forced exchange rates up to levels at which British industry is uncompetitive. The failure is acknowledged; the debate is only as to why it occurred. There are three positions: that the policies are theoretically unworkable and contradictory, that the instruments to implement them have not yet been established, and that all would be well if only a stronger political muscle and better judgment were ap-plied. But that controversy is not central to our argument.

What does matter is that Labour has matched the Conservative move to the right with its own turn to the left. The political and intellectual failure of the party's managerial center during the Wilson and Calla-ghan governments opened the way for the leftward swing. Clearly the ruling center left office with little sense of where to lead the party in the future and little appetite for a battle to control its future fortunes. The national party apparatus has long been dominated by the left, but there have been two important new developments: the left has captured the parliamentary party leadership and it has influence over the process by which M.P.s are selected. For the first time an incumbent M.P. will not have a virtually automatic right to run again for his seat but will have to be reselected. Consequently, the constituency itself will at last influence the choice of M.P. and presumably affect his or her behavior in Parliament. Arguably, what was once only party rhetoric is now becoming a central premise of government policy. A more abrupt swing toward nationalization and protection could be expected if the Labour party were returned to office. One ranking M.P. has said, however, that though the party would in fact attempt such policies, there need be no worry because the bureaucracy would simply refuse to implement them. Such a view will not allay many fears.

As the Conservatives preside over the declining economy and the Labour party moves to the political left, there is the possibility that the political mold will be broken, spawning a center party not shackled by the old debate. Certainly the emergence of the Social Democratic party suggested that the British electorate was not bound by the polar categories to which the elites of the two major parties have restricted the policy debate. A new party not constrained by the battles that created the interventionist apparatus in the 1960s and 1970s might be able to use that apparatus in new and more innovative ways. For now, however, the polar extremes of free markets and nationalization are implanted more strongly than ever in British politics.

The Unsettling Agenda and the Politics of Adjustment

In the two decades since supply management took its place on the political agenda, successive British governments have constructed an apparatus for state industrial intervention. That apparatus has involved creating mechanisms for the selective allocation of industrial credit. Those instruments have not, as in France, been linked to the allocation of credit by the financial system. Aid to industry came from the budget, not from a manipulation of the economy's flow of funds. This approach limited the scope of government's influence, made its industrial activities more public, and forced it to enter the market from the outside rather than acting through the financial system itself. The financial system served to limit rather than implement public policies of intervention. At the same time, the growing concentration in financial

227

markets has opened up the possibility of closer ties between industry and finance. Taken together, the changes in bureaucracy and finance have created a new potential for mobilizing Britain's industrial resources, a greater institutional capacity for harnessing the components of the economy to a state purpose. Yet the political will or consensus needed to direct such an effort has been dissipated in the struggle to create the basic administrative instruments for intervention. These instruments, by comparison with those in the French system, are very feeble even now. The technical reforms in the markets and in the institutions needed to establish promotional policies set the producer groups and the parties that tended to represent them at each others' throats.

The establishment of the NEDC—with the participation of industry, civil servants, labor leaders, and later financiers—suggests that institutions established in the pursuit of growth might well have produced a coalition for adjustment and change. Instead, however, the political parties and their respective constituencies divided not over the purpose that the interventionist apparatus should serve but over the much more basic question of whether it should exist at all. As the IRC and the NEB suggest, challenges to the traditional position of finance and business broke up that potential coalition. It was no accident that the effort to build interventionist institutions that would give government an expanded role in industry became a central point of conflict between Labour and the Conservatives. The new interventionist instruments operated as potential rivals to the preexisting financial system. As defined by the Labour left, they appeared as a challenge to private business. The arrangements in the financial system, with its division between industry and the state and finance and the state, had to be reordered. It was the institutional structure of the economy, the preexisting normalcy, that shaped the character of the political fight. The financial system, with its embedded privileges and position, was an obstacle to those who would promote state-led industrial change.

The state apparatus, consequently, wavered in purpose. For Labour, it chiefly served the leadership's effort to provide public direction and support for private redevelopment, but it also presented a challenge to private ownership from the left of the party. When in opposition the Conservatives have resisted this challenge to management's prerogative to chart an autonomous course, but once in office they have reconstructed and maintained the capacity to intervene on behalf of lame-duck companies. Neither party was able to find an enduring resolution of the state's role in the industrial marketplace. The problem of how state support might effectively be used to make British industry more

228

competitive was obscured by the challenge to privilege and position which the reforms represented. This conflict, along with the fight over the power of the labor movement in the factory and in politics, interfered with a political settlement of the terms of change, the issue that replaced the defense of sterling as the crucial obstacle to industrial growth.

Industrial adjustment—changes in who makes what, and how, in response to new market or technological conditions—has meant an expansion of the total product available to a society. Yet at bottom, an adjustment poses a distributional problem—who will bear the costs and who will reap the gains? A workable settlement requires a resolution at the electoral government level and also in the arena of producer institutions. Stable government policies and stable rules about financial, industrial, and labor markets are an indication that such a settlement has been reached.

The alternation of power between political parties in Britain and the flux within each party since the Second World War have prevented either party from dictating the terms of change. Was this alternation the underlying political problem? It might seem so when we consider the longevity of conservative governments in France and Japan, because these governments have facilitated changes in the market by resolving the terms of change. Yet in Germany party change has not interfered with industrial growth, and in Italy the long reign of the Christian Democrats has not permitted sustained governance of the economy. Apparently the answer lies not simply in continuity of rule but in the character of the parties and the terms of party competition. Rather than examining that problem here, let us consider the task that must be completed if adjustment is to proceed.

A settlement can be achieved in one of two ways: either groups that bear the costs of change can be excluded from interfering with policy or the operation of the market; or a settlement between the groups affected by change can be negotiated. When, as in Great Britain, there is an alternation of power between two parties of nearly equal strength, one of them based on a labor constituency and the other on a middle-class and business constituency, the political balance precludes a settlement by decisive victory. A negotiated settlement, however, requires not simply that the different groups have some set of common interests but that those common interests in fact dominate their dealings. The creation of an interventionist apparatus in the British political environment raised issues concerning both the distribution of burdens and the benefits of adjustment. In each controversy—including the most recent restructuring of NEB by the Conservatives which has led to the withdrawal of the labor unions—the question of managerial prerogatives has loomed as large as the technical problem of economic strategy. The efforts at institutional reform highlighted the issues that divided the groups and precluded a resolution based on joint interests.

The North Sea oil case illustrates how the institutional apparatus for distributing the national gains from oil bounty focused attention on the distributional problem rather than on the growth question. Growth, it was widely agreed, required a shift of national spending away from consumption and toward investment. The question was how the government gains from North Sea oil would be redistributed. Stripping away the technicalities, we see that there were two choices. First, the monies could go into the government coffers, in theory permitting lower tax rates and, as a result, higher corporate profits and investment. The operational difficulties, of course, would be to keep government from spending the money for other purposes or from reducing personal rather than corporate tax burdens. Second, the monies could be collected into a single investment fund and then lent or granted to industry. In this case the difficulty would lie in establishing the criteria on which the funds should be lent or directed to industry.

There was a political dilemma inherent in selecting an approach. For Labour, profits represented corporate exploitation of the society and a distribution of income toward private capital. Labour was willing to sacrifice the public expenditures that oil revenues might make possible but it was not willing to let higher investment depend on the judgment and purposes of industrialists. From Labour's point of view, a North Sea oil investment bank would have the advantage of openly demonstrating the connection between lost public spending and increased industrial investment. For business, however, the establishment of a multibillion pound investment bank with rights to allocate industrial credit selectively would constitute a direct challenge to its independence of business and to the free operation of financial markets. If such an investment bank had already existed, it could have been used without objection to distribute North Sea oil gains to industry, but the creation of such an institution from scratch was politically dangerous. The debate about North Sea oil policy is not an isolated case; rather it is typical of the way distributional issues surfaced to obscure common economic interests.

It was this failure to settle the terms of change that produced the appearance of "pluralistic" stagnation in Britain. Producer-group participation is not seen as a handicap in Germany or the Scandinavian countries, where the capacity to compensate the particular segments of the economy harmed by change is said to promote adjustment.[133] Since

Britain lacks both stable political direction and the institutional foundation for an industry-state alliance, interventionist policies have tended to degenerate into government grants of subsidies and protections. Under both Conservative and Labour governments, job support has seemingly taken precedence over industrial adjustment, and one might argue that the policies intended to prod growth were those that most often provoked resistance. Thus, for example, the British have found themselves defending a low-wage status quo rather than cooperating to create a high-wage future—the opposite of the German choice. Indeed, the bulk of government support in the forms of loans and grants in 1973–1974, before the full effects of recession had hit, went to declining industries and backward regions. The total was about 325 million pounds in that year, and some 35 million of that sum went to the shipbuilding industry.[134] In an effort to support the most distressed parts of the country, some areas have been designated development regions. Such regions have been so favored in the disbursement of funds that the real substance of British industrial policy has been to provide for troubled regions rather than to force or encourage adjustment by growing firms.[135] This pattern of state support for failing industries took shape after the First World War during the initial decline of the staple-goods producers that represented the livelihood of North Britain. Efforts to cushion such producing regions against unemployment became a defense of declining industry and vice versa. The result has been a tension between the goal of regional employment and that of industrial competitiveness—a tension evident in a recent struggle over the location of a semiconductor factory. The government had taken a stake in an American microelectronics industry and sought to use its shareholding influence to establish the plant in a region with high rates of unemployment. The company wanted to locate in Bristol and when it was subjected to massive political pressures to locate in a government-targeted development region of high unemployment, it threatened to break its partnership with the British government and return to the United States.

Support for the industrial status quo is evident also in the British government's intervention in labor markets, which has made these markets more rigid. Unemployment benefits paid for jobs lost through plant closings express the intent and consequences of the system. Such benefits reflect the notion that workers have property rights in their jobs, the result being that security has become an alternative to progress. One observer argues that the British arrangements have an emphasis and purpose different from those used in Germany. Whereas Britain tries to pay off its workers, Germany puts the greatest effort into finding them jobs. In Britain the bulk of funds for workers goes into individual cash compensation, into paying them for lost jobs. Security of employment thus becomes equated with holding a particular job, because there is little assurance of new jobs. "Security becomes synonymous with rigidity."[136]

Let us now summarize our argument. The British government was pushed by the pressures of industrial decline to seek an active role in promoting economic growth. The decline was not a postwar phenomenon—it had been underway for at least half a century—but the rapid emergence of Germany, France, and later Japan finally provoked the British government to make a concerted response. Its efforts at industrial promotion stumbled over institutional obstacles that restricted the range of policies available to it. Further complicating its task, however, was the fact that the effort to conduct a negotiated and later a state-led policy necessitated the creation of new institutions and the reform of old ones. These reforms were intended to expand the capacity of the British administration to act in the economy, but they only aggravated distributional conflicts that were already interfering with the objective of industrial expansion. We have argued that there are several ways of providing the political prerequisites of growth but that all of them depend upon a relatively stable resolution of the distribution of the gains and costs of growth. Such a resolution can be explicitly imposed by the state, produced by the market, or negotiated between the major social groups and producers. Britain found no solution to this central political problem. No solution could be imposed, and none was negotiated. The resulting distributional conflicts pressed all parties toward slowed adjustment and often toward an outright defense of the economic status quo. Put differently, the British government failed to set a political context in which the market could force the industrial changes required for expansion, and it failed to organize those changes itself. The British failure, in other words, has been as much political as economic.

CHAPTER FIVE

Generalizing the Argument: Japan, West Germany, and the United States

This chapter seeks to generalize the French and British experiences by examining three additional cases—Japan, West Germany, and the United States. The discussion of each country is abbreviated, the intent being simply to establish the plausibility of the proposed correlation between the system of finance and the model of adjustment. Japan, like France, has a credit-based, price-administered financial system. Both countries are examples of the model of state-led growth set forth in Chapter 2. Among the countries studied here, Germany is the one example of a credit-based, bank-dominated system; it fits the model of negotiated adjustment. The United States, which has a capital market–based financial system, is a case of company-led adjustment.

Our analytic task is to establish the relationship between national financial systems, which constitute a structural parameter in each national economy, and the political process of industrial change. We have contended that each of the three types of financial systems delimits predictably the way in which business and the state can act toward each other. Since the financial system influences both the capacity of government to exert industrial leadership and the character of the political conflicts about the government's economic objectives, it contributes to the pattern of politics which accompanies industrial development.

Though the political problems of adjustment are in some sense common to all countries, the ways in which they are resolved—the politics of industrial change—differ. Economic growth can occur within any of the three models of adjustment, since each defines a distinct process by which the political issues that accompany economic growth are resolved. Though growth can take place by several political roads, the failure to resolve the political conflicts will be an obstacle to inflation-free development. Since each model of adjustment endows government with distinct political capacities for economic action, a government may find its capacity more effective for dealing with certain kinds of problems than with others. It may also find that the effectiveness of its capacity varies considerably over time. These issues are addressed in the final chapter.

For now, in order to hold roughly constant the economic problems that the countries have had to confront politically, we shall consider France, Japan, and Germany as one set and Britain and the United States as a second set. The countries in the first set were relatively backward at the end of the Second World War and then developed rapidly. Those in the second set were more mature industrial economies at that point and were internationally dominant; they grew more slowly. As was stressed in Chapter 1, the division of these countries into two sets does not constitute an argument that one system of adjustment is more effective than another.

THE HIGH-GROWTH COUNTRIES: JAPAN, FRANCE, AND GERMANY

Whereas the German government tried to keep its distance from the market process, the French and Japanese governments actively intervened in the market to influence the fate of specific sectors and often of specific firms. The present discussion emphasizes what the French and Japanese experiences have in common and identifies the distinctively different role played by government and finance in the German case.

Japan

The French and Japanese experiences have important similarities, not the least of which derive from the structure of their respective financial systems and state bureaucracies. In our categorization, both countries have credit-based, price-administered financial systems and both are tied to state-led growth. The implementation of government industrial policy is facilitated by a credit-based industrial finance system, which allocates resources through state influence and administrative policies. In both cases, a conservative coalition that included elite members of the centralized state bureaucracy aggressively promoted the shift out of agriculture into industry, and out of low-wage into high-wage industrial sectors. That transformation was facilitated because state bureaucrats could manipulate credit, tax, and trade policies in pursuit of their goals. Policy for industrial development in each country has been formulated within a triangle of government bureaucrats, major companies, and banks; in each case the centralized bureaucracy has been somewhat insulated from detailed political parliamentary pressure and has been manned by a mandarin elite that stands first among equals. Indeed, Chalmers Johnson claims that in Japan the politicians reign but the bureaucrats rule. The triangle rests on bureaucratic and market structures but is riveted together by self-interest and career patterns.

The political settlements underlying growth have also had important similarities in the two countries, particularly from 1958 until the recent Socialist victory in France. Government has been dominated by conservative parties dependent for electoral survival on agriculture and traditional business. Consequently, agricultural enterprises and small businesses have been cushioned from change, with public expenditures for agriculture in the late 1960s representing 1.7 percent of the GNP in Japan and 1.6 percent in France and with special laws operating to protect small firms in both countries.[1] In both cases, union influence on policy has been limited although the marketplace and the firm-level organization of labor in each country is quite different. The difference in union organization meant that French labor was more able than its Japanese counterpart to blackmail the government with threats of disruption in order to obtain policy concessions.

Similar institutional structures and politics produced important parallels in the industrial policies of the two countries. Both governments mediated between the domestic economy and the international marketplace to foster industrial expansion, but successive French governments were more constrained in their tactics by international agreements and by companies that focused on the domestic market. The Japanese bureaucrats adopted "market-conforming" policies intended to help companies establish self-sustaining market positions in growth industries. In contrast, the French often sought to override the market by sheltering chosen companies from competition or by promoting favorite projects that did not fit into any strategic or commercial plan; in recent years, however, they have in specific cases sought to harness market forces to the purposes of the state, taking a lesson from the Japanese. The Japanese, committed to growth as a systematic priority, maintained an undervalued currency for a generation in order to promote exports, but the French had competing international policy purposes and did not systematically attempt the same monetary tactic. A case can be made that the French were also more constrained politically by the demands of their uncompetitive sectors. They provided extensive support to laggard sectors and firms and were less able to force them onto paths of competitive righteousness. Yet in each country, the state used such tactics as selective credit allocation to support the effort of expanding sectors to buy resources away from traditional uses. It can be argued that these tactics contributed to the patterns of inflation in both France and Japan. The two governments also sought to secure sources of raw materials and both explicitly arranged trade deals to pay for the imported production inputs. The policy differences between them turned more on the greater competitive strength of Japan's export sectors than on differences in political organization, state structure, or financial system.

The link between Japanese policies of state-directed development and the credit-based, price-administered financial system is the same as that which we explored in the French case. Finance was an important element in the state-led development strategy and a critical component in the emergence of the system of controlled competition. The Japanese case serves as strong evidence that a credit-based, price-administered financial system is a basic component of state-promoted industrial growth and adjustment strategies. In this discussion we will outline the system of business-state relations in Japan and examine the techniques of state promotional policies before explicitly considering the place of the financial system in the Japanese government's economic strategies.

The two images of the Japanese case that vie for our attention represent, at their most extreme, two competing cartoons.[2] The first image is that of Japan, Inc., the ordered and state-directed economy in which planning rules; the second, that of Japan the Land of the Triumphant Competitors, in whose intensely competitive domestic markets planning has, in reality, been of secondary importance to the initiatives of private businessmen.[3] The image of Japan, Inc., dates from the early years of reconstruction and is best represented by the development of the steel industry. State intervention in steel helped preserve the domestic market for Japanese companies, provided firms the funds to invest, staged investment to avoid oversupply, and often managed excess supply when it did occur. The image of Japan the competitive society was first projected by the sudden international success of Japanese companies in consumer electronics and automobiles. It has been reinforced by the inability of government to dictate the fate of textile manufacturers, auto assemblers, and consumer electronics firms.[4] The great financial resources of the successful auto manufacturers allowed them to break loose from the government's dictates, though part of their international

236

success depended on government intervention that reorganized the auto parts producers. Sony, which led the drive to introduce solid-state components in consumer electronics, stood outside the traditional arrangements between government and business. Textiles, an industry slated in government plans for continued decline, has prospered. At times the debate between the advocates of the two cartoons takes on a theological tone since the interpretation of Japan is used to confirm domestic policy prescriptions. Those who believe in the market discover competition and find evidence that supports their domestic ideological preferences; the would-be planners find MITI and take equal solace in the supposed benefits of Japanese government intervention. In fact, it is the particular interaction of state and market in Japan that is interesting.

The Japanese system, in my view, is one of controlled competition. There is every evidence of intense competition between firms but that competition seems to be directed and limited both by state actions and by the collaborative efforts of the firms and banks themselves. Though the state bureaucrats do not dictate to an administered market, they do consciously contribute to the development of particular sectors and they help in a detailed way to establish conditions of investment and risk which promote their long-term development and international competitiveness. An agency such as MITI (Ministry of International Trade and Industry) is not so much a strict director as a player with its own purposes and its own means of interfering in the market to reach them. Government industrial strategy assumes that the market pressures of competition can serve as an instrument of policy. It is not simply that the government makes use of competitive forces that arise naturally in the market, but rather that it often induces the very competition it directs.[5] It induces competition by creating the market for products and the conditions for high returns, thus seemingly assuring a profit and attracting the entry of many competitors. The competition is real, but the government and the private sector also possess the mechanisms to avoid "disruptive" or "excessive" competition. Such limits on competition include product specialization agreed on within a set of competing firms and the often-cited cartels to regulate capacity expansion in booms and cut-back arrangements in downturns.[6] The fact that these arrangements to manage the market often break down should not be taken as evidence that they do not operate or do not matter. In semiconductors today, as in steel a generation ago, these collaborative arrangements appear central to Japanese international success. In this setting, in which business collaborates as well as competes, the government appears as a marketplace actor, prodding here and promoting there.

The purpose of this system of controlled competition has been to generate expansion.[7] T. J. Pempel puts it directly: "The most central concern of the Japanese state, both prewar and postwar, has been economic development."[8] "It has been a developmental state."[9] From the beginning of the postwar era, the Japanese bureaucracy had a strong commitment to moving labor out of low-productivity sectors into high-wage industries, as well as to facilitating the move out of agriculture. The industrial structure that was built in the late 1930s and the 1960s resulted, at least in part, from this deliberate restructuring. As the share of labor-intensive light industry declined, capital-intensive heavy industries with higher wage structures grew.[10] The shift was promoted by government measures that channeled resources into those industries for which there was a growing domestic demand and potential economies of scale. The targets were increased production of machinery, metals, chemicals, and ships.[11] The diamond in Chart 5.1 shows the movement in Japan's shifting export mix, which Thomas Hout and Ira Magaziner explain as follows:

> The shape of the diamond represents Japan's export mix in successive periods. In 1959, Japan's exports were mainly unskilled labor-intensive and its diamond skewed toward the bottom. Throughout the 1960s, Japan's exports became more capital-intensive—steel, motorcycles, ships, etc. By the middle 1970s more complex products in the middle to upper areas of the diamond such as motor cars and color televisions became significant exports. This process is continuing as Japan's mix shifts toward high technology machinery and electronics industries. By 1985, the Japanese Economic Planning Agency hopes that Japan will have a structure similar to the structure of Germany's exports of manufactured goods in the mid-1970s.[12]

The shift in the composition of production occurred along with a sevenfold expansion of production in the twenty years since the end of the American occupation.[13] Whatever the measures—growth rates in GNP, per capita income, or worker output—it was an unmatched achievement.[14]

The constant theme of Japanese policy in these years was consciously to create comparative advantage in high-value-added industries rather than to remain focused on the labor-intensive industries that might seem appropriate to an economy with a scarcity of raw materials and capital. The decision to create a comparative advantage in capital-intensive and technology-intensive industries (iron and steel, petroleum refining, automobiles, industrial machinery, electronics, and electronic machinery are examples) was a political victory by MITI over, among others, the

Chart 5.1 Evolution of Japanese industrial structure

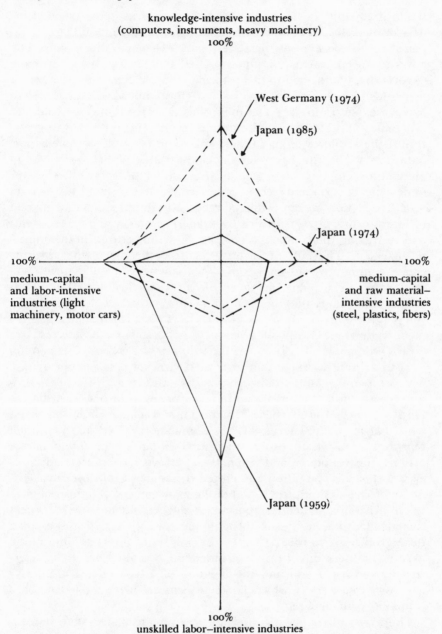

knowledge-intensive industries
(computers, instruments, heavy machinery)
100%

West Germany (1974)

Japan (1985)

Japan (1974)

100% ———— medium-capital and labor-intensive industries (light machinery, motor cars)

medium-capital and raw material–intensive industries (steel, plastics, fibers) ———— 100%

Japan (1959)

100%
unskilled labor–intensive industries

SOURCE: Japan Economic Survey, Economic Agency, 1974–1975, quoted in Ira Magaziner and Thomas Hout, *Japanese Industrial Policy* (Berkeley: University of California,
Institute of International Studies, 1981), p. 9.

Bank of Japan.[15] In the bank's view, the industries recommended for development by MITI were the "most inappropriate industries for Japan then in the eyes of the state theory of comparative cost."[16] The governor of the Bank of Japan argued that policy should promote exports that conformed to this principle of an international division of labor. MITI reasoned differently and chose industries that: (1) were likely to expand with increases in income; (2) offered the possibilities of economies of scale from concentrated investment; (3) would drag the rest of the economy along in their wake; and (4) could become export industries. "The theory underlying industrial structure policy was to place undeveloped domestic industries with little competitive power under the government's active interference and to build up a large-scale production system, while limiting entry into the domestic market of foreign enterprises with already established mass production systems and restricting the competition of foreign manufacturers in the domestic market.[17] The automobile case is the archetype of the effort to create comparative advantage in capital-intensive manufacturing sectors. Public investment laid down the infrastructure to permit a swift rise in auto usage, the domestic market was closed to outsiders, and a competitive auto components industry was established under government leadership. Competition between the assemblers did the rest.

MITI domination of industry in support of a policy of expansion worked as long as expansion generated growing profit opportunities. The competitive gains from such policies—measured by the fall in producer costs, domestic prices, and export prices—ran out, according to Hiroya Ueno, around 1967.[18] Interestingly, Chalmers Johnson maintains that in political terms MITI's domination ended in 1969, when Mitsubishi resisted its orders to restrict expansion in automobiles.[19] MITI's interventionist and promotional efforts have not ended, however. Instead, its attention has shifted to the new growth sectors, such as the electronics industries, and to the management of industrial transition situations. Equally important, the government now influences capital allocation indirectly through the banking system rather than through direct controls.[20] Clearly, the policies of direct administration gave way to less direct forms of intervention as the period characterized by reconstruction and the building of a base of heavy industry gave way to an era in which Japanese manufactured goods enjoyed a competitive advantage.

The government, acting through the semi-insulated state bureaucracy, has continuously formed its own view of the future of Japanese industry (and of the proper structure of specific industries) and then pursued that vision. It became a market player, using its capacities to advocate and to promote industrial development. The limits on its capacities should not deceive us about the extent of its influence, nor should the significance of the Japanese pursuit of actively created comparative advantage be underestimated. MITI policy involved a rejection of the limits of neoclassical equilibrium economics and a recognition of how government manipulation of the conditions of business competition generates national advantage.[21]

The Japanese government's promotional policies can be divided into two sets: (1) those controlling the links between the Japanese market and international markets; and (2) those manipulating the domestic firms to stimulate rapid expansion. Considering the first set, Pempel characterizes the Japanese state as an "official doorman determining what, and under what conditions, capital, technology and manufactured products enter and leave Japan."[22] The discretion to decide what to let in (and at the extreme what to let out) of Japan, permits the doorman to break up the packages of technology, capital, and control which multinational corporations represent. The Ministry of Finance operated selective controls over inward foreign investment. Foreign loans were encouraged but equity investment was not, and foreign efforts to control Japanese firms were actively discouraged. MITI controlled technology imports in order to force foreigners to sell raw technology in the form of patents, licenses, and expertise. Foreign firms were in general obliged to be content with royalty payments for the use of their technology, rather than with product sales in Japan. In sum, the government dictated the terms of access to the Japanese market and thus was able to provide Japanese firms a stable base of demand on which to build networks of competitive production and distribution.

The second set of promotional policies forced development by substituting an intense but controlled domestic competition for the pressures of the international market. The government actively encouraged such domestic competition by giving extensive support to expanding firms. Government policy helped provide cash for investment, tax breaks to assure cash flow that maintained liquidity, research-and-development support for technology, and aid to promote exports. These public policies changed the options of companies, helping them to justify large initial investments and providing the necessary funds. The speed of expansion in sectors such as automobiles and steel involved staggering investment sums. Whereas the Japanese produced only 160,000 cars in 1960, they were producing 3.1 million cars a year by 1970 and over 8 million a year in 1980. Such rapid expansion was of necessity debt financed, but neither companies nor banks could have managed the debt without special tax arrangements and a policy of diffusing lending risk.

Rapid expansion built on credit involves a high fixed cost and capital and thus creates serious cash-flow problems for companies. The Japanese tax system responded by permitting very rapid depreciation schedules, allowing the depreciation rates to exceed 50 percent for favored industries with strong export performance.

These government policies encouraged Japanese companies to view their investments as part of an integrated business rather than as a series of specific choices with discrete payoffs. This company bias toward long-term payback also encouraged superior production economies. Indeed, there appears to be a common pattern in Japanese business strategies across a whole range of sectors. An initial production volume is built on the domestic market and then steadily expanded through selective exploitation of market niches abroad. Those niches form the opening edge for export drives. Steadily increasing production volumes support the production economies that often make the Japanese the low-cost producers in the market. Indeed, in a wide range of sectors the Japanese use less labor than do producers in other countries, demonstrating a remarkable capacity to manage complex mass production processes. Government policies interact with corporate strategy and become more than a series of discrete subsidies; they affect the very nature of company strategies. The public and private objectives have converged because, as Kasuo Sato contends, business circles have seen industrial policy as a means of achieving higher profits.[23]

The easy availability of capital and technology within a protected market was bound to attract entrants. Indeed, since late Japanese entrants in an industry were apt to be closed out of the market, both by MITI policy and by the established positions of other firms, there was a veritable stampede to enter the new sectors.[24] In an expanding market firms competed for market share and the low profit rates of the larger firms reflected the intensity of competition.[25] MITI viewed the stampede for entry, which it had encouraged, and the resulting battle for market share, which limited profit, as excessive competition that had to be controlled, both to preserve the viability of the initial entrants and to assure market demand adequate to justify efficiently scaled plants for existing producers.

Thus, as intense as the domestic competition became, it was still controlled in many ways. One mechanism that worked to limit competition was joint planning of expansion, which helped to avoid excess capacity and to assure the introduction of plants of sufficient size to capture scale economies.[26] Such joint planning was very evident in steel. Similar policies were used later in the semiconductor industry.[27]

There was also a general awareness among competitors that when excess capacities emerged, either from overly optimistic judgment about the expansion of the domestic market or from a downturn in demand, the resulting "oversupply" would be managed. Firms would not be driven out of business. Indeed, one American businessman described the Japanese system as one in which the intense fight is to capture the largest possible share of the new demand in the market and in which shares of existing market demand are tolerated.

A second mechanism was used to diffuse the risk involved in the debt financing of rapid expansion. The corporate debt was parceled out among many banks, a procedure that limited the risk to each and gave all financial institutions a stake in the survival of heavily levered firms.[28] As in many operations in France, the Japanese financial community as a whole thus became committed to projects of national priority. American banks have lent to Japanese clients with debt levels they would not tolerate in American clients; they have perceived Japanese debt as being secured by government guarantees. The result is that the risks of rapid expansion to the banks are in essence managed and controlled, a situation that, ironically, intensifies the temptation for competitors to enter the market in the first place.[29] Indeed, the mechanisms of debt financing have led to steadily increasing debt levels, making firms and banks vulnerable to abrupt market changes that would endanger any large firms. A serious collapse of a highly levered firm could threaten the banks, not just the company in trouble or its suppliers. Since a bank collapse could have serious effects throughout an economy, the company's troubles become a matter of public policy. Despite seemingly risky corporate financial structures, the system remains stable because government concern with the well-being of firms in favored sectors is seen as an implicit guarantee of the bank loans made to them.[30] The system of debt finance is dependent on government policy as the *guarantor* of last resort.

The structure of business, as well as the system of state administration and policy, supports this arrangement of controlled competition. Before the Second World War the Japanese community had developed giant hierarchical firms, intercompany group linkages, and an international orientation. The business community was not only the vehicle but also the political support for the efforts of postwar development.[31] Equally important, the structure of business provided the basis of collaboration between firms—not so much because Japan is an economy of giant firms[32] as because a number of mechanisms drew the large firms together in common institutions. The trading companies, an early link between the insulated domestic economy and its external sources of supply, represent one such mechanism.[33] The Zaibatsu groupings of companies were dissolved during the American occupation, but groupings around large banks (*keiretsu*) have been established and now tie firms together. There are several forms of keiretsu, ranging from groups with close intercompany ties to loose arrangements that are basically financial.[34] Though the precise form or degree of operating cohesion in these groups is debated, the fact is that a majority of company stock is held by other companies or banks, an arrangement that provides still another set of intercompany ties.[35] The world of small companies is not an anarchy either, for many of the small firms are linked to larger companies as suppliers. (I am not suggesting that small firms are inevitably relegated to subordinate status; some independent small firms have grown to compete directly with the giants.) Lastly, though cartels are nominally illegal, a large number are in fact exempt from the general prohibition. In 1973 there were nearly one thousand authorized cartels. The bulk were small-business and export cartels (787), but there were a dozen depression and rationalization cartels as well.[36] These several forms of intercompany links provide the organizational infrastructure for controlled competition.

We must next situate the role of finance in the business system and assess its impact on the Japanese state's capacity to pursue its policy purposes. The financial system was not as crucial in the political victory for aggressive modernization in Japan as it was in France, but it played a similar role in the implementation of development policy. Hiroya Ueno contends that the financial apparatus was the *central element of promotional policy.* He argues that the fundamental strategy of the National Income Doubling Plan was "to concentrate funds of capital in key industries." "For this purpose," Ueno continues,

> in addition to utilizing public financial institutions, private financial institutions were placed under the strict control of the Ministry of Finance. *While tacitly establishing a principle that banks would neither be bankrupted nor go bankrupt, it regulated and directed financial activities so as to conform to industrial policy.* A significant point in this policy of concentrating and distributing funds is that, *in giving out industrial loans, private financial institutions decided on strategic industries and growth enterprises, most fundamentally along the judgment of MITI. This was tantamount to a governmental guarantee.*[37]

This view is shared by Henry and Mabel Wallich, who conclude that financial policy simply reinforced the preferences of the market by managing risk—socializing it, one might say.[38] For example, a short-term liquidity problem was not allowed to bankrupt a company as long as it had the capacity to remain solvent in the long run.[39] The operation of the financial system permitted the corporate overborrowing (of which more later) that made possible the rapid postwar growth. Though finance was by no means the only instrument of administrative discretion and intervention, it did permit expansion by providing the funds and diffusing the risk of investment. Moreover, it was central in influencing the direction of expansion.

We examine the financial system here to understand how it could be used to pump funds into expanding industries, to diffuse the risks to the banks that served as the pumps, and to nourish the firms that received the funds. Three features of the Japanese system are important to us: first, it is a credit-based system like those of France and Germany; second, it is structured primarily to finance industry; and third, as in the French system, prices in crucial markets are determined by government.

The Japanese have a credit-based financial system. The Inter-Bank Research Organisation concluded that "the securities markets in Japan do not play a significant role in raising funds for industry."[40] The pattern of industrial development before the Second World War did not leave much scope for securities markets. Indeed, stock issues represented only 3.8 percent of company funds in 1968.[41] Equally important, the stock market has become an intercompany and interbank market. That is, since company stocks are increasingly held by other banks and other companies, the stock market is not a means of raising new funds for industry from the household sector. Nor does the bond market provide an alternative to bank loans as the basic source of company finance. Because the government keeps interest rates low, the supply of funds in the bond market is limited, just as in France. "The government in effect has severely restricted access to the bond market for corporate borrowers by generally fixing rates on new issues at levels below those prevailing in the secondary market and by preempting for itself . . . a large part of the supply of the funds 'available' at these artificially low rates."[42] Since extensive bank financing of corporate expansion is available, companies and the government need not be troubled by the limitation on the securities market's capacity to raise funds. Debt financing, though, becomes self-confirming. It produces very fragile corporate financial structures with high debt-to-equity ratios. The levels of debt in companies, as measured by the debt-equity ratio, increased over the first twenty years of rapid growth; Table 5.1 shows the percentage of owner equity to total capital. These debt ratios make it more difficult to raise equity, but the close arrangements between banks, firms, and government make debt

Table 5.1. Percentage of owner equity to total capital in Japanese industry, 1950–1970

Year	Manufacturing	All industries
1950	31.4	26.9
1955	34.0	29.0
1960	27.6	22.6
1965	23.1	19.0
1970	19.9	16.1

SOURCE: Richard Caves, with Masu Uekusa, "Industrial Organization," in Hugh Patrick and Henry Rosovsky, eds., *Asia's New Giant* (Washington, D.C.: Brookings Institution, 1976), p. 479.

funding available even under these skewed conditions.[43] In essence, a credit-based system of corporate finance is hard to reverse, and Japan will doubtless maintain such a system for the foreseeable future. In fact, the system is so entrenched that some observers think that bank loans function as preferred stock, with the lender in fact having an assumed voice in corporate affairs.

Indeed, the Japanese financial system as a whole is oriented toward bank financing of the corporate sector with funds drawn from households. The system is dependent on *banks* as intermediaries between savers and users of capital. As we have seen, the securities market is limited but investing institutions are also underdeveloped. Nor do long-term credit institutions play the significant role they do in France. The crucial link in Japanese finance, therefore, is that between banks and corporations. Because public (government) debt is low and housing investment has been limited, industry has been the major user of bank funds. The major supplier of these funds has been the household sector. The distribution of loans provides a good measure of these relations. In the United States in 1973 corporations held 32 percent of loans to nonfinancial borrowers, whereas in Japan the figure was 73 percent.[44]

In this bank-oriented, credit-based system of corporate finance, the government exerts detailed controls over prices in a multitude of markets. The government's desire to control interest rates also leads it to encourage the flow of funds through institutions that can be controlled or whose lending habits can be predicted. The control of interest rates is crucial to the strategy of selective allocation and gives the government influence over the economy's financial flows. The market is kept in disequilibrium, which means that prices do not clear the market.

Controlled prices and selective intervention in industry go hand in hand. The Wallichs explains this clearly.

> The government's choice to rely on administrative control more than on market forces has reflected a traditional pattern. It may have presented some special advantages under postwar conditions of recovery and rapid growth, and it has fitted in with the government's preference for low interest rates. The desire to control allocation while keeping interest rates down made it advisable in turn for the authorities to keep funds flowing through institutions that can be controlled or that, like mutual banks and credit associations and cooperatives, will channel it to a known group of borrowers.
>
> In a flexible capital market, free from rigidities and compartmentalization, allocation techniques such as those practiced in Japan may not be particularly effective in increasing the supply of funds to the "favored" sector. As the government pushes funds into a sector, interest rates in that sector are likely to drop. This may cause suppliers to reallocate their funds to other sectors. In Japan there has not been much scope for such a mechanism until perhaps very recently. It seems reasonable to assume that because of rigidities, compartmentalization, and inflexibility of interest rates, governmentally sponsored allocation largely achieved its objective of increasing the supply of funds to the designated sector during most of the postwar period.[45]

Let us next consider how the system of bank credit in controlled markets generates state influence in the allocation of credit. The outlines of the system can be sketched quickly. First, the banking system as a whole is "overlent."[46] This crucial notion must be explained. A bank funds its loans with deposits and equity capital. Banks loan out a multiple of that funding base, creating money in the process. The multiples are set by law and prudence. Beyond this "core" the bank must borrow money to continue its lending. It is not unusual for a single bank to fund part of its assets through borrowings, but inside a closed financial system the net liabilities of borrowing banks should balance the net assets of lending banks. This is not the case in Japan. The banks as a set borrow from the central bank. Crucially, after the war there was no place to get funds except from the central bank; central bank lending thus served as an alternative to open-market operations in controlling bank liquidity.

Second, the system of industrial financing is based on bank lending, as discussed above. The companies are overborrowed or "highly levered," to use the term most often heard, and since alternative markets for industrial funds are underdeveloped, the companies can go only to the banks for funds.

Third, the market for industrial lending is structured by the government. Prices do not clear the market. "In postwar Japan, and particularly after 1955, the level of interest rates was kept low with the deliberate aims of reducing the cost of manufactured exports and stimulating investment."[47] *Prices in all but the very short-term money markets are artificially maintained by government.* An administratively established low interest rate can result in only one thing—an excess of demand for money. "Since the rates have been set at nonequilibrium level, the price mechanism cannot do its job, so that in the market for funds there is naturally an excess demand situation."[48] More people are willing to borrow at the price than are willing to lend and the outcome is a waiting line for funds. If markets cleared on their own, the price would rise, drawing in more funds and driving some borrowers away until the waiting line shortened. In this case, where prices are fixed, someone must decide the order in which demands are met. The question is who.

Fourth, the order of those standing in the waiting line is in the first instance decided by the banks. "The banks practiced a kind of credit rationing, selecting the most desirable clients on the basis of comparative profitability and growth rate among those seeking loan funds."[49]

Fifth, since part of the bank's funding must come from the central bank, the banks themselves are in an implicit waiting line: "Money is not supplied to any bank that is willing to acquire it through market transactions at the interest rate offered by the central bank, but it is allocated in a specific amount to a specific bank chosen by the central bank [authorities] from amongst those wishing to obtain high-powered money. In other words, for a given level of the official discount rate there is an excess demand from the commercial banks for scarce reserves and these are controlled at the Bank of Japan's loan window."[50]

This system is entirely different from the system of managing the money supply by the discount rate and reserve ratios which one finds in the United States. In Japan a rational banker *must* wish to follow the lead of the central bank. The government's industrial priorities of growth and exports will be met. The banks entangled with selected sectors will not be constrained by their ability to fund their loans, though banks in other sectors of the economy will be. "There is a tendency for city banks to meet the loan demands of export-oriented or investment-related concerns irrespective of any deterioration in their own fund position."[51] The system turns on itself. "As a result of the credit rationing which inevitably occurs due to the artificial low interest rate policy, the relationship between the Bank of Japan and the city banks, and in their turn the city banks and the export-oriented investment enterprises, is so inextricable that it preserves the over-loaned position of the city banks and the imbalance of bank liquidity."[52] Each element presented here depends on the others, and economic discretion in the bureaucracy is rooted in the arrangements of finance.

The U.S. Government Accounting Office presents its own summary of the system in these paragraphs:

> Since the capital market in Japan is underdeveloped, outside capital for corporate expansion until the last few years has come from the banking system, in which Japanese individuals overwhelmingly invest their savings. In a decision taken in the early postwar years, the Japanese government, as a stimulant to the economy, has chosen to keep interest rates below what for most of the period constituted market-clearing levels. This has meant that in most years more funds have been sought than are available to loan. Accordingly, capital investment funds have had in effect to be allocated with priority given to firms in "key" industries.
>
> How has the Japanese government been able to direct lending practices of private banks? It has been able to do so quite easily because during most of the period of high growth, there were such pressures on the commercial banks for funds that they loaned in excess of their stipulated ratio and had to borrow from the Bank of Japan to cover commitments. Japan's central bank is not an independent central bank, but one which follows Ministry of Finance policy. Therefore, the condition imposed for provision of the extra funds which the commercial banks were frequently seeking, was that the loan policy of the commercial banks be in accordance with government priorities.
>
> Commercial banks were able to get an explicit "reading" of the industries and companies which the government wished to favor from noting the companies to which the Japan Development Bank (JDB) made loans. The government made no attempt to supply all of the needs of companies in strategic industries through the JDB. In fact, the bank's loans were typically but a fraction of the firms' credit needs, but the JDB loan meant that the large commercial banks would then give these firms priority for funds.[53]

In sum, cheap loans create excess demand for credit. The available funds must be allocated by administrative discretion, which in the first instance is a choice of the major city banks. The ultimate source of discretion, however, flows from the central bank, which can selectively fund the excess of city-bank demand. There are no specific rediscounting facilities to enforce government preferences, as in France. The government lead is thought to provide additional security to loans in the form of implicit assurance that firms will not fail. This reinforces the government lead in lending priorities. The notion of administrative guidance, so bandied about in discussions of Japan, therefore rests not on some cultural propensity but rather on the dependence of firms on banks and the dependence of the banks on the government.

This financial system indeed served to move funds in the directions that the government indicated during the years of early development. Ueno has shown that shifts in the sectoral composition of public lending were followed by identical shifts in the composition of private lending.[54] We have described the mechanism by which guidance translates into lending decisions and have found evidence that the system works as predicted on an aggregate basis. As Ueno summarized the situation:

> Broadly speaking, the total supply of funds in Japan was controlled by the Bank of Japan, the level and structure of interest rates were artificially regulated by the Ministry of Finance, and *private funds were allocated, under the guidance of public financial institutions, by city banks which competed for market shares.* In this process, the Bank of Japan followed the guidelines of the Economic Planning Agency and the MITI and determined the total amount of funds so as to satisfy the demands to growth industries. At the same time, the Ministry of Finance maintained the low interest policy inasmuch as the policy did not lead to large deficits in the balance of payments or to sharp price rises.[55]

The credit-based financial system served the government as a powerful instrument of policy. The political and policy strategies of the Japanese government would have been difficult to accomplish within the constraints of a capital market–based financial system with freely moving prices and an elaborate securities market. The financial instrument in Japan served several purposes. Most generally, it helped force the household sector to bear the costs of expansion in the form of artificially low interest rates. At the same time, the system socialized those costs by diffusing or absorbing the risks of investment and corporate failure. It also reduced the price of expanding and stockpiling goods in anticipation of market development, which has been a constant Japanese market tactic. Access to credit was selectively manipulated to provide preference to favored sectors and to push the economy slowly toward capital-intensive and knowledge-intensive production. In all sectors there has been a constant effort to push and tempt firms onto what the government sees as the paths of competitive righteousness. The degree to which government's view prevails within particular sectors depends on the international competitive strength and financial position of their major companies. The government's view prevailed when companies needed capital, imported technology, and sought assistance in market development. In sum, the economy is not administered but the government seeks to act to affect the terms of competition in order to create the outcomes it favors. In essence, the state is another powerful economic player shaping market development in pursuit of competitiveness but not of profits. Finance is a vital instrument—in Ueno's view the crucial instrument—in the government's repertoire of domestic policies. The Japanese case closely parallels the French in which a credit-based, price-administered financial system is at the core of a state-led industrial strategy.

West Germany

Germany projects the image of a liberal market economy in which the most important decisions about the uses of the nation's economic resources are made by company managements driven by profit motivations and responding to price signals, not by bureaucrats following their plans or by politicians following their voters. Indeed, the German case has been used as evidence that if government would only ignore businessmen and workers in their demands to be protected from foreign competition and to be insulated from domestic change, inflation-free growth would result, benefiting those who bear the direct costs of adjustment. Successive German governments have in fact sought to pursue a policy of market-driven rather than state-led adjustment, avoiding government support for troubled industry more stringently than have their major trading partners. This determination to force the community to adjust to market changes, rather than to subsidize and protect it, was evident in the government's refusal to cushion the shock of the 1973 OPEC price hikes.[56] The required transfer of real resources out of consumers' pockets and into exports was accomplished quickly and with limited inflationary consequences. Overall trade surpluses were maintained and bilateral balances brought back into the black at the same time that inflation was kept below other national rates. It was a sharp contrast to policies elsewhere, which delayed these adjustments and, as a result, paid the price of inflation.

Though political virtue may well have been a contributory factor, the inflation-free nature of Germany's industrial resurgence was made possible by an industrial structure that was well suited to the needs of postwar competition. The German economic success suggests a second lesson: it is much easier to avoid protection and restriction when rapid growth does not involve major structural change within industry. Liberalism is the child of favorable economic circumstance and internationally competitive industry. Of all the fast-growth countries, Germany has required the least transformation of its industrial structure: its industries were well suited to the markets that began to emerge during

251

the postwar boom.[57] Indeed, its postwar industrial structure became the basis of export-led growth.[58] Thus, growing industries created a political base from which the government could refuse bailouts to industries in transition or decline. Past government success in forcing firms to make market adaptations made it easier to apply tough policies without sparking an immediate political reaction. An atmosphere that committed companies to market adjustment made it all the more likely that those companies would remain competitive.

This image of a liberal German economy—with individual and self-contained firms competing in market games umpired but not managed by government—is overdrawn in several respects, however. First, postwar Germany has never completely accepted the classical economic liberalism that condemns any tampering with the judgment of the market. The harsh prescriptions of liberalism are softened in Germany when the social disruptions caused by industrial change are judged to represent social and political costs that are simply unacceptable. Its policies for the coal and shipbuilding industries are examples.[59] Indeed, the Germans have made a principle out of this deviation from classical precept and have called this selected intervention intermingled with an elaborate welfare state "a social-market" system. The emphasis of their policy, however, is indeed on making firms respond to market signals and on making the markets work as effectively as possible by assuring that those signals are accurate. Second, although successive governments have not leaned toward public enterprise as an instrument of intervention, neither have they eschewed it for ideological reason. Finally, and more central to our purposes, German capitalism has about it a quality of organization, concentration, and centralization. Andrew Shonfield has labeled it "organized private enterprise." He summarizes the situation well: "There has been a powerful undertow throughout these postwar years which has irresistibly brought together pieces of economic power that were supposed to have stayed apart."[60] The industrial concentration and tendency toward centralization had to overcome considerable obstacles. The postwar occupation forces not only tried to keep business divided and small but also weakened the authority of the central government and divided power among the eleven "state" authorities.

The distinctive character of the German system of "organized private enterprise" depends on the combination of four elements: concentration, tolerated cartel-like arrangements, centralized semiofficial trade associations, and a tutelary banking system. From the beginning giant export-oriented firms had been instruments of industrial growth in many sectors of the German economy. As a result, the Germans never had to manage the politically delicate shift from an insulated economy of small-scale companies to an economy characterized by international competition between large corporations.[61] Concentration alone does not distinguish the German case from others, however. Giant firms and industrial concentration are typical of all advanced countries; some, like France, only came to them late. In many sectors, cartels—often organized in collaboration with the state—predominated. Despite intense Anglo-American occupation efforts to destroy the cartels, "mild cartel-like arrangements" have persisted in Germany.[62] Policy debate has asked whether particular cartels serve a useful public purpose, not whether they should exist at all. Organized arrangements between businesses were never viewed with automatic hostility, but were thought to provide elements of order in the unsteady world of market relations. As Karl Hardach puts it:

> The continued existence of mild cartel-like arrangements partly reflected the fact that, throughout Germany's industrial history, the academic and governmental attitude toward economic concentration in general, and cartels in particular, had in principle never been one of hostility. Quite in contrast to the Anglo-American view, which connected competitive markets with equilibrium and monopolistic situations with indeterminacy and disorder, it was held that unrestricted competition was "destructive" and that cartels were an "element of order." Apart from special-interest groups favoring cartels and largely apathetic and unorganized consumers, labor unions usually expected better job security from cartels than from unrestricted competition, or regarded the former as an intermediate stage in the industrial evolution toward socialism, while small producers frequently viewed cartels as protection against being competitively beaten down or swallowed up by larger firms. If one does not subscribe to the demonization of economic bigness and industrial concentration as an act of faith, there is indeed precious little evidence that in the long run cartelization exerted detrimental influence upon the growth of the German economy.[63]

Yet, like concentration, cartels are not a defining characteristic of Germany; they are common in France, Japan, and even in Britain.

The political counterpart of the cartel in Germany has been the trade association. These organizations link German business to the government in an elaborate and centralized fashion. The federal constitution gives these associations consultative or semiofficial status that draws them into policymaking. By insisting that only national trade associations be given such a role, the government forces the centralization of interest representation. German industry has long been "highly organized in a hierarchical system of industrial associations—dating back to imperial

253

Germany and enormously reinforced under the Nazi regime," and that system of organization "survived largely intact in the Federal Republic."[64] In the postwar years the Federation of German Industry (BDI) took over an organizational structure inherited from the Nazi regime which was based on thirty-nine federations. These associations consider the long-term concerns of industry to be their responsibility. The associations employ consultation rather than direction as the mechanism of coordination, but coordination there has definitely been. The banking system is the final element that makes for a system of "organized capitalism." "In this articulated industrial system," it is said, "the banks played from the beginning a major tutelary role. They were perhaps the most powerful force making for the centralization of economic decisions."[65] We will consider the arrangement of the banking system which makes for a negotiated or bargained industrial adjustment after we review the evolution of Germany's policy for industry.

German policy must be considered in two phases: the postwar boom and the period marked by commitment to readjustment, which dates from the late 1960s. It was to Germany's economic advantage that at war's end it was not necessary to make dramatic adjustments in the sectoral base of the industrial economy but only to reestablish and expand existing industries. As the German economy was reconstructed, the sectors that were important domestically were precisely those which were among the front-runners in international trade. Consequently, they enjoyed constantly growing markets. There is also evidence that the widespread rationalization of German industry which had occurred in the years before the war had laid the groundwork for postwar competitiveness.[66]

Until the basics of a market economy, including a stable currency and a political security for investment, were reestablished, however, these advantages remained mere potentials. Immediately after the defeat, of course, the Allied occupiers were determined to prevent the resurgence of what they saw as a deep-rooted German militarism and to recompense themselves for the war just completed. The political obstacles to German industrial reconstruction were large, as indicated by the fact that the Morgenthau Plan, which proposed a deindustrialization of Germany and an enforced return to agricultural life, was the focus of serious debate. Allied priorities shifted only when the threat from the Soviet Union took center stage. Even then, the political strategy of German economic redevelopment remained uncertain.

Thus, the policy of a "social-market" economy, which represented an abrupt turn toward price as the primary means of economic coordination and redevelopment, was by no means inevitable. At the time, the Allies were hesitant to release administrative control of the chaotic economy and the Social Democrats were pushing for extensive nationalization. In retrospect, the new policy was a repudiation of both the state-administered economy of the Nazis and the awkward and often punitive administration of the occupation. Several elements of the reconstruction of government and administration biased economic policy toward this arm's-length neoliberalism. The American emphasis on federalism gave extensive tax control to the State governments (*lander*) rather than to the central government. In an effort to assure itself funds, the central government ended up pushing for very high tax rates, thereby creating a situation in which exemptions from taxes were a powerful policy instrument. Tax exemptions, however, provide less room for detailed and selective intervention in the industrial sectors than the financial strategies of intervention in Japan and France afford. Similarly, the extensive independence of the central bank (the Bundesbank), which emerged in several phases, was a product of fears that government, in response to political pressures, would simply debase the currency. This autonomy of the Bundesbank cut the central government off from a direct regulatory or administrative role in the financial system—a role that is a prerequisite for the use of finance as an instrument of selective policy. Still, it was an economic policy that won the day for the would-be economic liberals.

In 1948 Ludwig Erhard, the minister of finance, moved simultaneously to establish a new currency and to lift many administrative controls. The dazzling and quick success of his program created political support for the social-market system he advocated. The currency reform presumed that a credible currency—one that again allowed money to represent a store of value and a basis of exchange—would unleash the economy. The intent was to expand the supply of goods and services rapidly, before the money demand created by a new currency translated into inflation. The Germans may simply have been lucky. The currency reform did spark a return to more normal economic functioning after years of black markets and shortages from hoarding. The turn to the market represented an escape from the trauma of the war and the subsequent occupation, periods during which government administration was associated with economic chaos. Undoubtedly, this policy triumph gave the Christian Democratic government considerable political leeway in implementing its economic strategy. Some observers maintain that the Marshall Plan saved the currency reform by infusing badly needed goods at a delicate moment. If so, the Marshall Plan served to entrench planning in France and social-market liberalism in Germany by adding to the maneuvering room and success of the governments then in power in each country.

255

Once reconstruction gave way to boom, the structural advantages of the German economy began to matter. Growth fed on growth, and policy was arranged to encourage development. In the decade or so that followed, the export sectors dominated policy, at least until growth made it necessary to choose between monetary control and an undervalued currency.[67] The exchange rate was consistently undervalued, in effect transferring resources from consumers to the export sector and encouraging industry to concentrate on new markets with new products. Tax policy was structured to permit the reinvestment of high profits. The political consequence was that rapidly improving productivity could sustain even higher wages, and that the costs of transferring resources from one sector to the next could be paid. As a result, workers displaced from one job could readily believe that other jobs were available. It is important to emphasize that throughout the postwar years German economic policy has rested upon a political consensus about policy and upon the operation of the market rather than upon an explicit political victory of one group that excluded the losers from power in politics and the markets. Such a consensus, based on a negotiated division of the national product, depends much more on favorable economic circumstances than does a politically imposed division of the spoils.

For more than a decade, rapid growth meant easy adjustment, while a commitment to effective adjustment facilitated growth without subsidy or intervention. The German trade surplus only began to recede in the late 1970s, despite the fact that since the middle 1960s the general increase in the value of the mark had raised the prices of German goods in international markets. The real test of German political commitment to follow the signals of the market and to limit government intervention has come since the late 1960s. Competition from newly industrializing countries in a range of traditional industries has surged, at the very time that rising wages and successive currency revaluations have cut into the price competitiveness of German goods. Pressures on traditional heavy industry and textiles from Third World manufacturers may have finally begun to outrun the capacity of German firms to respond to market adjustment. These changed economic circumstances create very new political problems—problems that Albert Bressand has summarized ably: "If it turned out that successful adaptation to a new international division of labor does not coincide with a successful employment policy, the question of what costs should be acceptable and who would bear them would come back to the forefront of the domestic debate."[68] Since policy has rested more on a corporatist alliance of producers than on the explicit victory of a party or social group, the delicate compensation required to sustain this consensus may be difficult to make during a period of real structural change in industry. Constructing a political alliance to replace the consensus of producer groups may prove difficult.

Yet for now, the traditional determination to resist demands for subsidy from declining industries appears to be holding firm. Government policy still seems to be based on helping companies move into defensible market segments in high-wage industries rather than on insulating them from competition or managing their adjustment. A clever administrative arrangement protects these against political interference. The Ministry of Economics, which has opposed subsidy on principle, manages sectoral and regional policy. Government support for positive adjustment—policies to shift resources into expanding sectors—is channeled through the Ministry of Technology. Thus, funds for research and development are managed through a technical ministry biased toward technological development, not through the Ministry of Industry, which is most vulnerable to the appeals of failing firms.[69] In sectors such as electrical engineering and electronics and mechanical engineering, government money has become a substantial portion of the national research effort. Project funding for research and development, excluding nuclear energy, space programs, and defense, grew dramatically from the late 1960s to the present, while indirect funding of research and development through tax incentives dropped. Government-industry committees selected the projects on the basis not only of their technical merits but also of their potential impact on the German competitive position and their ability to generate competitive high-wage industries.[70] The entire effort was seen as a partnership that would permit the application of big science in industrial sectors, the promotion of competitive business segments, and the development of technologies that would be crucial to long-term German growth.

The German government has spent substantially less money than the French on sectoral support to industry, whether measured in absolute terms or as a percentage of government support to industry. Such direct subsidy is the most likely to be protectionist. At current rates, the sectoral expenditures in the early 1970s represented about 35 percent of the industry budget in France and 16 percent in Germany. As noted, strong pressures for industry-specific structural adjustment policies have been sidestepped. Study groups urged by labor were set up outside the government altogether, where they would be less vulnerable to demands for detailed government involvement in industry affairs.[71] But one must not exaggerate. In coal, shipbuilding, and textiles, there are substantial assistance programs, though the evidence suggests that

257

the level of support for subsidy programs in textiles has been below that found in France and Britain. As in France, agriculture has been substantially supported, and despite technological modernization most farms remain small and uncompetitive. Businesses in small towns are protected against the giant department stores. Clearly, the government meets some claims for subsidy and protection, but agriculture and small business are seen as anomalies and not the centerpiece of a web of privileged market positions.

Whereas the French provided support for declining sectors, Germans provided regional assistance aimed at shifting resources out of declining sectors. Such regional support was an order of magnitude greater than that provided by the French. Those regional funds, managed by the Ministry of Economics, have been channeled to growth sectors.[72] The emphasis on finding competitive market niches for small firms in growth sectors, rather than favoring large projects conducted by large companies, is reflected in the substantial funds allocated to small businesses. Even at the regional level, where pressures to subsidize declining industries might be thought greatest, state governments have made their investments in the potential growth industries, and local alliances of business, banks, and government have been established for this purpose. In contrast to its counterparts in France and Japan, German labor has been a systematic force in policy and has collaborated in retaining and readjustment schemes. After detailing the government schemes to assist competitive industry, one industry analyst remarked that they worked because of good communication between the several producer groups and the segments of government. The interest-group and corporate alliance built in the first phase of the German boom, when growth fed itself, has been used as a policy instrument in this period of adjustment to a downward world cycle. Put differently, the structures of organized capitalism—the basis of a system of negotiated change—are evident just beneath the surface of what seems a liberal market economy.

The continued emphasis on market adjustment in German policy is suggested by the cases of textiles and steel. The federal government has provided no subsidies to the steel industry, despite the decline in the Saar and the Ruhr. Rather, it has encouraged local investment in mechanical engineering and has assisted the search for new steel technologies that will permit portions of the industry to remain competitive.[73] The industry itself has sought to confront its problems by market adjustment and internal rationalization. "In the mid-1960s . . . 85 percent of German crude steel production was in the hands of seventeen separate concerns. Now only six concerns produce 80 percent of the steel; and many of the producers have diversified increasingly from crude steel."[74] Significantly, the steel unions have responded to the crisis with reasonable restraint, and during the 1980 negotiating period they settled for increases of 6.8 percent instead of the 10 percent they had been seeking.[75] It is interesting to note that the German companies resisted the proposal for the declaration of a Europe-wide crisis in the steel industry—a declaration that would have permitted the Common Market's industry commissioner to impose cartel-like production restraints.[76] The Germans were more concerned with subsidies provided to steel by the British, Italian, and French governments than with drooping world demand. When the problem worsened in 1976, they responded by extending their existing rationalization groupings to include Deutschland Arbed (Luxembourg). Ultimately, a crisis plan was instituted at the community level, which permitted production agreements and reorganization plans. The German producers returned to profitability, albeit a fragile one. In sum, the Germans sought to respond to the steel crisis by market adjustment, new products, and new production organization, organized within the German steel community itself.

In textiles and apparel, the Germans have also been committed to free trade, despite the obvious decline of domestic employment in these sectors.[77] They have been better able to adapt to technical changes than British or French producers, having invested in new machinery in order to retain competitiveness. Nevertheless, the German policy against protection and subsidy "did lead to a severe contraction of the German [textile] industry, both in terms of output and employment and a move to offshore production."[78] This meant a loss of jobs, primarily for women and relatively unskilled immigrant workers. The fact that immigrant labor is an important source of the textile work force perhaps makes it easier for the Germans to maintain a firm commitment to free trade. The resulting unemployment can in part be exported, whereas in France the unemployed are generally native male workers.

Even this cursory review of postwar policy suggests the role "organized capitalism" has played in German adjustment. The secondary literature tells a story of industrial change negotiated at least in part among the several producer partners. The vital question is how deeply the system of organized capitalism actually affects the process of change and the choices that finally confront government. The literature implies that private organization acts as a safety net or first-aid station for firms in trouble. According to this logic, potential problems are dealt with in the private sector and few industrial crises present themselves as government policy issues.

We now turn to our primary concern—the role of the banks, the "prefects" in the German system of organized capitalism and the leaders in the process of adjustment which that system facilitates. The secondary literature demonstrates that the internal logic of the financial system does in fact press the banks into a deep involvement in industrial affairs. There is also anecdotal evidence that the banking system serves to nip corporate problems in the bud, before they become public policy issues. There are clear instances in which banks have taken industrial matters into their own hands and the evidence, though scanty, suggests that bank involvement is a central component of the private collective management of industrial change. We cannot establish, however, that these anecdotal cases form a consistent pattern that separates the German industrial adjustment from that of other countries. We can only speculate that private collective management changes the demands that industry makes on government, both by encouraging negotiated settlements of industrial difficulties and by reducing the calls for government protection.

The German financial system has two dominant characteristics.[79] First, it is a credit-based system of corporate finance. Like the systems in Japan and France, the transformation of savings into investment and the allocation of financial resources are dominated by the major banks and achieved primarily by loans. Second, the government does not intervene in a detailed way to affect the allocation of credit, either by quantitative intervention or by manipulating the relative prices in the various financial markets. As in France and Japan, the banks in Germany have close ties to industry; in Germany, however, resources are allocated in the markets by freely moving prices. In France and Japan, we have argued, prices are set by the government at disequilibrium levels, a procedure that generates the need to make quantity allocations by administrative priorities that are set by or at least influenced by government. As in all advanced countries, the German central bank intervenes to affect the level of prices and the volume of money, but it intervenes in market operations and resource allocation less than the central banks do in most other countries.[80] In Germany, intervention occurs through the manipulation of control ratios and through the discount rate, not through selective instruments or quantitative control. Moreover, the autonomy of the Bundesbank, which is centrally concerned with aggregate issues, simply reinforces the market character of the financial system. Since Bundesbank intervention in the markets is not intended to influence the allocation of credit and does not consciously and systematically manipulate relative prices, we do not need to consider it in detail here. The important consequence of the German approach to monetary management is that the banks are left as the preeminent actors in the transformation and allocation of financial resources.

The power of the German banks in industrial affairs rests on two pillars: their market power over the sources of finance for industry, and their legal right to own substantial stock in corporations and to exercise proxy votes for other shareholders. The distinction between these two sources of power is important because the exercise of equity rights by proxy or in one's own portfolio is entirely a legal matter, not strictly a matter of influence in the relations between financial markets. Germany is the only major country in which banks have extensive buildings of industrial equities.[81] But, if bank influence in industry rested only on a legal choice, not on a market compulsion, then legislative fiat could change the arrangement without overturning the operations of the German financial markets and the German system would not really represent a distinct case. It would be one of several other market-based financial systems—one in which banks are preeminent among other financial institutions and in which capital markets matter less.

The case that bank influence in industry does in fact derive from the structure of the financial system rests on the distinct place of banks, as a set, in the German financial markets. The argument does not hinge on the levels of debt which companies hold but rather on the routes through which they obtain that debt. The first structural element of the German system is the securities markets, whose limited size is suggested by the comparison made in Table 3.2 (see page 124). It is important to note that access to this limited equity market is dominated by the banks. The bond market, though seemingly more developed, is not an alternative source of funds for industry; again access is dominated by the banks. No less than three-quarters of domestic bonds outstanding at the end of 1975 were issued by banks, and of those nearly half were held by banks. Most bond funds are raised for government, with industrial and other issues accounting for only 3 percent of outstanding bonds.[82] In fact, German financial statistics, unlike those available for other countries, do not distinguish between kinds of debt. It appears that the distinction between bank loans and debt of all forms is simply a less interesting number in Germany than elsewhere. In essence, all routes to corporate external finance—loans, bonds, and equity—lead back to the banks.

Financial institutions other than banks play a smaller role in Germany than in the British and American systems. First, investing institutions are of less importance. In Germany the proportion of contractual

Table 5.2. Share of deposit-taking institutions in claims and liabilities with the
non-financial sector, end 1975 (percent)

Country	Liabilities	Claims
West Germany	61.5	60.1
France	71.7	48.3
Japan	68.7	58.1
United Kingdom	51.5	48.4
United States	57.3	51.8

NOTE: Liabilities represent deposits;
claims indicate loans.
SOURCE: Dimitri Vittas, ed., *Banking Systems Abroad* (London, Inter-Bank Research Organisation, 1978), p. 18.

savings to total savings is only about one-third of what is in the United States or the United Kingdom. Two factors help to account for this difference: (1) government retirement benefits are excellent in Germany and private pension accumulation is thus less significant, and (2) corporate pension fund reserves are generally retained by the companies as working capital and therefore do not enter the financial system.[83] Similarly, long-term credit institutions, which borrow funds in the capital markets, have a more limited role than in France and are not oriented toward industry.[84]

The major German banks therefore sit at the center of the system of corporate finance. They are universal banks, engaging in the widest range of activities on an extensive deposit base. (For a discussion of the distinctions between investment banks, merchant banks, and universal banks, see Chapter 4. These universal banks are more than simply a source of funds; they are the critical means of access to the capital markets. Historically, then, the German banks have been the nursemaids of industry. Jurgen Kocka has aptly described their role:

The major banks provided their industrial customers with long- and short-term loans, which constituted three-quarters of their balances in 1913 and were supplied primarily through a large number of small and medium-sized deposits that could be withdrawn on short notice. Thus the German corporate banks acted as mechanisms for the mobilization of scattered savings and channeled them into German industrial enterprises, *which depended more heavily on the capital market than their counterparts in Britain and the United States.* Gradually, as expansion and merger became more frequent and more significant than the establishment of new enterprises, long-term credit became the main basis of the banks' relationship with

industry. Their issues of shares and bonds on behalf of industrial enterprises usually came after cooperation in long-term credit arrangements
had been established. Increasingly, the large corporate banks became
more than purely financial intermediaries; they sought to monopolize the
financial arrangements of industrial concerns and to serve them with com-
prehensive policies "from the cradle to the grave." Because of their close
ties with industry, the banks began, in contrast to earlier decades, to seek
direct influence over manufacturing firms' high-level decisions.[85]

This pattern was well established around the turn of the century and
has eroded since then.[86] The ability of the large German firms to go
directly to the burgeoning international capital markets and the high
levels of postwar profits that fueled internal growth might be thought
to have accelerated the decline of the market power of the banks over
industry. Nevertheless, the limited importance of the securities markets
leaves the banks at the center of the system of external finance for
industry.

The case that bank influence rests primarily on legal arrangements,
instead of on market structures, is twofold. First, despite the significance of the banks, as a set, in relation to other financial institutions in
Germany, the banking sector is highly competitive and less concentrated than in France and Britain. Whether because of the postwar
restructuring or because of market forces already at work, the "big
three" banks came to have rivals. Although there are only six banks of
national significance (a situation similar to that in Britain and France),
twenty-nine German banks are among the three hundred largest in the
world.[87] In other words, banks that began from state or local bases have
expanded to have national and international significance. These banks
are important rivals to the national banks.[88] Competition between banks
diminishes the importance of any one bank in the affairs of an individual company. When there are bank competitors, the lending-based influence of the banks in industry is diluted. No single bank can exercise
power by denying a client access to finance.

Second, the legal environment encourages bank influence in industry
through the exercise of stock-voting rights.[89] There are no limits on
bank industrial holdings other than the prudential one of not allowing
a bank to bet its entire worth on a single company. In other words, a
bank can own 100 percent of any company (though in practice holdings are limited to a veto position of 24 percent plus one), but it cannot
invest the equivalent of its own equity in a single company. Remember
that a bank commands resources far in excess of the equity invested in
the bank. The size of the bank limits its ability to invest in firms. At the

263

same time, the banks can represent shareholders who deposit their shares with the banks. The portion of shares held in such accounts represents 85 percent of all privately held shares and fully half of all shares outstanding. Lastly, banks may loan proxy rights to each other, a communalism that can concentrate bank power. Voting power is disproportionately concentrated in the three largest banks, which in the 1990s voted 35 percent of the shares at the annual meetings of the seventy-four largest companies.[90] In an environment in which banks are the dominant financial institutions and in which the largest banks act as powerful shareholders, the fact that bank officers sit on the boards of the largest companies takes on particular significance. Writing in 1981, Richard Medley noted: "Of the 400 top companies in Germany, 318 have bankers on their supervisory boards. There are 570 bank executives on the boards of these 318 large companies: an average of 2 bankers on each board. The domination of the big three is displayed once again in this area. The banking industry controls 145 of the 1480 seats on the 100 largest companies, [and] the big three took 65 percent of these seats and 15 seats as board chairmen."[91]

Detailed studies of the circumstances of bank intervention in industrial affairs are required before we can distinguish which bank powers in industry are based on market structures and which are based on legal arrangements. When companies are operating profitably and successfully, they can find alternative bank sponsors without difficulty. Under these circumstances, the banks' legal voting power would be of greater importance than their economic market power. In such periods, however, the banks would have the least reason to be interested in intervention. When firms are in difficulty, however, the leverage of the lender grows and voting power simply implements and facilitates this influence. The role of banks in merger and takeover arrangements among profitable companies is an ambiguous case. We can conclude, however, that the financial markets spawned the system in which banks can vote stock, and that they provide the base from which bank influence is exerted.

Nearly every commentator on the German economy emphasizes the banks' capacity and willingness to intervene in industrial affairs. Typical perhaps is the view expressed by the Inter-Bank Research Organisation, an arm of the British clearing banks, in its comparative study of banking systems:

German banks have in general very close relations with industry. To a large extent, this is a reflection of the dependence of industrial companies on the banks for external finance. But the close relations are also the result of the preponderance of universal banking in Germany and of the significant industrial holdings of the big German banks. The banks as universal institutions have been able to play a major role in the financing of the reconstruction effort after the last war and of the subsequent expansion of German industry. They have also taken an active part in arranging mergers and takeovers and have occasionally used their strength to prevent the purchase of stakes in German companies by "undesirable" elements. More recently the banks have supervised the rescue of a number of companies, saving jobs and gaining considerable goodwill in the process.[92]

Newspaper headlines certainly provide prima facie evidence for this position, and every commentator has anecdotes and case histories to sustain the general proposition. A generation ago, Andrew Shonfield chose the steel industry as his example.[93] The recent intervention to restructure the troubled Telefunken company and the Deutsche Bank's refusal to allow Mercedes Benz to fall under foreign control reinforce this image that the banks patrol the borders of German industry. The implication of existing studies is that the banks make possible a more directed process of market-led adjustment, that in the face of intense international competition, private coordination can promote adjustment. Although the banks are no longer giving orders, as they did in the era of industrialization, they are at least able to coordinate the activities of industry and government on both regional and sectoral industrial issues.

Still, in drawing conclusions about the German case, we cannot go much beyond the contention that long-term bank financing encourages industrialists to take a longer view both by providing long-term capital resources and by substituting a longer-term view of industry needs for a concern with the short-run fluctuations of the stock market.[94] Even these propositions about the nature of the strategies firms adopt in the market rest mostly on assertion and not on systematic comparison. Few existing studies attempt to show the extent of banks' prefectural and tutorial roles or to examine their consequences; none offers an explicit argument as to how the banking system affects the choices of firms and government in industrial development and adjustment. Without such work we can only conclude that existing studies of the German case are consistent with the thesis of this book. The evidence supports our proposition that the negotiated character of German adjustment rests in large part on the role that the financial system assigns to the banks in industrial affairs, and that an arm's-length role for government is correlated to a market-based pricing system in finance.

The Slow-Growth Countries: Great Britain and the United States

In the postwar years, growth was not a priority concern in Britain or the United States but an objective to be balanced with defense, consumption, and the management of economic stability. In both countries, the government was really left out of the detailed strategies of private and public industry, a situation that even an extensive nationalized sector did little to change in Britain. First Britain and then the United States slipped in international market strength, a decline reflected in currency and trade figures as well as by growth and productivity indicators. This decline contributed to a reassessment of domestic priorities, particularly of the balance between investment and consumption. In Britain, although the growth and productivity rates accelerated in the 1960s, the economy fell further and further behind in international trade competition. At considerable political pain, Britain established and then partly dismantled a state strategy of industrial redevelopment (see Chapter 4). In the United States, rates of growth and productivity increase declined since the late 1960s, inflation has accelerated, and, for the first time since the war, American industry has faced intense foreign competition in its domestic markets. As a result, a debate on the proper role of government in promoting an industrial counteroffensive has become a central political issue. One important similarity between the two countries is that each has a securities market–based financial system with internationally oriented major banks. In both countries that financial system has constrained the government's capacity to intervene selectively in industry.

The United States

America's de facto policy for industry has three components: (1) autonomy for corporate management, guaranteeing freedom from outside interference and particularly from government intervention; (2) a basic consensus on the process of union-management conflict and collaboration, a consensus that though open to negotiation has, in practice, reserved to management the right to select production technologies and lay off workers; and (3) principled opposition to national and international trade restrictions which in practice accommodates demands for protection by specific troubled sectors. Market competition, price-driven adjustment, and government limited to regulatory functions would best describe the ideological principles behind the policy, but at all levels of jurisdiction the reality is an extensive web of ad hoc government policies that promote and control industry. Central government intervention is considered an exception and the myriad efforts of state and local governments to promote their own firms or attract plants are not seen as an industry policy. In a sense, then, Americans allow a multitude of industry policies to compete with each other while denying that they have any policies at all. But if industry policy is understood as a conscious federal strategy linked to tactics for the particular sectors, then it is indeed true that America has no policy.

The arm's-length political stance that the national government takes toward business rests on three structural elements: (1) the apparatus of government, which divides powers and makes the system responsive to particular interest-group demands; (2) the court system, which reinforces the fragmentation of policy and the ability of small groups to influence or block the government; and (3) the financial system, which stands at arm's-length from both government and business. Let us briefly consider each of these structural elements.

America, Stephen Krasner argues, has a weak state.[95] Among the advanced industrial countries, its executive bureaucracy has the greatest difficulty in formulating goals independent of those expressed by particular groups in the society. (In fact, some observers believe the porous nature of the American bureaucracy calls into question the very use of the term "state.") In implementing its purposes, the central executive has a limited range of tools to control these social groups. Indeed, when observers argue that ideological appeals are the most powerful weapon the executive has available (as evidenced by the tactics the Reagan administration used to force through its budget-cutting program), they are saying that the state as an organization has little power.

To support this view of a weak executive, Krasner mobilizes a body of generally accepted literature about American politics. In his view, "the central feature of American politics is the fragmentation and dispersion of power and authority."[96] The Constitution was structured to limit, not enhance, the power of the state executive. Within the executive branch, the president shares control of his bureaucracies with Congress. The large number of political appointments available with each shift in administration opens the bureaucracy to direct infiltration by groups concerned with specific agency decisions. The top officials of these agencies are often drawn from the groups affected by the agency. The legislature itself is fragmented, with power devolving to particular committees and in recent years to shifting and unstable congressional coalitions. The resulting alliances between congressional committees, particular interest groups, and individual agencies have been labeled "iron triangles," a notion that points to the insulation of issues from one another and the ability of narrowly drawn pressure groups to influence specific bits of policy. The result in the long periods of political routine is a series of disconnected individual policies, each reflecting the balance of social pressures more than the wishes of a central executive. A thousand small battles, relatively independent of each other, must be won before any broad policy can be implemented and secured. In the end, we have an economy that is shaped by myriad policies for industry without ever calling into question the principle of arm's-length government and corporate autonomy which we label free enterprise. Those who favor the system and its outcomes find comfort in the multiple routes of political access. Those less satisfied find the system dominated by private power or fragmented and incapable of action. Though the implications of the arrangements are judged differently, there is broad agreement on the system's operations.

The decentralized and independent judiciary also serves to constrain executive authority, as it was designed to do, by blocking its systematic and purposive intervention in the economy. In essence, the judiciary is a third party introduced into the dealings between business and the state. It cannot be controlled by the executive, and can in fact serve as a vehicle by which interests outside the limited alliances of bureaucrats and businessmen enter into their private dealings. The legal system confines executive discretion and restrains the ability of the central executive to compel action by other government officials, let alone by private business. It limits the executive in several ways. First, it encourages narrow delineations of agency mandates. Second, the uncertainty about the kinds of arrangements government and business can legally make inevitably complicates their negotiations; what government or business can do must often be determined by courts and, as a result, cannot be known for months or even years. Third, laws insisting on disclosures of information push business-state dealings into the light of day; even if they are legal, certain decisions may prove politically unacceptable if publicized. Finally, there exists a wide range of explicit constraints on what government can do with business and on the arrangements firms may make between themselves. These limits can be lifted by particular legislation, but this process is also time-consuming and generates a great deal of publicity. Even to recreate something like the Reconstruction Finance Corporation of the New Deal is to raise innumerable legal challenges to the permissible scope of government action.[97] Significantly, the system of trial by legal combat gives an adversarial character to business-state relations, since litigation—using the courts to block the opponent—is a readily available alternative to negotiation.[98] This position is widely understood by lawyers working on these issues.

> [An] adversarial framework . . . has traditionally governed relations between public and private sectors in the United States. Rooted in the basic Jeffersonian ideals, which are suspicious of both "big business and big government," this framework has evolved into a complex of laws and regulations designed to maintain the independence of, and distance between, American industry and government officials so that each sector can serve as a check on the discretionary power of the other.[99]

The financial system is the third structural element that limits the executive's capacity for direct industrial intervention. The system is decentralized and power is diffused into the market. "In the U.S. external capital is allocated among firms primarily by market mechanisms, and individuals invest directly in firms' assets."[100] A decentralized financial system with a strong securities market has contributed to the concentration of power and decision making in the corporation itself. Neither equity ownership nor loans offer instruments for banks or government to intervene regularly in shaping industrial outcomes or to challenge corporate self-governance. Indeed, the corollary is that it can be difficult to mobilize capital in the United States. "External capital flows directly in small bundles from many decentralized individuals to firms, so contacting sources is more difficult. Second, market prices in the U.S. are a strong objective indicator of firms' prospects and the process is less subject to persuasion than the Japanese administrative processes."[101] One need not accept the proposition that the market makes an ideal evaluation of companies to agree that the process insulates firms from outside influence. The U.S. government's role in industrial affairs is undoubtedly a consequence of the political history of America's industrialization, whereas the legal limits on bank involvement with industry were set by a series of political fights.[102] That is, politics shaped the financial system, in order to block the central government's domination of the economy and to prevent financial domination of industry. The American system is similar in structure to its British counterpart and differs sharply from the systems in the other countries we have considered. The similarities with Britain include: a highly developed securities market, which provides long-term funds for industry; the strength of the investing institutions, which nourish the securities markets; and the specialization of the deposit-taking institutions, which limits their involvement with industry by restricting their primary activity to short-term lending.[103] Differences from the British system include greater market competition and more complete autonomy from the political executive for the financial sector. The American system is closer to the ideal type of a securities market–based system of corporate finance than is the British. Let us now assess these elements of the American financial system in more detail.

The long-term financial requirements of the [American] corporate sector," according to Britain's Inter-Bank Research Organisation, "have been largely met by the securities market."[104] Table 3.2 (page 124) showed that both the bond and equity markets are of comparatively great importance in the United States and Britain. Since the bond market also serves to finance government, the equity market is most crucial to our argument. (The volume of funds raised in the bond market in the other countries listed in the table should not mislead us. Their governments also drink at the bond pool and their securities markets have only limited importance as a source of corporate finance independent of banks.) The nature of corporate access to these securities markets is just as important as their size. In the United States access is arranged for the most part by nonbank intermediaries such as brokerage houses—a fact that limits company dependence on banks for external funds. The presence of a strong securities market with independent brokers has tended to free companies from dependence on bank loans to raise long-term funds. The result is an arm's-length market relation with agents in the financial system rather than intimate institutional ties to intermediaries such as banks. As argued earlier, an extensive securities market encourages greater corporate autonomy from both banks and government.

The American and British securities markets are nurtured by funds from investing institutions, the importance of which is shown in Table 5.2. Such institutions are even more important as financial intermediaries in America than they are in Britain. In Table 4.2 (see page 192) the difference between liabilities and claims indicates the nonfinancial assets held by these investing institutions. The table shows that in America, a pension fund or similar organization acts more as an intermediary who puts money into other markets than as a direct investor who buys and manages a real estate portfolio. Writers like Raymond Goldsmith maintain that this characteristic makes the American market more "perfect" and more efficient.[105]

The deposit-taking institutions have a similar importance and function in the United States and Britain. Table 5.2 shows that these two countries form a set clearly distinct from France and Japan and arguably different from Germany as well.[106] The gap between claims and liabilities primarily represents funds channeled through long-term credit institutions. In other words, as discussed earlier, specialized deposit-taking institutions in France lend money to specialized lending institutions to which they are often connected. As Table 3.3 indicated (see page 126), these specialized long-term institutions are less important in the United States than in any other country. The figure in Table 3.3 that is relevant to our analysis is claims, or loans. The liabilities simply indicate funds directly deposited with these specialized institutions. In Britain, for example, the nationalized industry sector is largely financed through the National Loans Board, which is included in these figures.

The deposit-taking institutions have, by choice and by regulation, specialized in their functions and to some extent in their clients.[107] Figures on bank concentration really miss the point of this institutional specialization in the financial market. Thus, for example, savings and loans associations have funded housing mortgages and stayed out of industrial finance. Commercial banks, by contrast, have tended to make short-term loans to industry, relying on short-term deposits to do so. Evidently, such a divided system provides the saver a greater range of possible investments. Several other aspects of this specialization relate more directly to our argument. First, since the banks have been denied the right to hold substantial equity in any single corporation, they cannot exert influence as owners. Second, the banks do not control access to the securities and, as a result, they are influential primarily as short-term lenders. Third, since there is bank competition, the influence of any bank over firms that are not deeply in trouble is itself divided. Some authors emphasize the importance of bank-officer membership on the boards of major industrial companies.[108] Board membership does create networks of economic notables, but their leverage as representatives of the banks, rather than as individuals prominent in their own right, depends on the general place of banks in the financial system. In the United States, the potential leverage exercised by banks is limited and the power of bank board members is correspondingly restricted. Even more important, bankers sit on boards in their own right and not as agents of the banks.

Government intervention to regulate banks and control the money supply has not disrupted the market character of the American financial system. The critical point is that the complicated and divided regulatory structure simply acts to insulate the system from executive interference and discretion. Several features of the financial system are important. First, the American banking system is a two-tier structure of federal and state regulation. The National Bank Act of 1864 served to provide prudential banking to the East and more aggressive, risk-taking finance in the West. Second, for years even the federal regulatory structure was divided between the now-dominant Federal Reserve Board and the

Comptroller of the Currency. The ability of banks to "select" their regulator created a market in government regulations with the prize going to the low bidders, and it restricted central control by any one regulator. Third, the mechanisms of regulation have been market-oriented rather than administrative. This orientation is in part a matter of principle, but it is also a consequence of the dual and fragmented regulatory system that prevented the Federal Reserve from exercising direct authority over all financial institutions. "Greater emphasis has traditionally been placed on open market operations which affect the liquidity position of both member and nonmember banks than on changing reserve requirements of discount facilities."[109]

The Federal Reserve is autonomous from the political executive. Although it might run its own industrial policy, it cannot be used in any direct way as an instrument of federal government policy. The federal government, like the states, has intervened to make and guarantee billions of dollars of loans, many of which are handled through the Federal Financial Bank, an obscure government institution. The loan program, the financing of the federal debt, and general monetary management are separated from each other.

In sum, the American system is characterized by a multiple and fragmented arm's-length relation between the executive and the financial system, and an arm's-length market relationship between financial institutions and the industrial sector. It is conventional to assert that its structure is changing, for it always is, but in fact intrusion of foreign banks, the emergence of electronic banking, and the brokerage house merger move are now altering the American financial system dramatically. The current transformation will significantly reduce the present specialization of and the geographic restriction on large financial institutions, probably not stopping until the agglomerations are limited only in their right to handle equity issues. This will constitute a striking reversal of the restructuring undertaken during the Great Depression. The result will undoubtedly be greater concentration and less specialization of function, but whether these changes will lead to a more institution-dominated system, like that in Germany, is simply not clear.

There has been no political basis for a fundamental challenge to these structural arrangements that support an arm's-length role for government. Labor has not had the power or the inclination to oppose in any systematic way the basic autonomy of management, although the realm of managerial autonomy has been circumscribed by health, safety, and consumer legislation. The Chrysler case is exceptional because labor did demand a voice in corporate governance; but with the strength of organized labor waning in politics and in the market, the Chrysler settlement hardly marked the beginning of a new, politically significant trend. Regional political conflicts have also reinforced the federal government's hands-off stance toward business strategies. A basic feature of the American economy has been sectoral competition between American businesses backed by their state and local governments in alliance with pieces of the Washington machinery.[110] The regional character of American growth, reinforced by state and local promotion policies, works against the emergence of an explicit national policy for industry. In recent years, for example, political battles about the conflicting needs of declining industry in the North and growing industry in the South have led to a stalemate that has prevented the emergence of a clear policy of government interventions in industrial location. At least in the 1950s and 1960s, to foster development in the South was to accelerate the decline of labor-intensive industries in the Northeast and Midwest, whereas to prevent the decline and relocation of these sectors was to retard southern growth. The resulting deadlock can be seen in the empty character of American regional legislation, which offers programs for redevelopment but does not equip them with power and money.

Two trends do provide a limited impetus to reshape relations between government and business, however. The first trend is the expansion of business regulation for purposes of social policy. The earliest wave of such regulation sought to assure markets, or at least to prevent the giant firms emerging in the latter part of the nineteenth century from dominating the continental market. Antitrust legislation was the most vivid expression of this kind of regulation. Despite this populist intent, regulatory agencies were often captured (some would say created) by business, which used them as a means of controlling market competition. The more recent regulatory wave has tried to assure that the by-products of business activity do not damage the health and welfare of the public. Many believe that these regulatory efforts contributed to the slowdown in growth, because they forced firms to invest resources to comply with new standards and thus prevented the investments necessary to increase output. Confronted with this expansion of social regulation, businessmen can comply, negotiate, litigate, or even fight the political battle necessary to roll the regulation back. The reduction of regulation under the Reagan administration has postponed, though not eliminated, the effect of social regulation on the relations of business and government.

The second trend—intensified foreign competition leading to a decline in America's international trade position, both in the aggregate and in particular sectors—has made industrial development an issue of national debate; it has called into question both the structure of government-business relations and the distribution of income. In an insulated domestic market, the business struggle concerns the domestic distribution of wealth—a struggle in which regional conflicts predominate and a national policy can serve only to express the victory of one or another interest group. But when the troubles of industry stem from international trade competition, some kind of national response is required. State or local government cannot effectively address these international issues. From this perspective, the Lockheed and Chrysler cases, as well as the emergence of trigger-price protection for the steel industry, are not exceptions or anomalies but part of a new pattern in which the federal govenment is more actively involved in the detailed development of crucial industries. The limits on the American executive's capacity to intervene in order to shape industrial development are obvious in its responses to trade pressures. As domestic markets open to international competition, the government has several choices: (1) to accept the outcomes of market competition; (2) to try to influence the outcomes only through aggregate measures, such as taxes or monetary policies, which affect all sectors equally; (3) to shape the outcomes by intervening to support particular industries or sectors; or (4) to protect domestic firms, either by external protection or outright subsidy. (See Chapter 1 for a full discussion of government strategies.) The proposition here is that in the absence of an executive capacity to promote competitive adjustment or to cushion decline, one is left with a choice between protection and accepting the market outcomes produced by free trade. America's structural incapacity seems to leave the country especially vulnerable to international market changes. Given a political system open to interest-group influence, we would predict that accumulating international trade pressures will lead to extensive protection.

If the costs of protection or sectoral decline are considered to be too high, then constructing an interventionist apparatus can be an alternative. If an effort at systematic intervention were attempted in America, as it was in the British case, we could then consider whether a securities market–based financial system does indeed technically constrain the government's ability to pursue industry-specific objectives and whether it represents a political obstacle to creating a true interventionist system. For now, we must be satisfied with establishing the plausibility of the first proposition—that American policymakers are vulnerable to demands for aid and that their policy repertoire for responding to the problems of declining sectors or troubled firms is limited.

The United States used its postwar dominance to press for an open trading system. This policy aimed to create a world economy that favored free trade—an economy permitting the free flow of goods and finance. Restrictions on labor movements were retained. Our political and economic interests pushed in the direction our ideology pointed. An international economic regime that encouraged the expansion of international trade was thought to promote the interests of American firms, the American economy, and national security. Some observers argue that the United States encouraged not only an open trading system but also a specific form of domestic response to the expanding international economy. Both tax and trade laws encouraged the expansion of multinational business. That is, government policy encouraged companies to move production abroad rather than to export American goods.[111] For example, the trade laws were arranged so that when goods reentered the American market, American firms paid duty only on the value added abroad. Also, U.S. aid programs often facilitated the move offshore by helping developing countries establish reexport platforms. Other analysts, however, pointing for example to the treatment that has made it expensive to send American executives abroad, argue that policy has in fact tended to hinder overseas investment.[112] In many ways, the two sets of analysts simply address different time periods and different issues. That is easy, because as Fred Bergston, Thomas Horst, and Theodore Moran observe, "the U.S. has no consistent coherent policy toward foreign direct investment and multinational enterprises nor has it ever had one."[113] They conclude, however, that the balance of policy favors foreign direct investment, although the pro-investment tilt is being reduced:

This review of U.S. policy points to several conclusions. *First, there is no coordinated overall program.* Each individual measure affecting foreign direct investment, either directly or indirectly, had developed largely in a separate functional area, in response to problems in that area at a particular point in time. The government is not organized to coordinate the separate policies, and each agency is largely autonomous in managing the impact on foreign direct investment of policies within its area of responsibility.

Second, *these individual policies display a common theme; support of foreign direct investment by U.S.-based multinational enterprises, both by encouraging the investment itself and by defending the firms against adverse treatment in host countries.* The traditional government attitude is that there is a high coincidence between the interests of the multinational enterprises and the country as a whole.

In practice, the specific policy measures adopted toward foreign direct investment point toward different underlying objectives. Some seek to promote world welfare. Some seek to promote nontraditional objectives of the United States. Views vary as to the motives underlying the pro-investment U.S. approach. Interestingly, there has been no effort to apply optimum capital controls to promote the national economic welfare.

Third, *in a number of areas the pro-investment tilt is being reduced.* Doubts about the identity of interests between the firms and the country are increasingly translated into law.[114]

The present trade debate assumes the principle of free trade and requires that protection be justified as an exception to the rule.[115] This stance is a reversal of position held prior to the Hawley-Smoot Tariff Act of 1930, a period during which protection was the principle of policy and free trade in particular sectors required specific justification. The protectionist exceptions remain more numerous than one would expect given the current free-trade rhetoric. As American industrial preeminence has slipped, the number of sectors undergoing painful adjustment has increased. The pro-foreign-investment tilt of policy has encouraged firms in sectors such as consumer electronics to seek solutions to foreign competition by producing with cheap labor abroad rather than by innovating domestically. Other than invoking free trade and the market, the government has had no strategy of trade and development, no tactics of trade adjustment, and no effective policies with which to affect the course of domestic industrial development. Above all, the government has had no interpretation of the character of market events which would allow it to formulate a policy. As a result, industry is free to define the policy issues and choices.

Domestic intervention by the federal government simply has not been an alternative to trade restrictions; that is, it has not served as a means of derailing pressures for external protection. Rather than seeking to promote change or ease adjustment, sector-specific policies have in large part served to protect industries from foreign competition. The protectionist purposes of the specific policies contradict the free-trade principles pursued in more general policy. In a research project that investigated U.S. policy responses to foreign competition in a set of trade-impacted industries, my colleagues and I found that in all instances adjustment problems provoked protectionist policies.[116] The only recent exception was the Reagan decision in the summer of 1981 to lift restrictions on shoe imports in an attempt to placate traders after the imposition of restrictions on auto imports. With a few possible exceptions, government has not taken the initiative to help firms reach market competitiveness. Given the complexity of the problems and the array of strategies adopted by governments, the range of American policies is quite narrow. Indeed, the choice seems to be protection or no policy at all. And whether the policy instrument is protection or subsidy, the basic theme is the same: maintaining the continued autonomy of corporate management and decision making.

The tension between the principles of free trade and the particular policies of protection has been managed by restricting access to the American market on narrow grounds and for purposes that are as limited as possible. Yet the general proposition remains: the United States has neither an adjustment policy nor the apparatus for such a policy, and in their absence it is vulnerable to protectionist demands. The *Economist* of London expressed European frustration at this situation when it remarked that America hews to free trade when it is convenient and turns to protection when it isn't. As the set of trade-impacted industries grows, we might expect a protectionist coalition to emerge. In the Kennedy years, the passage of a general free-trade bill was secured by giving special treatment to the textile industry.[117] Today, steel, autos, and consumer electronics, to name just a few, join textiles on the list of industries seeking some kind of trade restrictions. But despite an avalanche of exceptions, the defense of the general principles of free trade hold firm. Supposedly, everyone understands the general risks of a trade war, but everyone pursues the specific exceptions that could provoke it. Though the executive has considerable power to resist protectionist pressures, one must ask how long the tension between principles of free trade and particular protectionist exceptions can be managed when protectionist demands are now being heard from vital industries?

American policy, then, has moved simultaneously toward free trade and protectionism. The divergence is no accident, because national policy and the needs of internationally competitive firms are served by free-trade policies whereas sectors threatened by imports can survive if given protection. Assuming that the choice is between free trade and market restrictions, the best predictors of the trade policies that affect a specific industrial sector are the needs and strategies of its dominant firms. The question is whether there is some systematic means of predicting what firms need, and what policies they will seek from government. Distinguishing between multinational and national firms can explain the pattern. In the face of intense foreign competition, the sectors dominated by multinational firms have still sought free-trade policies, using them to move offshore in search of cheap labor. At home, the major multinational firms in trade-impacted sectors have found themselves in political opposition to the labor movement, which seeks to maintain American production and save jobs. At the same time, na-

277

tional companies have tended to align with labor to gain some degree of protection.[118] This pattern is suggested by the responses of consumer electronics and steel sectors to foreign penetration of American markets. Let us consider them in turn.

In consumer electronics, government policies facilitated the strategies of the major multinational companies.[119] There was no evidence of any national purpose or goal separate from the demands of the firms. In the decade between the mid-1960s and mid-1970s, Japanese consumer electronics firms managed to drive their American competitors into a marginal position in the United States market for color television sets, the industry's most important product. The Japanese had rapidly adopted solid-state component technology as the basis of their product line. Although semiconductors had first been used in television sets by American companies, these firms were slow to diffuse them widely, instead holding on to tube-based manufacture. The Japanese used the semiconductor components to enter the market for small television sets, slowly moving into larger and more expensive products. Initially they competed on price—by offering both small sets and lower prices on larger ones. Japanese products were often distributed under American "house" labels, such as Sears. American companies tried to meet the price competition by moving traditional production offshore to cheap labor sources rather than by quickly redesigning products and production processes. That is, they tried to maintain their existing product and production structure by finding a cheaper worker. Because their strategy did not address the real problem—that the Japanese had made product and process innovations—the Americans found themselves at a long-term competitive disadvantage.

Beginning in 1968, labor, domestic producers, and component manufacturers applied pressure through Congress in an attempt to enlist government support for a response to the challenge of Japanese imports. But what this coalition, known as Compact (Committee for the Protection of American Color Television), really wanted was protection: it lobbied for restriction of the volume of imports. The multinational companies, which were trying to survive by moving production offshore, successfully opposed this protectionist effort by making direct appeals to the president. The mechanism of clause 807, which applied reimport duties only to that portion of value added during production abroad, was intended to give the multinationals an edge over foreign competitors in American markets. It was nearly a decade before the domestic producers managed to gain direct protection in the form of an Orderly Marketing Agreement (OMA), and by that time the market position of the multinational producers had changed; they had been

278

defeated by the Japanese. As in textiles and apparel, the OMA simply postponed the problem and pressed foreign companies into making the competitive adjustments that further strengthened their positions. Throughout this period the government had no view of its own concerning the competitive development of the industry. Consequently, it was in no position to do more than temporarily stave off the domestic industry's demands for protection by balancing them against the claims of the multinationals.

In steel, the dominant domestic producers sought and won protection.[120] Speaking for the industry, the major integrated producers claimed that unfairly priced imports and the extension of government social regulations were the main causes of their competitive difficulties. Whatever the problem of the integrated producers, it is important to remember that specialty steel producers and mini-mills remained internationally competitive. The "industry" as a whole was not in trouble; only certain types of producers had problems. The government, however, neither challenged the "industry" definition of the problem put forth by the integrated producers nor posed a competing interpretation. It did not propose any policy that would force the industry's evolution along more competitive lines and it did not force profits from protection to be reinvested in steel. By simply acquiescing to industry pressure for protection, the government in effect restricted itself to determining the form that protection should take. The technical protectionist arrangement that operated through 1980 was the trigger-price system, which set a floor on import prices based on an estimate of the production cost of the most efficient Japanese producers. The trigger price was revised in 1981 to offer protection against the European producers as well.

The government assumed that protection would restore corporate profits (which it did) and also that the companies would make competitive adjustments from the reinvestment of those profits (which only some companies have done). For example, United States Steel has apparently adopted a policy of investing outside the steel industry, whereas Bethlehem has decided to enter steel product lines in which it can create and maintain a comparative advantage. The justification offered for protection and profit-based industry rehabilitation was that the industry had been undermined by unfair competition—that it had been the victim of "dumping" by European and Japanese producers. A case can readily be made against the European countries—where portions of the steel industry survive because of government subsidy—but it is difficult to make the same case against Japan. Whatever the validity of dumping charges (their validity depends in part on the legal and economic definitions of dumping), the real problem was that American steel no longer had a strong competitive production position from which to meet its foreign rivals. There have been several attempts to explain why the American firms got into trouble. One explanation suggests that they missed the technological boat through organizational stubbornness. A second contends that an insulated oligopoly of American producers dampened the incentives for technological change. A third holds that though new American facilities were often more sophisticated than those built by the Japanese, the Americans did not build such facilities frequently enough. This slow expansion of American production left a stock of outdated facilities and saddled American producers with high average costs. Whatever the case, only a conscious program of revitalization could have reversed the shrinkage of the industry. The government did not develop or enunciate a strategy of its own but left developments to corporate choice. Given the incentives, many major firms used the high profit gained from protection to channel most of their investments outside the industry.

The common feature of American policies has been the presentation of corporate management autonomy in decision making. Whenever American industry has been jolted by international competition, the primary policy response has been to opt for protection in sectors populated by national producers and, often, to move production abroad in sectors populated by multinational firms. In some cases, such as textiles, protection has provided a cover beneath which some domestic producers moved offshore. Policy to restructure or redevelop industry has rested almost exclusively on self-defined industry choices; the assumption has been that increased profitability would permit companies to adjust.

The exception to America's arm's-length capitalism lies in the connections between industry and the military. Here the government is a buyer that influences industry—including plant location—as much by political as by technological logic. Government inevitably becomes entangled in the affairs of firms for whom it is the primary client. In the 1950s military procurement helped create a strong civilian commercial position in such goods as aircraft and electronics. Development of each generation of military bombers gave American producers an advantage in civilian aircraft competition. Even the Boeing 747, which originally was designed for commercial use, was given a boost by Boeing's initial interest in the jet transport–design competition that led to the ill-fated Lockheed C5A. Military procurement undoubtedly sped the development and diffusion of solid-state circuitry and computers in the 1950s, though direct research and development contracts were less important than funds for experimental production facilities. In the 1980s, however, the needs of the civil aircraft industry are not being met by the new military designs, and the direction of technological development in integrated circuits is being determined by the volume of civilian electronic purchases. Indeed, most military equipment now uses standard electronic technologies. Making the point more strongly, it can be argued that military purchases now distort rather than accelerate the rest of the economy.

Until recently, there has been no pressure from backward or declining sectors for an interventionist policy though the political support for such pressure could emerge from some troubled firms or regions. For example, Felix Rohatyn, the New York investment banker who has tried to mobilize support for such an effort is concerned with regional decline. Yet if such a policy were adopted as an objective, there would be serious institutional obstacles to implementing it. The points of market power and government influence in the American system are so numerous and scattered that it appears unlikely that the central executive could ever manipulate an active industrial policy. The federal structure, a fragmented and interest-dominated bureaucracy, and a multicentered financial system all contribute to this institutional incapacity for selective intervention. Clearly, the financial system does not account for the arm's-length role of government. In the American case, the system of finance was shaped by politics to fit the preferred economic system. A role for financial institutions in industrial management was explicitly blocked by legislation aimed at keeping business and banks apart. The result is a system of company-led industrial change.

Conclusions

These schematic presentations of the financial structure and its relation to the politics of industrial change in Japan, Germany, and the United States do not adequately express recent evolutions in the national financial systems. A full discussion would require us to assess whether domestic developments, such as the growing wealth and consequent autonomy of Japanese companies, or international developments, such as the ever more elaborate financial markets, are important factors in the evolution of the several national systems. The assumption here is that the existing structures will shape the specific domestic developments in a fashion that leaves us with three distinct types of financial systems.

PART III

CONCLUSION

CHAPTER SIX

Finance, Adjustment, and Political Crisis: Concluding Remarks

We have argued that structural differences in national financial systems contribute to the differing capacities of governments to intervene in the industrial economy. In the advanced Western countries financial markets as well as institutions act to constrain political choice. Markets are organized by price in response to supply and demand while institutions are organized by political or administrative hierarchy, but both influence politics in a similar way. The arrangement of the markets for finance helps shape the choices a government confronts, thus influencing the policies it adopts and the political process by which industrial change occurs.

Three distinct types of financial systems, each with specific political implications, were described in the first chapter. The three are: (1) a capital market–based system with resources allocated by competitively established prices; (2) a credit-based system with administered prices; and (3) a credit-based, bank-dominated system. The initial proposition was that a credit-based system with administered prices would facilitate government intervention in industrial affairs, whereas capital-market systems with competitive pricing would serve to shunt industry, government, and finance into insulated compartments. The British and French cases supported this hypothesis. The financial system was crucial to French industrial policy throughout the postwar years, and it was also a vital political instrument in the fight by a narrow elite to redirect the purposes of government policy toward industrial development. In Britain, the capital market acted as a constraint on government interventionist policies and was one element that created the political dichotomy of free markets and nationalization. British efforts to create interventionist policies challenged the existing financial market

285

Chart 6.1. Finance and the process of industrial adjustment

Type of financial system	Model of adjustment process
capital market with competitive prices	company-led
credit-based with administered prices	state-led
credit-based with price formation dominated by banks	negotiated

arrangement and opened up distributional conflicts that in turn undermined the efforts to create a national consensus in favor of industrial growth.

Because there are sharp limits on the generalizations that can be made from two case studies, we developed a second approach to test our arguments. Three models of the process of industrial adjustment were elaborated—state-led, company-led, and negotiated adjustment—and a correlation between them and the three types of financial systems was proposed. Thus, a capital market–based financial system would be linked to company-led growth, a credit-based system with administered prices would be linked to state-led growth, and a credit-based system with bank domination would be linked to negotiated change. In short, we reasoned that by knowing the financial system one could predict the nature of the process of adjustment.

The proposition that financial structure constrains government choices so sharply that it can influence the shape of the political process of adjustment is illustrated in Chart 6.1.

To evaluate this proposition, we added three more national cases—those of Japan, Germany, and the United States and assigned each of the five countries to a "model" of adjustment, illustrated in Chart 6.2. With the exception of Britain, our case analyses supported the proposition that one can make predictions based on the nature of the financial system. In Britain the capital market–based financial system which promotes arm's-length relations between business and government interfered with government efforts to direct the process of industrial change.

The relationships proposed here, it should be reiterated, assume that the growing importance of international financial markets does not undermine the importance of the national financial system in deter-

Chart 6.2. Finance and the process of industrial adjustment in five countries

Country	Financial system	Model of adjustment
Japan, France	credit-based with administered prices	state-led
United States	capital market	company-led
Germany	credit-based, bank-dominated	negotiated
Britain	capital market	unclear or ambiguous

mining *how* resources are allocated. That is, elaborate international financial markets may make it more difficult to insulate one national economy from financial developments in another national economy. High interest rates in the United States in 1981 and 1982, for example, have forced European interest rates up as those countries move to prevent an outflow of capital. Nevertheless, the structure of the domestic financial system still determines how international disturbances are translated into the domestic economy. Most important, while the international financial markets may represent a new constraint on government capacities to manage such economic aggregates as interest rates and money supply, they do not of necessity alter the channels through which financial resources are allocated. If those domestic channels remain in place, then the argument proposed here is not affected by the quite dramatic international developments of the past twenty years. Our argument also assumes that the national financial systems were not altered fundamentally during the thirty to thirty-five years after the Second World War.

The financial system is not, it should be evident, the only element of the political economy that influences the relations between government and business. This book argues only that financial systems must be considered when analyzing the politics of the economy in advanced countries. The institutions of politics and administration and the interests of the political groups that hold power, for example, quite obviously affect how governments and business deal with each other. The sections that follow have two tasks. First, they situate the financial system, and the constraints and possibilities for government action it represents, in relation to other pieces of the political system. Second, they place the line of argument developed here, that financial systems influence the relations between government and industry as well as the politics of industrial change, in relation to other analyses that take a different approach to the same problem.

FOUR VIEWS OF THE STATE AND THE ECONOMY

Situating the Problem of Finance

The contemporary literature contains four lines of argument, each with a distinct emphasis, which try to explain how government and business deal with each other: the first line of argument emphasizes the nature of the economic problem a country must resolve; the second emphasizes the interests of the political groups that hold power; the third emphasizes the institutional arrangements of politics and administration; and the fourth emphasizes the ideologies and world view of the politicians, bureaucrats, and businessmen about the proper roles of industry and the state. Some scholars propose a fifth approach, which emphasizes historical tradition as a distinct line of argument. In fact, however, a historical tradition of particular relations between government and business, such as the French legacy of state intervention, must be sustained through a continuity of the interests, institutions, or ideologies of those who govern. Historical tradition is not a mystical essence and it cannot constitute a separate category of explanation.

The first three explanations were considered in the earlier case studies and are incorporated in the following analysis of state behavior. We shall shunt aside the fourth category, ideologies and world views, for reasons worth explaining briefly at this point. Ideologies provide maps of what is possible and proper in political life.[1] They constitute world views and lenses through which experience is ordered.[2] Bureaucrats in states that attempt to force the development of their economies will have ideologies and world views different from those of bureaucrats in states that have stayed at arm's length from the economy. John Armstrong's excellent book *The European Administrative Elite* depicts this variation in Europe and demonstrates how values become entrenched in a bureaucracy's recruitment and socialization procedures.[3] There is no doubt that existing world views tend to reinforce existing operating procedures and that bureaucracies express the cultural values of the societies from which they emerge.[4] Yet when organizations and procedures are changed, the attitude of those working in them shift as well.[5] Our efforts to control our circumstances shape our ideas, but the ideas we hold at any moment mold how we see those circumstances and the range of actions open to us. This delicate balance between ideas and material conditions, however, simply need not be considered separately here. Since world views contribute to the continuity of institutional arrangements in politics and bureaucracy, they are thus subsumed in our analysis of institutions.

288

Explanation by the Nature of the Economic Problem

The first line of argument is that differences in the economic problems that confront a nation account for variations in the role of the state within that nation's economy. In other words, to determine the shape of a government's relations to industry, we should ask what market problems the firms and the nation confront. Those problems, according to this line of argument, determine the economic tasks the state must undertake and those tasks in turn dictate the institutional and political arrangements that will be constructed to perform them. But how do we account for the fact that when Britain's economic hegemony gave way to decline and Japan moved from backwardness to a place of leadership in international industrial competition, neither country experienced dramatic institutional upheaval. Indeed, the Britain of 1950 bears more resemblance to the Britain of 1980 than it does to the Japan of any given year—a situation that would seem to indicate that the institutional and political legacy outweighed economic problems in shaping the government's relations to industry.

Nevertheless, we can maintain a focus on economic circumstances if we argue that the way in which the problem of industrialization is resolved lays down, in each country, an institutional foundation that structures the way in which all subsequent problems are resolved. Alexander Gerschenkron has developed the best-known formulation of this position.[6] He proposes that the historical timing of a country's industrialization defines the economic tasks the society must accomplish and the policies that will prove to be workable solutions. A country's place in the historical sequence of industrialization establishes two dimensions of its situation. First, the moment of industrialization determines which industries must serve as that country's growth engine and the nature of that growth engine in turn determines the social, technical, and financial resources that must be mobilized for industrialization to be successful. Thus, when Britain industrialized, textiles were the leading industry. Since only limited resources were required to start up a textile firm, the individual entrepreneur could mobilize the funds, the work force, and the technology. When Germany industrialized in the latter part of the nineteenth century, however, steel had become a crucial part of the industrial base; and since steel production required large sums of money, mass work forces, and increasingly specialized scientific and technical knowledge, it was almost essential that the government and financial institutions play an active role in the process. Second, Gerschenkron points out that the early industrializers will have a competitive advantage in trade and military power over those who come later in the industrialization sequence. Consequently, the late industrializers must move quickly to amass substantial industrial strength. Governments will be pressed to speed this development as much by their concern for military security as by the promise of profits for entrepreneurs. They will assign a high priority to the military products of industry and mobilize their producers to provide them.

Thus, whereas individual entrepreneurs were central to Britain's early industrialization, banks and governments played a larger direct role in the development of the followers—France, Germany, and Russia. In Britain, for example, railroads were financed privately from the profits of earlier industrial investments. A slow and somewhat fragmented rail development could be tolerated. In Germany and France, however, governments and banks were drawn in to help raise the funds and to mobilize the work of building rail transport. By this logic, present-day relations between business and the state in an early industrializer such as Britain are dramatically different from those in a latecomer such as Japan because of the different ways in which each country resolved the problems of the initial stage of industrialization.

Gerschenkron, by considering the timing of industrial development, intends to explain why different institutions—states, banks, and entrepreneurs—have served to organize the process of industrialization. Other scholars following a similar line of analysis have made political arrangements their dependent variable. Latin Americanists, in an effort to account for the emergence of bureaucratic-authoritarian regimes in Brazil and elsewhere, argue that different economic problems pose different political tasks.[7] They seek to account for changes in political regime by tracing shifts in economic problems. The political regime rather than the entrepreneurial agent of industrialization is to be explained, but the logic of the argument is similar.

The economy, both at home and abroad, undoubtedly constrains the choices of business and government, delimiting a range of workable strategies for each goal. Yet, unless we believe that every situation can be perceived in only one way and can generate only a single solution, we cannot argue that the economic problems define the goals that are pursued or the strategies that are adopted. The goals and strategies of the state are decided by domestic political conflicts. For example, in the first part of the twentieth century France lagged behind Germany in industrial growth, yet the French state did not then lead the crusade for a rapid break with an agricultural past. That shift in policy came only after World War II. The economic problem did not call forth the political coalitions or the specific institutional arrangements required for state-led growth. Indeed, it is a weakness of Gerschenkron's argument that he does not consider that the state administration in his several cases differed dramatically for reasons entirely independent of the problem of industrialization. The autonomy that English society had won from the king permitted the entrepreneurial burst that produced the Industrial Revolution, whereas the power of entrenched state bureaucracies on the Continent made catch-up strategies possible. It is hard to imagine how the national sequence could have been different. The political response to an economic situation always has a political explanation.

Explanation by the Interests of Political Power Holders

The second line of argument maintains that whereas the problems a country confronts set the terms in which choices must be made and define the consequences of different decisions a government's actions depend on the personalities who govern and the nature of their goals. Thus we must consider the role of coalitions, interest groups, and political interests.

A governing coalition—a "grand majority" in Charles Lindbloom's phrase—sets the range of purposes for which state machinery may be used.[8] If national coalitions are to delimit the range of policy across a set of sectors, there must be either policies that constrain the choices to be made within each sector or a situation in which many of the same actors are involved in the decisions in each sector. Both may be the case. For example, general agreements to lower tariffs make it more difficult for firms in a specific industry to obtain protection from imports. In a centralized system like that of France or Japan, the same bureaucrats have a hand in the politics of many economic sectors. According to this line of argument, then, changes in the coalitions that govern the membership or the relative power of the coalition's constituent elements account for shifts in the basic directions of policy.

The purposes pursued by the partners in the coalition are defined as their "interests." "Interest" is a loose notion that implies a rational calculation of what the actor stands to gain; it is assumed that there is a direct link between market position and the calculations of political interests. The concept of interest serves as a simplifying assumption and a hypothesis for a range of writers which stretches from neoclassical economists and Marxists to behavioral political economists. They debate whether interests are something to be discovered empirically (in which case "interest" becomes another word for observed goals and "revealed" preferences) or whether interests are logically deduced from a consideration of the market position in which the groups find themselves. Those who argue that the nature of the governing coalition determines business-state relations must resolve several questions: What constitutes a social group acting politically? How are its interests identified and formed? Why do the several groups in a coalition combine? Unfortunately for simplicity and elegance, none of these questions can be resolved in an a priori fashion.

Let us explore one use of the coalition argument to see how these questions can be approached, turning to another work by Alexander Gerschenkron. The link between market changes and the reformulation of political interests and alliance is the theme of his classic examination of the creation of the alliance between industry and agriculture ("iron and rye") in the German Empire.[9] A flood of cheap grain from North America and Australia threatened both the Junkers and the smaller peasants and marked the beginning of a generation-long economic decline. These market changes produced a coalition between agriculture and big business, on the one hand, and within agriculture, between Junkers and peasants, on the other. The policy result was a sharp change in tariff policies which afforded protection from international competition to both industry and agriculture. The political price was the industrial sector's support for a regime run by the traditional agricultural elite.

The Junkers used politics to preserve existing production arrangements and the way of life that rested on them. The other available response to such changed market signals was market adjustment, a shift in what was produced and how. The Danes, in contrast, took the imported cheap grain, fed it to hogs and cows, and sold the pork and dairy products on the market. German peasants might have found such a market adjustment a solution to their problem, but decentralized dairy farming was not compatible with the large-scale grain plantations on which Junker social and economic position rested. The Junkers used their political resources to create an alliance with the peasantry which defined market protection as the solution to their agricultural problems.

Coalitions are not simply mechanical expressions of predefined and easily identifiable social divisions; they are political constructions, and the process of creating a coalition shapes the content of its objectives. To begin with, even the constituent groups of a coalition are themselves political creations. The social groups used as units of analysis to determine interests are not entities embedded in the social structure waiting to take on political form. We cannot speak a priori of an industrial class, when in fact the interests of its different sectors conflict sharply. Any business front will be divided on issues such as wage bargaining and foreign economic policy. Some firms can afford higher wage settlements or are pursuing export markets, whereas others depend on cheap labor, are fighting off imports, or are making deals with foreign producers. Nor can we solve the analytical problem by uncovering a bedrock social unit that can serve for political analysis by disaggregating to the level of the industrial sector. Different segments of each industry may move in different directions; knowing which sector a firm belongs to does not enable us to predict its political goals.[10]

The politically critical matter is, then, to define whose interests within a given industry define its political position. The American steel industry affords a clear example. Since 1977 the integrated steel producers (such as U.S. Steel, whose competitive position has deteriorated) have spoken for the entire industry, defining unfair foreign competition as the most important policy issue. By defining the issue in this way, they have diverted attention from their own internal problems and obscured the competitive strength of other domestic firms. The more efficient integrated companies, the mini-mill producers, and the specialty steel producers are in a stronger market position, but they do not have a strong political voice. The industry "problem" is thus a political expression of the needs of one segment of the industry. Politics, not the market, creates political interests. The political interests of each sector cannot be mechanically inferred; these interests depend on which types of firms control the industry associations and lobbies and on their own perception of their interests. The composition of an industry and its political interest, then, cannot be assumed any more than we can assume to know the composition of a coalition.[11] Political interests grow up around market positions, but there is no automatic tie between them.

"Secondary majorities" within particular policy areas are of more than secondary importance for in most cases they established what states actually do. Governing coalitions define broad lines of policy or approaches to policy, but the political groups organized around narrower political issues shape particular policies. To examine secondary majorities we must ask how particular groups are organized, what their channels of access to politics and bureaucracy are, and what the nature of political competition in a particular issue area looks like. Within each issue area—such as economic management, our concern in this book— there is a pattern of routine interchanges between the state bureaucracy and interest groups. The patterns of interest representation will be different in each country and often different in each sector of the same economy. Each pattern is maintained by institutional links between state bureaucracy and interest groups. Philippe Schmitter contends that these structures of interest representation have greater resiliency than other components of the political system, such as parties, electoral support, and coalitions.[12] The organization and powers of the state necessarily set the channels for influence; thus, if the institutions of the state remain constant, the modes of interest representation (which influence both the kinds of groups which will prosper and the kinds of policies which can be achieved) also remain constant. When state institutions change, the structured arrangements for interest representation shift as well. Suzanne Berger argues persuasively that the increased power of the French bureaucracy after de Gaulle's ascension to power in 1958 altered the kinds of interest associations which were successful in influencing policy and recruiting members.[13]

Indeed, those who control the state machinery can manipulate it to political advantage. The literature on "corporatism" has highlighted the active politician-bureaucrat who manipulates access to government and policymaking in order to construct interest associations that favor the purposes of the state executive.[14] These studies have emphasized one of two questions. The first concern is how elites who control the state machinery respond to political crisis. The central concern is who rules. Interest groups are manipulated to structure who can participate in politics and to define the terms on which such participation is possible. This slant has been taken by Alfred Stepan in his study of Peru[15] and by Charles Maier in his analysis of the recasting of bourgeois control in Western Europe after the First World War.[16] The second question—our focus here—is how to describe the routine interchange between state bureaucracy and interest groups which forms the process of economic management. Analyses of Western European policymaking in labor, agriculture, and industry have emphasized the state's manipulation of interest groups as it pursues economic policy. These analyses have focused not only on who can participate in politics but also on who is involved in policymaking. Evidently, politics and policy are cut from the same cloth and cannot be unraveled, but we can distinguish between political crises of participation or regime construction and the routine conduct of policy. In his analysis of postwar French agricultural policy, for example, John Keeler demonstrates that the state sought to alter the institutions of farmer-interest representation as part of its tactics for implementing new policies.[17] The new objectives were resisted by the old interest associations, agricultural syndicates that had grown up around the old policies and institutions. Part of the French policy strategy was to alter the syndicates to facilitate new government purposes. The centralized and insulated character of the political and administrative institutions facilitated this government strategy of reshaping the routine pattern of interest representation. The study of secondary majorities thus blurs into a study of the institutions of politics and administration, the third type of explanation to be considered.

In sum, this second line of explanation forces us to look at the groups that govern, at their interests and their organization. It derives propositions about state policy from the weight of the social and economic groups in the polity and from an analysis of their marketplace interests. The analysis of secondary majorities is concerned with how particular policies get constructed within each broad coalition. We need to know more than the political "weight" and market position of a group to predict what government will do. For example, equivalent levels of union membership may produce quite different goverment strategies toward labor in countries with different kinds of union organization.

Explanation by Institutional Arrangements

The third explanation views institutions themselves as forces in political life. Certainly it is an overstatement to claim that institutions are permanent features of any social and political topography to which actors in politics or the market must adapt. Any approach that obscures the conflicting purposes that produced institutions and the goals of the leadership that animates them would be misleading. On the other hand, institutions are not infinitely malleable, not mere facades hiding the reality of conflicts between political groups. By shaping the routes to power and the tools of administration, institutions help determine which political issues emerge as subjects of debate, which groups become allies in the ensuing fight, and how capable of acting on its interests a given coalition will be. The enduring brilliance of de Tocqueville's analysis of France is precisely that he captured the interplay between the institutional forms and the content of political conflict. There has been sufficient institutional continuity in France that the connections he drew between the form and content of politics still have meaning today. Likewise, part of the attraction of the literature on "corporatism" is its pursuit of the relationship between the institutional arrangements of politics and administration on the one hand and the formation of political interests and conflicts on the other. Existing institutional arrangements, in sum, are powerful forces in shaping political interests and the conflicts between them. Clearly, the argument about finance developed in this volume fits into these discussions.

Recently, some influential discussions of economic policy have turned to the notion of the weak and the strong state to account for government policies. Instead of focusing on "how" interests form and represent themselves to the state, this literature is concerned with the "capacity" of the state executive to get its own way when implementing policy. The purpose is to account for government's ability to mobilize and direct the resources of the society toward the ends chosen by the executive. These arguments about Western political economy draw their language and concepts from an earlier debate about the role of communist parties in state-dominated societies. In political economy the strong-state formulation tends to obscure the effect of administrative structures on political conflicts within the society.

Executive strength and weakness, in this view, are functions of the political structure, the internal coherence of the bureaucracy, and the relation of the bureaucracy to the legislature and to interest groups. Given sufficient support and commitment, any executive may be able to impose its will. The executive of a strong state should be able to do so on a more continuous basis across a wider range of sectors. Stephen Krasner puts it well:

The ability of political leaders to mobilize domestic resources is a function of (a) the structure of the domestic political system and (b) the convergence between public and private interests. . . . The defining characteristic of a political system is the power of the state in relation to its own society. This power can be envisioned along a continuum ranging from weak to strong. The weakest kind of state is one which is completely permeated by pressure groups. . . . At the other extreme [is a state] which is able to remake the society and culture in which it exists: that is, to change economic institutions' values and patterns of interactions among private groups. Such extraordinarily powerful states only exist immediately after major revolutions . . . (when) the society is weak because existing patterns of behavior have been shattered. . . . The domestic strength of the state can be indicated to answer three questions:
(1) Can the state formulate policy goals independent of particular groups within its own society?
(2) Can the state change the behavior of specific groups?
(3) Can the state directly change the structure of the society in which it operates?[18]

According to this model the U.S. government is weak because its executive authority is dispersed and because it is vulnerable to interest-group pressure. Japan and France are perceived as strong states because their executive bureaucracies are insulated from parliamentary and interest-group pressures. In France the essence of the strong state is expressed in nuclear policy, which neither the parliament nor any public groups have been able to influence substantially. When confronted with the Three-Mile Island accident in the United States, Giscard d'Estaing's government expressed indifference to the concerns of those wishing alternative nuclear policies. Since those outside the inner policy arena had no regular channels of influence on this issue, militant confrontation was the only alternative. (Indeed, protest as a tactic often reflects a group's lack of defined channels of influence or resources.)[19] Only after the defeat of a president and the remarkable victory of the Socialists was French nuclear policy reconsidered. In the end, the original decisions were confirmed.

Although the strong- versus weak-state formulation does make useful distinctions about the political capacity of the executives in different political systems, there are several difficulties with it that must concern us here. One difficulty is that a government's ability to act in one policy arena will be very different from its ability to act in another. Thus, France is a strong state in terms of energy policy but in the social services the bureaucracy is trapped in a morass; in welfare policy France is a weak state. The concept of a strong state–weak state continuum refers to a generalized capacity, not to specific abilities to carry out particular tasks. The policy tasks in each sector vary, as does the pattern of interest organization. Consequently, a state's "strength"—the ability to formulate and implement policy—varies with its capacity to execute these different tasks. There are two possibilities. First, there may be the same variation in capacity across policy sectors in all countries, social services being generally more intractable than industrial policy. Second, some states may be more effective at some tasks than others. For example, the British and the Swedes have evolved mechanisms to negotiate income policies, whereas the French would not even have attempted such a negotiation under conservative rule. If policy capacities vary by issue, then the undifferentiated notion of "strength" has little meaning.

Another difficulty with the strong state–weak state formulation is that in strong states, as Gourevitch points out, there is no way the theory can account for the orientation of state policy."[20] In weak states, the groups with access to or control over segments of policy are thought to set the orientation. In dealing with strong states, however, we are forced to argue without an explicit theory about how state directions are formed. The analytic problem is that one label, the state, embraces two actors—the political executive and the civil service or bureaucracy. The strong-state executive may sit atop a civil service that is semi-independent from daily pressures; thus, although it is not independent of politics, it can chart its own tactical course. To reformulate the strong-state argument, let us define the state as the national political executive and the bureaucracies that directly serve that executive office. This strong state manifests two characteristics. First, it is independent from continuous specific pressures exerted by particular political groups. The state does not simply reflect the wishes of groups that may have captured it; rather, it has the autonomy to develop its own policies and to evolve its own strategy for implementing them. Second, it has the capacity to act on groups in the economy and in society. Let us comment briefly on each of these characteristics.

The strong state has some autonomy because it can resist pressures both from its legislature and from nongovernmental interest groups. Its independence from the legislature is most crucially expressed in the budget; legislatures that must vote the budget as a whole (in France, for example) have few means of controlling the executive. Its independence from outside interest groups typically derives from the character of its bureaucracy; if the senior executive posts in the bureaucracy are filled from an elite civil service that forms a definable group, the ability of outside groups to place spokesmen in policy positions is limited. In Britain and France the political executive and bureaucracy have a similar independence from both parliament and interest groups. In both countries a centralized bureaucracy, staffed by an elite civil service, is responsible to an executive that has considerable autonomy from detailed parliamentary control. They differ, however, on the second characteristic of a strong state—the state's ability to act on the society, its ability to exert discretion. This ability turns on two elements. The first is the capacity to deny political access to unwanted groups, to determine which groups may organize or lobby government in the first place. The second is the ability to conduct market operations on a selective and private basis—an ability that enables the executive to maneuver in the economy. The argument developed in this book is that the structure of finance contributes to the state's capacity to act in the economy.

The Problem of Synthesis

The three explanations we have described clearly complement one another. The empirical task is to understand how they interrelate, not to select between them. How do we weave these notions of coalitions, interest groups, institutional arrangements, and state structures into a formulation that can permit us to interpret business-state interactions?

If we are to understand the development of industrial society, the analytic distinction between the political and the economic must be bridged. Power and money—politics and the market—are two ways to organize the use of resources: one can command goods and services or one can buy them. Certainly some institutions concern themselves primarily with the economic ends of production and distribution, whereas others pursue mainly the political goals of setting certain rules of play and compelling specific outcomes in the market. Yet at the same time, all these institutions have both marketplace objectives and political goals. The two activities cannot easily be separated. The logic of power (politics) and the logic of money and markets (economics) simply instruct us about different constraints on the same institutions. There is no pretense that we are building a general "theory" of government policy for industry here. Nonetheless, a coherent analytic approach requires that we focus on a single set of acts, examine the constraints on their actions, and then consider the logic of their choices and behavior.

Andrew Shonfield's remarkable book *Modern Capitalism* remains influential nearly twenty years after its publication precisely because it is built on such a unified conception of the advanced countries. His intent was to make plausible the notion of alternative strategies for controlling markets and industries, not to account for the national variations. For our purposes, the difficulty with the analysis in *Modern Capitalism,* as Philippe Schmitter points out, is that Shonfield tended to resort to argument based on national character and historical precedent.[21] Argument by historical experience states that there is a continuity, but it does not offer an explanation for it. In the view taken here, historical experiences are manifested in the current coalitions, institutions, economic circumstances, and ideologies of a country.

Drawing on the strong state–weak state continuum, Peter Katzenstein presents a more elaborated framework that attempts such a formal synthesis.[22] His intent, like that of his coauthor Krasner, is to relate domestic political structure to foreign economic policy. His discussion, though full of useful insight, obscures the limits of the approach. For our purposes, the central problem is that political concepts are used to discuss what are in large part economic phenomena. As a consequence, our approach is not able to consider either how economic situations translate into political interests or what capacities a government bureaucracy requires to intervene in economic affairs. These limits point to the need to introduce explicit arguments about market operations into the study of the politics of industry. Because Katzenstein's analysis has been influential, the limits of his analysis are discussed at length in a note.[23]

THE ARGUMENTS AND THE EVIDENCE

The preceding discussion suggests that to account for national adjustment strategies we had to consider (1) the government's institutional capacity to shape adjustment, (2) the marketplace problems of industry which would suggest the tasks government would have to accomplish and the interests that different social groups would pursue politically, and (3) the political power of different segments of business and labor. Evidence from the case studies in this book supports these alternative lines of argument, as well as the line of argument based on financial systems. After considering this evidence, this section then considers how these several approaches are related to each other.

Let us first consider variations in the arrangements of state administration. The proposition is that differences in the structure of the political executive will produce differences in the process of adjustment because such arrangements affect a government's capacity to construct a long-term economic strategy and mobilize economic resources to serve it. State-led strategies of adjustment require state structures that permit bureaucrats partial autonomy from parliament and from interest groups that attempt to influence them. They also require that bureaucrats have both the legal discretion to discriminate between firms when implementing policy and the administration and financial instruments to exert their will. Negotiated adjustment also demands a state with the capacity to formulate and implement a view of where the industrial economy should go. Without this capacity the state cannot be a negotiator, for it will have no notion of what to negotiate for. Thus, knowing that a country has a strong-state structure, we still cannot predict whether it will manifest a state-led or a negotiated pattern of adjustment. A weak state structure subject to influence by parliament and interest groups should foster company-led growth.

State structure, the independent variable, can be defined by three characteristics: the method by which it recruits the national civil service, the extent to which its power is centralized, and its degree of autonomy from the legislature.[24] These three characteristics, presented in Chart 6.3, suggest the capacity of senior executives to formulate their own view of the economy and industry and to impose those views on government policy.

These several elements can be combined into a single measure of a state's capacity for intervention. Thus, Japan and France have state structures favorable to intervention and compatible with state-led adjustment. The United States has a structure inappropriate to systematic intervention and compatible with a company-led pattern. Great Britain

Chart 6.3. Defining characteristics of state structure in five countries

1. Civil service recruitment of senior bureaucratic position	
Top positions recruited from civil service	Top positions filled by political appointments
France Japan Great Britain West Germany	United States

2. Power at the center	
Centralized national authority	Decentralized (federal) authority
France Japan Great Britain West Germany	United States

3. Executive autonomy from detailed legislative scrutiny	
Limited autonomy	Extensive autonomy
France Japan Great Britain West Germany	United States

has a structure that allows the central government to formulate a policy but does not have the discretion or instrumentality to implement it. The predictions about the relationships between state administrative structure and adjustment fit the evidence from the case studies summarized in Chart 6.4.

Let us next consider the notion that economic circumstances so circumscribe political choice that the situation will lead to predictable approaches to policy. For example, economic backwardness and economic decline will encourage the political executive to mobilize a national economic effort, whereas a secure position in the international economy will result in greater private autonomy and initiative. This hypothesis requires that we examine the economic situation of a country.

The economic position of the five countries we shall examine has shifted dramatically over the two generations since the end of the Second World War (see Table 6.1). In 1950 France and Japan were relatively backward economically compared to Germany, Great Britain, and the United States. In the postwar years the size of the agricultural work force was the most important measure of industrial backwardness and national trade position constituted a secondary measure. Since Japan and France both had large agricultural work forces, it appeared

Chart 6.4. State administrative structure and the approach to adjustment in five countries

State administrative structure	Actual approach to adjustment			
	State-led	Company-led	Negotiated	Ambiguous
Centralized executive: semiautonomous with extensive administrative discretion (predicts state-led adjustment) (cases, Japan and France)	Japan France			
Centralized executive: semiautonomous with limited administrative discretion (predicts ambiguous) (case, Great Britain)				Great Britain
Decentralized executive: semiautonomous central executive (predicts ambiguous) (case, West Germany)			West Germany	
Decentralized executive: limited autonomy, i.e., open to continuous and direct influence by social groups (predicts company-led adjustment) (case, United States)		United States		

that their economic structures required massive transformations. The French and German trade position was stronger than that of the Japanese. Moreover, it can be argued (as in Chapter 5) that the German trade position was artificially deflated in 1950 and did not reflect the underlying competitive potential of its reconstructed industry. Germany surged ahead because its economy required little reorganization. The greater the trade potential in the private sector the weaker the pressures on government to set the direction of development itself. The strategy of the finance minister Ludwig Erhard, was possible because the structure of German industry was sound. In this view Germany's economic situation was intermediate in 1950, standing between that of Japan and France at one end of a continuum and Britain and the United States at the other.

By 1977 the backward countries and Germany had surged forward in trade competition. These catch-up nations, however, are the most dependent on imported energy, and thus remain vulnerable to the external world. In Britain a precipitous decline in international power forced a debate over the mechanisms of revitalization and the premises of policy. Only recently has the United States faced external pressures on its collective economic well-being. Its trade deterioration has been

Table 6.1. Changing economic circumstances in five countries since 1950

A. Percentage of workforce in agriculture

Year	High	Medium	Low
1950	Japan, France	Germany	U.S., U.K.
1970		France, Japan	Germany, U.S., U.K.

B. World trade position (Percentage share of world manufactured exports)

Year	Weak 5%	5% Medium 10%	10% Strong 20%	20% Dominant
1950	Japan 3.4	France 9.9 Germany 7.3		U.S. 27.3 U.K. 25.5
1965		France 8.8 Japan 9.4	U.K. 13.9 Germany 19.1 U.S. 20.3	
1977		France 9.9 U.K. 9.3	Germany 20.8 U.S. 15.9 Japan 15.4	

C. Current dependence on imported oil (1980)

High	Medium	Low
Germany France Japan	U.S.	U.K.

slower and it has been less dependent on trade. Equally important, its long-term energy resource position is stronger than that of the other countries studied, despite its present partial dependence on imported oil. Thus it can be argued that for the United States, external economic pressures are not so compelling as to force a fundamental reconsideration of the system of company-led growth. In sum, the economic situation of the United States and Germany placed no intense pressure on their existing institutions for economic management. In France and Japan, the postwar economic situation created pressures favorable to some form of state-led development strategies; these pressures simply pushed them in the direction that their institutions and politics already pointed. In Britain, economic decline created intense pressures that produced a reassessment of the country's economic institutions and policies.

The evidence suggests the importance of each of these pieces of the political economy. Chart 6.5, which summarizes the evidence, suggests the relation we would expect to find between a country's financial system, its state structure, and its economic circumstances. The predicted relations are compared with the actual adjustment process of the

Chart 6.5. Patterns of industrial adjustment (predicted and actual) in five countries

Countries	Adjustment Model (predicted)	Adjustment Model (actual)
United States		company-led
capital-market finance	company-led	
fragmented, decentralized state structure	company-led	
economic dominance in postwar years	company-led	
Britain		unclear or ambiguous
capital-market finance	company-led, possibly state-led	
insulated state with limited discretion	state-formulated policy with no implementation	
declining economic position	state-led response	
Japan		state-led
credit-based, price-administered finance	state-led	
insulated state with discretion	state-led	
rapid industrial catch-up	state-led	
France		state-led
credit-based, price-administered finance	state-led	
insulated state with discretion	state-led	
industrial catch-up	state-led	
Germany		negotiated
credit-based, bank-dominated finance	negotiated	
decentralized state with civil service	company-led or negotiated	
industrial leader from mid-1950s but middle-rank economic power	negotiated or company-led	

several countries, based on the discussions in the preceding chapters. The political competition of groups within the economy is considered in a moment.

The evidence does suggest that each component considered here—financial system, state structure, and economic situation—represents an enabling condition for a particular pattern of industrial adjustment—a specific politics of industrial change. It can be argued that all three components were required for a particular model of adjustment to emerge. The British case suggests that when the economic problems to be resolved, the administrative possibilities for political action, and the arrangements of the financial system push in different directions, political conflicts that undermine the process of growth are the result. The significance of the components of a system depends on their relation to each other.

These elements—state administration, financial system, and economic circumstance—define the setting in which political fights occur. Economic circumstances specify the problems countries face, while state administration and financial systems specify something of a government's capacity to respond. The argument is that the institutional arrangements of market and administration structure the political conflicts over industrial change and economic policy. How groups must organize to achieve their objectives, who their allies will be, what their tactics must be, and what can be obtained from government will all be articulated by the organizational context—both economic and political—in which the fights take place.

Yet, evidently, the purposes of government and the outcome of conflict require explanation in terms of the interests, purposes, and political capacities of the groups affected by industrial development. How then do we tie these traditional concerns of political analysis to the discussion of institutions in this book? The first possibility is that we should group together those countries with common structural features that seemingly define a single model of adjustment. Within each set, variations in the power of the different social groups (such as labor and international business) would account for the purposes of policy. *How* political settlements were reached would be structured by institutional arrangements, but the *content* of those settlements would be settled by the relative power of the competing groups.

Several recent studies offer support for this view. Katzenstein examined the responses of a set of small European countries to international market pressures, all of which would be categorized here as instances of negotiated adjustment.[25] Their economic circumstances and political arrangements constrained the ways their governments could deal with economic crisis. Domestic adjustments to international market changes could not be avoided, and the costs of that change were distributed through explicit negotiation. In each of the small states he discussed, variations in the political power of labor and the different components of the business community accounted for differences in the types of market adjustments government supported and the character of the distributional bargains that were struck. Similarly, our analysis attributed the policy differences between the two state-led cases, Japan and

France, to variations in the domestic political strength of internationally competitive business and labor. Douglas Hibbs's effort to relate the social basis of governing parties—business or labor—to macroeconomic outcomes in a set of advanced countries provides additional evidence.[26] His proposition is that when in power, labor-based parties produce lower unemployment but higher inflation rates than business-based parties. The presumption is that government can weight monetary and fiscal policies to produce these different macroeconomic outcomes. What Hibbs does not explain is as interesting as his not unexpected conclusions. When labor-based parties were in power in Germany, inflation rates were consistently lower than those in France, which was governed by a business coalition. France and Germany represent structurally distinct cases in which, when accounting for their distinct macroeconomic outcomes, differences in the governing coalition matter less than structural differences in their economies. In other words, evidence from both Hibbs and Katzenstein supports our argument that variation in the power of social groups accounts for policy and economic outcomes *within* each national economy or adjustment model, rather than distinguishing between them. Factors other than the social basis of parties account for variation in both national economic outcomes and adjustment processes.

Institutions, nonetheless, are created as instruments of action and their organization reflects the political fights that established them and the goals of the leadership that animates them. An alternative proposition, therefore, is that variation in the relative power of social groups in the several countries does account for differences in the process of adjustment that typifies the politics of economic growth in each country. There is evidence for this argument and it must be addressed. In France and Japan, where labor was weak, we found state-led adjustment strategies, whereas in Germany a strong labor movement and the Social Democratic party supported a negotiated style of change. In the United States, the absence of any significant labor challenge to the political system and a fragmented state structure have prevented any systematic threat to business prerogatives and autonomy. Britain, finally, is a country seemingly caught inside a triangle defined by three points: business autonomy reinforced by a circumscribed bureaucracy and a capital market–based financial system; an insulated executive that could formulate and begin to implement a policy of state-led growth; and a strong labor movement with the power to claim a role in politics and the market but without the inclination or invitation to become a systematic partner in industrial change. The position of labor and business in these cases is different. We might argue that the variation in the power of different social groups during the political struggles that accompanied industrialization helps account for each model of change. The institutional arrangements of the modern economy and administration are thus the products of past conflict forcing us to undertake a kind of political archaeology in order to disentangle these developments.[27] For example, state-led growth that was still capitalist was one response to industrial backwardness: it hinged on market institutions that allowed large-scale mobilization of capital and political arangements that dealt labor out of power during rapid expansion. The consistency of the patterns of institutions and politics then has a simple explanation: the institutions were originally created to achieve particular purposes but once in place institutions are not infinitely malleable and will continue to shape the political struggles that follow. Thus, now that the Socialist left has come to power in France—strengthening the position of labor—will a state-led model of change take on characteristics of a negotiated model? A structural argument based on the arrangements of the executive, bureaucracy, and finance would predict that the Socialist victory will alter which groups are benefited by state action but that the system of state guidance will continue. We have suggested here that each national process of adjustment now rests on institutional and marketplace structures. Consequently, changes in social power will be reflected by changes in the groups that benefit from policy but they will not easily alter the basic political processes associated with industrial change.

A few preliminary propositions about each national case may now be offered. The state-led development in France and Japan was ultimately a conservative modernization in which agriculture and traditional business were sheltered from the consequences of development. In Britain, the inability to settle on a strategy for adjustment can be attributed in part to the fluctuation of power between political parties representing labor and business respectively, and to the relative balance of power between producer groups in the marketplace. What is still needed is an explanation of why the British could not work out a generally accepted agreement on the parameters of government policy and a consensus on the limits of production-group conflict. In Germany, a corporate bargain and a general acceptance of the market situation were not undermined by changes in the governing party. In the United States the strategic autonomy of corporations was not really challenged during the postwar years. Indeed, since politics is not organized on class or producer lines, an economic debate is not necessarily central to political life. As continued inflation and slowed growth have put pressure on the executive, a debate on the need to promote growth has begun in America, but only now is that debate becoming a policy struggle capable of organizing political conflict.

Though these four explanations of the national approach to adjustment highlight different independent variables—finance, state structure, economic situations, and governing coalition, they do not directly compete with one another. Rather, as argued earlier, each is an enabling condition for a particular model of adjustment. The case of state-led growth should serve to make this point clear. A broad economic challenge that affects the national position may induce efforts to use the state to promote economic restructuring and competitive adjustment to the market. Yet, unless there exists a state structure that can be used as an instrument of such a policy, the effort is likely to fail. If the state structure permits a coherent elite to define a line of policy, then a state-led initiative may be launched. Such an initiative can be implemented only if the proper instruments are available. In this case, a credit-based, price-administered financial system is a crucial enabling element. Indeed, as we argued in the French case, finance may be a weapon that permits an elite group to redirect economic administration toward interventionist developmental purposes. The financial system serves as the eyes and hands for the state's industrial brain. Indeed, the political meaning of a financial system cannot be understood in isolation but must be situated in relation to other institutional components of the economy and to the competing groups. In periods of economic adjustment, when the conflicts about control and organization of the economy and society are fought out in marketplace arenas as much as in electoral or legislative settings, financial institutions reveal clearly that they are allocative institutions—the scene and instrument of political conflict—whose behavior is not simply a technical but a political matter.

FINANCE ADJUSTMENT AND POLITICAL CRISIS

The question of relative national economic success lurks just behind our analysis of the variations in roles that government plays in industrial affairs and the processes of adjustment. Do the variations in the political process of adjustment—the balance between subsidy and promotion, the capacities for selective intervention, and the political mechanisms for establishing a settlement—substantively affect the industrial performance of these countries? A systematic argument relating the process of adjustment to the pace of industrial change is not really possible here. We can observe closely the effect of government policy within specific industries, perhaps assess the direction of policy in the economy as a whole, and even propose policy approaches that might be successful under specific industrial circumstances. But we cannot extrapolate those specific analyses to national growth processes without at least an informal model of each economy. Once it is clear that we cannot derive a general argument about economic achievement from our observations, we may point out some clear political implications that our research holds for discussions of national economic policy. This book has emphasized two roles that government plays in the economy: the establishment of the political conditions needed for the market to force industrial changes, and intervention to organize specific market outcomes. Let us consider these two roles in turn.

Establishing the Political Conditions for Market Development

We have contended from the beginning of this book that a stable settlement for distributing the gains and pain of growth is a political prerequisite for a smoothly functioning economy. If the distributional settlements are not stable, political conflict will continue until a new agreement is reached. Inevitably, the distributional battles will interrupt the routine functioning of the marketplace and make the institutions of the economy—such as the structures of finance and labor relations—the scene of overt political conflict. We have noted that governments can achieve a stable settlement of distribution in several ways: by consciously shaping the market to impose a particular distribution of the costs and gains of growth; by permitting the market to allocate them with only limited government intervention or compensation; or by negotiating an explicit settlement between the producer groups. In essence, the losers in the market must either be compensated by policy or excluded from policymaking. Each solution, each mechanism of reaching a settlement, is tied to one of our three models of adjustment. Since these imply different political strategies for industrial order, they also imply different political vulnerabilities. It is not so much that one political mechanism necessarily works better than another one at providing the political conditions for growth, but rather that each has its own distinctive advantages and problems.

In the state-led system, illustrated here by the French and Japanese cases, an explicit political strategy determined which groups would be compensated during change and which groups would bear the greatest burden. This distribution was systematically imposed by state manipulation of the market. More baldly, traditional industry and agriculture were protected and labor was squeezed; a conservative coalition had to be maintained and labor had to be excluded from policymaking. When the distributional outcome is a visibly political choice as well as a product of the marketplace, it invites a political challenge. Indeed, we argued that in France Giscard d'Estaing sought to promote a policy of "liberalism" that would make it appear that economic outcomes resulted from the workings of an essentially autonomous market. This "liberalism" had as much to do with an effort to bolster the legitimacy of economic outcomes as with any substantive withdrawal of the state from influence in the economy. Giscard failed in part because the policy provided no political explanation for the painful adjustments it seemingly compelled. Its political argument was limited to the technical claim that there was no choice.

Its need to enforce an explicit political victory makes the state-led system vulnerable. An imposed solution that excludes some groups is like a tightly wound spring: the tighter it is turned, the more likely it is to snap. The French have had to wind the spring tighter than the Japanese. In Japan the government's need to subsidize uncompetitive companies has been limited by the greater political strength of internationally oriented big business and the greater capacity of smaller-scale traditional firms to adjust to the market. At the same time, the Japanese labor market is fragmented. It is first divided between an organized secondary sector and a labor elite with lifetime employment, and that elite is itself divided into company unions. These divisions limit working-class political unity and diminish the threat that labor poses to conservative rule. The French Socialist victory can be viewed as the snapping of the spring of a state-led growth strategy conducted by a conservative coalition. The obvious question, soon to be answered, is whether state-led growth is simply a strategy of conservative economic modernization in a centralized and bureaucratic political system or whether it can be implemented with equal success by a Socialist left in a market economy.

In the company-led model of adjustment, individual firms make the basic strategy and production choices without interference. The government's role is to regulate the market and provide some limited assistance to those displaced by change. In principle, the workers and communities damaged by change have only limited claims to protection, but in practice they are often able to win compensation. Such compensation is quite distinct from the politically strategic bribery aimed at holding a growth coalition together, as in France, or from the more broadly negotiated settlements observed in some small corporatist democracies, such as Sweden. The American case may be one of the few pure examples of company-led adjustment.

There are two political vulnerabilities in the company-led system. First, as observers from Samuel Huntington to Mancur Olson contend, the accumulation of individual protections and compensations has ended up entangling the economy in a morass.[28] These compensations pose no particular crisis, however, because they emerge separately and not as a general political challenge. The crisis of democracy, in the view of Huntington and Olson, is the inability to resist those demands. The second vulnerability of the company-led system is that it lacks a center-point from which to shift the direction and priorities expressed in the routine accumulation of particular bargains. The policy reversal attempted by the Reagan administration in 1981 seemed to give the lie to these concerns; a sharp change has taken place and it is stripping away layers of social protection and privilege. However, the most important weapon in the first years of this fight was a broad ideological appeal, an appeal that gave momentary direction to a seeming surge of political conservatism. The Reagan economic battle, in fact, has dramatized the absence in America of state structures that provide executive leadership with administrative instruments to impose its preferences. In an atmosphere where the need to promote the productive apparatus of the economy is now generally acknowledged, the Reagan administration has mounted an ideological drive to generate the extra savings needed for industrial development by stripping away the social protections against market disruptions which were built up over generations. The political risk of these initiatives is that they have fractured the consensus on the need for redevelopment by precipitating a distributional battle. Since there are few mechanisms for enforcing the Reagan redistribution over time, and equally few for negotiating the distributional terms of a redevelopment effort, the routine of American politics can be expected to reassert itself. As it does, the Reagan victory could prove short lived and the American economy could stall on the distributional conflicts. Reorienting a decentralized political economy without dividing it by ideological conflicts is the present challenge to American policy.

The negotiated model of the adjustment, to which we assigned the German case, represents a system in which the distributional questions of the economy are explicitly confronted and resolved by a political bargain rather than through marketplace conflict. The problem with

this model is that a change in the nature of the growth problem necessitates the negotiation of a new political deal. Faced with internationally
changed markets, the government of a state-led system will try to maneuver consciously through the new political minefield; in the company-led model, individual firms will make their adjustments and their
choices will shift the distributional outcome. The difficulties of negotiating a new political bargain can be seen in recent Swedish troubles.[29]
Admittedly, the advent of a conservative Swedish government in 1976
for the first time in decades implicitly forced a renegotiation of the
existing political settlement, but the need for a new bargain had already arisen because of dramatic shifts in the Swedish economy's position in world markets. In earlier years, policies that sought to retrain
and shift labor from lower-value-added to higher-value-added jobs had
successfully matched the workers' desire for steadily rising wages with
the companies' need for secure niches in world markets. When an
entire set of Swedish industries became vulnerable to more intense foreign competition, however, the terms of the deal had to be altered. It is
possible to assume that the level of investment in the economy would
have to be raised through reduced dividend payout or reduced wages;
in sum, that the short-term gains of capital or labor (or both) would
have to change. Yet how does one strike a new national wage bargain
and at the same time make certain that wage restraint does not simply
relieve the burden on investors?

Reaching a new deal in uncertain economic circumstances can be
extremely difficult, even if all parties bargain in good faith. Steel negotiations in the United States in the early 1980s provide an example of
this problem. The American steel industry is preparing for both a
period of reinvestment in new equipment and a new round of wage
bargaining. Management has openly expressed its worries about present labor costs, which rose during the years when the American market
was insulated and have now become a clear competitive handicap in
international trade. The response of the president of the United Steel
Workers was revealing. He acknowledged that management's concern
over labor costs might be intended to convey the need for badly needed
modernization of steel mills. But if it was intended as a warning that
things were going to be tough in contract talks, he noted that a balance
in sacrifice by the USW and shareholders would have to be negotiated.
Any effort to use hard times to shift the returns between labor and
capital would be resisted. Determining what negotiations are actually
about when political and economic circumstances change is difficult.
Finding a "just" distribution becomes more difficult when the parameters within which a deal must be made are fluctuating or unclear.

There is more than one way of resolving distributional problems and no solution is exclusively market oriented, negotiated, or imposed. Negotiations can serve to impose solutions and in its own way the market is a political device for distributing economic resources. Those who would gain from industrial change can impose the costs on those displaced, bribe them into acquiescing in change, or work out an explicit bargain about the terms of development. These brief comments simply suggest the particular political vulnerabilities of the several approaches to settling the distribution of costs and benefits which have been discussed in this volume. The British case should make clear, however, that industrial paralysis will result if the distributional problem is not resolved in some fashion. Americans should not draw from the English experience the simple conclusion that rising public expenditures strain the private sector. Rather, they should conclude that unresolved distributional battles will unravel the industrial fabric and impede growth.

Indeed, this line of argument could be pushed one step further. We might consider not simply the political problems of maintaining a particular settlement but the economic character of the political settlement itself. Will the policy emphasis be on subsidizing uncompetitive activities and thereby resisting the market, or will it promote industrial growth and accelerate development occurring naturally in the market? I have argued elsewhere that the more heavily a settlement is weighted toward subsidy and protection, the greater the difficulty of sustaining inflation-free growth.[30] We might conclude that in recent years the increased pressure for industrial change and the diminished political capacity to carry it out (considered in Chapter 1) have pushed policy in the advanced countries toward economic subsidy and political conflict—a conclusion that would help to explain the conjuncture of inflation and stagnation since the end of the 1960s.

Government Strategies to Create and Maintain Market Advantage

Whereas government's first role in the economy is to assure that the market process continues, its second role is to undertake selective intervention to force or promote specific industrial outcomes. As we argued in Chapter 1, government policies can create or maintain competitive advantage for firms in international markets and over time can reshape the comparative advantage of the national economy. Government intervention does not necessarily retard or distort an otherwise perfect market. The meaning of interventions, we have suggested, must be considered in three different industrial contexts that concern governments: *growth* industries with linkages to the economy as a whole, *transi-*

tion industries seeking to survive in changed markets, and *declining* industries where no amount of investment could reestablish a competitive position. We have seen that government can help promote growth industries and often assure the survival of transition industries by providing the time and the investments they need to regain a competitive position in the market. But any enthusiasm for government intervention must be tempered by such evident disasters as Anglo-French Concorde and British Leyland. The possibilities of selective promotion often become the realities of general protection. It is evident that the technical capacity to intervene which we examined in the French and Japanese cases can be used for two very different purposes. In the Japanese steel and electronics cases, it served to promote internationally competitive firms and to create a comparative advantage in capital- and technology-intensive industries. French policies in the same industries, however, served to resist market forces and to preserve uncompetitive firms. The common thrust of intervention in France and Japan rests on similar technical capacities, but the diverging purposes—the differing mix of promotion and protection—reflect the different strengths of business and labor from country to country. The French government was more vulnerable than the Japanese government to political pressures to preserve the industrial past. One risk of an interventionist system, then, is that it will be used to subsidize and preserve uncompetitive firms rather than to promote development.

Even if an interventionist apparatus is intended to promote development, it may still be misused if incorrect marketplace judgments are made. The French and Japanese strategies of intervention are very different in character, and it may be that the French approach runs greater risks of misjudgment or abuse. The difference is that the Japanese adopt "market-conforming" policies, attempting to ride market forces toward their objectives, whereas the French policies have often had a distinctly administrative flavor, being attempts to dictate to the market. In the Japanese case, ordinary competitive developments served as instruments of policy, whereas in the French case they often appeared as obstacles to government objectives. In the 1960s French policies were often intended to impose particular product or production goals on an unwilling marketplace (although in more recent years French intervention has been more oriented toward marketplace success). French efforts were successful when the policy target was stationary; for example, when technological developments were slow-moving and the domestic economy could be insulated from the international marketplace. Such conditions gave the government time to mobilize a collective effort. But when there was a moving target, as in rapidly

314

evolving, high-technology industries that could not be insulated from international competition, technocratic intervention was not successful.

The Japanese system, which is not a cultural inheritance but an explicit political creation of the postwar years, is suited to rapid development and catch-up. The government could actively promote markets for new products. For example, drivers were trained and roads built to create demand for autos before the boom in auto production got underway. Tax incentives were given for the purchase of carefully chosen electronic goods that produced the volume of demand required to gain scale economies quickly. Abundant and implicitly guaranteed financing for favored sectors drew new entrants to the markets, and tax arrangements helped keep them solvent. The Japanese success cannot be discounted as an illusion of market manipulation. Ultimately, Japan's international strength has rested on innovation in the production of standardized mass goods, an innovation that reduced unit labor costs and the levels of expensive stocks held during production. The result has been both high quality and lower price. For a generation now, Japan has been the fastest of the followers, which is a very profitable position. Whether their system can work equally well in forging Japan a position as an industrial leader is another matter. The danger of the interventionist strategy—suggested by both the French and Japanese cases—is not only that the assistance for development will be diverted into subsidy, but also that state guidance may be more effective for organizing high-growth catch-up than for trailblazing into the future.

Some governments, such as the U.S. government, do not have the administrative capacities to mobilize industry toward state-selected goals or to prod firms into making necessary competitive adjustments. These countries are seemingly left with the choice between free markets and protection. When they try to help companies threatened by international trade, their assistance will most likely take the form of trade protection. Whatever the current difficulties in Britain and the United States, one must recall that the Industrial Revolution took place through entrepreneurial initiative, and that the reorganization of American capitalism into a continental system of giant, hierarchically managed corporations that became internationally dominant was also a private achievement. Much can be accomplished when a government supports industry through the creative use of policies that are aggregate in form but have well-planned sectoral consequences. For example, tax credits for incremental research-and-development investments can give an advantage to expanding companies that are developing new products and processes.

Such a tax arrangement does not require any selective decisions or knowledge on the part of government.

Yet, just as a more organized German economy challenged the British in the late nineteenth century, so a more organized Japan challenges the United States today. Our confidence in market mechanisms should not obscure the great power of government actions. The limits on arm's-length government policies become apparent when there are structural constraints on an industry's growth which require sector-specific policies to overcome market imperfections. For example, in many mature industries the failure or cutback of single large companies can lead to massive layoffs. Some protection is likely to be afforded. In mature industries with extensive sunken investment, trade protection that ostensibly provides time to manage adjustments often simply eliminates the incentive to do so. The problem is how to facilitate an industrial transition in the face of intense foreign competition. For such growth industries as computers and semiconductors, the question becomes what policies to adopt when foreign governments distort markets to promote the development of their own firms. Some argue that if the Japanese or French governments wish to subsidize our consumption of their steel we should graciously accept their offer. But those who would have the United States accept such subsidies must demonstrate two things. First, they must show that our economy and polity can absorb and respond to the dislocation provoked by the planned development of other national economies. It is quite possible that the gains that result from the lower product costs of imported goods may not exceed the additional adjustment costs they generate. Developed societies are not entirely plastic; they cannot simply be twisted this way and that without political repercussions. Second, the advocates of passivity in the face of policy-induced trade pressures must also show that our short-run gain is not our long-run undoing. State-promoted development abroad is an effort to gain an advantage in the industries that shape national development. Such state-led efforts are often misguided, but when they are well organized they represent serious competitive challenges to American companies. America is certainly not ready to substitute a system of state leadership for market and corporate initiative. Yet in an increasingly competitive international economy, the difficulties of promoting growth sectors and facilitating the competitive transition of temporarily troubled industries may force us to manage more creatively our market system, which rests so heavily on private initiative.

The alternative to state-led adjustment or privately initiated change with limited government compensation is a system in which the terms of industrial change are explicitly negotiated. The evidence, both anecdotal and systematic, gives such arrangements excellent reviews, not only politically but also technically. In many of the small European economies, negotiated bargains about the distribution of total production have contributed to long periods of strike-free development. In Sweden, retaining arrangements have apparently speeded adjustment by making labor markets work more effectively. In Germany, arrangements between government, labor, and industry which are organized around trade associations and financial ties have been credited with facilitating industrial transition and regional rejuvenation. Even in the United States, albeit on a more limited basis, the tripartite steel committees born of the steel plan of Anthony Solomon are sometimes credited with easing the transformation of that industry. All these negotiated arrangements accomplish two tasks. First, they dissolve resistance to change by assuring those affected that they will be accommodated in a new industrial order. Workers assured of new jobs are more willing to relinquish old ones or to train their own replacements. Second, by explicitly resolving the distributional problem, negotiated arrangements create an atmosphere in which the search for the common gains from industrial change can be made into a joint effort. If there is assurance that an effort will be made to accommodate all interests, then many of the seemingly fixed parameters within which change must occur can be eased. The jigsaw puzzle of change can be finished by deliberately reshaping some of the pieces.

For the most part, the countries in which negotiated change is a central component of adjustment are small or medium-sized nations. The social and political bases of negotiated change in these countries appear to be quite specific. First, they have centrally organized labor movements with a voice in government. (Effective centralization may depend on social and industrial homogeneity and limited populations, in which case a larger and more diverse society would have difficulty organizing collaboration.) Second, they exhibit a social corporatism based on bargains between centralized but encapsulated ethnic, linguistic, and religious communities. Third, they have some form of organized private enterprise that permits narrower sectoral or regional bargains. The smaller of the countries with systems of bargained change—such as the Netherlands, Sweden, and Denmark—are considered to be economically vulnerable because the size of their domestic markets limits the industries in which they can promote development, and the sectors in which industries are clustered are seemingly exposed to trade pressure from the developing countries.[31] Whether this system of bargained change is considered a deliberate response to that vulnerability or a fortunate conjunction of economic need and political capacity, it seems clear that the economic changes required in these countries are particularly suited to a system of negotiated adjustment. Political ossification—the formation of rigid structures that assure a place and voice to each segment of the community—may facilitate economic flexibility. Despite their seemingly vulnerable economic positions, the small northern European countries all have very high per capita incomes and, as a result, their firms are mostly in very high value-added segments of industry—even within ordinarily less attractive industries such as textiles and food processing. A strategy of finding market niches is a workable national solution in a small country, though not in a large one. Market niches limit the need to mount broad technological or commercial ventures and they reward the capacities to deliver reliable high quality and often specialized product applications to fixed deadlines.

Each of these systems of industrial change was produced by the fit between a nation's social and institutional configuration and the nature of the economic problems it faced. The United States and Britain were historically the entrepreneurs who held government at arm's-length from industry. Japan, France, and Germany gave an active promotional role to government in directing economic catch-up. In the postwar years Germany, whose structure had been altered by occupation and partition, became in part a quick-footed follower fitting into the world's market niches like its smaller European neighbors. Each of the three models of adjustment, then, reflects a solution to different problems.

The current challenges to each system are in many ways distinct. The fast-growth, state-led countries must apply the techniques that initially allowed them to catch up with the industrial leaders to the new task of promoting continued adjustment from a developed base. It can be argued that these skills at industrial promotion honed during the period of catch-up are being effectively applied to problems of adjusting to a troubled world economy. There is some evidence (presented in tabular form in notes) to suggest that in the years after the oil crisis France and Japan were able to adjust their production structures to the changed patterns of world demand more rapidly than other countries were. If this was in fact the case, we must ask whether their advantage stemmed from the unique capacities afforded by their bureaucratic-financial structure or whether it was the result of their being under more intense pressure to make the shifts. (Because of their oil dependence, France and Japan did in fact feel greater pressure to adjust than did the other countries studied here.) The adjustments they did make, primarily in industries that bend or cut metals, indicate their capacities for successful industrial catch-up. For the smaller countries that depend on a more negotiated style of adjustment, and even for the more powerful German economy, the economic dance will become more intricate, straining the capacities of even their flexible systems of bargained change. For Britain, which did not fit any one of our categories, the critical problem remains the same: to establish a system for resolving the terms of industrial change, to settle the distributional question that has paralyzed the economy and thus permit producers to focus on the joint gains of growth. That task may now be harder than at any time since the end of the Second World War. For the United States, the pure company-led case in this study, the challenge is clear and has two parts. The first is to maintain the capacity to innovate across a broad range of products and production processes, to continue to shape the industrial future. The second is to maintain advantage in a wide range of mature industries that provide the economy with ongoing employment and income.

Despite these real differences, the economic situations of the several advanced Western countries have steadily become more similar in the years since the Second World War. The domestic structural adjustments forced on them by international market shifts are becoming ever more alike, even if their specific domestic problems are different. Given this convergence in the tasks of economic management, the different systems of adjustment must be seen as nationally competitive strategies for mobilizing markets in a struggle between nations for the benefits of continuing development.

CONCLUSION

Yet, to conclude, we must place this discussion of the politics of industrial change in perspective. In the midst of an extended and serious economic slowdown, it is remarkable that we can talk at all about the relative capacity of these several countries to solve industrial adjustment problems. The last two extended worldwide economic downturns, in the late nineteenth century and the 1930s, produced dramatic changes in the very structure of political regimes across Europe. The stakes were not relative growth, economic well-being, and power; they were liberty and democracy. Certainly the current economic disturbance has not shaken society as those earlier downturns did and, consequently, the political reaction has been more muted. We should not conclude, however, that the present economic shocks are any less serious than their predecessors. The difference is that our economic and political capacity to absorb economic disorder has been vastly increased. Indeed, rather than bemoaning our failure to resolve the enigma of slowed growth and spiraling inflation, we should perhaps congratulate ourselves that severe economic shocks and conflicts have not degenerated into deep depression or intense trade war. Whatever the shortcomings of Keynes's insights for resolving the problems of our era, they provided powerful prescriptions for coping with the difficulties of his world. His insights suggested and justified policies that served to prevent demand from collapsing. In the half-century since the Great Depression, all the advanced countries have to one degree or another integrated the labor movement into politics and established a social-welfare network that cushions the economic shocks, giving us some assurance that a downturn will not become a collapsing spiral.

Many conservatives now fear that those social cushions against the dislocations of the market have become obstacles to industrial adjustment and growth. But we must not forget that the central purpose of the system of social protection was to prevent the desperation that springs from economic disorder. Liberals have come to value these protections as an entitlement akin to the rights of citizenship. The economic conservatives who would now restrict or dismantle them would do well to recall that even that protagonist of German unification under the Prussian state, Otto von Bismarck, established a social insurance system to reinforce conservative rule in Germany. Britain's difficulties in the spring and summer of 1981 should remind us all that social despair played an important part in the radical movements of the 1930s. Policies of economic management that propose to remove the protections that insulate us against social desperation should be examined from a political and not simply from a technical perspective. Until now the debates that have accompanied this extended period of economic adjustment have focused on policy, on the proper organization of the economy's institutions, and occasionally on the organization of work itself. The issue has been who should govern: which party or which leader. Though the search for new economic policies has not called into question the democratic regimes that now govern these countries, there is no reason to believe that our fragile political defenses against economic troubles can hold forever. We may find ourselves searching not for a formula for faster growth and lower inflation rates, but rather for a strategy to protect the integrity of our political system and our democratic values.

Appendix: Growth, inflation, and unemployment in five countries, 1954–1981

Year	Japan			France			West Germany			United States			United Kingdom		
	A	B	C	A	B	C	A	B	C	A	B	C	A	B	C
1954	5.7	6.0	1.5	4.2	0.0	1.7	7.7	0.0	7.0	-2.2	0.0	5.6	3.8	1.9	1.4
1955	8.6	-0.9	1.6	4.7	1.0	1.6	12.0	2.0	5.1	6.9	0.0	4.4	3.3	3.9	1.1
1956	7.5	0.4	1.5	5.9	2.0	1.1	7.2	2.5	4.0	2.2	1.5	4.2	1.6	4.9	1.2
1957	7.3	3.1	1.2	6.0	2.6	0.8	5.6	2.1	3.4	1.9	3.5	4.3	1.9	3.7	1.5
1958	5.8	-0.5	1.3	2.9	15.0	0.9	3.5	2.2	3.5	-0.5	2.7	6.8	0.2	3.0	2.0
1959	9.1	1.1	1.3	3.2	6.1	1.3	7.4	1.0	2.4	6.0	0.8	5.5	4.0	0.6	2.2
1960	13.1	3.5	1.1	7.2	3.6	1.2	8.9	1.3	1.2	2.1	1.6	5.5	5.2	1.0	1.6
1961	14.6	5.3	1.0	5.5	3.2	1.0	5.1	2.3	0.8	2.3	1.1	6.7	3.3	3.4	1.5
1962	7.1	6.9	0.9	6.7	4.8	1.2	4.4	3.1	0.7	5.6	1.1	5.5	1.0	4.3	2.0
1963	10.5	7.5	0.9	5.3	4.8	1.4	3.0	3.0	0.8	4.1	1.2	5.7	3.9	1.8	2.4
1964	13.2	3.9	0.8	6.5	3.4	1.1	6.7	2.3	0.7	5.1	1.4	5.2	5.2	4.0	1.8
1965	5.1	6.5	0.8	4.8	2.5	1.3	5.6	3.5	0.6	6.0	1.6	4.5	2.3	4.8	1.5
1966	10.6	5.1	0.9	5.2	2.6	1.4	2.5	3.4	0.7	6.0	2.9	3.8	2.0	3.6	1.5
1967	10.8	3.9	1.3	4.7	2.8	1.8	-0.2	1.5	2.1	2.7	2.8	3.8	2.6	2.4	2.3
1968	12.8	5.4	1.2	4.3	4.5	2.1	6.3	2.9	1.5	4.5	4.2	3.6	4.1	4.7	2.5
1969	12.3	5.2	1.1	7.0	6.5	2.3	7.8	1.8	0.8	2.6	5.4	3.5	1.5	5.3	2.5
1970	9.8	7.8	0.9	5.7	5.3	2.4	6.0	3.3	0.4	-0.1	6.0	5.6	2.2	6.4	2.4
1971	4.6	6.3	1.2	5.4	5.3	2.6	3.2	5.4	0.8	2.9	4.3	5.9	2.7	9.5	3.5
1972	8.8	5.0	1.4	5.9	6.2	2.7	3.7	5.5	1.1	5.8	3.2	5.6	2.2	6.8	3.8
1973	8.8	11.5	1.3	5.4	7.4	2.6	4.9	6.9	1.2	5.4	6.3	4.9	7.5	8.4	2.7
1974	-1.0	23.3	1.4	3.2	13.7	2.8	0.5	7.0	1.6	-1.3	10.9	5.6	-1.2	15.8	2.6
1975	2.3	11.7	1.9	0.2	11.7	4.1	-1.8	5.9	3.7	-1.0	9.2	8.5	-0.8	24.2	4.1
1976	5.3	9.4	2.0	5.2	9.6	4.4	5.2	4.5	3.6	5.6	5.8	7.7	4.2	15.8	5.7
1977	5.3	8.1	2.0	3.1	9.4	4.7	3.0	3.7	3.6	5.1	6.4	7.0	1.0	16.0	6.2
1978	5.1	4.2	2.2	3.8	9.1	5.2	3.6	2.7	3.5	4.8	7.6	6.0	3.3	9.0	6.1
1979	5.2	3.7	2.1	3.3	10.3	5.9	4.4	4.1	3.2	3.2	11.4	5.8	1.3	13.3	5.7
1980	4.2	7.7	2.0	1.1	14.0	6.3	1.8	5.5	3.1	-0.2	13.5	7.1	-1.9	18.4	7.4
1981	2.9	4.9	2.2	0.5	13.4	7.6	-0.3	5.9	4.3	2.0	10.2	7.6	*	11.9	11.3

Column A—Annual growth rate of Gross Domestic Product (constant prices)
Column B—Annual percent change consumer price index
Column C—Annual unemployment as percent of total work force
*figure unavailable

SOURCES: for growth rates—Organisation for Economic Cooperation and Development. National Accounts of the OECD Countries (Paris: OECD); for inflation—OECD. Main Economic Indicators (Paris: OECD); for unemployment—International Labour Organisation. Yearbook of Labour Statistics (Geneva: ILO).

Notes

Chapter 1. *The State in the Marketplace*

1. Paul McCracken et al., *Towards Full Employment and Price Stability* (Paris: Organisation for Economic Cooperation and Development [OECD], 1977). See the critical review by Robert Keohane, "Economics, Inflation, and the Role of the State: Political Implications of the McCracken Report," in *World Politics* 31, no. 1 (October 1978). Mancur Olson has argued this in unpublished papers. The political argument has been put in Michel Crozier et al., *Crisis of Democracy* (see note 2).

2. Michel Crozier, Samuel Huntington, and Joji Watanuki, *Crisis of Democracy* (New York: New York University Press. 1975).

3. Certainly the best-known work in this vein is that done by Philippe Schmitter, "Modes of Interest Representation," in *Comparative Political Studies* 10, no. 1 (April 1977), and by Leo Panitch, *Social Democracy and Industrial Militancy* (New York: Cambridge University Press, 1976).

4. See Fred Hirsch and John Goldthorpe, *The Political Economy of Inflation* (Cambridge: Harvard University Press, 1978), in particular the essay by Charles Maier; also Leon Lindberg and Charles Maier, eds., *The Politics of Inflation* (Washington, D.C.: Brookings Institution, forthcoming).

5. Gerhard Mensch, *Stalemate in Technology: Innovations Overcome the Depression* (Cambridge, Mass.: Ballinger, 1979).

6. Richard Blackhurst, Nicholas Manan, and Jan Tumlir, *Trade Liberalization, Protectionism, and Interdependence* (Geneva: GATT, 1977). I have argued this at length in "Inflation and the Politics of Supply," in Lindberg and Maier, *The Politics of Inflation.*

7. The various studies by the GATT Secretariat emphasize this point.

8. Blackhurst et al., *Trade Liberalization.*

9. I am grateful to Charles Sabel, who articulated many ideas remarkably well in his comments at the annual meeting of the Council of European Studies, Washington, D.C., April 30, 1982. This sentence is drawn from his notes.

10. Ibid.

11. The figures for Tables 1.1–1.3, and 1.7–1.9 are taken from Zysman, "Inflation and the Politics of Supply," and are included here as the Appendix.

12. Based largely on Zysman, "Inflation and the Politics of Supply."

13. In France, West Germany, and Japan, land-ownership patterns appear remarkably stable since the Second World War in terms of the number and proportion of (1) medium-sized farms (in spite of the overall decrease in the number of farms) and (2) proprietors (in spite of the overall decline in the agricultural labor force). In France the total number of farms decreased by 47% between 1942 and 1975 but the number of farms ranging from 20 to 50 hectares declined only slightly (and the number of those greater than 50 hectares increased). In West Germany the total number of farms decreased by 49% between 1949 and 1977, but the number of farms ranging from 20 to 50 hectares (and those greater than 50 hectares) increased markedly. The average farm size in Germany, however, is smaller than in France; yet even the number of farms ranging from 10 to 20 hectares declined only by 22%. In Japan, where the average farm size is extremely small, the total number of farms decreased by 20%, but the number of farms ranging from 2 to 3 hectares (and those greater than 3 hectares) increased substantially. In France owners have participated in the rural exodus in disproportionate numbers. Their disappearance stems from their death or retirement from marginal farms (see Gordon Wright, *France in Modern Times* 2d ed. [Chicago: Rand McNally, 1974], p. 445). In Japan, land-owners increased not only as a proportion of the agricultural labor force, as they did in France, but in absolute terms as well, from 3.82 to 4.16 million.

14. Edward F. Dennison, *Why Growth Rates Differ: Post-War Experience in Nine Western Countries* (Washington, D.C.: Brookings Institution, 1967).

15. Commissariat Géneral du Plan, *Rapport du Groupe d'étudier l'evolution des economies du tiers monde et l'appareil productif français* (Paris: La Documentation Française, 1978), p. 12.

16. Ibid., p. 25.

17. Ibid.

18. United Nations Economic Commission for Europe, *Structure and Change in European Industry* (New York: United Nations, 1977), chap. 3.

19. "When Steel Wages Rise Faster than Productivity," *Business Week*, April 12, 1980, pp. 144–48.

20. The pressure on a specific domestic economy, in comparison, is a function of the percent of energy imported as a percent of total need, the value of those incremental oil costs resulting as a percent of previous imports, the movement of its national currency against the dollar, and its domestic inflation rate. The relation of the national currency to the dollar matters because oil is denominated in dollars and a currency appreciating against the dollar means a reduced *real* oil price. Thus, France, Japan, and Germany all are major importers, but the burden on Germany and Japan has been reduced by their currency changes. Importantly, the adjustment for Britain is temporarily muted by its internal expansion in oil production. The impact will be felt in that country through higher energy prices and a changed composition of international markets.

21. Richard N. Cooper, *The Economics of Interdependence: Economic Policy in the Atlantic Community* (New York: McGraw Hill, 1968).

22. Christian Stoffaes, *La grande menace industrielle* (Paris: Calmann Lévy, 1978), pp. 64–70.

23. C. Michael Aho and Thomas O. Gayard, "The 1980's: The Twilight of the Open Trading System?" Report published for the Bureau of International Labor Affairs, U.S. Department of Labor (Washington, D.C.: Office of Foreign Economic Research, 1982).

24. Blackhurst et al., *Trade Liberalization;* Zysman, "Inflation and the Politics of Supply"; Commissariat Général du Plan, *Rapport.*

25. "When Steel Wages Rise Faster than Productivity"; Louis Turner et al., *Living with the Newly Industrializing Countries* (London: Royal Institute for International Affairs, 1980), p. 8.

26. "Steel Subsidies: Enough Is Enough," *Economist*, May 16, 1981, p. 27.

27. The data on autos are taken from David Friedman, "Beyond the Age of Ford: The Strategic Basis of the Japanese Success in Automobiles," in John Zysman and Laura Tyson, eds., *American Industry in International Competition* (Ithaca: Cornell University Press, 1983); and Ira Magaziner and Thomas Hout, *Japanese Industrial Policy* (Berkeley: University of California, Institute of International Studies, 1981).

28. The logic of the position developed here has similarities to that in Burton H. Klein, *Dynamic Economics* (Cambridge: Harvard University Press, 1977).

29. Raymond Vernon, ed., *The Technology Factor in International Trade* (New York: National Bureau of Economic Research, 1970); and Raymond Vernon, *Sovereignty at Bay* (New York: Basic Books, 1971).

30. In his varied works Joseph Schumpeter develops a similar notion which he identifies as the central driving force in capitalism. See *Business Cycles: A Theoretical, Historical and Statistical Analysis of the Capitalist Process* (New York: McGraw Hill, 1939).

31. Taken from my currently unpublished research.

32. Susan Strange, "The Management of Surplus Capacity: Or How Does Theory Stand up to Protectionism 1970's Style," *International Organization* 33, no. 3 (September 1979):303–334.

33. "Steel in the 80s," *The OECD Observer*, no. 103, March 1980.

34. John Zysman, "The State as Trader," *International Affairs*, 54, no. 2 (April 1978).

35. See the articles in Peter Katzenstein, ed., *Between Power and Plenty: Foreign Economic Policies of Advanced Industrial States* (Madison: University of Wisconsin Press, 1978).

36. Peter Kenen's discussion of international money is the basis of this observation. These discussions were presented at the University of California, Berkeley, in 1980.

CHAPTER 2. *Finance and the Politics of Industry*

1. John C. Carrington and George T. Edwards, *Financing Industrial Investment* (London: Macmillan, 1979).

2. Laura Tyson and Peter Kenen, "The Transmission of International Economic Disturbances: A Framework for Comparative Analysis," in Egon Neuberger and Laura Tyson, eds., *The Impact of International Economic Disturbances on the Soviet Union and Eastern Europe* (Elmwood, N.Y.: Pergamon, 1981).

3. Albert Hirschman, *Exit, Voice, and Loyalty* (Cambridge: Harvard University Press, 1970).

4. This section has been constructed from many bits collected while I have been trying to figure out how the politics of industry are shaped by finance and it makes no sense to list all of them here. The most important pieces can be found in any good text on finance, for example, Roland T. Robinson and Swayne Wrightsman, *Financial Markets: The Accumulation and Allocation of Wealth* (New York: McGraw Hill, 1974). The *Economist*'s briefs on money and banking are also a good introduction. The crucial pieces for me were: Jacques Melitz, "A Report on the Issue of Exchange Rate Determination" (Consulting Report to the OECD, December 1980), on France; and Yoshio Suzuki, *Money and Banking in Contemporary Japan*, trans. John Greenwood (New Haven: Yale University Press, 1980), on Japan.

5. Simon Kuznets, *Capital in the American Economy: Its Formation and Financing* (Princeton: Princeton University Press, 1961), p. 31.

6. John K. Galbraith, *Money: Whence It Came, Where It Went* (Boston: Houghton Mifflin, 1975), p. 19.

7. Ibid.

8. James M. Stone, *One Way for Wall Street* (Boston: Little, Brown, 1975), p. 18.

9. These models are based in part on inferences from the national cases. The two most easily available comparative studies are Dimitri Vittas, ed., *Banking Systems Abroad* (London: Inter-Bank Research Organisation, 1978), and James Galbraith, ed., U.S. Congress Joint Economic Committee, *Monetary Policy, Selective Credit Policy and Industrial Policy in France, Britain, West Germany and Sweden* (Washington, D.C.: GPO, 1981).

10. James Guy, "The German Stock Exchange," Institute of Business and Economic Research, *Working Paper* no. 45, August 1976; and James Guy, "The Stock Exchange, London: An Empirical Analysis of Monthly Data from 1960 to 1970," *Proceedings of the European Finance Association* (Amsterdam: North Holland Publishing Co., 1975).

11. Jacques Melitz, "A Report."

12. Ibid.

13. Ibid.

14. Chalmers Johnson makes a similar distinction between a regulatory and developmental state. The difference here is that a "player" state can intervene without necessarily having a developmental objective. The different language reflects our different empirical bases, France in my case and Japan in Johnson's. I would argue, however, that the "developmental" state is a subject of my category. See Chalmers Johnson, "Japan, Inc., Does It Exist?" in Kansai University of Foreign Studies, *Quest for Peace: American-Japanese Economic Relations* (Osaka: Kansai University of Foreign Studies, 1979), pp. 31–43.

15. Marc Roberts conducted this study when teaching at the Harvard University Department of Economics, but to my knowledge it has never been published.

16. Don Votaw, *The Six-Legged Dog* (Berkeley: University of California Press, 1964).

17. See for example, Fredric M. Scherer, *Industrial Market Structure and Economic Performance* (Chicago: Rand McNally, 1970).

18. John Keeler, "The Politics of Official Unionism in French Agriculture, 1948–1976" (Ph.D. diss., Harvard University, 1978). Also in Suzanne Berger, ed., *Organizing Interests in Western Europe* (New York: Cambridge University

Press, 1981); David Collier, ed., *The New Authoritarianism in Latin America* (Princeton: Princeton University Press, 1980); and Alfred Stepan, *The State and Society* (Princeton: Princeton University Press, 1978).

19. Mancur Olson, *The Rise and Decline of Nations* (New Haven: Yale University Press, 1982).

20. Arend Lijphart, *The Politics of Accommodation: Pluralism and Democracy in the Netherlands* (Berkeley: University of California Press, 1968).

21. Andrew Martin, "Labor Movement Parties and Inflation: Contrasting Responses in Britain and Sweden," in Galbraith, *Monetary Policy.*

22. Peter J. Katzenstein, "Economic Dependence and Political Autonomy: The Small European States in the International Economy" (Unpublished paper, Cornell University, Ithaca, N.Y.).

23. Martin, "Labor Movement Parties."

CHAPTER 3. *The Interventionist Temptation: The French Case*

1. See, for example, Shepard B. Clough, "Economic Planning in a Capitalist Society: France from Monnet to Hirsh," *Political Science Quarterly* 71 (1956):543; and Charles-Albert Michalet, "France," in Raymon Vernon, ed., *Big Business and the State* (Cambridge: Harvard University Press, 1974), p. 115. Elsewhere (p. 113) Michalet stresses the ambiguous status of planning at its inception.

2. François Caron, *An Economic History of Modern France* (New York: Columbia University Press, 1979).

3. Stephen Cohen, "Twenty Years of the Gaullist Economy," in William G. Andrews and Stanley Hoffmann, eds., *The Fifth Republic at Twenty* (Albany: State University of New York Press, 1981).

4. Alexis de Tocqueville, *The Old Regime and the French Revolution*, trans. Stuart Gilbert (Garden City, N.Y.: Doubleday 1955).

5. Peter Gourevitch, *Paris and the Provinces* (Berkeley: University of California Press, 1980).

6. See, for example, Ezra Suleiman, *Politics, Power, and Bureaucracy in France* (Princeton: Princeton University Press, 1974); and Ezra Suleiman, *Elites in French Society: The Politics of Survival* (Princeton: Princeton University Press, 1978).

7. See note 1 above.

8. See Charles Kindleberger, "The Postwar Resurgence of the French Economy," in Stanley Hoffmann, ed., *In Search of France* (New York: Harper & Row, 1963).

9. The Planning Commission depended on other ministries that retained control of the incentives and coercive powers the plan required. See Jean Monnet, *Mémoires* (Paris: Fayard, 1976), pp. 1, 285–290; and Stephen Cohen, *Modern Capitalist Planning: The French Model* (Berkeley: University of California Press, 1969), pp. 28–36. Monnet's closest assistants at the Planning Commission included at different times Robert Marjolin, Etienne Hirsch, Felix Gaillard, Leon Kaplan (all of whom had worked with Monnet during the war), Paul Debucrier, Maurice Aicardi, Jean Vergeot, Jacques René Rabier, Jacques Van Heimont, Jean Ripert, and Pierre Uri. It is interesting to note that though the

Planning Commission had some finance inspectors on its staff, it conspicuously avoided being "colonized" by the Grand Corps in the early years. See also Henry Ehrmann, *Organized Business in France* (Princeton: Princeton University Press, 1957). The research for this section was done by Jonas Pontusson in his work as a research assistant.

10. Peter Hall cites Monnet to this effect; see his "Economic Planning and the States: The Evolution of Economic Challenge as a Political Response in France and Britain," in Maurice Zeitlin, ed., *Political Power and Social Theory*, vol. 3 (Greenwich, Conn.: JAI, 1981). The quote is from Monnet, *Mémoires*, p. 301; see also pp. 277–281.

11. Monnet, *Mémoires*, pp. 302, 308.

12. See note 9 above.

13. Cohen, *Modern Capitalist Planning*, pp. 21–22.

14. Ehrmann, *Organized Business in France*, p. 285; Monnet, *Mémoires*, pp. 290–292.

15. Cohen, *Modern Capitalist Planning*, pp. 4, 89–90.

16. Ibid.

17. On the resistance of the banking sector, its failure to support the Plan's investment programs in the public sector, and the intervention of the Trésor to secure the collaboration of the banks, see François Bloch-Lainé, *Profession: Fonctionnaire* (Paris: Éditions du Seuil, 1977), pp. 104–106. It is unclear from Bloch-Lainé's account whether or not the Trésor's intervention preceded the creation of the Modernization and Equipment Fund in 1948, but this is of minor importance. The point here is not that there was no collaboration between the Planning Commission and the Trésor prior to the creation of the Modernization and Equipment Fund, but rather that the latter served to institutionalize such collaboration. See Jonas Pontusson, "The Origins of French Planning" (Unpublished paper, the University of California, Berkeley, 1979).

18. Ehrmann, *Organized Business in France*, pp. 285–290.

19. Ibid., pp. 289–290.

20. Ibid., pp. 287–288.

21. Andrew Shonfield, *Modern Capitalism* (London: Oxford University Press, 1965), chap. 7, develops this point.

22. Caron, *An Economic History*, pp. 49–54, 66–74; and J. S. G. Wilson, *French Banking Structure and Credit Policy* (London: G. Bell and Sons, Ltd., 1957), pp. 12–22, 121–129, 134–150, 265–279.

23. Wilson, *French Banking Structure*, pp. 280–289; Margaret G. Moyers, "The Nationalization of Banks in France," *Political Science Quarterly* 64, no. 2 (June 1947).

24. Bloch-Lainé, *Profession: Fonctionnaire*, p. 104.

25. Peter Hall, "French Etatism vs. British Pluralism: A Reconstruction of the Evolution of the Role of Economic Planning in France" (Unpublished paper, Harvard University, July 1978).

26. Two series of interviews were an important source for this discussion. The first series was conducted in 1976–77, some of them with Alan Butt-Phillips. The second series was conducted in the autumn of 1980, many jointly with Stephen Cohen and James Galbraith. Also important are two papers by Jacques Melitz: "A Report on the Issue of Exchange Rate Determination" (Consulting Report to the OECD, December 1980), and "The French Financial System: The Mechanism and Proposition for Reform" (Paper prepared for the American

Enterprise Institute Conference, "The Political Economy of France," Washington, D.C., May 29–31, 1980). *La répression financière* by Jean-Jacques Rose and Michel Dietsch (Paris: Bonnel, 1981), which was published after the completion of this manuscript, is, other than the Melitz piece, the only full analysis of the operation of the financial system which addresses the issues discussed here directly. Although it was not used in the preparation of this discussion, it is consistent with it in substance and detail.

27. François Morin, *La structure financière du capitalisme français* (Paris: Editions du Seuil, 1977), suggests this.

28. Nigel Adam, "L'état c'est nous," *Euromoney* (London), October 1980, p. 110.

29. Ibid., p. 113.

30. Caron, *An Economic History,* chap. 14.

31. This discussion is drawn from Adam, "L'état," and two rounds of interviews in the Trésor at four-year intervals.

32. Adam, "L'état," p. 125.

33. François Eck, "Le rôle monétaire et financière du Trésor: 1960–1974" (Thesis for the Doctorat des sciences économiques, Université de Paris I, 1975).

34. Christian Stoffaes, *La grande menace industrielle* (Paris: Calmann Lévy, 1978), p. 313.

35. Ibid., p. 129.

36. Ibid.

37. See, for example, N. Makuch, J. Peyne, and P. Prunet, *Le Crédit Agricole* (Paris: Berger, Levrault, 1978); and Jean-Claude Gaudibert, *Le dernier empire français* (Paris: Seghers, 1977).

38. This statement is from the text of an interview conducted by Butt-Phillips.

39. Banque de France, "Place des crédits à taux privilégiés dans le financement de l'économie," *Bulletin trimestriel de la Banque de France,* no. 35 (June 1980), annexe 2.

40. Jacques Melitz, "The French Financial System."

41. Interviews as noted in n. 26 above, Oct.–Nov. 1980.

42. Data to describe the French financial system have been drawn largely from three sources: two confidential analyses of the French system undertaken for the purposes of other governments, and Dimitri Vittas, ed., *Banking Systems Abroad* (London: Inter-Bank Research Organisation, 1978).

43. Vittas, *Banking Systems Abroad;* and Melitz, "The French Financial System," p. 5.

44. Interviews, 1976 and 1980; Melitz, "The French Financial System," pp. 7–8.

45. Melitz, "The French Financial System," p. 8.

46. B. I. Bayliss and A. Butt-Phillips, *Capital Markets and Industrial Investment in Germany and France* (London: Saxon House, 1980), p. 136.

47. Melitz, "The French Financial System."

48. Melitz, "The French Financial System," pt. B, p. 14.

49. Ibid., p. 11.

50. Donald Hodgman, *Selective Credit Controls in Western Europe* (Chicago: Association of Reserve City Bankers, 1976).

51. This quote is drawn from a confidential internal study of the French financial system done for a European central bank.

52. Banque de France, "Place des crédits," p. 29.

53. Ibid.

54. For excellent English-language treatments of the French elite, see Suleiman, *Politics, Power, and Bureaucracy in France,* and *Elites in French Society.*

55. Michel Crozier, *Bureaucratic Phenomenon* (Chicago: University of Chicago Press, 1964); Michel Crozier, *The Stalled Society* (New York: Viking, 1973); and Alain Peyrefitte, *Le mal français* (Paris: Plon, 1976).

56. John Zysman, *Political Strategies for Industrial Order* (Berkeley: University of California Press, 1977).

57. The evidence for this argument can be found in several sources. See, for example, Monnet, *Mémoires;* and Bloch-Lainé, *Profession: Fonctionnaire.* See also Kindleberger, "Postwar Resurgence."

58. This conclusion is based on Bloch-Lainé, *Profession: Fonctionnaire,* particularly chapter 4, and on a variety of interviews.

59. Caron, *An Economic History.*

60. Stanley Hoffmann, "Paradoxes of the French Political Community," in Hoffmann, *In Search of France.*

61. Cohen, "Twenty Years of the Gaullist Economy," p. 241.

62. Ibid.; Gourevitch, *Paris and the Provinces.*

63. Suzanne Berger, ed., *Organizing Interests in Western Europe* (New York: Cambridge University Press, 1981); and Suzanne Berger and Michael Piore, *Dualism and Discontent in Industrial Societies* (New York: Cambridge University Press, 1980).

64. Berger and Piore, *Dualism.*

65. Cohen, "Twenty Years of the Gaullist Economy" p. 241. This quote appears in the original manuscript. The reference to the pincer was eliminated in final editing.

66. Ehrmann, *Organized Business in France,* pp. 410–411. The industry that would have been most directly affected was textiles—the textile industry association under the leadership of Marcel Boussac (whose traditional business practices would finally lead to the collapse of his empire in the late 1970s) allied with the association of small businessmen.

67. Ibid., pp. 405–420.

68. Ibid.

69. Charles Maier, "The Politics of Inflation in the Twentieth Century," in Fred Hirsch and John Goldthorpe, eds., *The Political Economy of Inflation* (Cambridge: Harvard University Press, 1978), pp. 56–59.

70. John Zysman, "Inflation and the Politics of Supply," in Leon Lindberg and Charles Maier, eds., *The Politics of Inflation* (Washington, D.C.: Brookings Institution, forthcoming); and Maurice Levy-Leboyer, "The Large Corporation in Modern France," in Alfred Chandler and Herman Daems, eds., *Managerial Hierarchies* (Cambridge: Harvard University Press, 1980).

71. The classic statement of this position is Charles I. Schultze, *Recent Inflation in the United States,* U.S. Congress Joint Economic Committee Study Paper, no. 1 (Washington, D.C.: GPO, 1959), summarized in U.S. Congress Joint Economic Committee, *Employment, Growth, and Price Levels,* Hearing before the J.E.C., 86th Congress, 2d session (Washington, D.C.: GPO, 1960), pt. 7, pp. 2171–2175. This statement has been drawn on in Edward Shapiro, *Macroeconomic Analysis* (New York: Harcourt, Brace & World, 1966), pp. 526–528.

72. Levy-Leboyer, "The Large Corporation in Modern France," pp. 138–147.

73. Ibid., p. 138.
74. Ibid., pp. 138–147.
75. Ibid., p. 118.
76. Ibid., p. 119.
77. See John Sheahan, *Promotion and Control of Industry in Post-War France* (Cambridge: Harvard University Press, 1963).
78. Zysman, *Political Strategies,* chaps. 2 and 7.
79. Caron, *An Economic History,* p. 273.
80. Cohen, *Modern Capitalist Planning,* p. 4.
81. John Zysman, "The French State in the International Economy," in Peter Katzenstein, ed., *Between Power and Plenty* (Madison: University of Wisconsin Press, 1978); and Stephen Cohen, "Informed Bewilderment," in Stephen Cohen and Peter Gourevitch, *France in a Troubled World Economy* (London: Butterworth, 1982).
82. Melitz, "A Report"; and Melitz, "The French Financial System."
83. Levy-Leboyer, "The Large Corporation in Modern France," p. 118.
84. Diana Green, *French Policies to Promote Industrial Adjustment* (London: Crown, 1980).
85. Zysman, *Political Strategies,* pp. 33–50 and chap. 7.
86. Caron, *An Economic History,* p. 351.
87. Ibid.
88. Ibid.
89. This section is based on a set of twenty-nine interviews in French financial and government circles in the fall of 1980.
90. Part of this formulation is drawn from Cohen, "Informed Bewilderment."
91. Ibid.
92. Ibid.
93. Ibid., p. 26.
94. Ibid.
95. Suzanne Berger, "Lame Ducks and National Champions," in Andrews and Hoffmann, *The Fifth Republic at Twenty.*
96. Lynn Mytelka, "Structural Changes in World Trade Crisis and Adjustment in a Traditional Industry in France" (Paper presented at the American Political Science Association Meetings, 28–31 August 1980), p. 15.
97. Ibid, p. 25.
98. Robert Berrier, "The Politics of Industrial Survival" (Ph.D. diss., Massachusetts Institute of Technology, 1978).
99. This is reported by Gail Russell on the basis of her research on industrial adjustment in northern France.
100. Mytelka, "Structural Changes."
101. Stephen Woolcock, "The Problems of Adjustment in the Textile and Clothing Industry," Study group paper for the Royal Institute of International Affairs (London: Chatham House, March 1980).
102. Green, *French Policies,* pp. 66–85.
103. Mytelka, "Structural Changes," pp. 24ff.
104. Ibid., pp. 11.
105. Ibid., pp. 11, 25–29.
106. Ibid., sec. 5.
107. Ibid.; Green, *French Policies.*

108. Mytelka, "Structural Changes," sec. 6 and 7; Green, *French Policies;* Zysman, *Political Strategies.*

109. Woolcock, "The Problems of Adjustment."

110. Zysman, *Political Strategies,* chap. 7.

111. Green, *French Policies,* pp. 47–66.

112. Zysman, *Political Strategies,* chap. 7.

113. Green, *French Policies;* Cohen, "Informed Bewilderment."

114. These figures are widely agreed on; Green, *French Policies,* is one such source.

115. All sources mentioned here discuss this figure. It was confirmed by interviews conducted in the autumn of 1980.

116. Green, *French Policies.*

117. Ibid.

118. Ibid.

119. Ibid., p. 56.

120. Ibid.

121. Berger, "Lame Ducks."

122. Interviews confirm Berger's argument.

123. Green, *French Policies,* pp. 85–114.

124. Stoffaes, *La grande menace.*

125. The analysis of electronics is based on my own research in France and the United States.

126. The French system of aggressive trade is well understood. It is described in, for example, "The High Cost of Export Credit," *Economist,* 14 February 1981, pp. 78–79. The degree of intervention is spectacular. Seventy-eight percent of all credits for exports are subsidized. See Banque de France, "Place des crédits," pp. 26–41.

127. Banque de France, "Place des crédits," pp. 26–40.

128. Ibid.

129. Marc Maurice, François Sellier, Jean-Jacques Silvestre, "La production de la hiérarchie dans l'entreprise: Recherche d'un effet sociétal; comparaison France-Allemagne," (Aix-en-Provence: Laboratoire d'Économie et de Sociologie du Travail, October, 1977).

130. David Soskice, "Strike Waves and Explosions, 1968–1970," in Colin Crouch and Alessandro Pizzoro, eds., *The Resurgence of Class Conflict in Western Europe since 1968,* vol. 2 (New York: Holmes & Meier, 1978).

131. Michele Salvati advances this argument in "May 1968 and the Hot Autumn of 1969: The Responses of Two Ruling Classes," in Berger, *Organizing Interests.*

132. The studies at the American Enterprise Institute conference (Washington, D.C.) in May 1980 point to this, as do figures from Jeffrey Sachs, "Wages, Profits, and Macro-Economic Adjustment in the 1970s: A Comparative Study" (Paper presented to the Seminar on Capital and the State, Harvard University, September 1979).

Chapter 4. *The Unsettling Agenda: The British Case*

1. Richard Rose, *Do Parties Make a Difference?* (Chatham, N.J.: Chatham House, 1980), p. 77.

2. C. J. F. Brown and T. D. Sheriff, "De-industrialisation: A Background Paper," in Frank Blackaby, ed., *De-industrialisation* (London: Heinemann, 1979), p. 260; D. D. K. Stout, "De-industrialisation and Industrial Policy," in Blackaby, ed., *De-industrialisation*, p. 177.

3. The material on autos is taken from two sources: David Friedman, "Beyond the Age of Ford: The Strategic Basis of the Japanese Success in Automobiles," John Zysman and Laura Tyson, eds., *American Industry in International Competition* (Ithaca: Cornell University Press, 1983) and Peter J. S. Dunnett, *The Decline of the British Motor Industry* (London: Croom Helm, 1980).

4. Stout, "De-industrialisation," p. 176.

5. *Economist*, July 4, 1981, p. 13.

6. Stout, "De-industrialisation," pp. 178–186.

7. Ibid.

8. Anthony Peake, *Economic Growth in Modern Britain* (London: Macmillan, 1974), p. 27.

9. Richard E. Caves and Associates, eds., *Britain's Economic Prospects* (Washington, D.C.: Brookings Institution, 1968).

10. See Robert Bacon and Walter Eltis, *Britain's Economic Problem: Too Few Producers*, 2d ed. (London: Macmillan, 1978).

11. Ibid.

12. Samuel Beer, *British Politics in the Collectivist Age* (New York: Knopf, 1965), pp. 189–200.

13. David Soskice and Lloyd Ulman are conducting a study of labor development in the advanced countries. This study draws on their manuscript.

14. Leo Panitch, *Social Democracy and Industrial Militancy* (New York: Cambridge University Press, 1976); Douglas Hibbs, "On the Political Economy of Long Run Trends in Strike Activity," *British Journal of Political Science* 4 (April 1978):160.

15. Michael Moran, *The Politics of Industrial Relations* (London: Macmillan, 1977), chap. 5.

16. Ruth Collier and David Collier, "Inducements vs. Constraints," *American Political Science Review* 73, no. 4 (December 1979).

17. Moran, *The Politics of Industrial Relations;* Panitch, *Social Democracy.*

18. Robert Taylor, *The Fifth Estate*, rev. ed. (London: Pan Books, 1980), pt.2, "Varieties of Unionism," pp. 295–457.

19. Ibid., p. 258.

20. Soskice and Ulman, unpublished research.

21. Charles Sabel, *The Division of Labor: Its Progress through Politics* (Cambridge: Cambridge University Press, 1982).

22. Stephen Blank, "Britain: The Politics of Foreign Economic Policy, the Domestic Economy, and the Problem of Pluralistic Stagnation," in Peter Katzenstein, ed., *Between Power and Plenty* (Madison: University of Wisconsin Press, 1978).

23. Peter Gourevitch, "The Second Image Reversed," *International Organization* 32, no. 4 (Autumn 1978):903.

24. H. M. Drucker, *Doctrine and Ethos in the Labour Party* (London: George Allen and Unwin, 1979).

25. Rose, *Do Parties Make a Difference?* p. 47.

26. Drucker, *Doctrine and Ethos.*

27. Jacques Leurez, *Economic Planning and Politics in Britain*, trans. Martin Harrison (London: Martin Robertson, 1975), pt. 1.

333

28. Drucker, *Doctrine and Ethos,* chaps. 3 and 4; Reuben Kelf-Cohen, *Twenty Years of Nationalisation: The British Experience* (London: Macmillan, 1969), pt. 4.

29. Leurez, *Economic Planning,* pp. 61–67.

30. Drucker, *Doctrine and Ethos,* chap. 4.

31. Leurez, *Economic Planning;* Andrew Shonfield, *Modern Capitalism* (London: Oxford University Press, 1969), pp. 90–91.

32. See Samuel Brittan, *Steering the Economy: The Role of the Treasury* (London: Secker & Warburg, 1969): "Looking back on the documents and speeches of these years, one is struck by the extent to which economic policy was conducted on a year-to-year piecemeal basis. The allocation of scarce materials and of factory permits was, in Mr. Rogow's words, 'more often the result of interdepartmental negotiation and amateur judgment than of consistent and scientific planning.' The whole system was probably modeled on the traditional annual haggles which the spending departments have with the Treasury" (p. 109).

33. When Cripps, who had been minister of economic affairs, was appointed chancellor, he took with him to the Treasury his previous functions. The result was that responsibility for economic policy was divided: financial and budgetary policy was made at the Treasury and physical planning outside it. J. C. R. Dow, *The Management of the British Economy, 1945–1960* (Cambridge: Cambridge University Press, 1964), p. 14.

34. Beer, *British Politics,* pp. 189–200.

35. Leurez, *Economic Planning,* p. 63. In 1944, the *Economist* had warned: "The great defect of collectivism . . . is not that bureaucrats will control industry; it is that they will not control it but cede their duties to private monopolists."

36. For a discussion of the organization and functioning of the bank and the only minor effects of nationalization, see David R. Crowne and Harry G. Johnson, eds., *Money in Britain 1959–1969* (London: Oxford University Press, 1970); and Committee on the Working of the Monetary System, *Radcliffe Report, 1959* (London: Her Majesty's Stationery Office, 1959), pp. 109–128, 269–279. A spate of articles appeared in the late 1950s on the role of the bank, which were provoked by the convening of the Parker Tribunal and the Radcliffe Committee. See "The Bank Rate Tribunal Evidence: A Symposium," in *Manchester School of Economic and Social Studies* 127, no. 1 (January 1959), for an excellent collection of articles on the bank.

37. Leurez, *Economic Planning,* p. 45.

38. Vernon Bogdanor, "The Labour Party in Opposition: 1951–1964," in Vernon Bogdanor and Robert Skidelsky, eds., *The Age of Affluence* (London: Macmillan, 1970).

39. William M. Robson, *Nationalized Industry and Public Ownership* (London: George Allen and Unwin, 1960).

40. Kelf-Cohen, *Twenty Years of Nationalisation,* p. 30.

41. On Morrison and the public corporation, see Lord Herbert Morrison, *Government and Parliament: Inside,* 3d rev. ed. (London: Oxford University Press, 1964), pp. 258–266. Further on, he details the reasons for the establishment of the public corporation: "What are they? They are that we seek to combine the principle of public ownership of a broad, but not too detailed public accountability, of a consciousness on the part of the undertaking that is working for the national but not for the sectional interest, with the liveliness, initiative and a

considerable degree of the freedom of a quick-moving and progressive business enterprise" (p. 292).

42. Kelf-Cohen, *Twenty Years of Nationalisation,* chaps. 1 and 15.

43. *Economist,* June 20, 1981, p. 12.

44. Michael Pinto Duschnisky, "Bread and Caucuses: The Conservation in Office," in Bogdanor and Skidelsky, *The Age of Affluence;* and Paul Addison, *The Road to 1945* (London: Cape, 1975).

45. Nigel Harris, *Competition and the Corporate Society* (London: Methuen, 1972); and G. C. Allen, *British Industries and Their Organization* (London: Longmans Green, 1951), chap. 2.

46. For Macmillan's role in the Industrial Reorganization Leagues, see Harold Macmillan, *Winds of Change, 1914–1939* (London: Macmillan, 1966), pp. 371–372.

47. For Macmillan's position, see, for example, Harold Macmillan, *Reconstruction: A Plea for National Policy* (London: Macmillan, 1934).

48. Harris, *Competition and the Corporate Society,* p. 45.

49. Harold Macmillan, *Industrial Policy* (policy statement) (London: Conservative and Unionist Central Office, 1947); Macmillan, *The Right Road for Britain* (policy statement) (London: Conservative and Unionist Central Office, 1949).

50. See Y. S. Hu, *National Attitudes and the Financing of Industry* (London: Political and Economic Planning, 1975); Alexander Gerschenkron, *Economic Backwardness in Historical Perspective* (Cambridge, Mass,: Harvard University Press, Belknap Press, 1962) chap. 1; and E. J. Hobsbawm, *Industry and Empire* (Harmondsworth, Middlesex: Penguin, 1969).

51. Inter-Bank Research Organisation, *The Future of London as an International Finance Center* (London: Her Majesty's Stationery Office, 1973), p. 178.

52. Ibid.; and Wilson Committee Hearings, Committee to Review the Financing of Industry, *Progress Report* (London: Her Majesty's Stationery Office, 1973).

53. Inter-Bank Research Organisation, *The Future of London.*

54. Hu, *National Attitudes,* p. 35.

55. See Vivian Anthony, *Banks and Markets,* 3d ed. (London: Heinemann, 1979), p. 35.

56. John C. Carrington and George T. Edwards, *Financing Industrial Investment* (London: Macmillan, 1979), pp. 94–128.

57. Hu, *National Attitudes,* chap. 4. See Committee to Review the Functioning of Financial Institutions, Harold Wilson, chairman (hereafter referred to as Wilson Committee Hearings), *Evidence on the Financing of Industry and Trade,* vol. 1 (London: Her Majesty's Stationery Office, 1978), pp. 3–18, in which the Treasury provides statistics for internal and external financing. In the 1970–1975 period, the average percentage of external finance of total corporate finance for all industrial and commercial companies in the United Kingdom was only 32.11% (pp. 16–17). Stuart Holland attributes the self-financing tendency to a large multinational corporate sector in the United Kingdom that has attempted to resist all outside influences. See Stuart Holland, *The Socialist Challenge* (London: Quartet Books, 1975), pp. 80–82. The Treasury corroborates Holland to a certain extent, finding that the largest listed companies in manufacturing industries resorted to external financing for only 23.26% of total

financing requirements; see Wilson Committee Hearings, *Evidence*, vol. 1, pp. 14–15.

58. Hu, *National Attitudes*, p. 45; Carrington and Edwards, *Financing Industrial Investment*.

59. Carrington and Edwards, *Financing Industrial Investment*, pp. 94–128.

60. Ibid.; Hu, *National Affairs*.

61. Ibid.

62. See Committee on the Working of the Monetary System, *Radcliffe Report, 1959*, p. 109, which attributes the lack of external financing to factors in the structure of the market.

63. Wilson Committee Hearings, *Evidence*, vol. 1, pp. 58–59.

64. Wilson Committee Hearings, "Testimony of the American Bank Association," in *Evidence*, vol. 8.

65. Wilson Committee Hearings, *Progress Report*, p. 16; and *Evidence*, vol. 5 in which T. F. Tuke, chairman of Barclay's, repudiated the American distinction as follows: "No such distinction exists. . . . In the vast majority of cases covered by the clearing banks, we have a situation where one customer is dealing with one bank, and therefore there has grown up a special relationship between bank and customer, often over many years" (p. 195).

66. Anthony, *Banks and Markets*, p. 47.

67. See Marcello de Cecco, *Money and Empire: The International Gold Standard 1890–1914* (Oxford: Blackwell, 1974), pp. 85–87, for a brief discussion of the early workings of the merchant banks as financiers of commerce.

68. Pierre Moussa, "Les banques d'affaires, pour quoi faire?" *Revue des deux mondes*, October 1976, p. 44.

69. C. D. Foster, *Politics, Finance, and the Role of Economics: An Essay on the Control of Public Enterprise* (London: George Allen and Unwin, 1971), p. 164.

70. Dimitri Vittas, ed., *Banking Systems Abroad* (London: Inter-Bank Research Organisation, 1978).

71. Ibid., chap. 1.

72. This is based on documents and interviews; for a description of the history and functions of these institutions, see Wilson Committee Hearings, *Evidence*, vol. 4.

73. Ibid., Vittas, *Banking Systems Abroad*. The following figures are taken from Vittas, p. 22.

Shares of long-term credit institutions in liabilities and claims with the non-financial sector, end 1975 (percent)

Country	Liabilities	Claims
West Germany	12.8	23.5
France	8.2	32.9
Italy	9.1	29.9
Netherlands	5.0	19.5
Switzerland	1.3	2.4
Sweden	2.8	41.8
Japan	11.0	22.8
United States	5.5	7.9
United Kingdom	4.9	21.4

74. Anthony, *Banks and Markets;* Jack Revell, *The British Financial System* (London: Macmillan, 1973); Catherine Hill, "Finance and British Economic Policy," prepared for the House Committee on Banking and Urban Affairs (Washington, D.C.: GPO, 1981).

75. Anthony, *Banks and Markets,* p. 115ff.; see also Hill, "Finance." This point is implicit in Samuel Brittan's position in *Steering the Economy.*

76. Quoted in Hill, "Finance."

77. Ibid.

78. Jacques Melitz, "A Report on the Issue of Exchange Rate Determination" (Consulting Report to the OECD, December 1980).

79. Anthony, *Banks and Markets,* p. 12.

80. Ibid., p. 5.

81. Ibid., discussed in several sections.

82. See Dow, *The Management,* pp. 6–11; Richard N. Cooper, "The Balance of Payments," in Richard Caves et al., eds., *Britain's Economic Prospects;* J. H. B. Tew, "Policies Aimed at Improving the Balance of Payments," in F. T. Blackaby, ed., *British Economic Policy, 1960–1974: Demand Management* (New York: Cambridge University Press, 1978).

83. See Susan Strange, *Sterling and British Policy: A Political Study of an International Currency in Decline* (London: Oxford University Press, 1971), pp. 202–258, for an insightful analysis of how various components of the City, in cooperation with government, maintained the City's role as an international marketplace. See also Janet Kelly, *Bankers and Boarders: The Case of American Banks in Britain* (Cambridge: Ballinger, 1977), for the City's ability to increase its power through the attraction of foreign, and especially American, banks.

84. Committee on Invisible Exports (William M. Clarke, study director), *Britain's Invisible Earnings* (London: British National Exports Council, 1967).

85. See Wilson Committee Hearings, *Evidence,* vol. 5. pp. 224–226, and in particular p. 239, for Governor Richardson's oral testimony on the workings of the Industrial Finance Unit. Significantly, however, the bank still expects the market institutions to develop their own response. Witness the exchange between the committee and the deputy governor:

Deputy Governor:

Q: So you would not think it proper for the Bank to have a view about restructuring; restructuring will be done by the market.

A: If we thought that the restructuring was not, as it developed, providing a relevant answer to the gap which we saw, we should then be inclined to express a view.

(Sir Jaspar Hollom): Restructuring suggests a rather wholesale root and branch approach, whereby one takes the present system, retires to a back room, reorders it on paper, then promulgates it and expects people to fall in place. Much more, of course, we are concerned with working to improve the present structure where a deficiency of some sort occurs. Particularly, this has been the process we have followed in promoting the creation of specialist institutions to fill apparent gaps or possible gaps. This is much more the nature of the approach to restructuring we are likely to use.

86. See Max Weber, *The Protestant Ethic,* trans. Talcott Parsons (London: George Allen and Unwin, 1948).

87. Committee on the Working of the Monetary System, *Radcliffe Report 1959,* p. 109–110.

88. Aaron Wildavsky and Hugh Heclo, *The Private Government of Public Money; Community and Policy inside British Politics* (Berkeley: University of California Press, 1974); Brittan, *Steering the Economy;* Samuel Beer, *Treasury Control: The Co-ordination of Financial and Economic Policy in Great Britain* (Oxford: Clarendon Press, 1956), p. 66.

89. There is no dearth of material on the British civil service, especially after the Fulton Report on the Civil Service; see Committee under the Chairmanship of Lord Fulton, *The Civil Service* (London: Her Majesty's Stationery Office, 1968). For our purposes here, see Thomas Balogh's seminal critique, "The Apotheosis of the Dilettante: The Establishment of Mandarins," in Hugh Thomas, ed., *The Establishment* (London: Anthony Blond, 1959).

90. As Roger Opie writes ("The Making of Economic Policy," in Hugh Thomas, ed., *Crisis in the Civil Service* [London: Anthony Blond, 1968]): "The minister is free to choose, but only on the basis of the choice he is offered. . . . In the preparation and presentation of those alternatives the official has almost absolute power. He can, if he wishes, as he often does, limit the choice to two alternatives, rather than 'waste the minister's time' with half a dozen half-baked schemes" (p. 73). Richard Crossman has given us a fascinating account of his anxieties vis-à-vis his subordinates while minister; see *The Diaries of a Cabinet Minister,* vols. 1–3 (London: Hamish Hamilton and Jonathan Cape, 1973, 1976, 1977).

91. See John A. Armstrong, *The European Administrative Elite* (Princeton: Princeton University Press, 1973), pp. 237–245, 326–327.

92. Except when outside, economists are invited to serve for limited periods of time. However, as Wildavsky and Heclo make clear in *The Private Government,* "no one should underestimate the difficulty of bringing noncivil service advisers into government. Unless their reputations make them unassailable, they are likely to be regarded as amateurs who interfere with the workings of the machine without being able to improve it. They are the kind of people who create trouble without staying around to pick up the pieces. . . . Even the most successful outside advisers can be expected to survive little more than two years before being enveloped, rejected, or worn down by the established Civil Service" (p. 374).

93. Roy Harrod writes: "Professor Beer reckons 1947 a critical date, when Sir Stafford Cripps, having been for a brief period Minister of Economic Affairs, also became Chancellor, taking his responsibility for economic planning and his set-up with him. It could be argued that in the saving of the country from a jarring discordant form of socialism, harsh bureaucracy . . . the bringing of economic planning—under the auspices, I don't know whether it would be fair to say under the nose, of Sir Stafford Cripps—into the sphere of the sage and mellow influence of Treasury traditions was a much more decisive step than the conservative victory in 1951" (cited, without reference, in Balogh, "Apotheosis," p. 113).

94. Balogh, "Apotheosis," p. 37.

95. Armstrong, *Economic Administrative Elite.*

96. Ibid., p. 301.

97. Sven Steinmo, "The Policy of North Sea Oil: The Legacy of Arm's-Length Government" (Unpublished paper, University of California, Berkeley, 1979).

98. Ibid.

99. Charles Maier, "The Politics of Productivity: Foundations of American

International Economic Policy after World War II," in Katzenstein, *Between Power and Plenty*.

100. Michael Stewart, *The Jekyll and Hyde Years: Politics and Economic Policy since 1964* (London: Dent, 1977), pp. 208–209.

101. David Marquand, "The Challenge to the Labour Party," *Political Quarterly* 46, no. 4 (October–December 1975):399–400.

102. Beer, *British Politics;* Stewart, *The Jekyll and Hyde Years,* pp. 241–247.

103. Leurez, *Economic Planning;* Stewart, *The Jekyll and Hyde Years,* pp. 47, 92.

104. Keith Middlemaas, *Politics in Industrial Society* (London: Andrew Deutsch, 1979), p. 413.

105. Brittan, *Steering the Economy,* pp. 148–153.

106. This discussion is drawn from Stewart, *The Jekyll and Hyde Years;* Leurez, *Economic Planning;* and Michael Shanks, *Planning and Politics: The British Experience, 1960–1976* (London: George Allen and Unwin, 1977).

107. Middlemaas, *Politics in Industrial Society,* p. 413.

108. Shanks, *Planning and Politics,* p. 32.

109. Stephen Blank, "Britain: The Politics of Foreign Economic Policy," in Katzenstein, *Between Power and Plenty*.

110. Frank Longstreth, "The City, Industry and the State," in Colin Crouch, ed., *State and Economy in Contemporary Capitalism* (New York: St. Martin's Press, 1979).

111. George Brown, *In My Way* (London: Victor Gollancz, 1971), p. 100.

112. Ibid., p. 113.

113. Shanks, *Planning and Politics,* p. 35.

114. Ibid., p 35.

115. See for example Anthony Howard, ed., *The Crossman Diaries: Selections from the Diaries of a Cabinet Minister, 1964–1970* (London: Methuen Paperbacks, 1979); also Brittan, *Steering the Economy:* "The really serious mistake of the Labour Government, after both the 1964 and 1966 elections, was to refuse to admit that a choice between devaluation and relying on accompanied deflation had become necessary. The result was an eventual devaluation, which in all but the technical sense was forced, at the worst possible time internationally, when resources not only of foreign exchange, but of confidence, patience, and credibility had all been nearly exhausted. Trying to get the best of both worlds, the Government succeeded in achieving the worst" (p. 188).

116. See Shanks, *Planning and Politics;* Leurez, *Economic Planning;* and in particular Mereick Brian Garland, "Industrial Reorganization in Britain" (senior honors thesis, Harvard University, March 1974).

117. Stewart, *The Jekyll and Hyde Years,* p. 98.

118. Garland, "Industrial Reorganization," p. 98.

119. Harold Wilson, *The Labour Government, 1964–1970: A Personal Record* (London: Weidenfeld and Nicolson, 1971), p. 202.

120. Andrew Graham, "Industrial Policy," in Wilfred Beckerman, ed., *The Labour Government's Economic Record: 1964–1970* (London: Duckworth, 1972), p. 195.

121. Trevor Russell, *The Tory Party: Its Policies, Divisions, and Future* (London: Penguin, 1978), p. 94.

122. Stewart, *The Jekyll and Hyde Years,* p. 137.

123. Shanks, *Planning and Politics,* p. 80.

124. The empirical evidence is clear in Shanks, *Planning and Politics,* and Stewart, *The Jekyll and Hyde Years.* The intent was verified in interviews.

125. This argument is drawn originally from a paper by Frank Longstreth for a conference on capital formation at Harvard Center for European Studies, Harvard University, 1975. It is confirmed, for example, in "International Economic Performance and Comparative Tax Structure," Department of Economic and Business Development, Office of Economic Policy, Planning, and Research (San Francisco, Calif., January 20, 1981).

126. Leurez, *Economic Planning,* p. 178; Shanks, *Planning and Politics,* p. 75.

127. See Wilson Committee Hearings, "Hearings with the Merchant Bank," in *Evidence,* vol. 5, p. 87, for evidence on this subject.

128. Similarly, NEB itself was a copy of the Italian IRT, a state holding company. See Stuart Holland, ed., *The State as Entrepreneur* (London: Weidenfeld and Nicholson, 1972), written as much for political propaganda as for academic analysis.

129. These internal documents were never published.

130. The best sources on all these details are the Wilson Committee Hearing volumes.

131. Ira Magaziner and Thomas Hout, *Japanese Industrial Policy* (Berkeley: University of California, Institute of International Studies, 1981).

132. Hill, "Finance and British Economic Policy."

133. Katzenstein, "Economic Dependence and Political Autonomy: The Small European States in the International Economy" (Unpublished paper, Cornell University, Ithaca, N.Y.).

134. Alan Whiting, "Overseas Experience in the Use of Industrial Subsidies," in National Commission for Manpower Policy, *Reexamining European Manpower Policies,* Special Report no. 10 (August 1976); originally from Department of Industry, *The Economics of Industrial Subsidies* (London: Her Majesty's Stationery Office, 1976).

135. This statement serves to put on the record this author's interpretation of developments in three industrial sectors: textiles, steel and autos. The auto case in particular reflects a range of the issues discussed here.

136. Santosh Mukherjee, *Through No Fault of Their Own* (London: Macdonald, 1973), p. 18.

CHAPTER 5. *Generalizing the Argument: Japan, West Germany, and the United States*

1. Organisation for Economic Cooperation and Development, *Inflation: The Present Problem* (Paris: OECD, December 1970), p. 97.

2. This point was nicely presented by Peter Katzenstein in "State Strength through Market Competition" (Paper presented to the Council on Foreign Relations, Working Group on Industrial Policy, New York, April 1980).

3. Philip H. Tresize, with Yukio Suzuki, "Politics, Government, and Economic Growth in Japan," in Hugh Patrick and Henry Rosovsky, eds., *Asia's New Giant* (Washington, D.C.: Brookings Institution, 1976). The authors cite Norman MacRae's article "The Risen Sun" (*Economist,* May 27, 1967), as representative of the Japan, Inc. position. Unfortunately, by using a straw man, Tresize and Suzuki undermine the plausibility of their own position.

4. These industry references are based on several basic sources; see Ira Magaziner and Thomas Hout, *Japanese Industrial Policy* (Berkeley: University of California, Institute of International Studies, 1981). As business analysts, their work on sectoral issues is particularly revealing. It is an elaboration of an earlier work by Eugene J. Kaplan, *Japan: The Government-Business Relationship* (Washington, D.C.: U.S. GPO, 1972). See also John Zysman and Laura Tyson, eds., *American Industry in International Competition* (Ithaca: Cornell University Press, 1983). The essays on auto, steel and electronics directly consider the Japanese cases in some detail. Kasuo Sato, ed., *Industry and Business in Japan* (White Plains, N.Y.: Sharpe, 1980), has good analyses of autos and steel. Katzenstein, "State Strength through Market Competition," provides interesting materials on textiles, computers, and steel. Tuvia Blumenthal, "The Japanese Shipbuilding Industry," in Hugh Patrick, ed., *Japanese Industrialization and Its Social Consequences* (Berkeley: University of California Press, 1976), presents a good study of shipbuilding.

5. The weakness in Katzenstein's formulation in "State Strength through Market Competition" is that he understates the degree to which the forces of competition are themselves state generated.

6. Y. Miyazaki, "Excessive Competition and the Formation of Keiretsu*Ktsu*," and "The Japanese-Type Structure of Big Business," in Sato, *Industry and Business in Japan.* See also Michael Borrus, James E. Millstein, and John Zysman, "Trade and Development in the Semiconductor Industry," in Zysman and Tyson, *American Industry in International Competition;* and Richard Caves, with Masu Uekusa, "Industrial Organization," in Patrick and Rosovsky, *Asia's New Giant.*

7. This is very evident in the excellent monograph by Ira Magaziner and Thomas Hout, *Japanese Industrial Policy.*

8. T. J. Pempel, "Japanese Foreign Economic Policy," in Katzenstein, ed., *Between Power and Plenty* (Madison: University of Wisconsin Press, 1978), p. 139.

9. Chalmers Johnson, "The Internationalization of the Japanese Economy" (Unpublished paper, University of California, Berkeley, 1981).

10. Hugh Patrick and Henry Rosovsky, "Japan's Economic Performance: An Overview," in Patrick and Rosovsky, *Asia's New Giant.*

11. Magaziner and Hout, *Japanese Industrial Policy,* p. 8.

12. Ibid.

13. Tresize and Suzuki, "Politics, Government, and Economic Growth," p. 455.

14. Edward F. Denison and William K. Chung, "Economic Growth and Its Sources," in Patrick and Rosovsky, *Asia's New Giant,* p. 67.

15. Hiroya Ueno, "The Conception and Evaluation of Japanese Industrial Policy," in Sato, *Industry and Business in Japan,* p. 382.

16. Ibid., p. 376.

17. Ibid., p. 396.

18. Ibid., pp. 410–415.

19. Johnson, "The Internationalization of the Japanese Economy."

20. The theoretical case is argued in John Zysman and Laura Tyson, "American Industry in International Competition," in Zysman and Tyson, *American Industry in International Competition.*

21. Ueno, "The Conception."

22. Pempel, "Japanese Foreign Economic Policy," p. 139.
23. Sato, "Introduction," in Sato, *Industry and Business in Japan.*
24. Caves and Uekusa, "Industrial Organization," pp. 493–494.
25. This is a widely cited fact and can be found in both Caves and Uekusa, "Industrial Organization," and Sato, *Industry and Business in Japan.*
26. Caves and Uekusa, "Industrial Organization," p. 492.
27. See Borrus, Millstein, and Zysman, "Trade and Development in the Semiconductor Industry."
28. See, for example, Sato, "Introduction," p. xiii.
29. This point is argued later, but see Caves and Uekusa, "Industrial Organization," p. 488.
30. Ibid.; Ueno, "The Conception"; Katzenstein, "State Strength through Market Competition"; Tresize and Suzuki, "Politics, Government, and Economic Growth."
31. See Tresize and Suzuki, "Politics, Government, and Economic Growth." The support of big business is a central part of their argument that MITI followed pressures rather than structured the economy.
32. Levels of concentration in Japanese economy as a whole and of sellers in specific markets are as high as in the U.S. economy. See Caves and Uekusa, "Industrial Organization."
33. See Kozo Yamamura, "General Trading Companies in Japan," in Patrick, *Japanese Industrialization and Its Social Consequences.*
34. Y. Miyazaki, "The Japanese-Type Structure"; and Yusaku Futatsugi, "The Measurement of Interfirm Relationships," in Sato, *Industry and Business in Japan.*
35. Miyazaki, "The Japanese-Type Structure"; Futatsugi, "The Measurement of Interfirm Relationships."
36. Caves and Uekusa, "Industrial Organization," p. 487.
37. Ueno, "The Conception," p. 384.
38. Ibid., p. 274; Henry C. Wallich and Mabel I. Wallich, "Banking and Finance," in Patrick and Rosovsky, *Asia's New Giant,* p. 252.
39. A recent publication of the U.S. Congress Joint Economic Committee examines the Japanese financial system from the vantage of financial intermediation. That analysis does not directly bear on this discussion but confronts the economic problem of whether controlled markets are efficient. It in essence redefines that problem without undermining this analysis. See Eisuke Sakakibara et al., *Japanese Financial System in Comparative Perspective* (Washington, D.C.: U.S. Congress Joint Economic Committee, 1982).
40. Dimitri Vittas, ed., *Banking Systems Abroad* (London: Inter-Bank Research Organisation, 1978), p. 279.
41. Ibid., p. 267.
42. Miyazaki, "The Japanese-Type Structure," p. 267.
43. Ibid., p. 305.
44. Vittas, *Banking Systems Abroad,* p. 5.
45. Wallich and Wallich, "Banking and Finance," p. 266.
46. Ibid; Yoshio Suzuki, *Money and Banking in Contemporary Japan,* trans., John Greenwood (New Haven: Yale University Press, 1980), chap. 1.
47. Suzuki, *Money and Banking,* p. 37.
48. Ibid., p. 45.
49. Ibid., p. 46.

50. Ibid., p. 215.

51. Ibid., p. 17.

52. Ibid.

53. General Accounting Office, *United States–Japan: Trade Issues and Problems* (Washington, D.C.: GPO, 1979).

54. Ueno, "The Conception," pp. 400–407.

55. Ibid., p. 403.

56. Alain Cotta, *La France et l'impératif mondial* (Paris: Éditions du Seuil, 1978).

57. Karl Hardach, *The Political Economy of Germany in the Twentieth Century* (Berkeley: University of California Press, 1980), p. 173, is one of several authors who emphasize this point. See also Gustav Stolper, Karl Hauser, and Knut Borchardt, *The German Economy, 1870 to the Present*, trans., Tony Stolper (New York: Harcourt, Brace and World, 1967), chap. 7.

58. Michael Kreile, "West Germany: The Dynamics of Expansion," in Katzenstein, *Between Power and Plenty*, p. 192.

59. Ibid.

60. Andrew Shonfield, *Modern Capitalism* (London: Oxford University Press, 1965), p. 241. See also Georg Kuster, "Germany," in Raymond Vernon, ed., *Big Business and the State* (Cambridge: Harvard University Press, 1974).

61. Jurgen Kocka, "The Rise of the Modern Industrial Enterprise in Germany," in Alfred Chandler and Herman Daems, eds., *Managerial Hierarchies* (Cambridge: Harvard University Press, 1980), traces the development of giant industrial firms in Germany.

62. Stolper et al., *Germany Economy*, chap. 7; Hardach, *Political Economy*, chap. 7.

63. Hardach, *Political Economy*, p. 148.

64. Shonfield, *Modern Capitalism*, p. 240.

65. Ibid., p. 247.

66. See Mary Nolan and Charles Sabel, "Class Conflict and the Social Reform Cycle" (Unpublished paper cited in Hardach, *Political Economy*, p. 33).

67. Kreile, "West Germany."

68. Albert Bressand, "The New European Economies," *Daedalus* 108, no. 1 (winter 1979).

69. This information is drawn from an unpublished study of the German adjustment process done by the Boston Consulting Group for the Swedish government.

70. Ibid.

71. Ibid.

72. Bressand, "The New European Economies."

73. Boston Consulting Group study, plus interviews with private analysts of international steel industry conducted in 1979.

74. *Financial Times*, May 16, 1980, p. 21.

75. Ibid.

76. Loukas Tsoukalis and Antonio da Silva Ferreira, "Management of Industrial Surplus Capacity in the European Community," *International Organization* 34, no. 3 (summer 1980).

77. Ibid.; Woolcock, "The Problems of Adjustment in the Textile and Clothing Industry," Study group paper for the Royal Institute of International Affairs (London: Chatham House, March 1980).

78. Tsoukalis and da Silva Ferreira, "Management of Industrial Surplus Capacity."

79. This section is based on several works: Peter Readman, *The European Money Puzzle* (London: Joseph, 1973); Vittas, *Banking Systems Abroad;* James Maycock, *European Banking: Structures and Prospects* (London: Graham and Trotman 1977); James Medley, "German Monetary and Industrial Policy," forthcoming as a report of the U.S. Congress Joint Economic Committee for the House Committee on Banking.

80. Vittas, *Banking Systems Abroad,* p. 58.

81. Ibid.; Y. S. Hu, *National Attitudes and the Financing of Industry* (London: Political and Economic Planning, 1975), p. 52; John C. Carrington and George T. Edwards, *Financing Industrial Investment* (London: Macmillan, 1979), p. 160. All these authors misplace their emphasis.

82. Vittas, *Banking Systems Abroad,* p. 69.

83. Ibid., p. 66.

84. Ibid., p. 69.

85. Kocka, "The Rise of the Modern Industrial Enterprise," p. 90.

86. Ibid.

87. Maycock, *European Banking,* chap. 4.

88. Ibid., p. 44.

89. Medley, "German Monetary and Industrial Policy."

90. Ibid.

91. Ibid.

92. Vittas, *Banking Systems Abroad,* p. 80.

93. Shonfield, *Modern Capitalism,* pp. 255–259.

94. This argument is typical of Hu, *National Attitudes,* and Carrington and Edwards, *Financing Industrial Investment.*

95. Stephen Krasner, "United States Commercial and Monetary Policy: Unravelling the Paradox of External Strength and Internal Weakness," in Katzenstein, ed., *Between Power and Plenty.*

96. Ibid., p. 61.

97. Ira Millstein, "Comments on Proposals for a New Reconstruction Finance Corporation: Possible Antitrust and Conflict of Internal Problems (Colloquium on Government's Role in Large Business Failures, Columbia University Center for Law and Economic Studies, May 15, 1981).

98. Ibid.; see also Weil, Gotshal, and Manges, *An Overview of the Legal Environment for Government Industrial Policy in the United States,* prepared for the Office of Technology Assessment, 1980; and Ira Millstein and Salem Katsh, *The Limits of Corporate Power* (New York: Macmillan, 1981).

99. Millstein and Katsh, *The Limits of Corporate Power,* p. 3.

100. Vittas, *Banking Systems Abroad,* p. 308.

101. Ibid., p. 307.

102. Ibid., p. 308.

103. Ibid., p. 307.

104. Ibid., p. 308.

105. Ibid., p. 25; Raymond W. Goldsmith, *Financial Intermediaries in the American Economy since 1960* (Princeton: Princeton University Press, 1958).

106. Vittas, *Banking Systems Abroad,* pp. 18ff., 22.

107. Ibid., p. 309.

108. David M. Katz, *Bank Control of Large Corporations in the United States* (Berkeley: University of California Press, 1978).

109. Vittas, *Banking Systems Abroad*, p. 309.

110. John Zysman, "Research, Politics, and Policy: Regional Planning in America," in Suzanne Berger, ed., *The Utilization of the Social Sciences in Policy Making in the United States* (Paris: OECD, 1980).

111. Ibid.; Robert Gilpin, *U.S. Power and the Multinational Corporation* (New York: Basic Books, 1975).

112. Millstein and Katsh, *The Limits of Corporate Power*, chap. 3.

113. C. Fred Bergsten, Theodore H. Horst, and Thomas Moran, *American Multinationals and American Interests* (Washington, D.C.: Brookings Institution, 1978), p. 16.

114. Ibid., p. 31.

115. This section is drawn from several sources: Raymond A. Bauer, Ithiel De Sola Pool, and Lewis Anthony Dexter, *American Business and Public Policy: The Politics of Foreign Trade*, 2d ed. (Chicago: Aldine, 1972); Krasner, "U.S. Commercial and Monetary Policy"; Robert A. Pastor, *Congress and the Politics of U.S. Foreign Economic Policy* (Berkeley: University of California Press, 1980); I. M. Destler, *Making Foreign Economic Policy* (Washington, D.C.: Brookings Institution, 1980); and Stephen Cohen, *The Making of United States International Economic Policy* (New York: Praeger, 1977).

116. John Zysman and Laura Tyson, "American Industry in International Competition," in Zysman and Tyson, *American Industry in Internatinal Competition*.

117. Ibid. See the pieces by Michael Borrus and James E. Millstein in this volume. They are responsible for this observation.

118. G. K. Heilener, "Transnational Enterprises and the New Political Economy of U.S. Trade Policy," *Oxford Economic Papers* 29, no. 1 (March 1977).

119. James E. Millstein, "Decline in an Expanding Industry," in Zysman and Tyson, *American Industry in International Competition*.

120. Ibid.; Michael Borrus, "Slow Growth and Competitive Erosion in the U.S. Steel Industry," in Zysman and Tyson, *American Industry in International Competition*.

CHAPTER 6. *Finance, Adjustment, and Political Crisis: Concluding Remarks*

1. Suzanne Berger, Peter Gourevitch, Patrice Higonnet, and Karl Kaiser, "The Problem of Reform in France: The Political Ideas of Local Elites," *Political Science Quarterly* 84, no. 3 (September 1969).

2. Charles Sabel, *The Politics of Work and Workers in an Age of Fordism* (New York: Cambridge University Press, 1981).

3. John A. Armstrong, *The European Administrative Elite* (Princeton: Princeton University Press, 1973).

4. Michel Crozier, *Bureaucratic Phenomenon* (Chicago: University of Chicago Press, 1964); Kenneth Jowitt, "An Organizational Approach to the Study of Political Culture in Marxist-Leninist Systems," *American Political Science Review* 48, no. 3 (September 1974); John Zysman, *Political Strategies for Industrial Order* (Berkeley: University of California Press, 1977), chap. 6.

5. Zysman, *Political Strategies*, chap. 6.

6. Alexander Gerschenkron, *Economic Backwardness in Historical Perspective* (Cambridge: Harvard University Press, Belknap Press, 1962); James Kurth, "The Political Consequences of the Product Cycle," *International Organization* 33 (Winter 1979):1–34.

7. David Collier, ed., *The New Authoritarianism in Latin America* (Princeton: Princeton University Press, 1980); Guillermo O'Donnell, *Modernization and Bureaucratic Authoritarianism: Studies in South American Politics* (Berkeley: University of California, Institute of International Studies, 1973).

8. Charles E. Lindbloom, *Politics and Markets* (New York: Basic Books, 1977).

9. Alexander Gerschenkron, *Bread and Democracy in Germany* (Berkeley: University of California Press, 1943).

10. See John Zysman and Laura Tyson, eds., *American Industry in International Competition* (Ithaca: Cornell University Press, 1983), in particular the studies of textiles, steel, and consumer electronics.

11. These arguments are similar in character to Barrington Moore's historical analysis, *Social Origins of Dictatorship and Democracy* (Boston: Beacon 1966).

12. Philippe Schmitter, "Modes of Interest Representation," *Comparative Political Studies* 10, no. 1. (April 1977).

13. Suzanne Berger, "The French Political System," in Samuel H. Beer et al., *Patterns of Government: The Major Political Systems of Europe*, 3d ed. (New York: Random House, 1973).

14. Alfred Stepan, *State and Society* (Princeton: Princeton University Press, 1977). This is not the only definition. The label "corporatism" has been so widely used that we must clarify its usages. In one set of usages, the term implies community representation—that is, representation by economic sector or social community—and the internal self-management of each component group. Relations between these groups are conducted according to bargains rather than being set by the market or the state. Thus, in the French department of Finistère, the rural elites attempted to create agricultural cooperatives as a means of retaining their traditional position by avoiding dependence on state policies (see Suzanne Berger, *Peasants against Politics* [Cambridge: Harvard University Press, 1972]). Organizing peasants politically along these functional lines, elites were able to influence agricultural management and political behavior in the region. As an ideology, the guiding image of corporatism is one of harmony within social community, which is gained by setting the secondary conflicts that separate mutually dependent sectors.

Such visions have often guided conservative political strategies, in which elites sought to control or to create institutions of political governance and economic management which would allow them to shape affairs within their sector and insulate the corporate group from national political institutions. These goals of internal control and insulation distinguish corporatism from "clientelism," another strategy for preserving traditional social relations in the modern political world. Clientelism refers to the particular chain of contacts that link individuals through a hierarchy of personal ties to national political institutions. Corporatism, by contrast, is a group strategy instead of an individual one, and has insulation, not intermediation as its goal. Sometimes, as in the case of Finistère, the intent is to shun the state, not to be tied to it. In the case of Vichy France, the intent was to reconcile and regulate the competing groups. The implication of this usage is that the social groups are politically autonomous and have a socially legitimate existence. The community and its parts exist and organize themselves apart from the state (see Stepan, *State and Society*).

A second usage of "corporatism" emphasizes the ties the state establishes to these social groups and its liability to manipulate them. "Corporatism," writes Stepan, "refers to a particular set of policies and institutional arrangements for structuring interest representation. Where such arrangements predominate, the state often charters or even creates interest groups, attempts to regulate their number, and gives them the appearance of a quasi-representational monopoly along with special prerogatives. In return for such prerogatives and monopolies the state claims the right to monitor representational groups by a variety of mechanisms so as to discourage the expression of 'narrow' class-based, conflictual demands" (p. 46). Stepan says that in this second usage the initiative lies within the state.

15. Stepan, *State and Society*.

16.. Charles Maier, *Recasting Bourgeois Europe* (Princeton: Princeton University Press, 1975).

17. John Keeler, "The Politics of Official Unionism in French Agriculture 1948–1976 (Ph.D. diss., Harvard University, 1978); see also Keeler, "Corporatism and Official Union Hegemony," in Suzanne Berger, ed., *Organizing Interests in Western Europe* (New York: Cambridge University Press, 1981).

18. Stephen Krasner, "United States Commercial and Monetary Policy" in Peter Katzenstein, ed., *Between Power and Plenty* (Madison: University of Wisconsin Press, 1978).

19. See Stanley Hoffmann, "The Ruled: Protest as a National Way of Life," in Stanley Hoffmann, ed., *Decline or Renewal: France since the 1930s* (New York: Viking Press, 1974).

20. Peter Gourevitch, "The Second Image Reserved," *International Organization* 32, no. 4 (autumn 1978).

21. See Schmitter, "Modes of Interest Representation."

22. See Peter Katzenstein, "Conclusion: Domestic Structures and Strategies of Foreign Economic Policy," in Katzenstein, *Between Power and Plenty*.

23. Katzenstein's argument is in two parts. First, he proposes that the objectives of policy are set by ruling coalitions. "Such coalitions combine elements of the dominant social classes with political pawnbrokers finding their institutional expression in the party system and in a variety of institutions a step removed from electoral competition—government ministries, industrial associations, and large public or private corporations" (p. 306). In the tradition of Gerschenkron, Moore, and Gourevitch, Katzenstein implies that the interests of dominant groups determine the direction of policy. As we have seen, however, identifying a coalition's membership does not allow us to forecast its policy goals in any mechanical way. Nor does it provide an explanation of why one group rather than another determines policy. Second, Katzenstein argues that goals set by ruling coalitions are implemented through policy networks. Differences in policy networks imply that the instruments and thus the possibilities of state action are different in the advanced countries. It is implied but never specified that what is at stake is the state's ability to define society's purpose and to mobilize the political and economic resources necessary to achieve it. The strength and attraction of this approach is its effort to connect arguments about the organization of representation and policy making with the political

conflicts that underlie policy. It seeks to link the corporatist and strong-state arguments to the coalition analysis. Moreover, by adopting a structural stance, it offers the promise that system characteristics can be used to distinguish national experiences.

The analytic problems emerge from the way in which the policy network is defined and from the separation of policy formulation from policy implementation. Institutions become reified, and since structure and politics are divided, it is hard to see them interact. The influences of institutions on political conflicts is obscured, as are the consequences that political battles have for the institutions themselves.

When national political structures are characterized and differentiated by *system-level characteristics* rather than by the characteristics of particular political actors in the system and the specific constraints on them, we cannot understand how interests are formed. Actor interests and resources based on their place in the political system and the market cannot be related to what they want from government. Policy networks, we are told, reflect the links between the state and an undefined concept of "society." These structures differ with the degree of differentiation between the state and society and the degree of centralization of each. A clear and operational definition of the two concepts is not offered—not as a result of an oversight, but because such a definition has meaning only in relation to the characteristics of specific actors and choices. It is, for example, not clear what falls in the category of state and society or what behaviors are expected to differ. Should public firms be treated as part of the state or part of the society, and what meaning does differentiation have in Britain, where a substantial part of the economy is in the public sector? Is a labor movement that is nominally centralized but in which crucial choices about wages and working conditions are made on the shop floor to be treated as centralized or not?

Three specific problems result from this formulation. First, like the argument based on the strong state–weak state dichotomy, this centralization-differentiation formula considers whether the state bureaucracy can manipulate the behavior of domestic actors to achieve foreign economic policy goals. The implication is that as state and society become more centralized, the ties between state and society tighten and the capacity for such internal leadership increases. Implicit in this approach is the assumption that the content of policy and the form of policymaking are consistent across a wide range of issues and, as a result, that national predictions can be made without reference to the task at hand. The concepts of centralization and differentiation are not related specifically to a capacity to act—either in general or in a particular case. Furthermore, the links between system characteristics and their outcomes in terms of policy content are not specified. Thus, French industrial strategies were successful in energy, effective but ultimately limited in steel, but ineffective in electronics and irrelevant in machine tools. More broadly, the supposedly strong French state is perceived by Michel Crozier (*Bureaucratic Phenomenon*) as the centerpiece of a "stalemated" society, incapable of direct action. Japanese policy in electronics was effective in establishing an internationally competitive industry whereas French policy damaged the same industry. In both examples, there is a similarity in form but a difference in the content and outcomes of policy. These system characteristics do not relate structure to outcomes. Most critically, we do not know what capacities a government requires to intervene.

A second problem with system-level analysis is that it prevents us from examining the seats of power in the economy or the politics of control over marketplace outcomes and industrial structures. Such an approach does not allow us to understand how interests are formed, how social groups combine into coalitions to carry on their purposes, or what institutional positions and organizational arrangements give them the capacity to act. Policy formulation and implementation become separate realms rather than the interconnected reality that they are. Unless the concept of institutional structure is linked to the concept of ruling coalitions, we cannot see which elements of the society have an interest in which aspects of its structure or how their purposes are implemented, either through existing structures or by effecting changes in those structures. Indeed, this approach reifies structures, converting them into given characteristics without providing an account of how they emerge, why they change, or how they affect outcomes. The system characteristics become frozen in a nominalist and static view.

Finally, the centralization-differentiation schema makes it virtually impossible to analyze how state policies affect the market positions of groups, or to understand how their market positions push them to pursue policy objectives in the institutional setting. It precludes an examination of industrial structure and marketplace operations, and therefore cannot describe their influence on politics. For example, a half-dozen firms may dominate an industrial sector; each may be dependent on the government but independent of its peers. In this case the state may be able to dominate market developments but the system will nevertheless be decentralized. If a centralized trade association is composed of thousands of small firms, however, the state may find its power more circumscribed. Centralization does not describe marketplace choices or the character of business-state interactions. From the economic literature, the appropriate concept is "concentration"—the power of the individual firm in relation to the market. Again, we are unable to link government policy strategies to the marketplace choices and behavior of groups in society. Economics and politics remain isolated from one another. Any useful structural approach must retain a capacity to analyze the interests of actors, their capacity to act, and their influence on the structure.

24. This is a synthetic interpretation based on a variety of sources, including Armstrong, *European Administrative Elite;* Ezra Suleiman, *Power, Politics, and Bureaucracy in France* (Princeton: Princeton University Press, 1974); Aaron Wildavsky and Hugh Heclo, *The Private Government of Public Money* (Berkeley: University of California Press, 1974); Hugh Heclo, *A Government of Strangers* (Washington, D.C.: Brookings Institution, 1977).

25. Peter J. Katzenstein, "Economic Dependence and Political Autonomy: The Small European States in the International Economy" (Unpublished paper, Cornell University, Ithaca, N.Y.).

26. Douglas A. Hibbs, "Political Parties and Macroeconomic Policy," *American Political Science Review* 71, no. 4 (December 1977).

27. Suzanne Berger, "The French Political System," chap. 1.

28. Samuel Huntington, "The United States," in Michel Crozier, Samuel Huntington, and Joji Watanuki, *Crisis of Democracy* (New York: New York University Press, 1975); Mancur Olson, *The Rise and Decline of Nations* (New Haven: Yale University Press, 1982).

29. See Andrew Martin, "Labor Movement Parties and Inflation: Contrast-

ing Responses in Britain and Sweden," in James Galbraith, ed., U.S. Congress Joint Economic Committee, *Monetary Policy, Selective Credit Policy and Industrial Policy in France, Britain, West Germany and Sweden* (Washington, D.C.: GPO, 1981).

30. John Zysman, "Inflation and the Politics of Supply," in Leon Lindberg and Charles Maier, eds., *The Politics of Inflation* (Washington, D.C.: Brookings Institution, forthcoming).

31. Katzenstein, "Economic Dependence and Political Autonomy."

Index